Based on fresh research and presented with verve and insight, this study of Africa's pioneering evangelical theologian, Byang Kato, represents a singular contribution towards a better, fuller understanding of Kato, his life and his legacy. It also represents an essential resource towards understanding the theological life of Africa's evangelical community during the past half century. The author engages both with Kato's own writings and with a considerable array of other literature relevant to the inquiry. He also addresses probing questions relating to Kato's continuing significance, assesses with considered judgment, and encourages adjustments in common perceptions and misperceptions. This volume will be a benchmark for all Kato research going forward.

Paul Bowers, PhD
Former Director,
Association for Christian Theological Education in Africa (ACTEA) and
International Council for Evangelical Theological Education (ICETE)

Byang Kato is arguably one of the greatest African evangelical theologians in recent years. In his theological fights against syncretism he is famously quoted to have said, "Let African Christians be Christian Africans." With this statement, Kato was simply saying, in as much as Africans ought to radically leave tradition when they become Christians, they should do the same with Western culture, in ensuring that Christianity in Africa should not be westernized. Kato was the first African General Secretary of the Association of Evangelicals in Africa (AEA). He is credited for a clear cut vision road map that has led to where AEA is currently. When asked what his vision for Africa was in 1974, Kato answered;

"African Christianity is being consumed by a dreadful disease. We must find a cure for our *theological anemia*."

In the hour following that statement Kato spelled out four tools that he believed would support steady, responsible development of genuine Christianity across Africa:

1. We need evangelical African scholars writing and publishing African theology.
2. We need graduate schools in theology so that our best students do not leave the continent in order to learn: one school in French-speaking Africa in the west and another in English-speaking Africa in the east.

3. We need a journal. African scholars of theology will seek a place to publish their ideas and read the responses of their evangelical peers across the continent.
4. We need an accrediting agency to set standards of theological education and monitor the progress of schools in order to maintain those standards. Scholars throughout the world will want to know what African-educated theologians think about Jesus.

All these four vision pillars have been institutionalized and are now the infrastructural apparatus of the AEA. He was a man in the right place and at the right time. A visionary and a scholar of note, and an evangelical.

It is for this that Dr. Aiah Foday-Khabenje's intensive labour on the life journey of this African intellectual and theological general is worth my endorsement. Aiah's book is a laboratory or information bank, a mine of an important jewel of evangelical theology. Every evangelical will do well to have it in order to avoid common pitfalls and to fortify mainstay biblical conscience for the current generation and future posterity.

Master Oboletswe Matlhaope, PhD
General Secretary,
Association of Evangelicals in Africa (AEA)

Byang Kato: The Life and Legacy of Africa's Pioneer Evangelical Theologian is a rare gem that discusses the contributions of a very important African figure and the father of African evangelicalism. African Christianity owes its vibrancy to men and women who were unwavering in their theological beliefs and ethos. Although he died at a very young age, Dr. Byang Henry Kato left an indelible mark in African Christianity that must be told, retold, protected and celebrated. Christian leaders, pastors, students and historians will find this book a rare resource. I highly recommend it without reservation.

David Tarus, PhD
Executive Director,
Association for Christian Theological Education in Africa (ACTEA)

Byang Kato

The Life and Legacy of Africa's Pioneer
Evangelical Theologian

Aiah Dorkuh Foday-Khabenje

ACADEMIC

© 2023 Aiah Dorkuh Foday-Khabenje

Published 2023 by Langham Academic (Previously Langham Monographs)
An imprint of Langham Publishing
www.langhampublishing.org

Langham Publishing and its imprints are a ministry of Langham Partnership

Langham Partnership
PO Box 296, Carlisle, Cumbria, CA3 9WZ, UK
www.langham.org

ISBNs:
978-1-83973-667-4 Print
978-1-83973-890-6 ePub
978-1-83973-891-3 PDF

Aiah Dorkuh Foday-Khabenje has asserted his right under the Copyright, Designs and Patents Act, 1988 to be identified as the Author of this work.

All rights reserved. No part of this publication may be reproduced, stored in a retrieval system or transmitted, in any form or by any means, electronic, mechanical, photocopying, recording or otherwise, without the prior written permission of the publisher or the Copyright Licensing Agency.

Requests to reuse content from Langham Publishing are processed through PLSclear. Please visit www.plsclear.com to complete your request.

Scripture quotations marked (NLT) are taken from the Holy Bible, New Living Translation, copyright © 1996, 2004, 2007, 2013, 2015 by Tyndale House Foundation. Used by permission of Tyndale House Publishers, Inc., Carol Stream, Illinois 60188. All rights reserved.

Scripture quotations marked (RSV) are from Revised Standard Version of the Bible, copyright © 1946, 1952, and 1971 National Council of the Churches of Christ in the United States of America. Used by permission. All rights reserved.

British Library Cataloguing-in-Publication Data
A catalogue record for this book is available from the British Library

ISBN: 978-1-83973-667-4

Cover & Book Design: projectluz.com

Langham Partnership actively supports theological dialogue and an author's right to publish but does not necessarily endorse the views and opinions set forth here or in works referenced within this publication, nor can we guarantee technical and grammatical correctness. Langham Partnership does not accept any responsibility or liability to persons or property as a consequence of the reading, use or interpretation of its published content.

Contents

Abstract xiii

Acknowledgements xv

List of Abbreviations xvii

Chapter 1 1
Introduction
   General Background for the Study 1
      Introduction 1
      Synopsis of Kato's Life and Ministry 2
      The Socio-political and Cultural Context of Kato's Ministry 4
      Emergence of Evangelicalism in Africa 6
      Kato and Intra-evangelical Debates on Continuity 12
   Problem Statement 14
   Research Questions 14
      Main Research Question 15
      Sub-questions 15
      Hypothesis 15
   Importance of Study 16
   Research Design and Methodology 18
      Research Design 18
      Methodology 22
   Delimitations of the Study 26
   Overview 27

Chapter 2 29
A Synopsis of the Life and Times of Byang Kato
   Introduction 29
   Sources of Information for the Biography 30
   Socio-political and Cultural Context of Kato's Time 32
   Birth and Early Childhood 36
   Dedication as Fetish Priest and Rite of Passage to Manhood 40
   Conversion to Christianity, Spiritual Formation and
      Elementary Education 44
   Marriage and Family Life 50
   Further Education 54
      Bible College at Igbaja (1955–1957) 55

  Undergraduate Education at London Bible College
   (1963–1966)..56
  Postgraduate Studies at Dallas Theological Seminary
   (1970–1973)..58
  Vocation and Ministry..61
   Bible Teacher 62
   Media and Writing Career...66
   Pastor and Denominational Leader 70
   General Secretary of AEA...74
  Background to Theological Debates 78
  Global Engagement 79
  Kato's Tragic Demise 81
  Byang Kato's Accomplishments 85
  Failures and Deficiencies of Kato 88
  Conclusion 89

Chapter 3 93
Byang Kato's Theological Legacy in Biblical Hermeneutics, African Christian Identity and Evangelical Theological Education
  Introduction 93
  Kato's Hermeneutics...100
   Kato's Biblicism 101
   Kato's Exegetical Approach...104
   Application of Scripture to Specific Issues Kato Confronted....109
  Kato's Contribution to African Christian Identity 133
  Kato's Contribution to Evangelical Theological Education in
   Africa..151
  Summary of Kato's Theological Legacy...163
  Kato's Theological Pitfalls 166
  Current State of the Church in Africa in View of Kato's
   Theological Legacy...170
  Contemporary Resonance of Kato's Hermeneutics, Identity
   and Theological Education 174
  Legacy of Mission and Culture Debates 180
  Conclusion...182

Chapter 4 185
Theological and Biblical Foundations for African Christian Identity, Hermeneutics and Evangelical Theological Education
  Overview 185
  Tenets of Evangelicalism as Background to Kato's Theology...........186
  Historical Sketch of the Development of Evangelical Orthodoxy....190

    Classical Ecumenical Approach to Christianity 190
    Biblical Orthodoxy in the Reformation Era 197
    Evangelical Hermeneutics 199
    Contemporary Evangelical Hermeneutics 201
Theological and Biblical Foundations of Kato's Theological
    Legacy 211
    Foundations of Kato's Biblical Hermeneutics 211
    Foundations of Kato Contribution to African Christian
        Identity 233
    Foundations of Kato's Contribution to Evangelical
        Theological Education 253
    Summary and Conclusion 260

Chapter 5 263
A Model for Biblical Fidelity in African Evangelical Christianity
    Introduction 263
    Outline of Kato's Theological Construct 268
    Description of Kato's Theology 271
        Soteriology (Personal Conversion) 271
        Christian Formation (Radical Discipleship) 276
        Bibliology (Bible-centred Christianity) 280
        Christology (Christ-centred Christianity) 284
        Ecclesiology (Christian-African Identity) 287
        Missiology (Apologia for Biblical Christianity in Africa) 295
        Eschatology (Second Coming of Christ) 302
        Pneumatology (Power of the Holy Spirit and the Spirit
            World of the Cosmos) 306
    Summary 317

Chapter 6 319
Summary, Conclusion and Recommendations
    Introduction 319
    Summary of the Study 320
        Summary of Chapter One 320
        Summary of Chapter Two 322
        Summary of Chapter Three 324
        Summary of Chapter Four 327
        Summary of Chapter Five 329
    Conclusions of the Study 330
    Contributions of the Study 334
    Recommendations of the Study 335

Bibliography 339

List of Figures

Figure 1: Map of Nigeria Showing Northern Nigeria and the Middle Belt in the 1960s...34
Figure 2: Photo of Byang Henry Kato 38
Figure 3: An African Hermeneutic – A Four-Legged Stool 204

List of Tables

Table 1: Drawing a Parallel between ATR and the New Generation Christianity...173

Byang Henry Kato
used by permission

Abstract

This study is an analytical biography of a pioneering church leader – Byang Henry Kato (1936-1975) – in shaping African evangelicalism. The study explores Kato's life story and theological legacy to contribute to leadership development and the maturing of the church in contemporary Africa. Specifically, the study explores Kato's biblical hermeneutics, Christian African identity and contribution to evangelical theological education in sub-Saharan Africa, using empirical and qualitative approaches, literary review and field interviews.

Kato was immersed in African traditional religion as a child and was on course for succeeding his father as fetish priest when he converted to the Christian faith. He rose from that humble beginning to become a world class evangelical leader and scholar before his tragic death by drowning. Kato was a young Nigerian theologian and the first African general secretary of the Association of Evangelicals in Africa (AEA), among other roles. He is renowned as the father of evangelical theology in sub-Saharan Africa.

Kato stood against the formidable ecclesial establishment of his time to contend for biblical fidelity over nationalistic loyalty. Kato's angst about the incipient syncretistic universalism in the church in Africa resonates with current secularism, pluralism and spirituality which tends to undermine the gospel. He raised an alarm and warned the church in Africa about theological pitfalls and advocated for discontinuity with the African traditional religious worldview, especially aspects that were inconsistent with Scripture. What Kato's warning amounts to then is constant awareness and vigilance, and his prophetic voice needs to be heard again.

In an era when Africa has become the heartland of Christianity, the eminent pitfall is for the fastest growing church to become the fastest declining church. The need is for an authentic paradigmatic Christian expression. The church must be on guard to contend with the tendency for human culture, with secularistic worldviews lurking at the door of biblical Christianity. Kato's hermeneutics and theological legacy has much to contribute as a panacea to the new generation Christianity. This study sought to synthesize Kato's biblical theological insights – the Kato theological construct – important for disciple-making and maturation of the church in Africa.

Acknowledgements

Research obligation has its way of acknowledging those whose hard work informed the research, and these are all appropriately acknowledged in the bibliographical section. Without these, the tedious and hard work would be discounted. I have some others who are not listed in the bibliography, but these are so important that the academy reserves a very special place for them – the acknowledgement page in the front section of the work. I would like to take the opportunity to say "ekushe," "kabo kabo" and "wainguie" (these are my heart languages to special people who live in my heart). Translated in English, it is simply "thank you very much."

I would not have been able to do this work without the support of my wife, Olufumilayo, and children: Nornie, Ndeana, Nema and Nafachima. I am because you let me be. My extended family in Kenya, home away from home, have always been an encouragement. These include my dear colleagues at the Association of Evangelicals in Africa and the pastorate and members of the Liberty Christian Centre of the Redeemed Gospel Church Inc.

I am very grateful to all my respondents, for their willingness and lively dialogue on Byang Kato, the subject of this study. These included Kato's surviving family members, his former colleagues and acquaintances from varied backgrounds. I had the rare privilege to be mentored by a Ghanaian British medico theologian, Dr. Annang Asumang. He is a clinician in intensive care medicine in the UK, as well as a senior scholar at the South African Theological Seminary, with pastoral duties in at least two church congregations in the UK, where he preaches regularly. Notwithstanding his very busy schedule, I always received my scripts, thoroughly scrutinised, ahead of time! *Medase*, dear mentor and brother. I look forward to meeting you in person one of these days.

The COVID-19 era was a revelation in many ways. The South African Theological Seminary (SATS), which had mastered the art of offsite education, with a team of excellent faculty and administrative staff, became the "ivy league" for online education, especially for theological education at a tertiary level. The lockdown period was a God-given opportunity (which is not the same as saying COVID-19 was sent by God to punish a rebellious world) for me to get on with this research and writing. It also saw many schools at a standstill and crying for help to migrate online. Many had neither the know-how nor the resources to do anything. SATS proved to be ahead of its time and well adept to reaching the world in this virtual space. Thank you all for your excellent and God-honouring services.

List of Abbreviations

AACC	All Africa Conference of Churches
ACT/PEMA	Africa Christian Television/Proclamation de l'Evangile par les Medias en Afrique
ACTEA	Association for Christian Theological Education in Africa (previously, Accrediting Council for Theological Education in Africa)
AEA	Association of Evangelicals in Africa
AEAM	Association of Evangelicals in Africa and Madagascar
AIC	Africa Inland Church
AIU	Africa International University
A Level	Advanced Level
ATR(s)	African traditional religion(s)
BBC	British Broadcasting Cooperation
BD	Bachelor of Divinity
CEF	Child Evangelism Fellowship
CLMC	Christian Learning Material Centre/Christian Learning Materials for Children
DTS	Dallas Theological Seminary
ECWA	Evangelical Church Winning Africa/Evangelical Church Winning All (previously, Evangelical Church of West Africa)
EFMA	Evangelical Foreign Mission Association
FATEB	Faculté de Théologie Évangélique de Bangui
GCE	General Certificate of Education
ICCC	International Christian Council of Churches

ICETE	International Council for Evangelical Theological Education
ICOWE	First International Congress on World Evangelization
IFMA	International Foreign Mission Association
MDiv	master of divinity
NAE	National Association of Evangelicals
NEGST	Nairobi Evangelical Graduate School of Theology
NGC	New Generation Christianity
NIV	New International Version
O Level	Ordinary Level
SIM	Sudan Interior Mission/Serving In Mission
STM	master of sacred theology
TEE	theological education by extension
ThD	doctor of theology
UK	United Kingdom
USA	United States of America
WCC	World Council of Churches
WEA	World Evangelical Alliance
WEA-MC	World Evangelical Alliance Mission Commission
WEF	World Evangelical Fellowship (now the World Evangelical Alliance)

CHAPTER 1

Introduction

General Background for the Study

Introduction

Byang Henry Kato (1936-1975) hailed from the predominantly Christian area of Kaduna State in Northern Nigeria. As a child, he was dedicated as a fetish priest, became a Christian at the age of twelve and, at the time of his death, was reputed to be the father of evangelicalism in the contemporary church in sub-Saharan Africa.[1] However, current theological discourse in Africa has failed to acknowledge the immense contribution that consideration of the theological legacy of Byang Kato could make to that discourse and to the maturation of the church from an evangelical perspective. Bowers reveals existing gaps in exploring Kato's contribution to evangelical Christianity in Africa, arguing:

> One might think that all there is to know about Kato has already been well rehearsed over the years. But not so. The fact is that not everything relevant about Kato has yet been adequately surfaced or sufficiently pursued. There is still room for further fruitful inquiry, rich opportunity for further professional research and exposition.[2]

---

1. Kapteina, "Formation," 70–71; Ngong, "Material," 128; Haye, *Byang Kato*, 17.
2. Bowers, "Byang Kato," 5.

Of particular interest in this study are Kato's life history, biblical hermeneutics, understanding of African Christian identity and contribution to evangelical theological education. In his writings, he warned the church in Africa of incipient syncretism and universalism and advocated for sound evangelical theology.[3] He outlined a blueprint to rescue authentic biblical Christianity in Africa from syncretism. It would appear from a broad assessment of the current state of Christian witness and praxis in many parts of Africa, that these preoccupations of Kato have contemporary salience. A summary of some of the pertinent background issues, such as the nature of the socio-political milieu which nurtured the common outlook of sub-Saharan African churches of his time, as well as the internal differences among the sub-Saharan Christian theologians which sharpened his own theological worldview, will provide the context for this study and specifically indicate why an analytical biography of Kato is long overdue. Prior to that, I set out a synopsis of Kato's life and ministry.

Synopsis of Kato's Life and Ministry

Born and raised in Kwoi, rural Northern Nigeria, Kato had an appreciable immersion and experience in African traditional beliefs and practices. As a child, he was exposed to traditional religious beliefs as fetish priest before conversion to the Christian faith. He had a blended educational experience; that is, he was educated in a regular mission school and at the same time self-taught. Kato studied on his own and took correspondence courses to sit and pass the General Certificate of Education (GCE) Ordianry and Advanced Level examinations to gain entrance to Igbaja Bible College and the London Bible College, respectively.[4] He raised a family of his own, with a Nigerian spouse and three children, in the same community in which he was born. He also worked among his compatriots as a teacher, had a career in print

---

3. Syncretism: What Kato described as syncretism was the attempt by proponents of African theology to discover what the traditional religions were saying and to wed those pre-Christian, pre-Muslim religions with contemporary faith; an attempt to synthesize Christianity with African traditional religions. Kato *Theological Pitfalls*, 55. Universalism: According to Kato, universalism means the belief that all will eventually be saved, whether they believe in Christ now or not. Kato saw these two concepts (syncretism and universalism) as heresies and focused on bringing these to the attention of the church in Africa.

4. Haye, *Byang Kato*, 30, 34.

media as a writer and counsellor, and was a pastor before launching on the international scene for further education and ministry.[5]

The peak of Kato's short earthly career was his role as the first African general secretary of the Association of Evangelicals in Africa and Madagascar (AEAM) – now Association of Evangelicals in Africa (AEA).[6] As general secretary, Kato also held the position of executive secretary of the AEA Theological Commission.[7] Kato's work and contribution to the church earned him the distinction of being called the father of evangelical theology in Africa.[8] Kato's role as general secretary of AEA lasted only about two years before he died a tragic death by drowning in the Indian Ocean in Mombasa, Kenya.[9]

He is remembered for his concern about the theological trends and malaise in the church in sub-Saharan Africa and his vision about possible solutions to certain theological pitfalls. He took a critical and radical view of the theological trends espoused by many of his fellow African theologians, like John Mbiti, Bolaji Idowu and Harry Sawyerr, among others. Kato, for example, had concerns about the uncritical merging of African traditional religious beliefs with Christianity and about beliefs and practices of African Christians that were inconsistent with the Bible: "Whether we call it Christo-paganism, syncretism or universalism, it makes little difference. The fact remains that New Testament Christianity is threatened in the continent due to theological and biblical ignorance."[10]

He planted the seeds for evangelical theology in his seminal work *Theological Pitfalls in Africa*. Among other contributions, Kato crafted the blueprint for evangelical theological education in Africa.[11] His plan resulted in the establishment of the first two postgraduate theological schools to serve the whole of sub-Saharan Africa; the Accrediting Council for Theological Education in Africa (ACTEA, now the Association of Christian Theological Education in Africa), an institution for the standardization and accreditation

---

5. Bremen, *Association of Evangelicals*, 36–48.

6. For consistency, and to avoid confusion, all future references to the AEAM/AEA will use the current abbreviation. From its inception in 1966, AEA was known as AEAM until 1993.

7. Bowers, *Theological Education*, 2.

8. Kapteina, "Formation," 61.

9. Haye, *Byang Kato*, 91.

10. Kato, *Theological Pitfalls*, 1.

11. Nystrom, "Let African Christians."

of theological education; and the Christian Learning Materials Centre (CLMC, now Christian Learning Materials for Children), which produced curriculum and Sunday school materials for the nurture and development of children by the church.[12] Kato's contribution to theological education went beyond Africa; he made an important contribution to the global evangelical church as well.

A comprehensive and critical evaluation of Kato's life and ministry no doubt includes, but is not restricted to, the socio-cultural factors that shaped his worldview, as well as his formative experiences before and during his time as a minister of Christ. It is to a brief summary of this that I now turn.

The Socio-political and Cultural Context of Kato's Ministry

The mid-twentieth century, an era of emerging independent nation states in Africa, was an important turning point, not only in the political sense but also in religious, philosophical, theological and ontological terms. Africa's quest for independence from colonial rule had implications for African Christians' perceptions of selfhood and dignity, Christian identity and biblical hermeneutics.[13] African Christian identity in this study refers to the composite worldview and self-understanding of the sub-Saharan African Christian.

Being a vast continent, with multiple different cultural identities, it is somewhat problematic to speak of a single African Christian identity. Nevertheless, it is reasonably safe to speak of a sub-Saharan African identity, given the roughly contemporaneous shared experiences of Christianity, colonialism and political independence in the region. The North African section of the continent may be excluded from this identity, as it had a radically different historical Christian experience non-contemporaneous with the sub-Saharan region, and it currently has a much more ingrained Islamic culture, very different from the rest of the continent. Accordingly, this study is restricted to the sub-Saharan region

Pan-African nationalists' quest for political independence and self-rule in sub-Saharan Africa was therefore in tandem with the church's desire to be

---

12. Bowers, "Byang Kato," 4–5;

13. Ezibo, *Re-Imaging African Christologies*; Nyende, "Church"; Turaki, *Engaging Religions Worldviews.*

self-governing, self-propagating, self-supporting and self-theologising.[14] The search for authentic African Christianity, devoid of Western vestiges, thus became a common demand by some in theological circles.

As African peoples asserted their selfhood, any aspect of their lives that appeared to have been shaped by Western influence was viewed with suspicion. Religion is particularly central to the African psyche, and Christianity, which had spread during the colonial era through the effort of Western missionaries, was therefore subject to scrutiny. John Mbiti underscores the need for African theologians to weigh in on this and writes:

> Missionaries who began the modern phase of Christian expansion in Africa, were more concerned with practical evangelism, education and medical care than with academic theological issues, and not prepared to face serious encounter with either the traditional religions and philosophy or modern changes taking place in Africa. The church here now finds itself in the situation of trying to exist without a theology.[15]

A particular strand of African Christian theological discourse emerged towards the end of colonialism and the advent of independent nation states, which therefore tended to be nationalistic. Burgeoning African Christian theologians, especially those closely associated with the academic centres on the continent, like Mbiti, Sawyerr and Idowu, tended to focus on the need to de-eurocentralise or decolonise the inherited theology from European missionaries.[16] They proposed a brand of Christian practice that blended African traditional beliefs with Christian faith. Kato opposed this trend, thus originating a vigorous debate that came to shape and characterise his theological mission. Kwame Bediako, for example, spends a substantial part of his magnum opus, *Theology and Identity*, criticising Kato's opposition to the focus of African theologians. These theologians appear to have argued for a Christian identity which ultimately was more Afrocentric than biblical, whereas Kato argued for a more fully shaped biblical worldview.

---

14. Adeleye, "Development," 378; see also Mbiti, *African Religions and Philosophy*; Bediako, *Theology and Identity*.

15. Mbiti, *African Religions and Philosophy*, 232.

16. Ndiaye, "Investigation," 8; Sakupapa, "Decolonising Content," 406–424; Adamo, "Christianity," 1–10; Bediako, *Theology and Identity*, 386–425.

While Kato was committed to the Africanisation of the church, he was concerned about heresies and advocated for sound biblical understanding, matching Christian profession with practice. He argued for African Christians being "Christian Africans."[17] Essentially, Kato's argument was that the Christian identity was first in priority over national or ethnic identity or Africanness. He advocated for a discontinuity from traditional beliefs for the African Christian, especially regarding attaining salvation. Thus, African evangelical Christianity began to establish its own unique orientation that diverged from that established by others.

Emergence of Evangelicalism in Africa

The Reformation movement and Protestantism in the sixteenth century were synonymous with evangelicalism. However, in the last five hundred years of the Protestant church, various traditions and denominations have emerged. Evangelicalism, which cuts across different denominations, has taken on a distinct identity within other traditions in the church and mainstream Protestantism. Nevertheless, the precise meaning and identity of evangelicals is confusing, and thus the need for understanding who evangelicals and especially African evangelicals are. This no doubt goes to the heart of Kato's contribution. In his disputations, he contributed to African understanding of evangelical, and biblical, Christianity.

Problem with definition of evangelical or evangelicalism

The word "evangelical" is derived from the Greek word *euangelion*, which means the "good news." In this case, it refers to the good news of the gospel of Jesus Christ.[18] Evangelicalism has been popularly defined by David Bebbington's quadrilateral characteristics: (1) conversionism – the belief that people need new life or to be born again; (2) activism – the need to propagate the gospel; (3) biblicism – the inspiration, infallibility and inerrancy of the Bible; and (4) crucicentrism – the crucifixion of Christ on the cross for salvation of people.[19]

---

17. Kato, "Critique of Incipient," ThD diss., 296.
18. Wolffe, "Who Are Evangelicals," 25; cf. Stott, *Evangelical Truth*.
19. Bebbington, *Evangelicalism*, 3–19.

However, the specific meaning and usage of "evangelical" over time has been varied and become contentious. Evangelicalism as a tradition of Christianity is currently an emotive label and some well-meaning evangelical Christians do not want to identify themselves as such.[20] The definition for evangelicals is even more nebulous when American Christianity is generally associated with evangelicalism. Kunhiyop alludes to this enigma when he states: "Others who see themselves as defenders of evangelical and biblical Christianity suspect that African Christian theology must inevitably be liberal and syncretistic. But *African* is no more a synonym for liberal than *American* is a synonym for *evangelical*."[21]

The church in Africa is also not spared from the confusion and imprecision about the meaning and identity of evangelicals.[22] Yet, it is exactly in this area that Kato's contribution to a concise definition of the word "evangelical" – certainly as it may be applied to the African Christian – comes into its own. To begin with, lack of understanding in regard to Kato's contribution to theological discourse in Africa is also true about the definition, and therefore the contribution of evangelical theology in general.[23]

From its founding in 1966, the Association of Evangelicals in Africa (AEA) struggled with divisions among the evangelicals, namely, separatists versus conservatives and historic, Pentecostal and American versus the rest.[24] However, what emerged as consensus for evangelical beliefs and what Kato asserted as non-negotiable beliefs were the following: (1) the infallibility of God's revelation in the Bible; (2) the virgin birth of Christ; (3) his vicarious death; (4) his bodily resurrection; and (5) the personal, visible future return of Jesus Christ.[25] This definition was clarified by Tiénou, when he added:

> In the complex and varied picture of African Christianity, evangelicals are to be found among the established and recognised denominations such as the Anglicans, the Methodists,

---

20. James, "Tony Campolo;" cf. Ewell, "What Evangelicals Believe," 48.
21. Kunhiyop, *African Christian Theology*, xiii.
22. Adeyemo, "What Are Evangelicals," 5.
23. See Breman, "Association of Evangelicals," 19–29; Shaw, *Kingdom of God*; and Adeyemo, "What Are Evangelicals," 5–12.
24. Breman, "Association of Evangelicals," 35.
25. See Kato, "Challenge of Evangelicalism"; cf. Breman, "Association of Evangelicals," 27; Adeyemo, "What Are Evangelicals," 7–8.

the Lutherans, and the Presbyterians, as well as among the numerous so-called mission and independent churches of the continent. Historically, evangelicals are those who were faithful to the gospel of Jesus Christ. They understood it to include: (1) Humans' sinful condition before a holy God; (2) humans' need for salvation; (3) revelation of the grace of God in Jesus Christ; (4) the authority of the inspired Scriptures; (5) the necessity for a birth from above or regeneration and (6) justification through faith alone, apart from works.[26]

Fifty years after the founding of the AEA, the imprecision and diverse perception of evangelicals continues. In his keynote address at the jubilee celebrations, for example, the president of the AEA, Goodwill Shana, stated:

The evangelical identity in Africa, while it has enjoyed steady growth and a credible reputation, has in recent times, suffered setbacks and confusion arising from the proliferation of churches and church leaders who share most, if not all, the fundamental doctrinal beliefs of evangelicals but have embellished them with counter-poised beliefs, doctrines and religious activities. These pseudo-evangelicals have embraced many aberrations including hyper prosperity, pseudo-prophetic shamanism, hyper supernaturalism, or miracles often resulting in personal deification and veneration of these charismatic leaders.[27]

The current imprecision in defining the term "evangelical" mirrors Kato's original challenge. Thus, a close analysis of Kato's approach to the problem at the dawn of African evangelicalism is likely to yield some pointers as to how to address the current challenge.

Beginning of evangelical theology

Kato derives his importance from being a leading voice and actor for evangelical theology.[28] The recent history of theological scholarship can be traced back to the late 1950s and early 1960s. The Protestant church in sub-Saharan

---

26. Tiénou, *Theological Task*, 10.
27. Shana, "Our Evangelical Identity," 4.
28. Ngong, "Material," 127; cf. Shaw, *Kingdom of God*, 330; Kapteina, "Formation."

Africa, starting with the first Christian settlement in Freetown in the late eighteenth-century, was evangelistic in doctrine and practice.[29] With the arrival of missionaries, the practice and liturgy of the church was shaped and led by Western expressions.

In the middle of the last century, agitation by Africans to break the shackles of colonialism and attain independence was an important preoccupation for African leaders and scholars. Some African theologians started theologising as independent thinkers and espoused Africanness, African values and an African understanding of Scripture. However, some people in the church embraced liberal views about the Bible and exalted traditional religious belief systems above biblical teachings. Some of the home churches in the West of missionaries in Africa became liberal or modernistic. These began to question the fundamental "doctrines of God, Christ, the Bible and salvation"[30] The writings of their theologians were influencing universities across the world to undermine biblical orthodoxy.

The birth of the World Council of Churches (WCC) in 1951, following the two world wars, and its support for the historic churches in Africa exacerbated the perceived concerns of incipient liberalism or universalism. The All Africa Conference of Churches (AACC) established in 1963 served as a major partner of the WCC on the continent and thus was viewed with suspicion by many within evangelical circles. African evangelicals, therefore, felt the need to be united, to be founded on sound doctrine and to maintain the historic Christian faith.[31]

The sponsorship of the WCC included scholarships to African students to study abroad in liberal theological institutions. Citing from a 1965 WCC service programme and list of projects, Kato wrote: "In 1965, AACC projects in Africa looked for 726,500 U.S. dollars from the World Council of Churches."[32] Furthermore, Kato noted: "Besides the massive support of projects in Africa, a sizeable number of African students are sent overseas each year for further education."[33] In an interview with a key evangelical leader

---

29. Walls, *Cross-Cultural Process*, 28; cf. Adeyemo, "What Are Evangelicals," 17–18.
30. Adeyemo, 18.
31. Kato, *Theological Pitfalls*, 138–151; cf. Adeyemo, "What Are Evangelicals," 18–23.
32. Kato, *Theological Pitfalls*, 139.
33. Kato, 139; cf. Bangura, "Tracking the Maze," 117.

in Sierra Leone, Rev. Dr. Joseph Saidu Mans, the researcher asked why the founding denominations of the Evangelical Fellowship were still members of the Council of Churches in Sierra Leone, fifty years after the Evangelical Fellowship's founding. He revealed: "We go to the Evangelical Fellowship for spiritual nurture and fellowship and to the Council of Churches for resources and scholarship to train our pastors."[34] This sponsorship scheme fuelled the suspicion of evangelicals like Kato.

However, while people like Kato were not against training, they were concerned about the liberalism of the schools these African leaders were going to in Europe and America and the influence of their liberal and philosophical tendencies on the church in Africa upon their return. The training included theological education with the aim of entrenching liberal ecumenism, which brought a "poisonous element" to the continent, according to Kato.[35] Kato further stated: "It is unrealistic to expect so many students from the Third World to digest Aquinas, Tillich, or Cone, and return home unaffected. It is naïve to expect the World Council of Churches to make such a massive investment in Africa without influencing African thinking."[36]

At the core of the concern of evangelicals in Africa and in other parts of the world, about liberal ecumenism, was the call by the German Philosopher, Friedrich Nietzsche, before the end of the nineteenth century, that "God is dead!"[37] This was a deduction from the influence of Enlightenment philosophy. The idea of God was no longer relevant to enlightenment. This is remarkably like the contemporary era of secularism – the tendency to exclude God from human affairs or our world. The philosophical approach to doing theology – the so called "higher criticism" of liberal theology – was on the rise in theological departments in Western universities and denominational seminaries. This caused the theological compromise of the ecumenical movement: the deity of Christ was denied; the Bible was no longer relevant for many in the church; some called for changing the gospel to make it more relevant; there was a call for a moratorium on receiving missionaries from

---

34. Rev. Dr. Joseph Saidu Mans (First national president of the Evangelical Fellowship of Sierra Leone) in discussion with author, Lunsar, Sierra Leone, June 2008.

35. Kato, *Theological Pitfalls*, 140; cf. Kabongo, "Africanisation of Missiology."

36. Kato, *Theological Pitfalls*, 140.

37. Fuller, *People of the Mandate*, 20.

abroad; and the promotion of a social gospel was more of a priority than proclaiming the gospel for salvation.[38]

Thus, the AEA (then AEAM) was established in 1966.[39] The key function of the AEA and the constituent National Evangelical Fellowships was to connect, equip and be a representative voice for common action.[40] With the birth of AEA, the way was paved for evangelicals to mount theological training programmes at all levels in the church.[41] Central to this development was Byang Kato. His assessment of the church in Africa was that it was ailing from "theological anaemia."[42] The prognosis of the ailing church that Kato highlighted included the following: liberal ecumenism; many no longer taking the word of God at face value; a dubious type of cultural revolution; the simmering down of the first love that had characterised the first generations of Christians in Africa; and the major weakness of ignorance of basic biblical doctrine. Liberal theology under the guise of African theology was seeking to solve the theological ignorance.[43] Kato believed sound theological education, undergirded by the Bible, was the greatest need of the church in Africa.[44]

Kato's contribution towards evangelical theological education in Africa is well attested. Several theological schools, such as Nairobi Evangelical Graduate School of Theology (now Africa International University) in Kenya, the ECWA Theological Seminary in Jos, Nigeria, Faculté de Théologie Évangélique de Bangui in the Central African Republic and several others, have each erected some memento as a memorial to Kato.[45] However, Kato has received both praise and scorn for his theological views in African theological circles,[46] creating a lot of debate even within evangelical circles, another area to which I now turn.

---

38. Fuller, 20–21.

39. Kato, *Theological Pitfalls*; Bremam, *Association of Evangelicals*; Bowers, "Theological Education".

40. Foday-Khabenje, *Synopsis*, 6.

41. Kato, "Africa: Facts."

42. Kato, *Biblical Christianity in Africa* 11; cf. Kato, "We Are," 6–7; Kapteina, "Formation," 64; Bangura, "Tracking the Maze, 109.

43. Kato, *Theological Pitfalls*.

44. Kato, "Critique of Incipient," ThD diss., 53.

45. Bowers, "Byang Kato," 1; cf. Kapteina, "Formation".

46. Ngong, "Material," 128.

Kato and Intra-evangelical Debates on Continuity

Another aspect of Kato's legacy is his role in debates within the African evangelical community itself that enabled a sharper definition of evangelical theology. Right from the start, Kato took a clear and categorical view regarding the nature and relationship between Christianity and African traditional religions, and of continuities and/or discontinuities between African traditional beliefs and Christian faith. Kato's discontinuity view sparked off a debate in African theological discourse, and this inevitably reflected itself in the question of what constituted an authentic African Christian identity. Kato pitched his arguments against leading African Christian identity proponents like Bediako, Mbiti, Sawyerr, Musharhamina and Idowu, among others. Kato's opposition to the "continuity" proposition led to him being portrayed as naïve and, sometimes, as a mouthpiece for Western missionaries.[47]

The continuity/discontinuity debate, still prevalent in theological discourse in Africa, had to do with the value placed on ATR beliefs in Christian reflections. This debate is also about the line between contextualisation and syncretism.[48] Proponents of continuity base their argument on general revelation of the Supreme Being, or God, in nature, history and people's conscience. There is some element of the divine nature of God in ATR, since all people are created in the image of God. Change of religion does not alter this divine pursuit.[49] While acknowledging the divine image borne by all peoples, and elements of the manifestation of this in ATR, Kato argued this was not enough for salvation and advocated for discontinuity. He based his argument on the supremacy, all sufficiency and finality of Christ's atoning death and resurrection which made ATR unnecessary.[50]

Many of Kato's opponents within Christian theological circles took the view that Western missionaries disdained African spirituality and introduced Christianity in Africa dressed in their own cultural cloaks. Kato's opponents objected, and rightly so, to representative Christianity being determined by what was typically Western. Like Walls, they complained: "The doctrines, liturgy, ethical codes and social applications of the faith were those prominent

---

47. See Bediako, *Theology and Identity*; Bowers, "Byang Kato"; Simango, "There Is"; MacDonald, "Critical Analysis."
48. See Simango, "There Is"; Kakabo, *African Theology*.
49. Simango, "There Is," 7.
50. Kato, *Theological Pitfalls*; cf. Simango, "There Is," 7.

in the West."⁵¹ They in effect criticized the wholesale adoption of European culture and institutions: "The Christian community gathered in buildings looking like European parish churches, wore European dress and lived lifestyles influenced by European models."⁵² Shades of this criticism were directed towards those evangelicals like Kato who were less vocal in their objection to the colonial missionaries. Bediako asserts:

> Byang Kato was most notable as the dissenting voice in the chorus of positive evaluations of African pre-Christian religious heritage. But in Kato's case, his response was complicated by a theological posture which rendered his appreciation of the heritage from the past problematic. His great achievement, however, consisted in a persistent affirmation of the centrality of the Bible in the theological task. Kato thus contributed a viewpoint of cardinal importance, even though his own acultural conception of theology in fact defeated the very purpose of theology as the struggle with culturally rooted questions.⁵³

This is quite an important quote as it betrays three aspects of the nature of the differences of opinions between Kato and Bediako (and presumably some of Kato's other opponents): (1) the debate on continuity/discontinuity in relation to African traditional religion and Christianity, (2) the extent and prominence to be given to the Bible as basis of Christian theologising (hence biblical hermeneutics), and (3) how culturally bound theological reflections need to be in the African context. Kato's critics thus felt his theological contribution was inconsistent with independent thinking and lacked appreciation for African values and contextualisation.

However, followers of Kato hail him for providing a sharper definition of African Christian identity and believe he had an important message for the church in Africa. Evangelicals in Africa remember Kato for his theological legacy.⁵⁴ He is remembered for his biblical views on Christian identity and practice, and his contribution to evangelical theological education in Africa.

---

51. Walls, *Cross-Cultural Process*, 85.
52. Walls, *Missionary Movement*, 103.
53. Bediako, *Theology and Identity*, xviii.
54. See Bowers, "Byang Kato"; Ferdinando, "Christian Identity"; Shirik, "African Christians"; MacDonald, "Critical Analysis."

Kato did not only make a diagnosis but also prescribed a cure for the theological malaise impacting the church of Africa in his time.[55] A critical analysis and re-appraisal of the issues Kato contended with and of his unique contributions offer important avenues for appreciating the heritage of evangelical Christianity in Africa and bring clarity to evangelical self-understanding.

Moreover, the issues of Kato's time highlighted above have significant parallels with the contemporary church in sub-Saharan Africa. Crucially, there are questions of African Christian identity, evangelical hermeneutics and, significantly, the nature and future of evangelical theological education in the continent.[56] Accordingly, this study argues that a critical analysis of Kato's legacy will make original contributions which have the potential to enhance evangelical Christianity in the African context.

Problem Statement

Contemporary evangelical discourse in sub-Saharan Africa, especially on evangelical hermeneutics, evangelical theological education and African Christian identity, has failed to consider the immense contribution Byang Kato's theological legacy could make on enhancing that discourse and the maturation of the church. The purpose for this study is to critically analyse the biography of Byang Kato and his theological contribution to biblical hermeneutics, African Christian identity and evangelical theological education and to identify important theological lessons for the enhancement of sound biblical reflection, leadership development and Christian practice on the continent.

Research Questions

This research seeks to investigate and articulate a portrait of an African Christian leader, his legacy and the influences that shaped his biblical worldview and how he lived this worldview out. It aims to study how he developed from a fetish priest, dedicated as a child, to become an important evangelical

---

55. Bangura, "Tracking the Maze," 110.

56. Shirik, "African Christians," 132; cf. Young, "New Breed"; Turaki, *Engaging Religions*; Bangura, "Tracking the Maze"; MacDonald, "Critical Analysis."

Christian leader. The research explores Byang Kato's biblical hermeneutics, African Christian identity and vision for theological education and faithful biblical practice without compromise in the church in Africa. To achieve this goal, I sought to find answers to the following questions.

Main Research Question

What theological contribution does an analytical study of Byang Kato's life history and theological legacy of biblical hermeneutics, understanding of African Christian identity and contribution to evangelical theological education make to contemporary biblical Christianity in sub-Saharan Africa?

Sub-questions

To investigate this main question, I explored the following sub-questions:

1. Who was Byang Kato and what social, cultural, political and theological contexts and influences shaped his theological formation and views?
2. How did Kato's message on biblical hermeneutics, African Christian identity and Christian education impact evangelical Christianity in Africa during his lifetime?
3. What is the biblical and theological foundation for Kato's message on hermeneutics, African Christian identity and evangelical theological education?
4. What can the contemporary sub-Saharan church learn from Kato's life and theological contribution to biblical hermeneutics, Christian identity and evangelical theological education in shaping evangelical theology in Africa?

Hypothesis

Given the place of Kato as one of the pioneers of evangelicalism in the church in Africa in modern times, he made a unique contribution to the shaping and development of evangelical Christianity. Thus, this study assumes that an analytical study of Byang Kato's life history, legacy and message regarding biblical hermeneutics, theological education and African Christian identity will provide a corpus of unique theological constructs that are important for enhancing contemporary biblical Christianity, by matching confession with practice, for the maturation of the church in Africa.

Importance of Study

One of the crying needs of African Christianity today is to consider the writing of its history as an authentic subdiscipline within church history. African Christian biography forms an important part of that history and is pivotal in that exercise.[57] In view of the dearth of literature on key African Christians, Omulokoli states: "Given the critical role of African Christian Biography in the writing of African Church History, it is important that it should be undertaken seriously and urgently as top priority."[58] This research is an attempt to respond to this critical need, especially within the African church's evangelical tradition.

Kato's theological development, biblical views and contribution to evangelical theological education is important historically and in the context of the search for appropriate contextualisation and development for the church in Africa. The debate about what constitutes authentic African Christian identity and the question of "continuity" and "discontinuity" does not seem to have disappeared. Questions are still being raised about African culture and biblical Christianity.[59] African theologians therefore need to hear Kato's reticence and misgivings regarding continuity and his proposals for a cure of syncretistic practices in the church afresh. Africa is at the heart of global Christianity and African Christianity must be paradigmatic and authentic.[60]

Notwithstanding Kato's contributions, very little is written about him and his particular contributions to evangelical theology, beyond passing commentaries focusing on his singular opposition to the doctrine of continuity between aspects of ATR beliefs and Christianity popularly espoused by other pioneering African theologians of his time. Comprehensive research on the life and ministry of Kato may reveal other important information that may be of interest to the contemporary church.

---

57. Omulokoli, "Priority of African," 7.

58. Omulokoli, 7.

59. See Palmer, "Byang Kato: Theological Reprisal"; Chalk, *Making Disciples*; Nihinlola, *Theology*; Conteh, *Essays*.

60. Johnson, Zurlo, Hickman and Crossing, "Christianity 2018."

Despite serving as a key source for information about Kato's contributions, Breman only devotes thirteen pages of her work on the history of the AEA to Kato.[61] Bediako also has a chapter on Kato, but this is predominantly devoted to criticism of Kato's opposition of the continuity proposition and his insistence on the centrality of the Bible in Christian theological reflection, which Bediako somewhat pejoratively characterises as "bibliology."[62] The only complete biography of Byang Kato is by Sophie de la Haye, but this is a popular version of Kato's life and has little from a critical historiographical or theological perspective. Several other works on Kato are relatively modest treatments of Kato, mostly articles in journals, periodicals and magazines.[63] However, MacDonald's PhD thesis was focused on Kato's demonology, a fraction of Kato's theological contribution.[64]

The main writing of Kato himself is a book published by the title *Theological Pitfalls in Africa*. The rest of his work was in the form of articles, speeches, letters, reports and written statements, not all of which have been publicised or adequately analysed for their contributions. This results in a lack of coherent appreciation for his unique contributions. Sadly, the voice of Kato on biblical orthodoxy was silenced by his premature death, and it would appear as if his theological message was also drowned in the Indian Ocean and interred with his remains in Nigeria, his home. However, it will be argued and evidenced in this thesis that the legacy of Kato has a crucial role to play in theological reflections and certainly cannot be ignored by the contemporary church in Africa.

Furthermore, what constitutes Kato's theological legacy has not been well defined. The motivation for this research, therefore, was to explore the life, ministry and theology of Kato with a view to assessing his contribution to evangelical theology, and how the contemporary church in Africa could benefit from that contribution. The current growth of the church in Africa has also revealed newer deviations from biblical Christianity, both moral and

---

61. Breman, "Association of Evangelicals." See also Breman, "Portrait."

62. Bediako, *Theology and Identity*, 416.

63. See Tiénou, "Problems"; Tiénou, *Theological Task*; Tiénou, "Understanding African Theology"; Bowers, "Evangelical Theology"; Bowers, "African Theology"; Bowers, "Byang Kato and Beyond"; Ferdinando, "Christian Identity"; Kapteina, "Formation"; Palmer, "Byang Kato: Theological Reappraisal"; Turaki, "Theological Legacy"; and Shirik, "African Christians."

64. See MacDonald, "Critical Analysis."

doctrinal, which in many ways mirror some of the contextual circumstances of Kato's time. So, for example, the situation of the church in Africa is aptly described as a church that is a mile long and only an inch deep, and the growth is said to be a swelling rather than a healthy growth. There is the proliferation of all kinds of churches, fraught with all kinds of theological pitfalls.[65]

Furthermore, biblical illiteracy is a cause for concern in the church in Africa, leading not only to syncretic practices but distorting the biblical vision of prosperity in favor of self-aggrandisement in what has become known as the "health and wealth gospel" or the "prosperity gospel."[66] There is thus an important need for exploration of Kato's theological legacy in order to draw lessons for contemporary authentic African Christian identity and sound biblical practice in the church in Africa.

Research Design and Methodology

The plan for the research is in two parts: the design and methodology. The design describes the type of research and outlines the different steps that were sequentially followed to accomplish the goal. The methodology describes the instruments used to collect the relevant information or data, motivated by the research questions. In addition, I use this section to provide the philosophical justifications and framework which shaped the design and methodology.

Research Design

This research is an analytical biographical study of the life and theological legacy of a key African evangelical Christian leader, Byang Henry Kato. The study falls within the discipline of historical theology.[67] Historical theology, according to Domeris, is the contextual study of the development of Christian theology over the centuries.[68] While in most instances historical theology might be interested in the historical development of particular theological philosophies, it is sometimes also interested in the lives and contributions

---

65. Osei-Mensah, "Why PACLA," 20; cf. Niringiye, *The Church: God's Pilgrim People*, 2; Mokhoathi, "From Contextual Theology"; Cole, "State of Theological," 1–11.

66. Adeleye, *Preachers*; Niringiye, *Church*; Simango, "There Is."

67. Smith, *Integrated Theology*, 138; cf. Lassig, "Toward a Biographical Turn," 147.

68. Domeris, "Historical Theology," 192.

of individual theologians who helped in shaping that history.[69] Identifying the contributions and especially the legacy of important historical figures is essential. Not only does this provide the contextual background to the historical development of Christian doctrine in particular geographical regions, but it also serves as an evocative mirror for contemporary reflections. Also, self-definitions from adherents of the theological ideas are of interest to the discipline of historical theology.

This research belongs to this category of study in the theological disciplines, exploring as it does the life and contributions of Byang Kato, an evangelical leader, in shaping evangelical theology in Africa. Given the range of issues for consideration, the study adopts an interdisciplinary approach, involving historical, sociological and theological methods.[70]

A problem with biographical accounts is hagiography, where the subject of a biography is unduly revered without the prerequisite critical analysis or engagement with the sources.[71] However, in terms of scholarship, classical theological biographies like those of Saint Augustine, Luther, Wesley, Dietrich Bonhoeffer and a wide range of theologians, make sound theological contributions.[72] These speak more about God and the struggle to be faithful to God than they do about the individual.[73] In that way, the reader may have a feeling of resonance between her own life and that of the subject of the biography. Following a number of decades in which biographies were sometimes regarded as contentious because of uncertainties about their crucial historiographical methodologies, there is now a strong revival in regarding them as providing important windows to historical studies.[74] As Lassig astutely argues, "Historiography has shifted from concentrating on structures and numbers to a cultural history that is sensitive to the individual, the unique, and the non-typical, and thus must bring 'people' back into history."[75] The same argument may be made with regards to mapping out the development of doctrines in

---

69. Meserve, "Biography as Theology," 227–230; cf. Fergusson, *New Blackfriars*, 131; Van Tonder, "Towards."
70. Haokip, *Can God Save*, 4.
71. Greggs, "Confession of Stanley," 315.
72. Meserve, "Biography as Theology," 228.
73. Greggs, "Confession of Stanley," 316; see also Cockerill, "Bible."
74. Lassig, "Toward a Biographical Turn," 145; cf. Kaeser, "Biography."
75. Lassig, "Toward a Biographical Turn," 147.

church history, as well as identifying how influential individuals have helped shape the trajectories of Christian theological reflections.

The current study seeks to follow the basic premises of current historiographical principles. In making a case for biography as an acceptable research model, Brekus states:

> One of the distinctive features of the modern world has been its reliance on experience as the basis of knowledge. Perhaps it is not surprising that Americans have become increasingly fascinated by the varieties of personal experience as they have become less certain about the meaning of human life. When we read about other people's experiences, we try on different models of selfhood, experimenting with different identities and gaining a richer sense of the possibilities for our own. Experience offers us a way to determine the truth or, at least, our own personal truths.[76]

Brekus further points out that the strengths of the biography are in its narrative style, evocative descriptions of the past, focus on individual uniqueness, and questions about experience. She points out that these can become weaknesses, however, if not balanced by historical analysis. It is against this firm theoretical background that I employed the tenets of an analytical biographical method in this study to critically analyse Kato's life and historical circumstances for an interpretive pattern and application in contemporary contexts.

This main approach to the biographical analysis is therefore also a qualitative single case study.[77] According to Creswell, "case study is an in-depth exploration of a bounded system (e.g. activity, event, process, or individuals) based on extensive data."[78] The theoretical foundation for case studies is in the fact that important lessons can be learned from a single case.[79] The case study is an invigorating method for vicariously learning from the lived experiences of others.[80] Cases are learning tools that present narratives of real lived experi-

---

76. Brekus, "Forum," 9.
77. Barnes, "F. F. Bosworth," 86.
78. Creswell, *Educational Research*, 465.
79. Sensing, *Qualitative Research*, 143.
80. Sensing, 147.

ences so that others can benefit from the experiences of the subject.[81] Another aspect of the case study approach is its potential for furnishing insights into contemporary issues. In other words, they enable the historian not just to examine the past in the light of the present, but also to seek ways in which the past may speak to the present. Since this research is not just interested in the past but also in how the past informs the present, the case study method offers immense advantages for this project.

Of significance are the debates and critical engagements with other theologians of Kato's time since this tends to sharpen and clarify Kato's beliefs and stance. As it is now nearly forty-five years since Kato's death, this research also explores current views about Kato's theological corpus held by his opponents. This helps in assessing the states and shifts of theological thinking in Africa.

The study is also exploratory, aimed at developing an in-depth understanding of Kato's life and biblical hermeneutics as an instrumental case study.[82] Thus, the approach is descriptive, qualitative and, to a limited extent, ethnographic. As the researcher, I am also one of Byang Kato's successors at AEA, even though several decades exist between us. Nevertheless, my access to information and to people who were Kato's contemporaries and family members, as well as similar experiences in my own life, enhance the in-depth exploration of Kato's life and theological contributions.

The study was carried out in five steps. The first step describes the research problem and plan. Second, the study outlines a historical analysis of the life and ministry of Kato, with particular attention to areas of contribution (i.e. hermeneutics, evangelical theological education and African Christian identity) and to how Kato addressed the dissonance in belief and practice in the church in sub-Saharan Africa. Third, I sought to thoughtfully outline Kato's legacy regarding his theology and biblical hermeneutics, understanding of African Christian identity and contribution to evangelical theological education in Africa. The fourth step critically engages with the biblical and theological basis for Kato's theological themes. In the final step, the thesis formulates a theological model in response to the main research question on the relevance of Kato's theological legacy for contemporary challenges to

---

81. Sensing, 156.
82. Creswell, *Educational Research*, 465–484.

Christianity in sub-Saharan Africa, offering practical biblical guidelines for biblical Christianity in the African context.

Methodology

Each step outlined in the section above, designed to respond to the research questions, used appropriate methodologies and instruments for collecting the necessary data for analysis and interpretation. Generally, literary review, empirical field interviews and textual analysis were used in the study. In the first step, analytical, dialogical and comparative tools such as academic libraries and internet software were used in reviewing relevant material to describe the problem and to outline a plan of the research. The second and third steps involved an analytical biography of the life of Byang Kato. Case study tools included review of Kato's published and unpublished work. Other biographical materials were examined, such as the Kato Memorial Lectures, and other works on Kato such as those by Breman, Haye, Bediako, Bowers, Shirik and Ferdinando, among others.[83] Also, interviews were conducted with people who knew him and could provide relevant information about his life and ministry.

Interviews are a way to gain insight into issues through understanding the experiences of the participants and the subject matter. "As a method of inquiry, interviewing is consistent with people's ability to make meaning through language."[84] It is satisfying to biographical researchers who are interested in others' stories. Interviewing covers a range of practices, from structured interviews with pre-set and closed-ended questions to open-ended and unstructured questions.[85] The interviewees included a purposive sampling of surviving family members and professional colleagues. Examples of these interviewees include Kato's widow and daughter in Nigeria and professional colleagues of Kato's such as Paul Bowers and Yusufu Turaki, among others. The interviews were semi-structured and open-ended. A total of ten people from various backgrounds, ranging in age from sixty-two to ninety-five, were

---

83. Breman, "Association of Evangelical"; Haye, *Byang Kato*; Bediako, *Theology and Identity*; Bowers, "Byang Kato and Beyond: The 2008 Byang Kato Memorial Lectures 1"; Bowers, "Evangelical Theology in Africa: Byang Kato's Legacy"; Shirik, "African Christians"; and Ferdinando, "Christian Identity."

84. Seidman, *Interviewing as Qualitative Research*, 7.

85. Seidman, 9.

interviewed. What they all had in common was their knowledge of, and encounters with, Kato. Two of the interviewees were theological scholars and each had written at least a couple of published articles on Kato. Kato's sibling, spouse and daughter, as well as a childhood friend who was a mate in the rite of passage initiation and the king of the Jaba ethnic people in Kwoi, Kato's birthplace, were interviewed. Respondents also included three others, including a fellow missionary in Nairobi and two other people from the WEA network who first met Kato at the First International Congress on World Evangelization in Lausanne, Switzerland, in 1974.[86] Data collected from these interviews were captured in handwritten notes and used as important sources of information in the study.

It was providential that Kato's wife, who had survived him as a widow for forty-four years, died at eighty, under two months after I met her in Kaduna at the home of her daughter. I was in Kwoi, Kato's birthplace, 22–23 March 2019, where Kato's half-brother, childhood friend and the king were interviewed. However, Kato's widow had taken ill and been taken to Kaduna City by her daughter, where I met her on 23–24 March 2019 for the interview. Mrs. Jummai Kato's death was announced on 8 May 2019. Oral transmission has the disadvantage of distortion of facts with time and subjectivity.[87] However, this is a critical source of historical information in Africa.

The fourth step deployed a survey of some relevant literary works on biblical hermeneutics and exegetical analysis of selected biblical texts that were key to Kato's formation, to articulate the biblical understanding of the theological themes. Examples of these passages include Genesis 6:9–7:24, a passage which first connected Kato to Christianity; Jeremiah 8:11–22, a passage he preached on; and Philippians 4:13, one of his favourite verses in the Bible.[88] Theological resources such as Bible commentaries, encyclopaedias, Bible dictionaries, books and journals were also used to anchor the biblical understanding of these themes.

Finally, the fifth step included a reflective analysis and synthesis of biblical and theological insights generated by the data produced from the literary

---

86. It was desirable to have Kato's seminary classmates among those interviewed but the researcher could not find any at the time of field research.

87. See Omulokoli, "Priority of African."

88. Haye, *Byang Kato*, 24.

and field research. This final step responds to the main research question, identifying Kato's theological corpus.

The sources of information required for this research were twofold: (1) literary works or written sources and (2) interviews (oral histories). The literary sources included Kato's work and a bibliographical collection made available by ACTEA, among other written sources. Each source was evaluated for its historical authenticity and reviewed to collate necessary data for the research. Data was also generated from field interviews, using semi-structured interviews with open-ended questions. This had the advantage of some flexibility and allowed for in-depth probing to indeterminate responses while ensuring access to information that was essential to the study. The interview prompts were based on Kato's theological themes and any aspects of his life the respondents wanted to talk about. The responses were recorded, transcribed and coded by theme for analysis and interpretation. Most of the interviews were conducted via face-to-face meetings, and when this was not possible, interviews were done through video conferencing or WhatsApp calls and email.

Serious consideration was given to organising focus group discussions, which have a high potential of yielding more insights than one-on-one interviews. However, given that several of the participants were older and scattered in different parts of Africa and outside Africa, it was not possible to do a group discussion. However, the lack of focus groups was mitigated by the amount of time and in-depth discussion I had with some key respondents. I spent half a day talking about Kato with Dr. Paul Bowers in his home in Charlotte, North Carolina, in the United States, and about the same amount of time with Professor Yusufu Turaka in Jos, Nigeria. I spent two nights with the Kato family members, one night each in Kwoi and Kaduna. I was back in Kwoi two months later, in May 2019, for the funeral of Mrs. Jummai Kato and connected with the family again and engaged in more discussion about Kato, in line with research objectives.

There are ethical concerns about the use of interviews for research. Interviewing as a process may, for instance, theoretically turn others into subjects whose words are appropriated for the benefit of the researcher.[89] However, these concerns were mitigated by ensuring strict compliance with

---

89. Seidman, *Interviewing as Qualitative*, 7.

ethical requirements for participants.[90] In the first place, interviewees in this research were considered as equal partners and participants in the project.[91] They voluntarily consented to take part in the research and were treated with respect and confidentiality. They were happy to be identified, and trusted me to quote them with discretion if necessary. They were adequately informed about the purpose for and benefit of the research and were assured of the confidentiality required for their participation. While the kind of responses to the open-ended questions were not pre-empted, participants were informed about the nature of the interview, the length of the interview and a mutually agreeable timeframe to accommodate the convenience of participants was agreed upon for the exercise.

As one of Kato's successors at AEA, I endeavoured to be objective in my assessment of Kato's theological position and mine on the one hand, and the biblical and theological material in the academy on the other. Kato and I have thirty-four years between us at AEA, from the time of his death in 1975 to my assumption of office as AEA general secretary in 2009. Two other general secretaries have served between us. My interest in Kato arose when I first read the historical background of Africa International University (then, the Nairobi Evangelical Graduate School of Theology), an AEA institution in Nairobi. In the brief historical sketch, I ran across multiple mentions of Kato as the visionary of the school, which was founded in 1983, eight years after Kato's death. I advocated to have the history rewritten, arguing that it might not be a fair reflection of the institution's history and thinking that the account was unfairly biased towards Kato. However, that ACTEA and FATEB had similar histories and memorabilia associated with Kato fed my curiosity and left me wanting to know more about who Byang Kato was and why he was so revered and remembered. I came across Christina Breman's dissertation, *The Association of Evangelicals in Africa*, and for the first time got to know a little more about Byang Kato, further increasing my curiosity.

Unfortunately, I could not find a single work on Kato on the shelves of AEA schools, apart from background mentions in historical sketches and inscriptions upon memorial structure. My curiosity turned to vexation when I had the privilege to endorse a handbook, edited by Brian Stiller and others,

---

90. Creswell, *Educational Research*, 588.
91. Seidman, *Interviewing as Qualitative*, 8.

under the auspices of the WEA: *Evangelicals around the World: A Global Handbook for the 21st Century*. A section of this book mentions eight people from Africa as "evangelicals you would want to know."[92] Unfortunately, Byang Kato is not among the eight people mentioned. Ironically for me, this time I felt the opposite of what I had felt about the AIU history. I sensed the need for a more comprehensive scholarly work exploring Kato's life and contribution in the church in sub-Saharan Africa. Shirik underscores this need and writes: "It appears that while his critics have misunderstood him in some aspects, his supporters also have not paid enough attention to his theological conviction and articulation."[93] Given the advantage I had in being involved with the various institutions that continue to remember Kato, and given my access to his close surviving family members and colleagues, I opted to undertake this research, and hence the ethnographic nature of the study.

Delimitations of the Study

This study is a single case study and limited in scope in terms of its generalisability. The research focuses on Byang Kato's key experiences and key messages. However, the focus relates to only three key areas of theological issues identified in the study (i.e. biblical hermeneutics, African Christian identity and contribution to evangelical theological education).

Given the cultural diversity in Africa, the traditional and cultural issues into which Kato endeavoured to bring biblical insight are limited in scope for application to all sub-Saharan Africa. Given the diversity among the different denominations in the church as a whole, and even among evangelicals, it is difficult to apply a single case to all. However, the apparently extensive influence of Kato's pioneering work on the evangelical church in Africa is worthy of study, and it represents an important contribution to classical or standard Christianity in the region.

The study has a focus on Africa, but there is not a single Africa. A discourse on Byang Kato (1936–1975) as a pioneer of African theology and the African church may seem a travesty, given the role of Africa in the Bible and in the shaping of classic Christianity. Following the establishment of the church

---

92. Hickman, "Evangelicals," 227.
93. Shirik, "African Christians," 131.

in Palestine,[94] North Africa was the next important centre of Christianity. Therefore, this discussion is limited to sub-Saharan Africa, where the history of the church tends to be limited to the last two centuries. Though sub-Saharan Africa itself has multiple cultural identities, experiences and challenges associated with Christianity are similar enough to allow it to be treated as a region, even if North Africa is to be excluded.

Overview

My research is carried out in six steps, with each step corresponding to a chapter as follows:

1. *Introduction*. This chapter describes the research problem, purpose, importance, hypothesis, design and methodology. The problem description includes a sketch of the background to the study, including past and current practices in the church, to illustrate how Christian beliefs or professions compare with practice and how this impacts the church and is being addressed. The theoretical foundations and justifications for biographical study as an aspect of historical theology is also articulated.

2. *A Synopsis of the Life and Times of Byang Kato*. This chapter sets out the life and ministry of Byang Kato. How he developed from traditional fetishism as a boy to become a leading evangelical Christian leader. This is a narrative of the life story of Kato, his childhood, education, adulthood and ministry before his demise. The chapter also provides important socio-cultural and political contextual information about Kato's biography. Kato's accomplishment and failures are also highlighted.

3. *Byang Kato's Theological Legacy in Biblical Hermeneutics, African Christian identity and Evangelical Theological Education*. This chapter examines Kato's understanding of these three themes and how he applied them in practice and their impact on the church. The chapter draws on data from the literary review and field research. It gives an overview of some of the issues Kato contended

---

94. Oden, *How Africa Shaped*.

with in theological debates for insights about his hermeneutics and Christian identity. Kato's contribution to theological education in sub-Saharan Africa and beyond is also highlighted. The contemporary resonance with Kato's time is also explored. Efforts are also made to relate the discussion with current notions, influenced by the legacy of some of Kato's critics, that are circulating in some sub-Saharan African evangelical institutions, such as the Akrofi-Christeller Institute of Theology, Mission and Culture. In so doing, the arguments and warnings Kato enunciated while he was alive are brought to bear again in the contemporary setting.

4. *Theological and Biblical Foundations for African Christian Identity, Hermeneutics, Evangelical Theological Education.* This chapter involves assessment of Kato's biblical perspectives and exegesis of three biblical passages that shaped Kato's life or he used for preaching, which serve to ground the dialogue and are crucial to understanding his theological legacy. These include the following texts: Genesis 6:9–7:24; Jeremiah 8:11–22; and Philippians 4:13–19. The chapter outlines some standard theological and biblical approaches, against which Kato's messages are assessed for orthodoxy and relation to the historic Christian faith. A key aspect of this chapter is the critical engagement of Kato's theological opponents who found significant continuity between African worldviews and the mainstream Christian worldview.

5. *A Model for Biblical Fidelity in African Evangelical Christianity.* The research culminates in formulating a framework for a unique theological model for harmonising a profession of Christian faith and practice in a contemporary African context. This chapter essentially outlines the contours of the theological corpus that characterises Kato's theological contribution for evangelical orthodoxy in the African context.

6. *Summary, Conclusion and Recommendations.* The final chapter offers a summary of each of the five preceding chapters, highlights findings of the project and concludes with recommendations for further research.

CHAPTER 2

A Synopsis of the Life and Times of Byang Kato

Introduction

This chapter outlines the life and ministry of Byang Kato, from childhood through adulthood. The research explores how as a boy he was raised in traditional religious beliefs and practices in an African context in Kwoi, the local government headquarters of the Jaba people in Northern Nigeria, and became in adulthood an outstanding evangelical Christian leader in the global church. A portrait of Kato is painted, depicting various phases of his life, including birth, childhood, transition to adulthood, conversion and spiritual formation, education, family life, vocation and tragic demise. This chapter outlines the various influences that shaped Kato's life and how he in turn influenced the church and people in Africa and beyond.

Kato is remembered as the father of evangelicalism in Africa, with exceptional achievements in his short life of thirty-nine years. According to Bowers, "Kato was no obscure, second-rate individual operating at the fringes of world Christianity. In evangelical structures of the time, he was a well-regarded member of its inner global leadership circles."[1] Kato's influence and contribution went beyond polemics. He had a few important firsts in his life and ministry, which set him apart. Unveiling his personality, beliefs

---

1. Bowers, "Byang Kato and Beyond" 4.

and self-identity is of interest and is an inspiration for disciple-making and leadership development in the church in Africa.

Kato's biography is studied with particular emphasis on his theological legacy, especially regarding his biblical hermeneutics, conception of African Christian identity and contribution to theological education in Africa. The question of identity in theological discourse is important in the African context. A person's self-identity is mostly shaped by his or her personal experiences, society's assessment and the internalisation of other people's judgements.[2] Therefore, the socio-cultural, religious and political context plays an important role in the development of self-identity.[3] How Kato weathered extenuating circumstances to become an outstanding Christian leader is worth exploring.

Sources of Information for the Biography

The main sources of information for this study were accessed from a comprehensive bibliography on Kato compiled by Christina Breman and made available by ACTEA.[4] The primary source was Kato's works – his books and papers. Secondary sources included several scholarly articles by Bowers, Palmer, Tiénou, Shirik, Ferdinando and Turaki, among others. Some information was also retrieved from AEA archives. Other works relevant to the study also include John Stott's *Evangelical Truth: A Personal Plea for Unity, Integrity and Faithfulness* (2003), Thomas Oden's *The Rebirth of Orthodoxy: Signs of New Life in Christianity* (2015) and *The Rebirth of African Orthodoxy: Return to Foundations* (2016), Christopher J. H. Wright's *The Mission of God: Unlocking the Bible's Grand Narrative* (2006), Elizabeth Mburu's *African Hermeneutics* (2019), Kwame Bediako's *Theology and Identity* (1992), Yusufu Turaki's *Engaging Religions and Worldviews in Africa* (2020), and a popular biography of Kato by Sophie de la Haye, *Byang Kato: Ambassador For Christ* (1986). Many of Kato's papers, along with Haye's biography, were not necessarily peer reviewed or evidence-based scholarly papers. They were either speeches or sermons, many of which were neither dated nor paginated. However, Kato's

---

2. MacKinnon and Heise, *Self*, 164; cf. Kuwana, "African Leadership."
3. MacKinnon and Heise, *Self*, 163–198; cf. Horowitz, "Self-Identity."
4. See Breman, "Association of Evangelicals," 505–512. See also Breman, *Byang H. Kato*.

magnum opus, *Theological Pitfalls in Africa*, the published version of his doctoral thesis, along with the thesis itself, was also reviewed. Data was also derived from field interviews with people who knew Kato.

The study and writing of African church history are based on a multiplicity of sources. Oral data is particularly important in the African context.[5] Important historical information may be stored in the minds of people, ready to be recalled but not available otherwise in a discernible manner. When this information is not gleaned in a timely manner, it is lost through death and buried with the individuals whose memories held it. Many of Kato's contemporaries had already passed at the time of this study. Nevertheless, a few survivors of Kato – friends, colleagues and family members who knew him — were interviewed.

The reliability of oral history has been a subject of debate and there are concerns about the limitations of human memory, even if those narrating the events were intimately involved.[6] Interviews generate oral information, which is complimentary to documentary data.[7] Surviving contemporaries of Kato may not be many, and it was important they communicate relevant information that may not be found in existing historical records before they passed on. Perks and Thomson state: "Oral history has had a significant impact upon historical practice in the second half of the twentieth century. It has democratised the study of the past by recording the experience of people who have been 'hidden from history.'"[8]

To mitigate the concerns about reliability, the semi-structured approach of posing open-ended questions allowed the respondents to voice their experiences without any constraint from the researcher's perspective. These respondents were interviewed one-on-one, did not care whether or not they were anonymous, and spoke freely and articulately in responding to questions on any issue.[9] These interviews generated data as part of gathering relevant information for analysing Kato's theological legacy. Next, I highlight the background into which Kato was born and was shaped.

---

5. Omulukoli, *Priority of African*, 7.
6. Perks and Thomson, *Oral History Reader*, 3.
7. Sensing, *Qualitative Research*, 103.
8. Perks and Thomson, *Oral History Reader*, ix.
9. Creswell, *Educational Research*, 217–218; cf. Hirsch, "Culture and Disability," 214–223.

Socio-political and Cultural Context of Kato's Time

Kato was born and raised during the colonial era in Nigeria (1900–1963), and he witnessed the end of colonial rule when Nigeria gained independence from Britain in 1963.[10] He also lived through the Nigerian Civil War, or Biafran War, fought between the federal government and the secessionist state of Biafra, from July 1967 to January 1970. The state of Biafra was mostly the homeland of the Igbo tribe or people from Southern Nigeria who felt they could not co-exist with the North-led federal government.

Northern Nigeria was divided into two different regions: the far north, dominated by Islam with Fulani and Hausa being the main people groups, and the Middle Belt region to the south, dominated by traditional African religions, with several ethnic groups. The far north of Nigeria is surrounded by Islamic countries with links to Egypt and the Maghreb (that is, western North Africa, such as Algeria, Morocco and Libya) and influenced by Arab civilisation. Before the arrival of the British rulers in Nigeria, Islamic colonialism in the early 1800s imposed its religion, expanded slave trade and created a polarised society in that part of Nigeria. There was a social divide between Muslims and non-Muslims, with the former being the dominant force and subjugating the latter. This stratification created a dominance-subordination relationship. The non-Muslims were treated as second class citizens by the Muslims.[11] Due to the ongoing Boko Haram incidents in Northern Nigeria, there have been a lot of studies exploring the historical socio-political context of the region.

With the divide-and-rule doctrine of British colonialists, the same division the Islamic occupiers before them created – a dominance-subordination relationship between powerful Muslims to the far north and the non-Muslims southward, in the Middle Belt and further south – was institutionalised.[12] At the same time, the two different societies – the Muslim North and the non-Muslims to the south and closer to the Middle Belt – were merged into a single political region (i.e. Northern Nigeria).[13] The Muslim North was the region first occupied by the British imposition, and they used the Islamic

---

10. Turaki, *Tainted Legacy*, 113.
11. Byimui, "Toward Christian-Muslim," 22; Turaki, *British Colonial Legacy*; Abar, "Islam."
12. Turaki, *Tainted Legacy*, 2.
13. Turaki, 23–24.

rulers as their viceroys to rule the rest of the country to the south through indirect rule, a strategy commonly used by British colonialism, setting up one group of indigenes against another and using a particular faction to exercise control over their compatriots at the behest of the British.[14] This is essential for understanding the current religious tensions and conflict in Northern Nigeria, and their genesis.

The Middle Belt, dominated by traditional ethnic groups, was merged with the North, and its peoples subjected to ethnic and religious hostility, slavery and wars of territorial expansion and annexation.[15] Culturally, Northern Nigeria was mostly Islamic and not so open to Christian missionary endeavours compared to the southern part of Nigeria. The ethnic people who did not convert to Islam were lower in social status; some were denied their basic rights and land. "Islamic colonialism and slavery were crucial in defining the religion, culture, ethnicity and general social life of the region."[16] The imposition of the Islamic culture virtually replaced the traditional African culture. Contrary to current popular belief, "Christianity did far more to preserve African languages and promote African identity than Islam did."[17] The divisions and injustices created in the region by the Islamic leaders were reinforced under British colonial rule, and at the time of independence, the non-Muslims were not any better off than they had been, and they continued to be subordinated by the Muslims.

---

14. Turaki, 74–76.
15. Turaki, *British Colonial Legacy*, 24; cf Maigadi, "Christian Faith."
16. Turaki, *British Colonial Legacy*, 9.
17. Turaki, 43.

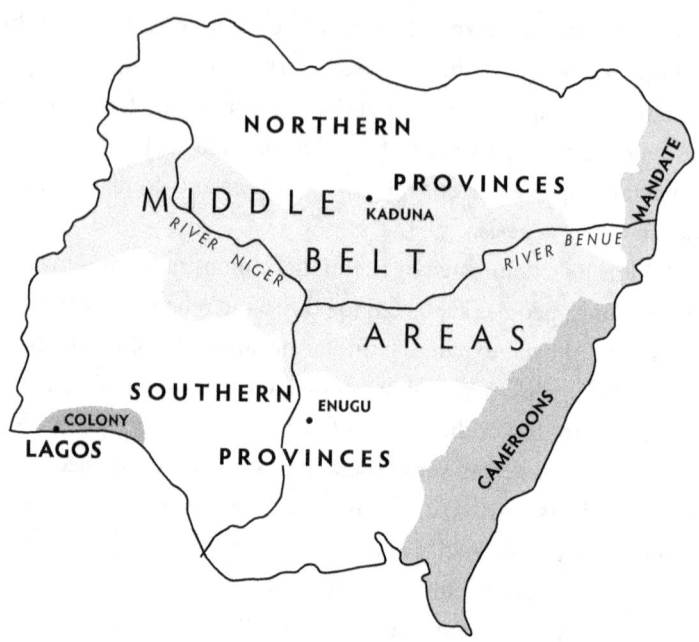

Figure 1: Map of Nigeria Showing Northern Nigeria and the Middle Belt in the 1960s[18]

Kwoi, the birthplace of Kato, is presently the administrative headquarters of the Jaba local government area in Kaduna State in the southern part of Northern Nigeria. This region was associated with the Middle Belt where the Jaba ethnic group is found.

> With an estimated over 350 ethnic groups speaking different languages, Nigeria is not only the most populous country in Africa, but it is also the most multi-ethnic society in Africa as well. Such ethnic diversity makes ethnicity an important element in the life of each ethnic group because it provides each group with a positive sense of self-identity, security, self-determination, and belongingness.[19]

The Hahm or Ham ethnic group is popularly referred to as Jaba people by the Hausa.[20] The Hausa language is the dominant language of the people

---

18. Turaki, *British Colonial Legacy*, 81.
19. Maigadi, "Christian Faith," 29.
20. Kato, *Theological Pitfalls*, 27.

of Northern Nigeria and the second language of the other ethnic groups in Nigeria. Jaba has remained as the most popular name for the Ham people. Jaba people are believed to be descendants of Africa's earliest civilization, the Nok culture, an early Iron Age civilisation dating back to 400 BC. The archaeological discovery of the Nok terracotta heads, beginning in the 1920s and 1940s, points to the existence of Nok culture, which dates from 500 BC to AD 200,[21] and establishes a firm link with the modern Jaba people in the Kwoi local government area.[22] The Jaba was one of the ethnic groups that was resistant to Islam and mostly followed African traditional religion. They were therefore a target in Islamic raids to enforce Islam and to capture slaves. The Middle Belt as a whole has been a target for attacks by Isamist jihadists from the North as it stands in the way between Northern Nigeria and the southern region, which is mostly Christian.

Kwoi was one of the earliest settlements for Christian missionaries in Northern Nigeria, especially those from Sudan Interior Mission – now Serving In Mission (SIM) – since 1910. SIM, a conservative evangelical North American missionary organisation, founded in 1893, is a leading evangelical mission agency in Africa. SIM founded the ECWA denomination (Evangelical Church Winning All, formerly Evangelical Church of West Africa). In terms of denominational beliefs, ECWA is dispensational pre-millennialist and emphasises water baptism by immersion. Christianity was more acceptable to the Jaba people than Islam, a further reason for the Islamic aggression even today. This is the church that Kato was baptised into, and in which he had his discipleship and basic Bible and theological training before his undergraduate and postgraduate training abroad. The multi-religious and political context were a factor in shaping Kato. His experience of the Islamic influence and the Hausa's subjugation of smaller ethnic groups (including the Jaba) on the one hand, and treatment by the Western colonial systems and the missionary influence on the other, were pivotal. There were also the traditional, religious and cultural factors of his birth and upbringing. His lifestyle, as for most African peoples, was communal.[23]

---

21. See Abar, "Islam"; Byimui, "Toward Christian-Muslim."
22. Kato, *Theological Pitfalls*, 28.
23. Maigadi, "Christian Faith," 84–85.

The cultural influences in the Nigerian context are to some extent typical of other nations in sub-Sarahan Africa, and it is against this background that Kato developed his biblical faith and dared to have a lone voice on a wide range of issues. The religious tensions contributed towards shaping his boyhood self-image and ministering as a Christian may have emboldened him. The more his context is understood the less difficult it is to understand Kato's development.

Birth and Early Childhood

Kato was born on 23 June 1936 in Kwoi, a rural town of about fifteen thousand people in the Sabzuro section in Kaduna State.[24] The Jaba people with their Nok ancestry have lived in the archaeological Nok area for at least two thousand years. There are no myths of migration from any other place. Folklore suggests they came from Bitaro, which is only four miles away. They also look to Njeng, twelve miles away, for their religious ancestry.[25]

Kato's birth, nurture and childhood experiences, culminating in the rite of passage from childhood to manhood, may exemplify the experience of a traditional African child. Kato was the first child and son, therefore the heir apparent, of Heri and Zawi Kato. Kato's middle name, Henry, was an anglicised version of the father's name, Heri.[26] The father was the fetish priest of a local deity known as Pop-ku.[27] A few months after Kato's birth, he was dedicated as fetish priest, destined to succeed his father.[28] Worship of a deity is common in African traditional religions. Belief in a Supreme God as creator of heaven and earth and with power to kill is acknowledged in African traditional religions.[29] However, the Supreme Being and creator seems to be far removed from day-to-day reality, and people relate to lesser gods in their worship, a distortion of the valid concept of a Supreme Being in the

---

24. Baba, "Profile of Dr. Byang"; cf. Haye, *Byang Kato*, 17.
25. Kato, *Theological Pitfalls*, 28.
26. Alemu Kato in an interview with author in Kwoi, 22 March 2019.
27. Baba, "Profile of Dr. Byang." According to Kato, fetishism refers to a created object used by worshippers of African traditional religions. For example, use of charms and amulets believed to inherit special spiritual powers for protection against malevolent spirits. However, fetishism is only an aspect of the ATRs as a whole. Kato, *Theological Pitfalls*, 21–22.
28. Haye, *Byang Kato*, 17.
29. Kato, *Theological Pitfalls*, 19.

Judeo-Christian faith.[30] African spirituality or worship of the deity by African peoples has been referred to by various terms: animism, idol worship, paganism and heathenism, witchcraft, fetishism, magic, juju, primitive religion or ancestral veneration. A more comprehensive nomenclature for African religions is "African traditional religions" (ATRs). There is no single religion of African peoples; rather, there are multiple religions of different ethnic groups.[31] Although there are differences in the ways the diverse ethnic groups do their ritual and cultic worship, some common features can be identified and therefore an assessment of a particular African traditional region may provide an understanding of what ATR is. Thus, Kato describes the characteristics of Jaba religion as an example of ATR.[32]

According to Kato "Jaba do not have the fully-developed polytheism scholars sometimes claim for West Africa. But they do have the concept of a Supreme Being, a notion of future life, and some views of sacrifice."[33] However, "the chief object of their worship is not Nom, the Supreme Being. Apart from verbal references, nothing in practice is done in connection with Nom. They do not worship Nom though they have him constantly in their language."[34] Thus, like many other African cultures, the Supreme Being is approached through intermediaries or idols. Kato demystifies African traditional religions, which bring fear and control the lives of people. According to Kato, worship of the deity was humanistic, and its motivation was material benefits. The cult promised power and control and protection.[35] The ultimate goal is neither the glory of the Supreme Being or even of the lesser gods, but that women and children may serve the needs of men.[36] Followers believe that the world is full of spirits that are out there to hurt people, and there are hardly good spirits.[37] So, the life of the Jaba person is dominated by fear. The graveyard is believed to be filled with the spirits of the dead roaming about; places of fear are numerous, including trees. So, at harvest, first fruits are

---

30. Kato, 27.
31. Kato, 16–28.
32. Kato, 28–69.
33. Kato, 29.
34. Kato, 33.
35. Kato, 38; cf. Turaki, *British Colonial Legacy*, 37–39.
36. Kato, *Theological Pitfalls*, 47.
37. Kato, 47.

placed at the tombs or under a tree before human consumption. Failure to do so is to one's peril, incurring punishment from the spirits.

Exorcism is part of Jaba belief and practice. Some people specialise in casting out the evil spirits, and rituals are associated with some sacred articles such as a drum, calabash and a locally made string instrument like a guitar.[38] The exorcism is done at night and requires lots of food, singing and incantations, with the fetish priest calling the name of the spirits in the possessed. The possessed and women from the village would then break into dancing to the tempo of music and singing from the exorcist. The dancing would go on for at least two hours; the possessed would then fall down as if in a coma, apparently out of exhaustion. They would wake up later revived and strengthened in the belief that the spirit had now left them. If the person is ever troubled by the spirits again, the exorcising practice is repeated. The Jaba religion and the world of the spirits could have had substantial impact on Kato and his attitude to mysticism.

Figure 2: Photo of Byang Henry Kato[39]

---

38. Kato, 49.
39. Used by permission

Kato bears in his physical body and lifestyle, elements of authentic traditional African identity, epitomised by the prominent tribal marks he wore on his left temple (see figure 2 above). African traditional marks caused by body piercing and cuts are not merely for fashion; these have spiritual connotation and are inflicted with some blood-letting rituals with religious and social functions.[40] The marks were not only for fashion but also were marks of identity, protection from evil and were meant to be medicinal.[41] One of the characteristics of African traditions, with religious connotations, is the practice of bloodletting and the permanent scars that those raised in a typical African religious tradition carry on their bodies for the rest of their lives. The two slits or traditional marks on either side of Kato's temples gave him an authentic cultural identity.

Kato survived seven siblings who perished, and his community believed he was saved or spared by the evil spirit or devil.[42] Every effort was made to make young Kato grow up, appeasing the gods for his own safety. He learned how to offer the first harvest of the crop at a shrine at the base of a sycamore sacred tree where the spirits were believed to dwell, and he also learned the art of offering sacrifices to the deities.[43] Relationship with and worship of the clan gods was based on fear and not love, unlike the God of the Bible, about whom worshippers are admonished: "Love the Lord your God with all your heart and with all your soul and with all your mind" (Matt 22:37). Kato had a sound knowledge of African traditional religions from his experience as a Jaba priest.[44] Kato was also influenced by some cross-cultural values when he encountered missionaries and experienced life in the church and the mission school.

---

40. Turaki, *Christianity and African Gods*, 92.
41. Cullivan, "Meanings," 1.
42. Kato, "From Juju"; cf. Turaki, *Christianity and African Gods*, 18.
43. Haye, *Byang Kato*, 17.
44. Kato, "Critique of Incipient," ThD diss., 28–67.

Dedication as Fetish Priest and Rite of Passage to Manhood

African traditional religious beliefs hold that the world is permeated with spirits and divinities who influence every aspect of a person's life for ill or for good. Rituals are means of appeasing these divinities and spirits. Diviners and witch doctors are believed to be close to the spirits and tend to go to extra length in the observance of rituals to appease the gods.[45] Rituals like child dedications were to confer on the child special blessings from the gods and avert curses. Also, rituals of this nature, in the traditional sense, are covenantal, and in Kato's case, required "bloody sacrifices, exorcism, curses, and trial by poison."[46] Dedication was a ceremony marking the devotion of the child back to the gods of the clan. This could well have been the case for Kato, and the tribal marks on his temple could have been incised as part of the dedication ritual.

Dedication as fetish priest was cultic and a cardinal feature of ritual worship, among other rites such as confession, prayers and sacrifices to deities, communal meals, ritual washing, ancestral veneration and blood-letting for ablution.[47] According to Sawyerr, blood is life and is therefore used to establish, preserve or restore a blood-covenant relationship between all members of the family and between the deity or spirit and the worshippers.[48] Sawyerr goes further to observe that the worship of ancestors and divinities by Africans falls short of Christian worship, in terms of liturgy and cult or way of worship.[49]

Some preachers today would call for deliverance at conversion to Christianity to nullify the influence of the spirits and divinities to which the person was dedicated as a child. There was no such deliverance ritual or ceremony in the case of Kato. At his conversion, he believed he had been saved from his past and trusted the efficacy of the salvation Jesus offers when people trust him. Kato appeared to be reticent about charismatic expression and teachings about the Holy Spirit by some in the church. One wonders

---

45. Kunhiyop, *African Christian Theology*, 108–109.
46. Nystrom, "Let African Christians."
47. Sawyerr, *Creative Evangelism*, 119–121.
48. Sawyerr, 121.
49. Sawyerr, 128–129.

whether this was because of the spiritism he experienced in the Jaba religious practices, especially aspects that were inconsistent with the Bible.

Early childhood education shapes belief, values and accomplishment in the whole of life, helping children to realise their full potential. The formative stages are categorized into four: infancy, early childhood, middle childhood and later childhood.[50] At each stage of the child's life, a foundation is built for the child's physical, spiritual, intellectual and emotional well-being. The dedication of baby Kato was a commitment to nurture the child into fetish practices. Cultural and historical traditions are transmitted orally from one generation to another.[51] Byang acquired the skill for offering sacrifices to the deities which inhabited votive objects and was dedicated as a fetish priest a few months after his birth. His nurture was oriented to this goal. His father was mentoring him and he was undergoing rites of passage preparing him for his destined vocation.[52]

The rite of passage into manhood required living in the jungle for one hectic week, out of the reach of women and non-initiates, who were made to believe that the young initiates had been swallowed by the devil. The seclusion and exclusion from non-members, mostly women and children, was also meant to arouse fear in the women and children, who were made to believe that the initiate was in company with the devil. While this may sound like a hoax, some engagement of ancestral spirits and deities, together with blood sacrifices, are characteristic features of rite of passage rituals: "The mothers were required to provide enough food and drink for the devil until the devil's stomach was so full as to vomit the young men out."[53] The boys themselves would be indoctrinated to reinforce their invincibility and ensure they kept the secrets of the rituals for a lifetime.

Activities in the bush included indoctrination, disciplinary programmes, skilful arts (e.g. fishing, farming and warfare), life skills to prepare the young boys for manhood, and oath-taking not to divulge the secrets of the goings-on in the bush to non-members of the men's society. Ikwubuzo observes: "Some

---

50. Semenye, *Let Children Come*, 39–49.

51. Kenyatta, *Facing Mt Kenya*, xvi.

52. Haye, *Byang Kato*, 17; cf. Ferdinando, "Christian Identity"; Janssen, "Initiation and Passage."

53. Haye, *Byang Kato*, 18; cf. Janssen, "Initiation and Passage"; Ikwubuzo, "Rites of Passage," 143.

of these cultural patterns of life are of mythic dimensions in that they reflect the myth that bind the society together in its people's psychological, social and religious activities."[54] These were valuable forms of education that established the young adult as a responsible citizen. However, the underlying secrecy and hidden motivations and deceptions in the guilds may have contributed to these traditional systems and forms of education being endangered in more recent times.

The late childhood period in a person's life is an important formative period of development when values and beliefs are firmly implanted for a lifetime.[55] Demonstrating traits of traditional fetish cultural beliefs would be expected in the later life of Kato. In his writings, Kato stated his cognitive experience and knowledge of the Jaba traditions.[56] Kato, like other Jaba tribal boys, was ready for the transitioning rite from boyhood to manhood at the age of ten. At this stage of late childhood or puberty, the young person is spiritually prepared and open to instruction and able to discern what is right or wrong with an enquiring mind.[57] The goal of the initiation rite of passage was to prepare the young man for manly responsibilities, ready to start and run his own family. The ritual was a test of manhood through drills and rough life in the bush. Generally, traditional education emphasised comprehensive aspects of human endeavours. The rite of passage also included training in other adult skills like warfare, marriage, parenting and leadership. The young man was prepared and given the opportunity to prove his readiness as a grown-up person.[58] The initiates who had now graduated as men would return to the village from the bush amidst the singing, drumming, dancing and feasting of the entire village, along with guests from neighbouring villages.[59] Kato's experiences described here are familiar in African folklore and literature, for example in the work of Camara Laye, Chinua Achebe and others in the African Writers Series.[60] Thus, these experiences may typify what an

---

54. Ikwubuzo, "Rites of Passage," 140.
55. Semenye, *Let Children Come*, 47–49.
56. Kato, "Critique of Incipient," ThD diss., 30.
57. Semenye, *Let Children Come*, 48.
58. Jusu, "Rites of Passage," 1838; cf. Ikwuagwu, "Initiation," 62.
59. Haye, *Byang Kato*, 17–18.
60. The African Writers Series is a collection of 359 books written by African writers and published by Heinemann between 1962 and 2003.

average African boy went through, certainly in Kato's time. These experiences are important factors in shaping one's worldviews with implications for one's perspective on Christianity. Kato was thoroughly shaped and mentored in the tradition of his father and was ready to succeed the father.

Kato's birth, childhood and rite of passage to manhood typify experiences in African traditional religious belief systems. He did not just read or hear about African traditional religion, but he had a real immersion in the belief system from the earliest possible and most impressionistic period of his life. To illustrate the indelible impact of childhood impressions, Kato writes:

> As a child I used to be very afraid of a graveyard. I am still not sure that I would be happy to spend a night in a cemetery. I think this fear comes from my pagan background, because I grew up believing that the spirits of the dead come back to haunt the living. This is a universal belief among heathen societies. But is it true? Do dead people come back as spirits?[61]

Although he had been tested physically, spiritually, mentally and emotionally through the demands of the cultic rituals and had been conferred with manhood, the budding adult was still in the formative stages, at the tender age of ten to twelve years old, and open to other influences that could shape him for life. However, it would be inappropriate to treat the young initiate as a child. The gap between a child and an adult is huge; it is not about chronological age but rather the cultural status the boy would now assume after his rite of passage. The child had grown through the impressionistic phase of life, acquiring conduct through imitation and prone to accept all that he had been taught with tender conscience, a strong impulse to obey and a God-consciousness.[62]

However, much of missionary education ignored traditional education and focused more on spiritual and less on social life.[63] Formal schooling and attending Sunday school provided Kato the opportunity for encounter with and conversion to Christianity. Essentially, the Western educational curriculum focused on literary work, based on reading, writing, arithmetic

---

61. Kato, *Spirits*, 3.
62. "Evangelism Is."
63. Ogunbado, "Impacts of Colonialism," 55.

and Bible knowledge, and aimed at producing Christians who could read the Bible. Also, the education in colonial times was aimed at preparing people to serve as clerks, agents and interpreters in the colonial administration and commerce.[64] The initial objective of the missionary schools was gospel work among the natives. However, the colonial government gave financial assistance and exercised control over the schools which "formed the foundation upon which the educational systems of most African nations are built today."[65]

Kato had a comprehensive immersion in his formative years, educated in both the world of traditional culture and in the world of missionary education influenced by the colonial government. Kato found purpose for his life in committing to living out the truth of his new faith without compromise in elementary school.

Conversion to Christianity, Spiritual Formation and Elementary Education

In later childhood, Kato had an encounter in his village with a lady missionary, Mary Haas of the Sudan Interior Mission (SIM).[66] In 1954 the independent SIM-related churches in Nigeria came together to establish a single indigenous evangelical denomination known as the Evangelical Church of West Africa, now known as the Evangelical Church Winning All (ECWA). This was in Kato's last year in primary (or elementary) school. The ECWA church is currently one of the largest evangelical church denominations in Nigeria, with a membership of over ten million.[67] It has been the dominant denomination in the Nigeria Evangelical Fellowship since its founding in 1965. The SIM missionary lady visited the village square many times and attracted the community through playing music on a gramophone which was placed on a rock in the town square, close to Kato's home in Kwoi. This was how Kato was first attracted to missionary activities and encounters. Mary Haas did not only play music but also preached the gospel in the language of the local people, or more likely in Hausa, the *lingua franca* in Northern

---

64. Ogunbado, 54.
65. Sulaiman, "Internationalization in Education," 86.
66. Haye, *Byang Kato*, 18.
67. "ECWA History," ECWA, ECWA Information Office, http://www.ecwa.org.ng/ecwa-history/.

Nigeria. For the first time, Kato heard the gospel in his own language.[68] This enhanced understanding and may have made an indelible impression. The local church was also not far from the square and the Kato homestead. Kato also got interested in gospel stories he heard in Sunday school at the church. The gospel message Kato heard in the village square several times from the missionary, in his own language, was reinforced when Kato got enrolled in the elementary school, built by missionaries, at the age of twelve. Regular schooling in the missionary school would be a distraction for the plans of Kato's father. It was not surprising therefore that, for nearly a year, the father resisted the idea of enrolling his son in a Christian missionary school. Ironically, it was the grandfather who prevailed on Kato's father for the young grandson to enroll in the Christian school, thus jeopardizing the succession of the fetish priesthood tradition.

Kato's heart was stirred when he heard a Bible story, told by his Nigerian teacher, about Noah and the ark and God's plan of salvation in saving Noah and his family (Gen 6:9–8:22). Kato's understanding of the story made him come to appreciate the human need for salvation from the devastating consequences of sin and the way of salvation offered by God in Jesus Christ. He saw the need to make a personal choice of accepting Jesus Christ as his Saviour that day, to escape the wrath of God as a sinner.[69] Testifying about his conversion, Kato writes:

> Finally a day came when I knew I had to decide what I would do. I had to face these facts: Juju could not save my soul. Juju demands bloody sacrifices – often human sacrifices. Juju demands torture, keeps women and children in fear. Juju priests claim they have the power of life and death over anyone who fails to give the required number of goats, rams, and cocks. These priests are a terror to everyone![70]

Kato was interviewed by a journalist on a tour in Europe about his faith and why he became a Christian. Kato's response was:

---

68. Haye, *Byang Kato*, 18.
69. Breman, "Association of Evangelicals," 37; Haye, *Byang Kato*, 19.
70. Kato, "Devil's Baby," 13.

> Well, when I was without Christ, I was of course religious – religious in the sense of worshipping idols. But when Jesus Christ was presented to me, I realized that He was the Way of Life – not just a way, but the only Way, and so I asked Him to come into my heart, in order that when I die, I may be sure of going to be with Him in heaven.[71]

While Kato felt forgiven by God and was now free from the consequences of sin, he incurred the wrath of his father and suffered the consequences. He was deprived of his livelihood; his father stopped feeding him and providing clothing for him. However, Kato endured the ordeal, and as the first son of three, he had responsibility to mentor his two younger half-brothers and work on the family farm.[72] Counting the cost for discipleship and following Christ was real and experiential. Kato's conversion to Christianity meant a rejection of the traditional religious practices he had been nurtured in since infancy. The decision to become a Christian angered his father and aggravated the punishment meted out to the young Kato; he got beaten and denied food.[73] The implications of Kato turning his back on cultural status would have far-reaching consequences beyond immediate livelihood and punishment.

This is the fate of many young people, especially those on the continent from Muslim backgrounds for whom Kato's experience is an inspiration. Accepting the Christian faith in school initially, Kato did not feel anything different had happened to him, apart from the punishment from his father who was hurt by his son's conversion. Quoting Kato, Haye writes: "I was a Christian, but I knew constant failure. My testimony was a mockery to the name of Christ."[74] This was an apparent reference that he was still living the old life of sin and had not experienced any change the new faith promised. The turning point in his spiritual journey and encounter with the Christian faith was when he got convicted of his sins through listening to the preaching of the gospel during a SIM church conference in 1953 when he was 17. The speakers for the week-long conference and revival services were Gin

---

71. Kato, "African Perspectives," 1.

72. In Kato's context, and indeed in many African cultures, these are real brothers. However, the term "half-brother" is used to let the reader understand that the other two boys were from a different wife of Byang's father.

73. Breman, "Association of Evangelicals," 37.

74. Haye, *Byang Kato*, 20.

Mai-Gari and Andarawus, African pastors from SIM-related churches. These held to traditional values and beliefs generally characterizing evangelical Christians. The theme of the revival meetings was holiness and a call for repentance from sin.[75]

Kato felt convicted by the Holy Spirit through the message and was moved to tears in repentance, to the point of sacrificing anything to follow Christ. He took off his shirt and laid it on the altar as a sacrifice and contribution towards the effort of the African Missionary Society for sending out missionaries.[76] He was also convinced about the voice of God and that God wanted more than the sacrifice of a shirt. God wanted his whole life and his commitment to go out as a missionary himself. According to Haye,[77] Kato surrendered to God and invited him to use him as he would. In interviews with several respondents, this pietistic tendency of Kato was mentioned, and respondents spoke about his passion for the evangelistic work of the church and also his generosity to people even at the expense of his own family. In an interview with Rev. Adamu Kato, for example, he said that every time Kato returned from a trip back to the town, it took him nearly two hours to get from the drop-off point to his home, a distance that would ordinarily take less than thirty minutes. He would stop by every household to greet the people and often to evangelise them.[78]

Following Kato's conversion and encounter during the revival services, when he made a recommitment to faithfully follow Jesus, there was a marked change in his life. This was also a time of great revival in the church in Nigeria and in West Africa in general.[79] He was keen to attend Sunday school classes. He learned how to listen to God's word, and how to apply God's word to his own life. Kato looked forward to the Sunday school lessons, not only to hear the word of God but also as a way of learning and improving his English language studies. He taught other boys what he learned from Sunday school and even went to neighbouring villages to share the message he had learned. Kato was serious about following Christ as a disciple and about helping others

---

75. Haye, 20.
76. Haye, 20–23; cf. Breman, "Portrait," 138.
77. Haye, *Byang Kato*, 20–27.
78. Interview with Rev. Alemu Kato, brother of Byang, in Kwoi, 22 March 2019
79. Breman, "Association of Evangelicals," 38.

follow Christ in obedience to the Great Commission of Jesus Christ to make disciples of all nations and people (Matt 28:19–20). Kato also joined the Boys' Brigade, an interdenominational uniformed Christian youth organisation with a goal of character formation through the use of semi-military discipline with Christian values. He was also involved with Youth for Christ. By the age of eighteen, he was a company leader (presumably in the Boys' Brigade), promoted to the rank of sergeant for hard work and leadership.[80] The regimental training of the Boys' Brigade was meant to reinforce obedience and faithfulness to the Christian teachings youth received in school and church. Kato was particularly sensitive about drawing the line between traditional religious aspirations and what was authentically biblical Christianity.[81] With Kato's spiritual immersion in both African and Christian religion, he was knowledgeable enough to make comparison and make informed choices.

The beginning of Kato's spiritual journey was influenced by his father and grandfather on one hand and on the other by Mary Haas and various Nigerian teachers, especially the one who taught the story about Noah's ark which contributed to Kato's conversion to Christianity. Hearing the gospel in his local language from evangelical missionaries and the disciplinary drills of the Boys' Brigade all helped to shape Kato. Just like his traditional dedication and initiation experiences, Kato was baptised and became a communicant member of an evangelical SIM-related local church. He read the Bible with enthusiasm and regularity. He searched Scripture to discern the mind of God and looked to it for guidance for his faith and conduct. Like his grasp of previous religious beliefs, Kato was quick to understand his new faith. He chose to abandon his former religious worldview, associated with his old sinful life, and unequivocally embraced the Christian biblical view. This is particularly important given the dominance of traditional religious worldviews in the church in Africa.[82]

It is noteworthy that Kato stayed at home with his parents even when his parents objected to his new religious faith. The tendency in this kind of context was dualism. Most of the fetish priests were happy for their children to be engaged with the education and other opportunities offered by the foreign

---

80. Haye, *Byang Kato*, 23.
81. Kato, "Critique of Incipient," ThD diss., 33.
82. Chalk, *Making Disciples*, 11.

missionaries so long as the children continued to also participate in the fetish rituals at home. Accordingly, Kato's continued stay at home must have been challenging in his early years as a Christian. He must have been involved in day-to-day negotiations of this difficult situation of balancing two masters. Therefore, this kind of situation is likely to have contributed to developing his Christian character, appraisal of the value of ATR culture compared to his Christian faith and, thus, his contrary view from others in theological discourse later in his life. Recalling the bitter memories, Kato states:

> My father cursed and swore. He got so angry that he swore by his juju never to buy me any more clothes. Both my parents cursed and abused me. I was very frightened and worried, but they did not care. Believe me – people who serve juju are hard hearted, cruel, wicked, and bloodthirsty. They are cruel to those who dare to oppose them. They try by all means to put terror into the minds of all who do not follow them.[83]

His encounter with the gospel and discipleship as a young Christian proved to be effective and transformative and could be an important lesson for the church in Africa today.

Kato started primary school in earnest at the SIM school in Kwoi in 1948.[84] Starting his formal education was an important turning point. Though he was only a twelve-year-old boy, his cultural and life experiences had prepared him for manhood. As a young man, he was still open to being nurtured by other value systems. As an adult in the traditional sense, he was now in the position to fend for the family and assist his father on the farm. Apart from concern that schooling would be a distraction from his fetish priestly role, responsibilities for farming and the livelihood of the family was another of his father's concerns and objections to Kato enrolling in missionary school.

Kato's commitment to his schoolwork was exceptional. He balanced his time between work and studies. He worked on his father's farm in the morning, attended school in the afternoon and worked part-time for missionaries in the evening, to earn money to pay school fees and buy school supplies.[85]

---

83. Kato, "Devil's Baby," 13.
84. Haye, *Byang Kato*, 114.
85. Haye, 19; cf. Breman, "Association of Evangelicals," 135.

He learned how to cultivate crops like ginger, turmeric, bambara beans, cocoyam, cassava, millet and sorghum for subsistence.[86] Notwithstanding the hectic work schedule, Kato excelled in class and was often ranked the top student.[87] The current king of the Jaba people in Kwoi, Kpop Dr. Jonathan Danladi Gyet Maude, was Kato's classmate. In an interview he confirmed that Kato was always top of the class. Kato's primary education laid a solid foundation, and he propelled himself to Bible college, a tertiary institution, skipping secondary school.

Marriage and Family Life

Kato first met Juma Rahila Gandu (a.k.a. Jummai), who would eventually become his spouse, in Sunday school, and they attended the same primary school. Jummai was also born in Kwoi, on 22 May 1939, to His Highness Mal Gandu Maude and Dabo Kambo, and was a princess, daughter of the king of the Jaba people, known as the Kpop Ham.[88] Jummai was raised by her grandmother. Her mother, Dabo Kambok, had been kidnapped by a famous businessman, Kobo Nimen, when the king and father of Jummai died and when Jummai was only two years old.[89] Jummai's grandmother loved Kato for being a Christian young man, and she was instrumental in encouraging her granddaughter to date Kato. Kato was in his third and final year at Bible college at Igbaja when he and Jummai Rahila Gandu married. They wedded on 26 January 1957.[90]

Byang's union with Jummai brought together two influential African traditionalists: the one from a traditional ruling house and the other from a traditional fetish background. Jummai was of Jaba aristocracy and a princess, daughter of the Kpop Ham. Kato had been transformed from a fetish priest to a preacher of the gospel of Jesus Christ. The Bible places importance on these community positions: priest and queen. The priest exemplified God's values and tasked to teach God's precepts to the people, while the monarch lived

---

86. In an interview with Mrs. Jummai Kato, in Kaduna, 23 March 2019.
87. Breman, 138.
88. Breman, 139; Haye, *Byang Kato*, 36.
89. Jummai's funeral booklet, Kwoi, 25 May 2019; Haye, *Byang Kato*, 25.
90. Haye, 25–26.

these values out and enforced them in the family and community. Jummai would be remembered for her sternness and forthrightness,[91] and Byang for his hard work, sense of purpose and commitment to the things of God.

When Kato got married, he was finishing his three-year diploma programme at Igbaja Bible College. He had also commenced home studies in earnest to prepare to sit O-level and A-level exams from London, in order to qualify for matriculation into university. His new bride had also enrolled in the women and pastors' wives' programme. Before the end of the year of their wedding, their first child, Deborah, was born on 20 October 1957. Their marriage was blessed with three children, a girl and two boys: Deborah, Jonathan and Paul, respectively, in fairly quick succession. Jonathan arrived on 19 December 1958 and Paul, the third and last child, followed on 11 October 1960.

The rigorous and ambitious educational pursuits of her husband and the early arrival of three children in quick succession allowed Jummai only modest formal education. She provided support for her husband when he was away, and she did more in raising the children and looking after their home.[92] Nevertheless, she attended the Girls' Christian Training Institute in Kwoi and did several short-term courses, including the Child Evangelism Fellowship Institute in Paris, the Pitman Examination, the British Red Cross Society, London, the St. John Ambulance, the National Youth Programme and the Girls' Brigade. With her typing skills, she did her husband's typing and served as typist for SIM. She was matron for the ECWA/SIM Teachers' College girls' dormitory, and she would be remembered for a long and active service for the Girls' Brigade in Nigeria.

Kato raised his family on Christian values. He observed a daily discipline of Bible reading and prayer time at home, involving the whole household. All three children came to personal faith in Jesus at the age of eight, seven and six, respectively.[93] He involved the family in his pastoral and preaching ministry as much as possible. Deborah recalled, in an interview, how he would often mention them, the family members, to illustrate or recount experiences to

---

91. Several people interviewed and those who gave tributes at the funeral of Jummai Kato on 8 May 2019, including her children and members of the Girls' Brigade in Nigeria, mentioned her sternness and forthrightness.

92. Haye, *Byang Kato*, 32.

93. Haye, *Byang Kato*, 139.

make a point in his preaching. He was fond of calling the family onto the stage to sing before his sermon. "Apart from the whole family coming together for prayer, we were trained to read the Bible and pray on our own, using devotional materials," Deborah said.[94] This is corroborated by Haye's interview with Deborah. At breakfast, their dad would ask them, "Have you had your devotions?," before they had the corporate family devotions.[95]

The family would also pray together at bedtime. Kato narrates how his second son and last child came to faith during one of the evening prayers. The Scripture reading was about the second coming of Jesus Christ (Matt 24:37–44). Paul, the youngest child, asked whether he would be taken away or left behind when Jesus returned. Kato used the opportunity to illustrate the gospel to the young child leading him to accept Jesus Christ as his saviour.[96] Kato took time to teach his children about Jesus Christ and was convinced this was the greatest need for every person and the duty of every believer to tell others about Christ. According to Deborah, two of his favourite subjects, which rang through his sermons or speeches, were leadership and salvation. And he would mention Yakubu Gowon as his favourite leader, then the head of state of Nigeria. Oladipo names Gowon among the fifteen most exemplary and influential Christian leaders in Nigerian public life.[97]

Kato demonstrated a balanced view of his experiences, rejecting what he considered idolatry but also recognizing positive values of the traditional system that stayed with him. According to Deborah, he was known for "hard work, discipline, and [being] very focused." His mantra, which he told the children all the time, according to Deborah, was: "Hard work does not kill."[98] This was a way of inculcating studiousness in the children's schoolwork and at home. Also, the children were trained to share in the domestic chores. Each one of the three children had an assigned task they were responsible for, and they were expected to excel in both their home assignment and schoolwork. Kato wanted to give the children a good education, and they all went to Rift Valley Academy, the famous school in Kenya for the children of

---

94. Interview with Mrs. Deborah Bature, Kato's Daughter, in Kaduna, 23 March 2019.
95. Haye, 112.
96. Kato, "How I Won," 15.
97. See Oladipo, *Exemplary Christians*.
98. Deborah Kato-Bature, in an interview with author on23 March 2019, in Kaduna, Nigeria.

missionaries. He also opened an account in the USA, where he started saving for the children's education. The children generally remember him for his sternness and his love for his people. Their home was also open to strangers and friends and often used for fellowship, Bible study and prayer meetings.

In response to a question about culture, Deborah revealed how their American friends believed he was a chief because of his fondness for wearing his *babban riga* (big gown), the traditional Hausa attire. He also liked traditional food from Kwoi, even on his travels and away from home. He did not spare the rod when disciplining the children, even in America. According to Deborah, he was, in many ways, a traditional Jaba man. However, Daborah said he showed humility and servanthood in his leadership. He was accessible to all in the village and led many to the Christian faith, including his parents and siblings.

Notwithstanding his exemplary family life, with the exigencies of Kato's preoccupations and career path, there were concerns about his frequent absence from home. The spouse was often left on her own, with the burden to care for the young family.[99] To his credit, Kato made intentional effort to spend quality time with the family when he was home and created space for fun and play. At the time of his death, in 1975 when he was aged just thirty nine, the family was together at an exotic retreat centre on a beach on the Indian Ocean near Mombasa for a family holiday and to celebrate the birthday of one of the boys. (Only Deborah was missing, having travelled to Nigeria for vacation.)[100] Kato had gone swimming with the two boys on the nearby beach when he met his tragic death by drowning.

Jummai Kato (1939–2019) died an octogenarian and survived her husband by forty-four years. At her funeral on 8 May 2019, the senator of Kaduna State, Northern Nigeria said: "As a princess many prominent men would have loved to have her as a wife, when her husband died at a very young age, but she would not give in to any possible suitors, in reverence for husband's memory and legacy which she kept intact." Similarly, the general secretary of the Association of Evangelicals in Africa re-echoed similar sentiments and said: "If the Church could look up to the late Rev. Dr. Byang Kato for theological polemics and disputations, Mama Jummai provided us the practical

---

99. Haye, *Byang Kato*, 35.
100. Haye, 91–96.

theology of widowhood, single parenting, resilience, virtue, modesty and faithfulness."[101] The AEA general secretary further stated:

> Jummai obviously became the key for unlocking the treasures that appeared to have been drowned in the Indian Ocean and interred with the remains of the then burgeoning theological figure, who would then be remembered as the father of evangelical theology in Tropical Africa. Mama Jummai's widowhood lasted 44 years, longer than the entire lifetime of the husband.[102]

Jummai Kato is credited for co-owning and preserving the theological vision and legacy established with her late husband for the benefit of the theological institutions in Africa.[103]

Further Education

Kato's choice of career would appear to have been predestined, given that he was dedicated as a fetish priest a few months after his birth. As a young man he chose to go to Bible college when he completed primary school. This time the training was as a religious leader in the Christian church and as a Bible teacher and preacher, a training he would further pursue abroad, attaining a terminal degree in theology. In an era when many leading African Christians lived a life of religious pluralism, resorting to traditional religious practices of divination or witchcraft when in stress and anxiety,[104] Kato's detachment from this non-Christian and traditional belief system, and his quest for authentic biblical Christianity, was an exceptional African contribution to the global church.

In the 1950s–1960s, Christianity in Africa was at the crossroads, with the resurgence of African consciousness and the shaping of African Christian thought and practice. Most of the scholars of that time bought into the

---

101. Senator Haruna Zego Azeez, Senator of Kaduna State (1999–2003), Tribute to Jummai Kato at funeral in Kwoi, 8 May 2019

102. Aiah Foday-Khabenje, General Secretary, Association of Evangelicals in Africa, Tribute to Jummai Kato at Funeral in Kwoi, 8 May 2019

103. Tribute by Prof. Randee Ijatuyi-Morphe, provost, Jos Theological Seminary and ECWA College of Education, Jos, Nigeria, to Mrs. Jummai Kato at her funeral, Kwoi, 25 May 2019.

104. Sawyerr, *Creative Evangelism*, 19.

Christian consciousness a strand which was decidedly postcolonial, while Kato appeared to have prioritised biblical Christianity. That was the beginning of evangelical Christianity in sub-Saharan Africa. Kato became a leading voice and advocate for sound biblical beliefs, with important contributions to evangelical theology on the continent. His quest for theological training started at Igbaja Bible College in Kwara State in Nigeria, then continued when he went to London Bible College in the UK and later pursued postgraduate studies at Dallas Theological Seminary in the USA. All three institutions played no small part in shaping Kato's distinctive evangelical self-understanding.

Bible College at Igbaja (1955–1957)

Kato demonstrated adult qualities while he was still a child and in primary school, evidenced by his hard work and the way he handled his responsibilities. He proceeded to study theology after finishing primary school, in preparation for work in the church, as he had committed himself to serve God as a missionary. With the assistance of the local ECWA church in Kwoi, Kato enrolled at Igbaja Bible College in 1955.[105] The Igbaja Bible College, established in 1941, was an important SIM theological training institution in West Africa. Initially, its focus was on training in Biblical interpretation and preaching. It would go on to be the first higher education institution of learning in Nigeria for the training of homebred African pastors and Christian educators. The Igbaja Bible College of Kato's day is now ECWA Theological Seminary Igbaja, offering post-graduate and doctoral degrees in theology. Many prominent evangelical Christian leaders and scholars, like Tokumboh Adeyemo, Victor Babajide Cole, Yusufu Turaki, Danfulani Kore, Musa Gaiya and Femi Ilesanmi, are among the illustrious alumni of the institution.

Skipping the normal educational stages and opting for a basic Bible college training was characteristic of evangelical missions. The mission organisations did not encourage more advanced biblical or theological training.[106] However, one of the issues that Kato took to heart was sound education, especially biblical education, at the highest level of scholarship. He would not settle for less. As in his primary school days when he stayed after school to work for missionaries to make money for fees and books, Kato continued to work and

---

105. Breman, "Portrait," 139.
106. Foday-Khabenje, *Synopsis*, 110–112.

study from early morning until late evening to earn money for the family.[107] In spite of all the family responsibilities, Kato excelled in his course work.[108]

On graduation, Kato returned to Kwoi with his family and lived and taught at the Kwoi Bible School. The Bible school in Kwoi was another SIM-established Bible training school for the training of pastors. As a Bible school teacher, he wanted to advance his education, but this required further general education to qualify for matriculation to a higher institution for an undergraduate degree. To attain the requisite entry qualifications, he resorted to independent studies on his own and passed the O and A Level GCE exams in 1961 and 1963, respectively, and was qualified for university matriculation.[109]

Undergraduate Education at London Bible College (1963–1966)

Now armed with his A Level qualification, Kato looked beyond what Igbaja offered him in terms of higher theological education. He was immediately able to gain admission to the London Bible College (LBC) in England. The SIM/ECWA scholarship board offered him a grant for the studies, at the time the most expensive scholarship the board had ever granted, knowing the value and quality of education this would bring to the mission.[110] London Bible College, now known as London School of Theology, was and is a world class evangelical theological school, established in 1943 in the heart of London. Established as a united action by evangelical Christians from all denominations in the UK, the institution was devoted to evangelical scholarship of the highest standard possible. The school was loyal to the entire trustworthiness of the Bible, without reservation of any kind. Its purpose was to equip men and women in the scholarly and practical knowledge of the Bible, and to train them for the work of the gospel – pastoral, evangelistic, teaching and missionary services. It is international and interdenominational, and it is the largest theological college of its kind in Europe. London Bible College did

---

107. Haye, *Byang Kato*, 25–26.
108. Haye, 28.
109. Haye, 115.
110. Haye, 35–36.

not only train for scholarly and academic excellence but also for character formation and practical abilities for missionary work in the world.[111]

Kato's enrolment at LBC in 1963, as the first person from tropical Africa to ever be enrolled, was itself an important achievement. Kato pursued the diploma in theology and continued on to earn, in 1967, the coveted bachelor of divinity (BD) degree from the University of London, the university to which LBC was affiliated for the awarding of degrees. Kato was the first LBC student from tropical Africa to graduate with a University of London BD.[112]

When Kato sailed to London to commence his studies, Jummai was left to look after the three young children in Kwoi. In the following year Jummai joined him in London, and the three children were left in the care of relatives.[113] While Byang worked to complete his BD, Jummai enrolled in a certificate course in home economics at the YWCA. She studied home management, sewing and culinary arts. She was also involved with the British Red Cross and attained certificates in first aid. She took evening classes in typewriting. Both Byang and Jummai worked as host and hostess at an Inter-Varsity Fellowship hostel to earn extra money.

The London Bible College curriculum allowed for evangelistic activities outside of campus and Kato was actively involved in outreach, going with teams down south of London to Devon. Their home in London was also opened to their fellow Nigerian students in London. God used Kato's preaching and witness to bring people to faith in Christ, among them local British people and fellow Nigerians. Kato successfully completed his studies in 1966, and he and his spouse were ready to return home to Nigeria. However, on their way back home, they passed through Paris to attend the Child Evangelism Fellowship Institute for a three-month training course for children's ministry workers/teachers. Both Byang and Jummai were qualified children's ministry workers.[114] This was an important step given the importance of children's ministry in the church, though little attention or investment was made by the church in this area of ministry. The family would be

---

111. "London Bible College 1960s Photographic Slideshow," Hail the Librarian, 19 April 2019, video created from materials held in the archive of the London School of Theology, accessed 27 July 2019, https://www.youtube.com/watch?v=74bNsou_Dyc.

112. Breman, "Association of Evangelicals," 40.

113. Haye, *Byang Kato*, 40.

114. Haye, 40–42.

the immediate beneficiary of this when Byang was able to lead all three of his children to Christ when they were united again. Kato returned home to teach at his alma mater, Igbaja Bible College, in 1966. However, this was not the end of his academic training; he later opted to go abroad again, this time to the United States of America for postgraduate studies.

Postgraduate Studies at Dallas Theological Seminary (1970–1973)

Being the first student at London Bible College from tropical Africa to be awarded a University of London BD was enough for Kato to establish himself as a theological leader on the continent. However, Kato could not be contented with a first degree; he took advantage of the next opportunity, and proceeded to the USA for graduate studies in theology. In 1970 he gained admission to Dallas Theological Seminary (DTS), a well-known conservative evangelical theological school, to pursue the degree of master of sacred theology (STM), and completed the two-year programme in a year, with honours. He also won the Loraine Chafer Award that year for proficiency and the best grades earned in systematic theology. He immediately enrolled in the doctoral program and attained a doctor of theology (ThD) in 1974. Kato's completion of his course in record time was another first for a student from Africa at DTS.

Dallas Theological Seminary, founded in 1924, is a world class evangelical theological school. It is unreservedly committed to the inerrancy of Scripture as God's word. It affirms the "doctrines of evangelical orthodoxy in the framework of premillennial dispensational theology, derived from a consistent grammatical-historical interpretation of the Bible."[115] DTS prides itself on its Bible-centred curriculum. All students are expected to take a course on all sixty-six books of the Bible. The seminary also values a missions focus, and it suspends a week of classes annually to observe a world evangelisation emphasis. Also, it is known for its rigorous theology programmes and strong emphasis on biblical languages, Hebrew and Greek, to develop exegetical skills basic to the inductive examination of Scripture.[116]

---

115. Breman, "Association of Evangelicals," 41–42.

116. "About," Dallas Theological Seminary, accessed 27 July 2019, https://www.dts.edu/about/.

Kato saw the need for advanced theological education in Africa. He strove to achieve this for himself, and then to highlight biblical scholarship for the evangelical church in Africa. Addressing this need for the church in Africa, Kato said that "the battle was for the mind."[117] He further stated:

> Theological education available so far for any of these varsity grads has a strong view of African religions and culture. Almost all the 68 universities of the continent have a department of religions, where one can obtain up to a Ph.D. A search for peaceful co-existence among religions seems to be the basic concern of these institutions. Thus, the graduates have come out with a call for softer and friendlier approach to Islam, African Religions and other faiths.[118]

Thus, Kato was motivated to promote biblical theological education at the highest levels of scholarship for the evangelical Christian community in Africa, and thus his quest to pursue a doctorate in theology himself.

The topic for Kato's doctoral thesis was "A Critique of Incipient Universalism in Tropical Africa." The thesis was published in 1975, a year after his graduation, by Evangel Publishing House, Kisumu, Kenya, with the title *Theological Pitfalls in Africa*. This work turned out to be Kato's seminal contribution, or the magnum opus, of his theological literary work.[119] The dissertation was an important contribution to scholarship, being the singular contribution from an African evangelical perspective among a number of burgeoning theologians from a more liberal direction of thought. Kato's purpose was to alert the church in Africa about unhealthy trends taking shape in theology in Africa at the time. His perception was that conservative evangelical biblical Christianity was under threat, and he saw the need to encourage the church to conserve biblical orthodoxy. He states: "the pride of culture and undue respect for African Traditional Religions have already started to lead some churchmen astray."[120] The dissertation recommended a ten-point plan as guide to the preservation of biblical Christianity. Kato's work sparked some controversy and disputations in African theological discourse

---

117. Kato, "Africa: Facts."
118. Kato.
119. Bowers, "Byang Kato"; Breman, "Association of Evangelicals," 368.
120. Kato, "Critique of Incipient," ThD diss., ii.

that have not gone away. Kato's message and contribution to this theological discourse in Africa will be dealt with more extensively in the next chapter.

While at Dallas, Kato not only excelled in his academic work but was also outstanding in social interactions and relationships with people. He won the Four-Way Test Award, granted to the student ranked highest for personal relationship inside and outside the seminary, who demonstrated a consistent Christian life and outstanding leadership qualities.[121] Kato deemed this to be his best accolade, and it motivated him to live up to the expectation.[122] These virtues were collaborated by Paul Bowers, a colleague and friend from Igbaja Theological Seminary.[123] With Jummai, Byang also started a Good News Club for children from the neighbourhood for Child Evangelism Fellowship activities. They recorded eight children coming to faith in Christ, and the children became a link between the Katos and the children's families, enabling them to establish a discipleship relationship with these families.[124]

Kato opened the way for DTS to admit more students from Nigeria. His immediate successor at AEA was Tokunboh Adeyemo, also from Nigeria, who followed Kato at Igbaja and then at DTS.[125] As a DTS graduate student, Kato was offered a teaching assistantship and taught a course in missions and African Christianity at the seminary. He continued to be on the faculty at Dallas as visiting instructor after his studies were completed and he returned to Africa. With his training, Kato then also became a champion for quality theological education not only for his fellow Africans but also for Western missionaries coming to work in the mission field. According to Haye,[126] Kato said: "The day when just anything will do is past. Spirituality is no substitute for ignorance. A missionary should possess knowledge that can contribute to the progress of the country." His aspirations for the church were not just about the typical evangelical preoccupation of saving souls. He wanted to see the whole person transformed by the gospel of Jesus Christ. He was now well trained to return home with his family and serve his church and country and, indeed, Africa and beyond.

---

121. Breman, "Portrait," 140.
122. Breman, 140; cf. Haye, *Byang Kato*, 66.
123. Bowers, "Byang Kato, 3.
124. Haye, *Byang Kato*, 67.
125. Breman, "Association of Evangelicals," 366.
126. Haye, *Byang Kato*, 68.

Vocation and Ministry

Byang Kato's active working ministry dates from 1958, following the completion of his course at Igbaja Bible College, and continues up to his demise in 1975. This period covers the late colonial era in Nigeria, Nigeria's attainment of independence, and the first decade and a half of Nigeria's early self-rule. Nigeria attained independence in 1960, and the first decade of independence was marked by a violent military coup in 1966 and a civil war (1967–1970). This was the context of Kato's growth and rise as a Christian leader. These were challenging times with lots of disruption to normal life.

Between 1958 to 1963 Kato taught at Zabolo Bible Training School and Kwoi Christian Training Institute, then worked at the offices of the popular Christian magazine *African Challenge* in Lagos (now *Today's Challenge*). He proceeded to London for his undergraduate studies from 1963 to 1966. On his return from his studies in London in 1966, he was posted to Igbaja Seminary and Bible College as a tutor. The following year he was elected as the general secretary of the ECWA Church in Nigeria, the post he relinquished in 1970 to proceed to the United States for graduate studies. This was another admirable move by Kato. Many church leaders would consider the prestigious position of head of a denomination to be the apex of their ministerial career, and going back to become a student would be rare. In the first place, it was exceptional for Kato to have ascended to this position at age thirty-three, and to voluntarily relinquish it to go back to school with a family of five was unusual. However, this was a mark of Kato's commitment to theological education, as well as his attitude toward leadership and the trappings of high office. While completing his doctoral work, he was appointed in February 1973 as the first African general secretary of the Association of Evangelicals in Africa and Madagascar (now Association of Evangelicals in Africa), a post that he continued to hold until his tragic death in Kenya on Friday, 19 December 1975, at the age of thirty nine years.[127]

Although his time on earth was relatively short, the scope of his work and accomplishments was wide and would be remembered for generations. The following sections highlight more details about the full-time employment and positions he held, all within the ministry of the church and particularly with the SIM/ECWA Church and the Association of Evangelicals in Africa.

---

127. Haye, 91–97.

Bible Teacher

Kato's teaching vocation can be traced back to the time he started going to Sunday school and Boys' Brigade. Whatever he learned in school he would teach other boys in his neighbourhood who were not privileged to go to school, especially reading, writing and Scripture verses he had memorised, both in English and Hausa. "Eagar to improve his English, he attended an early morning Bible Class on Sundays. After church, he would go to a village to teach the boys God's Word."[128] A contemporary of Kato, now in his eighties, said in an interview in Kwoi: "Kato made me to be a better person and a farmer; he taught me to read my Bible in Hausa, and today I am an elder in the church and one of the leaders in the choir."[129] Baba Leo, as the interviewee is commonly known, is a member of the ECWA Central Church choir and plays a local musical instrument, known as "molo," in the church.

After graduating from Igbaja Bible College, Kato was appointed as a teacher at the SIM Bible Training School in Kwoi. He taught in English and also in Hausa, the main language spoken in the northern region of Nigeria. At the Bible Training School, he also revived the ailing Boys' Brigade and started the Youth for Christ programme. The school provided a platform for him to reach out to young people. He introduced extracurricular activities like games and drama. His work attracted young people to the church and "the church grew fantastically."[130] His superiors and faculty colleagues were well pleased with him. He looked out for needs in the school and was engaged in finding solutions to meet those needs. He was also always concerned that his people were built up in the Lord. He started a church paper or bulletin and a school choir and took his students out on Fridays to the marketplace for evangelism. On Sundays, he preached at outstations and sometimes in the main ECWA church, which had an average attendance of about one thousand people. He was licensed as pastor while at the Kwoi Bible Training Institute.

Kato also did some farming to augment the relatively meagre salary he received as a teacher. Kato's teaching approach was commendable, providing cognitive, pedagogic and practical learning experiences for his students.

---

128. Haye, 22.

129. Mallam Leo Lim, interview with author, Dakachin Sab-Zuro, Kwoi, Jaba Local Government Area, Kaduna State, 22 March 2019.

130. Haye, *Byang Kato*, 28–29.

Teaching, mentoring, coaching, preaching, farming and private studies occupied his time, and he lived a very productive life. Kato was involved with his people.

On Tuk-Ham Day in Kwoi, Kato celebrated the cultural ceremony in a way that would be consistent with his Christian faith. The Tuk-Ham is an annual cultural festival celebrated around Easter to mark the beginning of the farming season. The festival, celebrated with music, dance and feasting, is said to date back to 900 BC, under a theocratic ancestral religion.[131] It is also the day of Ham, when the king, the Kpop-Ham, honours the deities of the Ham or Jaba people. Such festivals are not just social functions; they are also religious functions and include the pouring of libations and veneration of ancestors and intermediary gods, practices Kato stood against in his theological disputations. Aware of the spiritual implications, which were contrary to his faith, Kato would instead organise an evangelistic festival or outing and mobilise his friends to go up the mountain to pray.[132] On Easter day itself, Kato established a practice of rising early in the morning to go up the mountain to see the sunrise. He mobilised friends and family members to march with him to the mountain top, observe the rising of the sun, sing hymns, proclaim the gospel message and say prayers before returning to the village. Kato was not just an academic theologian, or a Christian on Sundays, but he endeavoured to live out his faith, notwithstanding social pressures from extended family members and the community. He also looked for innovative ways of showing respect for others and practising his faith without compromise. He was very much respected in his township and the community as a whole and continued to be engaged with both.

In 1966, Kato returned to Igbaja Bible College as a teacher after attaining his BD in London. The school was now offering a four-year seminary degree programme for the bachelor of theology degree. His courses included one in African religions.[133] It is important to note that Kato took seriously traditional African thought and religious practice long before his work rejected "African theology." His rejection was not necessarily a disdain for African thought and

---

131. Ham Cultural Heritage (website), accessed 28 July 2019, http://www.hamculturalheritage.org.

132. Interview with Alemu Kato, 22 March 209, Kwoi..

133. Haye, *Byang Kato*, 50.

values; his contention and rejection were based on the definition and goals for "African theology" which its main proponents established at the time.[134] According to Haye, Kato provided a clear understanding for his students and stated: "In the context of African traditional religions, the worship is merely an indication of an honest craving for God, which can be fulfilled only in the biblical revelation through the incarnate Christ who died and rose again. This should be the preoccupation of the Church in Africa."[135] Furthermore, he taught his students:

> Whatever would reflect the glory of Christ in his Church in Africa, and make the African feel that "this is *my* faith" should be promoted. If there are any alien beliefs or practices mingled with Christianity, the answer is not to throw away the baby with the birth water. Rather, we should purge biblical faith in Africa for the Africans, since it is as much an African religion as it is a European religion.[136]

His theological work, including his doctoral studies would be hinged on this understanding for the rest of his life. Kato demonstrated consistency in what he said and in what he did.

Kato again changed ministry role and location after one year at Igbaja Bible College, when he was elected as ECWA secretary general in 1967. But he continued to return to Igbaja as an adjunct faculty member. His influence as a teacher at Igbaja had some outstanding impact on both colleagues and students. According to Haye, when Tokumbo Adeyemo, as a student, listened to Kato during one of his return visits to Igbaja, Adeyemo wanted to be like Kato and regarded him as a mentor. Some years later Adeyemo wrote in the foreword of Haye's biography of Kato:

> I was a theological student when I had the privilege of hearing Kato, the prophet, for the first time. . . . He predicted that for the next ten years (i.e. from 1972) the battle for the Church in Africa would be theological. He was right! His emphasis was twofold: the trustworthiness of the Word of God against all theological

---

134. Kato, *Theological Pitfalls*, 53–68.
135. Haye, *Byang Kato*, 50.
136. Haye, 51.

liberalism, and the proper contextualisation of theology in the African setting without adulterating the Gospel. It was his challenge that God used to propel me into the ministry.[137]

It was remarkable that Adeyemo actually succeeded Kato as AEA general secretary after the latter's tragic death and became the embodiment of Kato's theological vision and implementation.

Another great impact Kato made was working with Paul Bowers, an SIM missionary on faculty at Igbaja with a PhD from Cambridge in biblical studies. He would later recruit Bowers to serve as the founding coordinator of the Accrediting Council for Theological Education in Africa – now the Association for Christian Theological Education in Africa (ACTEA).[138] This dream was realised after Kato's death, as Paul Bowers went on to establish ACTEA in 1976. Bowers would move on to pioneer setting up the International Council for Evangelical Theological Education (ICETE) under the World Evangelical Alliance. According to Bowers, ICETE itself was a theological initiative rooted in Kato's vision and his role as chair of the WEA Theological Commission before his death.[139]

Kato's teaching career also included his time in the USA, when he served as a teaching assistant during his studies and also taught a course in missions. After his graduation, he returned to DTS as an adjunct professor.[140] He continued to give lectures in various schools around the continent and abroad, such as Nairobi University in Kenya,[141] Institute for Advancement of Calvinism in Potchefstroom, South Africa[142] and Ibadan University in Jos, Nigeria,[143] among others.

At a time when many church leaders gave little priority to children's ministry, Kato made time to minister to children. The investment in children at this level of leadership in the church was revolutionary and perhaps another first for Kato. Addressing evangelical leaders as guest speaker at the first

---

137. Adyemo, in a Foreword, *Byang Kato: Ambassador of Christ*. 11–13.
138. Bowers, *Theological Education*, 10, 21.
139. Bowers, 10.
140. Breman, "Association of Evangelicals," 42.
141. Kato, "Black Theology and African", 1–10.
142. Kato, "Creating Facilities", 1.
143. See Kato, "Written Theology."

AEA General Assembly in 1969, Kato spoke on the theme "The Youth and the African Church." The text was "Remember now thy Creator in the days of thy youth" from Ecclesiastes 12:1a. Kato stated:

> This great injunction presupposes that the youth has already got something to REMEMBER. Before we expect the youth to do his own part. Therefore, the parents, the teachers, and other Christians responsible for bringing up children must be sure that they have given the youth something – the word of life which generates faith that accepts the free gift of eternal life. Here we want to see if the Church of Christ in Africa is fulfilling its task in filling the minds of the youth with something to remember.[144]

Kato's focus on children and youth was important, given the strategic nature of ministry to young people. Studies show that over 80 percent of born-again Christians got saved when they were children and the circumstances leading to their salvation were also influenced by fellow children.[145] Kato understood this and brought this to the attention of the church leaders. One of the projects of the AEA Theological Commission, envisioned by Kato, was the Christian Learning Materials Centre (CLMC). The CLMC produces theologically sound and culturally relevant Sunday school curriculum and materials for distribution in Africa.

Media and Writing Career

In 1959 Kato was asked to join the *African Challenge Magazine* production team in Lagos, then the bustling capital city of Nigeria. He was responsible for responding to readers' inquiries and offering counselling and guidance for those who needed help. The magazine received about two thousand enquiries per month, seeking counsel and help. Kato responded to the writers by return letters, and during this time he developed his communication skills.[146] He had developed a keen interest in writing and had worked on the school magazine during his time at Igbaja Bible College and on the church paper.[147]

---

144. Kato, "Youth." 1.
145. Brewster, *Child, Church and Mission*, 4; cf. Bush, "4/14 Window," 3; "Evangelism Is"; cf. Mwithi, *Parenting with Purpose*.
146. Haye, *Byang Kato*, 31.
147. Haye, 26–29.

He cultivated a habit of writing a journal and a diary, recording details like prayer points, sermons, reflections on lectures or messages he preached, travel schedules and the different tasks he would be doing.

The editor-in-chief at *African Challenge Magazine* was affirming of Kato's contribution, and he was offered an opportunity for further training in journalism for a career in the media house. Kato turned down the offer because he was convinced that his call was in pastoral ministry, and he would rather have more theological training for the ministry of the gospel. He convinced his boss that he would still be able to write articles for the magazine as a pastor.[148] This was exceptional insight, as not many pastors in Kato's day would see themselves as writers and contributors of articles to magazines. Indeed, Kato, the pastor and theologian, wrote several articles on various subjects, and a few booklets written by Kato were also published by African Christian Press and Evangel Publishing House.

As general secretary of AEA, Kato had over 2,000 people in his directory for circulating communication through the ordinary postal system. Even with the internet, the number of people on the AEA emailing list in 2015, forty-five years later, did not match Kato's ordinary mailing list. The current AEA directory has about 1,500 people on their emailing list, according to the AEA communication officer.[149] AEA had a couple of regular publications. One was the AEA newsletter, *Afroscope*. Another was *Perception*, which presented occasional theological papers published for circulation. He wrote a booklet, *The Spirits*, published by African Christian Press, and *African Cultural Revolution and the Christian Faith*, published by Challenge Publications, plus the book edition of his doctoral thesis, *Theological Pitfalls in Africa*, published by Evangel Publishing House. He also wrote sermons and other materials for public presentations.[150]

Kato was a prolific writer. He not only wrote for the church or for Christian magazines, but he also wrote open letters to the press for the public, in which he sometimes boldly and courageously addressed contentious issues. For

---

148. Haye, 31.

149. The author confirmed this in a discussion with the AEA communications officer, who keeps a record of all AEA contacts.

150. A bibliography compiled by Christina Breman includes over 90 works. Some of these are short papers, sermon outlines and notes, and his doctoral dissertation, which was the most significant scholarly work that Kato produced before his early death. See Breman, *Byang H. Kato*.

example, following a General Assembly of the WCC held in Nairobi in 1975, and hosted by its regional counterpart, the AACC, the press published an open letter by Kato that was critical of the WCC and AACC. Kato wrote:

> There are certain structures in the church with which you should be familiar. You have no doubt heard about the World Council of Churches (WCC) which held a big General Assembly here November 23 to December 10. Over 2000 delegates representing 280 different churches from around the world met to discuss the theme, "Jesus Christ Frees and Unites." The World Council of Churches and its affiliated body, the All Africa Conference of Churches (AACC), represent what is known as Ecumenism. Their main concern is unity, and it does not matter very much what a person believes as long as he calls himself Christian.[151]

Kato went on to highlight what he said were erroneous views expressed during the conference which he wanted the readers to be aware of and outlined fundamental differences between evangelicals and non-evangelicals. This was his last piece of writing and was published posthumously. In the build up to the WCC General Assembly in Nairobi, the *Target Newspaper* carried stories about the seeming differences between ecumenicals and evangelicals, with the caption "'Evangelicals' deny fighting WCC Assembly."[152] Kato would not be silent; and wrote a rejoinder back to the editor. In his opening paragraph, Kato wrote:

> Please allow me to comment on the article that appeared in the October 19–26, 1975 issue of TARGET under the caption, 'Evangelicals' deny fighting WCC Assembly. By putting the word Evangelicals in quotation marks in this title, you give the impression of having some reservations in recognising the Association of Evangelicals of Africa and Madagascar (AEAM) as truly evangelical. We wonder why.[153]

---

151. Kato, "An Open Letter in Today in Africa." 1.
152. "'Evangelicals' Deny Fighting WCC Assembly," *Target*, 19–26 October 1975d.
153. Kato, "Africa's Evangelicals." 1.

He wrote personal letters to friends and partners as well. also, he kept record of his salary and how he spent his money.[154] Kato's writings have been the main source of information for what we can learn about his life and the past. In Kato's curriculum vitae,[155] the following are listed as his publications: contributor to *Christ the Liberator*, the report of Urbana '70; editor of *ECWA News* (Nigeria); consultant for Hausa New Testament revision; author of articles in *Africa Now, Evangelical Missions Quarterly, Kesho, Moody Monthly, Theological News, Today's Challenge* and *World Vision*; editor for *Afroscope* and *Perception*; and author of *The Spirits, African Cultural Revolution and the Christian Faith* and *Theological Pitfalls in Africa*.

Thus, Kato's literary work goes beyond his magnum opus, *Theological Pitfalls in Africa*, for which he is well known. In the first fifteen months of publication – that is, from October 1975 to December 1976 – Kato earned (posthumously) USD 2,236 in royalties.[156] That is quite impressive, even by current standards, and more so then. The list of publications also reveals that Kato's literary output was not only scholarly and abstract but engaged with contemporary and current issues.

Furthermore, we live in an era of information, when the media and the minister's skills in engaging society is so important. Kato took communications seriously and laid the foundation for evangelical scholarship and writing. Hippo Books, an imprint of Langham Literature, currently partners with the AEA to produce scholarly theological materials from Africa. Many of these works have a mention of Byang Henry Kato in their bibliography. Haye credits Kato for the continuing growth of the AEA. John Langois, who was on the staff team of the World Evangelical Fellowship Theological Commission during Kato's time, in 1974/5, credited Kato for the continuing growth of the AEA after his death, stating of Kato: "He was able to spearhead that organisation as a natural leader to whom Africans could relate. His academic success gave him standing. His uncompromising stand for biblical Christianity did much to strengthen evangelicals in Africa with a new confidence in the face of liberal and syncretistic pressures."[157]

---

154. Haye, *Byang Kato*, 60.
155. Curriculum Vitae for Dr. Byang K. Kato. Retrieved from the AEA archives.
156. Letter from Evangel Publishing House to AEAM Administrator, 31 May 1977, 171/77, Achieved at AEA Office in Nairobi, Kenya.
157. Quoted in Haye, *Byang Kato*, 105–106.

Apart from works of individual scholars, the AEA sponsored the publication of a one-volume Bible commentary in 2006 – the *Africa Bible Commentary* – with a team of seventy scholars and pastors. The AEA also collaborated with Oasis International to produce the *Africa Study Bible*, work that involved hundreds of Africans. Kato could be given some credit for laying a solid foundation for evangelical scholarly writing in Africa, which continues to thrive. Literary theological work was part of Kato's pioneering vision and strategy for the ministry of AEA.

Pastor and Denominational Leader

At the heart of all his life, Kato demonstrated a call to the ministry of the church. He chose to be a minister of the gospel, and for that reason, he went to Bible school to attain the highest-level qualifications as preparation for ministry. He did not only train to acquire skills and competencies to minister but also to train other pastors, church leaders and believers everywhere to do the same. Whether he was in public engagement or on the editorial team of a media house or in the academy as teacher, scholar or disputant, his message was clear: the good news of Jesus Christ is the only way for salvation.

While he was still teaching at Igbaja Bible College, Kato came into the ECWA limelight when he attended the General Church Council in 1967 and served as an interpreter for the Hausa speaking delegates from the north of the country. He was elected as the general secretary of ECWA at the meeting. He was the first person from the North to hold the post. At the age of thirty-three, he left the Bible college and moved to the ECWA headquarters in Jos, from where he worked as general secretary. He was ordained as a minister of ECWA at the Bishara 1 local congregation in Jos in 1968. He did more pastoral ministry as a licensed pastor prior to his official ordination than he did as an ordained minister when the call was to provide leadership for the denomination at headquarters. However, his passion for the pulpit and evangelism was not diminished despite his leadership and administrative tasks. He continued to see teaching and preaching as his primary call.

As general secretary of ECWA, Kato had an oversight role for 1,200 local congregations, several educational and medical institutions, and personnel including eight hundred pastors and one hundred missionaries in the ECWA/

SIM network in Nigeria.[158] Kato's tenure as general secretary coincided with the Nigerian Civil War. ECWA, as the local church denomination, was taking over more responsibilities from SIM. The war, among other factors, restricted the movement into Nigeria of foreign nationals or missionaries. Pastors and other church workers and their families in the war zone were cut off from headquarters in Jos.

Among other of Kato's responsibilities, ECWA was increasing involvement in relief interventions, along with their SIM partners. They launched three operations for emergency relief items, including medical items, food, clothing and resettlement items such as seeds and tools for food production. Operation Good Shepherd, located near the war zone, was a medical centre, Operation Dorcas provided clothing for the war victims, and Operation Blacksmith involved local blacksmiths to produce farming tools like hoes and shovels, distributing them to resettling victims, with seeds and yam tubers for food production.[159] The programmes were also accompanied by evangelistic efforts like the sharing of tracts, counselling, preaching and the mobilising of relief food items from churches. On one visit to the war zone, Kato preached to a congregation of two thousand troops in Enugu.[160] When the war ended in 1970, ECWA also embraced contributing to the implementation of the government's triple-R programme of Reconciliation, Rehabilitation and Reconstruction. ECWA's involvement in the peace and reconciliation programme after the civil war was in psycho-social and trauma counselling. Kato was personally involved in counselling and ministering to people. He visited his members in the war-torn region three times. The third visit was to reunite and celebrate with those who had been cut off from headquarters during the war.

That a conservative evangelical church could be involved with social intervention to the extent that Kato allowed was commendable. It was particularly noteworthy that Kato's relief intervention initiatives happened in the pre-Lausanne era – that is, before the First International Congress on World Evangelization (also known as the Lausanne Congress) in 1974, when there was a paradigm shift in the evangelical vision of evangelism and social

---

158. Haye, 56, 58.
159. Haye, 54–55.
160. Haye, 55.

action and a theology was articulated to embrace both of these as integral to the mission of the church. ECWA's involvement in social intervention was a departure from the practice of the then conservative church's sole focus on evangelism and church planting, leaving social interventions to parachurch agencies. However, pinning gospel tracts on clothing before distribution in Operation Dorcas, which had its base in Kato's living room, could be problematic.[161] Humanitarian workers may frown at this and consider it as proselytism. Nevertheless, there is still ongoing discussion in evangelical circles about best practice for integral mission in the church.

In a moment of rest and recuperation, Kato watched a documentary of SIM missionary adventures in taking the gospel of Christ around the world. It was called *They That Are of Faith*. According to Haye, this was another turning point for Kato. He was left in tears and wrote in his diary:

> I shed more tears than I have done in any religious service I could remember. The challenge – love of the white man for me – forced me to ask, "What have I done for my brothers?" I prayed and fasted. As I studied the Word, I realised that with God's help I shouldn't let anything stand in the way of my fellowship with the Lord – be it food, friends or sex.[162]

This informs Kato's attitude to the missionary enterprise. When many scholars, for nationalistic reasons, were not so complementary about missionary work because of missionary attitudes to ATR, Kato was deeply grateful for their work and the extent of the sacrifice they made to propagate the gospel. This does not in any way mean that Kato was not aware of the lapses of the Western missionaries of that he was not critical about their work.[163] As a matter of fact, he would often pick on his missionary colleagues when he insisted on the quality of work, especially educational standards for church leaders. He was, for instance, critical about missionaries with poor educational backgrounds. If there was one area where Kato had conflict with both missionaries and local colleagues, it was in his uncompromising stance on issues of integrity, standards and encouraging the pursuit of higher education

---

161. Haye, 54.
162. Haye, 55–56.
163. Haye, 68, 70.

for church leaders.[164] Kato was convinced about the need to put together an organisational plan for his work when he attended a management seminar. He put together a five-year plan that was endorsed by the ECWA board in 1968. The next five years saw this plan implemented and most of the goals were achieved. Predictably, goals included the doubling of baptized converts and the training of leaders from Bible school to doctoral levels.[165] He also put together a pastors' manual as guide to liturgies and ordinances of the church and other administrative guidelines.

Kato had his first contact with AEA when he was included in the SIM/ECWA delegation to the AEA First General Assembly in 1969. It took place in Limuru, Kenya, the venue of AEA's birth three years previously. Kato was also one of the plenary speakers, and in cognisance of his work with children and youth, he was asked to speak on the topic of Christian education.

Kato was a lifetime learner; he saw the need for further education. Notwithstanding his enviable BD from London, he contemplated further advanced studies. The opportunity came when the professor of world missions at Dallas Theological Seminary in the United States, George Peters, visited Nigeria as a guest of SIM. Dr. Peters facilitated seminars for ECWA pastors and leaders. The emphasis of the seminars was administrative and management competencies for church leaders, spiritual maturity and the need to develop faculty and scholars for the Bible colleges. This struck a chord with Kato, and he engaged the visitor after the seminar and eventually submitted his application to pursue a two-year master of sacred theology course at DTS and was admitted. He informed the ECWA board of this and declined renewal of his contract as general secretary of ECWA. Kato left for postgraduate studies in 1970. His pastoral role in terms of preaching and teaching continued informally during his studies in the US, and his next full-time appointment would be with AEA.

---

164. In a conversation with a respondent and one of the leaders of ECWA it was revealed that Kato did have clashes with some missionaries, and local leaders as well, on his uncompromising stance on standards, and opened the way for higher education for many young people during his tenure as general secretary of ECWA. Some of these are still in leadership or have retired from leadership positions in ECWA.

165. Haye, *Byang Kato*, 58.

General Secretary of AEA

Byang Kato was guest speaker at an AEA Christian Education Strategy Conference in 1973, which was also the last year of his doctoral studies in the USA. The topic of his presentation was "The Needs and Problems Facing Christian Education in Africa." The Christian Education Strategy Conference was followed immediately by the second General Assembly of AEA. AEA (then AEAM) had its roots in the endeavours of two associations of missionary societies – the International Foreign Mission Association (IFMA) and the Evangelical Foreign Mission Association (EFMA) – which had worked together in Africa since the early 1960s with the purpose of establishing national and regional evangelical fellowships in Africa.[166] According to Breman, this was to counter the influence of the World Council of Churches that sought to unite the churches in Africa as one church organisation and were sponsoring African leaders to study theology in liberal schools abroad.[167]

AEA provides the different evangelical denominations and organisations in Africa with a platform and relational space for common identity, action and voice, so there can be synergy and effectiveness in accomplishing the mission of the church – salvation from the scourge of sin and the transformation of society in accordance with God's purposes. It is a service agency for national evangelical fellowships, churches and theological schools aimed at equipping the local church for effective witness and transformation of their communities and the wider society through the gospel. Membership also includes missionary agencies based in Africa and international Christian non-governmental organizations (NGOs) focused on development. Founded in 1966, AEA headquarters are in Nairobi, Kenya, where it is registered as a society or charitable Christian organization. AEA currently comprises forty national evangelical fellowships in Africa. AEA is also one of the regional associations of the global evangelical movement, the World Evangelical Alliance (WEA). The basis for unity and membership is affirmation of the historic Christian faith and the authority of the Holy Scripture as the inspired word of God, inerrant and infallible in all it affirms as originally delivered.[168]

---

166. Breman, "Association of Evangelicals," 6.

167. Breman, 6–7.

168. See the website for the Association of Evangelicals in Africa (https://aeafrica.org/) for more information.

During the second AEA General Assembly, Kato was one of the officials elected to lead AEA in the ensuing period. Kato was unanimously elected as the general secretary and chief executive of the movement, the first African, and only the second person, to be appointed to the post.[169] The post had been vacant for the previous three years, as AEA could not find a suitable candidate following the resignation of the first general secretary, Kenneth Downing, an American missionary from the Africa Inland Mission. The assembly also approved the formation of an AEA Theological Commission, and Kato was elected as its executive secretary. He would be famous more for his role and achievements as executive secretary of the AEA Theological Commission than for the avant-garde post of AEA general secretary.[170]

Kato's dual appointment conflicted with his declared purpose for pursuing further studies: academic leadership for his church's theological seminary at Igbaja. A compromise was struck when the AEA General Assembly approved ECWA's request for him to become an adjunct faculty member at Igbaja for at least two years, and they graciously released him to serve AEA. Kato returned to the USA to pack and relocate his family back to Africa. He returned to AEA's headquarters in Nairobi, Kenya, to assume work for AEA, and received his ThD in absentia.[171] In Nairobi the family was accepted into local church membership at the Nairobi Baptist Church on Ngong Road.

As general secretary of AEA, executive secretary of the AEA Theological Commission and adjunct faculty at Igbaja, Kato had a hectic traveling schedule, teaching, preaching, writing and speaking. Kato was clear about AEA's objectives, and he set out to accomplish his task as the organisation's chief executive. Kato stated the purpose of AEA:

> The AEAM exists as a service agency to the national fellowships, churches and theological schools. It assists in a wide variety of evangelical projects and has helped sponsor such activities as seminars promoting church growth, church management, "New Life for All" and theological education by extension. It has also

---

169. Breman, "Portrait." 141.
170. Breman, 141.
171. Breman, 141.

sponsored writers' workshops to produce programmed texts for pastoral training.[172]

This succinct summary of the AEA's agenda could be assessed to be the most profound contribution of the AEA in over five decades of existence. Kato criss-crossed the continent, visiting almost every African country,[173] meeting church leaders, speaking at conferences, and lecturing in colleges and seminaries. In the Central Africa Republic (CAR), for example, he met the then head of state, Emperor Jean-Bedel Bokassa I, to share his vision and the need for a place to build an evangelical theological school for the training of church leaders in francophone Africa. He succeeded in having his request granted when the emperor offered a seven-acre plot of land in the nation's capital, Bangui, near the national university.[174]

Kato had articulated a theological vision and programme for the training of leaders on African soil to address the theological pitfalls he had identified in his doctoral research. The plan included establishing two graduate theological schools to serve the French-speaking and English-speaking regions of Africa, respectively. He envisioned a curriculum designed to be relevant to issues on the continent and a standard of scholarship that would equip leaders to counter the heresies and promote biblical Christianity in the young church in Africa. The plan also included promoting research and the publication of African theological reflections. He also included an institution to ensure maintenance of standards, accreditation and support for the development of evangelical theological schools. This is how the first two evangelical theological graduate schools in sub-Saharan Africa were founded, namely the Faculté de Théologie Évangélique de Bangui (FATEB) in the Central Africa Republic, established in 1977 for the francophone region, and the Nairobi Evangelical Graduate School of Theology (NEGST) – now the Africa International University – in Kenya, established in 1983, for the anglophone region. Also, AEA established the Christian Learning Materials Centre (CLMC) in Kenya to provide sound theological Sunday school curriculum. AEA also owns Africa Christian Television (ACT/PEMA) in Abidjan, Cote d'Ivoire, with outreach to other francophone countries. In addition, it sponsors the Association

---

172. Kato, "Africa's Battle," 55.
173. Breman, "Portrait," 114.
174. Haye, *Byang Kato*, 77.

of Christian Theological Education in Africa (ACTEA), which provides accreditation and other services for quality assurance to affiliated schools for sound theological education in Africa.

In the nearly three years that Kato served as general secretary of AEA, he grew the number of national evangelical fellowships from eight to sixteen, representing ten million Christians in Africa, with only three colleagues on staff.[175] The voice of evangelicals became recognisable and heard across Africa and beyond, and the AEA changed from being a small side-line fellowship for the interaction of evangelicals to an influential continental organization within world Christianity.[176] In his assessment of Kato's achievements, his successor, Tokumbo Adeyemo, said:

> Under his [Kato's] leadership within the space of less than three years before his tragic death, AEA doubled its membership, improved the quality of its publications and services and thus became a force to reckon with. He literally placed the name AEA on the ecclesiastical map of Africa. For my first three years in office, the only way people knew what I was doing and the organisation I was working for was to mention the name Byang Kato.[177]

During Kato's time, two prime properties in Nairobi were also acquired for the work of AEA, through assistance from the Africa Inland Mission, in whose name the properties were held in trust until 2010, when the title deeds were transferred to AEA's name.[178] These included two villas on a 1.2-acre plot near the city centre in Nairobi, which served as AEA offices and residence for the AEA general secretary, and an 0.8-acre plot in another part of the city, Riara Road, which was developed by his successor as staff houses.

However, he did not see the actualisation of the theological projects. The theological graduate schools, FATEB and NEGST, were both established after Kato's death. Although he was instrumental in recruiting the first director for ACTEA, Paul Bowers, it was not until 1976, the year after Kato's death, that ACTEA officially started operations.[179] Kato can certainly be granted

---

175. Breman, "Portrait," 146.
176. Haye, *Byang Kato*, 106; cf. Breman, "Association of Evangelicals ," 146–147.
177. Adeyemo, "Byang Kato," 8.
178. AEA Board Minutes of 28 November 2010, archived at AEA Offices in Nairobi, Kenya.
179. Bowers, *Theological Education*, 2.

credit for the establishment of these AEA projects even though the projects, successfully implemented after his death. Indeed, as it happened, there was a three-year gap between Kato and Adeyemo, his immediate successor.

Background to Theological Debates

Kato's debates against theological systems, including ATR and some of its proponents – John Mbiti, J. K. Agbeti, Bolaji Idowu and Harry Sawyerr, among others – was an important factor of Kato's prominence in African theological discourse. Ferdinando states, "By his opposition to the AACC and theologians like Mbiti and Idowu, Kato was taking on the African ecclesiastical and theological establishment. He disagreed in print with those whose academic credentials were already established, risking opprobrium and ridicule."[180] Kato highlighted ten areas that he saw as challenging biblical Christianity in Africa and the motivation for his work in addressing these.[181]

Kato asserted that what was emerging as African Christian theology was imprecise and was at best a theology of decolonisation, an amalgamation of Black theology and Ethiopianist theology.[182] Thus he argued that the emerging African theology was unbiblical and that the aim was to synthesise Christianity with ATRs, which he said was syncretistic.[183] Kato therefore argued against Mbiti's alleged supposition that ATRs constitute a well-organised system, and that the ATR worshipper has not only known God truly, but that he has worshipped him.[184] However, Kato noted: "Mbiti did not concede the possibility of salvation in ATR but holds the view of salvation for all men on different ground."[185] Kato would identify this ground as universalism.[186] Kato was also opposed to Mbiti's assertion that "traditional religions neither send missionaries nor make proselytes; their strength lies in being fully integrated in all departments of human existence. As such, they cannot and need not

---

180. Ferdinando, "The Legacy of Byang Kato," 6.

181. The ten-point summary of Kato's theological concerns are enumerated in chapter three of this work which deals with Kato's disputations. See also Kato, *Theological Pitfalls*, 11–17.

182. Kato, *Theological Pitfalls*, 53–55.

183. Kato, 55–56.

184. Kato, 69.

185. Kato, 56.

186. Kato, 57.

be completely wiped out so long as those who follow them are alive."[187] Mbiti was making a case for the Christian faith being continuous with African traditional religious beliefs and that the two are bound to go together. The "Theology of Peaceful Co-existence," according to Kato, was championed by Bolaji Idowu, whose thesis was that Africans believed in one God, and who explained away the pantheons of gods and objects of worship as only mediums to the one Supreme God.[188] Another concern was Harry Sawyerr, who posited that "the prayers of African Christians might in the providence of God lead to the salvation of their pagan ancestors."[189] Kwame Bediako, after the death of Kato, did an important appraisal of Kato's work on the question of contextualisation and African Christian identity.[190] This work, among others, also contributed to the sustained debate about the relationship between ATR and Christianity.

Based on the nature of these issues and the calibre of his opponents, Kato developed character and distinctiveness. His opponents were distinguished heads of religion departments in leading universities in West and East Africa following independence in the early 1960s.

Global Engagement

Apart from his studies in the UK and USA, while he was still a student himself, Kato was plenary speaker at Urbana 1970, the Inter-Varsity Student Missions Conference in the USA, with an audience of over twelve thousand students.[191] As general secretary of AEA, Kato led the African contingent to the historic First International Congress on World Evangelization in 1974. The Lausanne Congress was an important gathering of evangelicals that brought together 2,700 people from 150 nations of the world. In the estimation of *TIME Magazine* at the time, it was "possibly the widest-ranging meeting of Christians ever held."[192] The meeting was convened by evangelist Billy Graham

---

187. Mbiti, *Concepts of God*, xiv.
188. Kato, *Theological Pitfalls*, 91.
189. Sawyerr, *Creative Evangelism*, 112; cf. Kato, *Theological Pitfalls*, 179–180.
190. See Bediako, *Theology and Identity*.
191. Breman, "Portrait," 141.
192. Billy Graham, "The Beginnings of the Lausanne Movement": https://lausanne.org/our-legacy

and delegates were drawn from every known evangelical organisation. The objective of the conference was to create a movement for the evangelisation of the world – taking the whole gospel to the whole world.

Kato spoke on two topics at the Congress: (1) "Evangelism Opportunities and Obstacles in Africa" and (2) "The Gospel, Cultural Contextualisation and Religious Syncretism."[193] As will be analysed in subsequent chapters, these two topics were among his most significant contributions to the development of African Christian theological thought from an evangelical perspective. He is certainly credited as the first to introduce the subject of contextualisation in evangelical theological discourse.[194] Ironically, Kato's critics perceived him to be against contextualisation because of his opposition to the brand of African Christian theology that was promoted on the continent. However, Kato made clear that his contention was rather with any belief or practice, in the name of contextualisation, that was not consistent with Scripture. He went on to state his understanding of contextualisation: "By contextualize, we mean to make Christianity truly relevant in our situation and to make the African view himself welcome in the church. By that we are not dealing with the content, we are only dealing with a mode of expression."[195] He further stated:

> The eternal nature of God's Word covers the modern space age as well. While the thought patterns of God's revelation may and should be expressed to the Christians of various cultures in the manner they should understand, they should not be changed for the benefit of the hearer. Rather, the hearer should be taught some of the strange concepts. If the African or the Asian can be taught that egg is more nourishing than cassava or that there is vitamin in sunshine, he could be taught that salt is a symbol of righteousness.[196]

---

193. Haye, *Byang Kato*, 80.
194. Bowers, "Byang Kato," 4.
195. Kato, "Presentation at meeting of leaders of the National Evangelical Association of USA" in Washington, January 1975, 9.
196. Kato, "Contextualisation of the Gospel: Theological Perspective", 1–2, (1975?).

Kato's presentation provoked further discussion after the 1974 Lausanne Congress by the Lausanne Theology Working Group and hence popularised the discourse on the subject of contextualisation in theological scholarship.[197]

Following the initial gathering of evangelicals from one hundred and fifty countries in Lausanne, a committee was set up to continue to mobilise and sustain the collaboration of evangelicals around the world for world evangelisation. Kato was elected to serve on the newly formed Lausanne Continuation Committee of the International Congress on World Evangelisation. He was also chosen to serve as vice president of the World Evangelical Alliance (WEA)[198] and became chair of the newly formed WEA Theological Commission.[199] According to Breman,[200] Kato himself acknowledged that his life had been enriched by the opportunity of meeting and connecting with top evangelical leaders from around the world through these networks.

Kato's passion for sound theological education was demonstrated by his personal development and training, and his establishment of theological institutions in Africa. He also shared in the vision of the WEA Theological Commission for the establishment of a similar body for evangelical theological schools globally, culminating in the founding in 1980 of the International Council for Evangelical Theological Education (ICETE).[201] He was also a member of the Advisory Council of the Asia Theological Association.[202]

Kato's Tragic Demise

Kato died by drowning in the Indian Ocean on 19 December 1975, at the age of thirty-nine. Given Kato's hectic schedule as general secretary throughout the year, he saw the need to take some time off to relax at a beach resort in Mombasa, and also to use the time to prepare for his next trip abroad. He went to the resort with his family, except his daughter Deborah, who had left days before for Christmas vacation in Nigeria. On the fatal day, he went swimming with his two boys in the morning while his wife stayed at the

---

197. Haye, *Byang Kato*, 80.
198. At that time the World Evangelical Fellowship (WEF).
199. Bowers, "Byang Kato," 4; Breman, "Portrait," 145.
200. Breman, "Association of Evangelicals," 417.
201. Bowers, "Byang Kato," 4.
202. Breman, "Portrait," 145.

residence busy preparing a meal for the family. The day was also the seventeenth birthday of the elder son, Jonathan. At lunch time, the boys preceded him to the residence, leaving him to come on his own. Curious that he had not come home to listen to the BBC news at 1:00 pm, as he would normally do, they went looking for him. But their search proved to be in vain – their father was nowhere in sight. The family raised alarm about his whereabouts. Eventually the reality of his having drowned in the waters of the Indian Ocean was confirmed when the drowned body was recovered the next morning.

The news of Kato's tragic sudden death shocked the church around the world, and left the people of Kwoi, Kato's hometown, in disbelief:[203] "News of Dr. Kato's death spread rapidly and cables and letters by the hundreds poured into the AEA office from every continent."[204] The funeral service attracted hundreds of people. According to Haye, "The Boys' and Girls' Brigades formed a guard of honour stretching from the airport to the church, seven miles. A cavalcade of fifty-five cars followed the plain, wooden coffin in a slow procession to the church, where 1,200 people had packed inside, with many more sitting and standing outside."[205]

The result of the post-mortem was inconclusive about the cause for Kato's drowning. He was known to be a good swimmer and speculations about his death were varied. The suggestion of him being bitten by a poisonous fish was dismissed on grounds that there were no marks on his lifeless body. Another suggestion was that he might have died of exhaustion, given the frenzy of activities he was engaged in before retreating, and the work he was continuing to do for his overseas trip the following year. His people believed that his death was not an accident, but he must have been attacked by someone physically or through witchcraft.[206] One reason for the various conspiracy theories about the cause of Kato's death was due to the fact that the corpse, according to the people of Kwoi, was fully clothed when it was retrieved from the water. In a letter, dated 13 February 1976, the SIM area director in Jos, Nigeria, Harold Fuller, wrote to the AEA administrative secretary, Jim Halbert, requesting an explanation in a quest to dispel the speculations. He states:

---

203. Breman, 143.
204. Haye, *Byang Kato*, 102.
205. Haye, 98.
206. Breman, "Portrait," 142–143.

The people of Kwoi cannot imagine that Byang Kato drowned by accident. They cannot understand why he was fully clothed, with his shoes on. Because they had heard he had many "enemies" (which term had been used metaphorically in connection with those who opposed his evangelical stand), they think that someone must have attacked him. Any detailed information which you can send, including a coroner's report, will help dispel these notions.[207]

Jim Halbert, who was standing in for the substantive AEA administrative secretary, Eric Maillefer (who was on furlough), wrote in response to Fuller's inquiry:

Byang was not fully clothed. He had on his swim trunks, tennis shoes and his glasses. At low tide you can walk out on the coral from the shore, but it is wise to wear tennis shoes because some of the coral has sharp edges, and also because there are two types of fish which are poisonous. He always wore his glasses when he did not intend to swim. However, this time he changed his mind and did swim with the glasses. However, they were not on his body when it was found.[208]

Nonetheless, the cultural assumption among the Jaba people and many other African peoples is that nothing happens by natural causes. Kato wrote:

When I was a boy, a court of assizes was a regular practice in our family. Since nobody dies of natural causes according to the Jaba philosophy of life, an adequate cause must be sought in order to know how to try to save a sick child. So if a child was sick in the family, my grandfather would call for an early morning meeting to investigate the matter. He would use the language of pleas and threats for the culprit to make himself known. Anyone who knew the supposed witches seeking to devour the child

---

207. Harold Fuller, Sudan Inland Mission Area Coordiantor in Jos, Nigeria in a letter to the AEA office in Nairobi about the concern raised by Kato's relatives in Kwoi, Nigeria about the cause of Kato's death, on 13 February 1976 (archived at the AEA offices in Nairobi, Kenya).

208. Jim Halbert, a Missionary from the African Inland Mission who acted as Administrative Secretary for the AEA when the substantive office holder was on leave, in a letter responding to Harold Fuller's inquiry (achieved at the AEA offices in Nairobi, Kenya).

was to declare it. Our grandfather would conclude, "If this sick boy dies, the culprit among you who has collaborated with the witches to snatch away one of us will face the same fate.[209]

In any case, the widow was able to convince the family to accept Byang's death as the sovereign will of God and quelled the quest for divining through African traditional religious means so that evil would befall Kato's presumed killers.

The corpse was flown from Kenya back to Nigeria and to his hometown for burial. The Jaba people in the Kwoi local government area had never seen so many landings of small aircrafts on the air strip. Forty-four years later, the day is still remembered by the frequency of the plane landings, which was unlike any other time in Kwoi.[210] A long motorcade followed the funeral hearse from the air strip to the ECWA church in the centre of the town. The funeral and burial took place in the church compound. The Boys' and Girls' Brigades mounted a guard of honour. The one-thousand-seat congregation had an overflow in equal number, with representatives from the evangelical community around the world at the funeral service.

Bruce Nicholls was a well-known theologian from New Zealand based in India as a missionary researcher and theological educator. He was the executive secretary of the WEA Theological Commission when Byang Kato was its chair. He paid this personal tribute to Kato:

> I, with many, could not help asking why our heavenly Father had permitted such a tragedy, as it seemed that this was the hour when Africa needed him most. He was undoubtedly the most outstanding evangelical theological leader in Africa. Byang was a skilled biblical exegete, theologian and apologist. . . . Byang was a twentieth century prophet, somewhat in the school of an earlier African, Tertullian; for while he was identified with Black Africa in its cry for liberation against unjust oppression, he was fearless in his denunciation of all liberal theology and

---

209. Kato, *African Cultural Revolution*. 13

210. During field interviews in Kwoi, people in their forties made reference to "that man for whose burial so many planes landed here in Kwoi," without even making any reference to the man's name.

philosophy that deviated from the authority of the Bible as the word of God.[211]

Bruce Nicholls further stated: "We were together for the WCC Assembly in Nairobi.[212] I grew to respect the clarity of his understanding of the issues being debated. Within the limitation of his status as an observer, he entered fearlessly into debate. . . . Byang was also a preacher and a pastor."[213] Byang Kato was survived by his wife, Jummai, and three children, Deborah, Jonathan and Paul, and the extended family. Jonathan and Jummai subsequently joined him in death in 2015 and 2019, respectively.

Byang Kato's Accomplishments

Byang Kato was an accomplished young man, a husband, father, pastor, teacher, preacher, prophet, visionary leader and evangelist. The people interviewed for this study recalled how Kato impacted their lives and the warmth and godly life of his family. His witness saw his children, parents and other family members come to the Christian faith and convert from African traditional religions.[214] What Kato did manage to accomplish before his untimely death was to set the stage for theological work among evangelicals in Africa, namely by initiating the AEA Theological Commission and its various projects.[215] He laid the foundation for the bulk of AEA's ongoing task.

Kato was the leading voice for evangelical Christianity in Africa at that time. In the foreword to Kato's biography by Sophie de la Haye, Tokumboh Adeyemo writes:

> He was a prophet. Like prophets before him, his voice was that of a lonely man in theological wilderness of his day. His life as a prophet was marked by courage, boldness, moral purity and discipline. His message was forthright, powerful, uncompromising

---

211. Breman, "Portrait," 144.
212. Kato had declined a formal invitation as a fraternal delegate to bring greetings to the WCC Assembly in Nairobi (1975), but instead requested to attend the assembly as an observer, a lower status, given to people who were not necessarily in close communion with the WCC.
213. Breman, "Portrait," 144.
214. Haye, *Byang Kato*, 44–45.
215. Kapteina, "Formation," 72.

but always compassionate. As often true of prophets, Kato lived before his time.[216]

Palmer writes: "Byang Kato was a prophet in the early 1970s. He called attention to dangerous trends in Africa and worldwide. Although he was not without mistakes, his basic message was and still holds true."[217] Kato believed biblical Christianity taking root in tropical Africa was under threat by liberal teachings in the church and was "the first African evangelical to attempt to engage with the African intellectual world, to participate in the principal intellectual project of African Christianity in his day. And the first to provide a published contribution in that effort."[218]

Kato had seen his community transformed by the Christian gospel and had personal experience of transformation: "The true gospel that has transformed the lives of some 30 per cent Jaba people must not be adulterated."[219] Like Kato himself, Kato's tribal people, the Jaba, had experienced the transformative power of the Christian gospel, and Kato was committed to preserving that true gospel that he had received as a child. Kato said, "What is desired for Jaba goes for the continent and the world."[220]

Kato's life and ministry represents a classic case for authentic African Christian theological reflection, from a predominantly African worldview shaped by the philosophical religious framework of ATR. He saw the need for sound theological training to equip church leaders to defend the Christian faith so that people would not be led away from the faith by heresies. Kato argued for Christianity that was truly African and truly biblical.[221] He asserted that Christianity must baptise African culture and it is erroneous to reverse the order. He rejected veneration of ATR and affirmed the uniqueness of the gospel of Christ which alone provides the way for salvation.

Kato's life is an example and a model for African Christians in navigating socio-cultural and religious belief systems and living out an impactful Christian life. Breman observes that Kato had no examples of African

---

216. Adeyemo, "Byang Kato," 11.
217. Palmer, "Byang Kato: Theological Appraisal," 16.
218. Bowers, "Byang Kato," 5.
219. Kato, "Critique of Incipient," ThD diss., 33.
220. Kato, 33–34.
221. Kato, *African Cultural Revolution*. 15

theologians he could follow for himself.[222] His work in this regard, in his era, was a pioneering feat. His most outstanding contribution to African Christian theology was his insistence on the centrality of the Bible.[223] Kato's leadership was inspiring, courageous and dared to go where others had dared not go. He also confronted what he considered to be worldly. He acknowledged the lordship of Christ in his personal life, as evidenced in his family worship and a God-driven life.[224]

Kato's influence and contribution went beyond Africa. Shirik affirms:

> Kato's strength also lies in that he was able to speak beyond the confines of Africa. I, as an Asian, more than four decades separated from Kato, and with very different challenges and struggles, can affirm many of the things he affirms. He and I can read the Scripture together to come to a common understanding. In this aspect too, he has bequeathed to his readers a compelling argument that all theologies must not be contextual to the degree that they have no universal resemblance and application. God speaks to us through his words sometimes differently, but not contradictorily. Our cultures can enrich our reading of the text, but they can also blind us from seeing the truth. Kato seems to have a profound understanding of both the limitations of culture and the universal applicability of the text.[225]

This is an important citation in underscoring the importance of Kato's biblical understanding. The message of the Bible has a universal appeal, across cultures, ethnicities and races. While Kato wanted African Christians to understand and appropriate the message of the gospel, he wanted to do it in a way that did not trap the message in traditional African attire so that it would have no appeal to other cultures.

Included among his many accomplishments were the establishment of renowned theological institutions, the growth and increase in number of national evangelical fellowships in the region and the acquisition of properties in Nairobi for the establishment of AEA headquarters, and the same in

---

222. Breman, "Association of Evangelicals," 417.
223. Bediako, *Theology and Identity*, 413.
224. Breman, "Association of Evangelicals," 416–417; Shirik, "African Christians."
225. Shirik, "African Christians," 150.

Bangui, the home of the first evangelical theological graduate school in sub-Saharan Africa. His legacy included the mentorship of many future evangelical leaders; including Tokunboh Adeyemo, who succeeded Kato as general secretary of AEA.

Notwithstanding the achievements of Byang Kato, he was a "sinner saved by grace." He did have failures and shortcomings. At thirty-nine years of age, Kato was youthful and was still maturing and gaining wisdom. He needed more time to build on the foundations he had laid. There was some room for improvement.[226] It is to some of Kato's apparent lapses that I now turn.

Failures and Deficiencies of Kato

Despite Kato's brilliant career, he had his own pitfalls. Criticising a dead man is not an African thing to do. However, this is a critical analysis of an individual life, and viewing both sides of the person, his strengths and weaknesses, in tension, authenticates the person's humanness. One of the regrets Kato himself admitted was when he left his family for further studies in the UK. His wife followed him a year later and each of the three young children were left with different relatives to look after them, in three different cities. When the couple returned to Nigeria after their studies, they were heartbroken at the state and health of the children. According to Jummai, they were emaciated and were not in robust health,

Kato was faced with the same situation four years later after the couple's return from the UK, when he had to leave the family again to go to the USA for postgraduate studies. However, this time he endeavoured to have the whole family join him later in the USA. While they lived together as a family in Nairobi during his tenure with AEA, Kato spent a lot of time away from home on ministry assignments. In the not quite three-year tenure (Feb. 1973–Dec. 1975), Kato travelled to almost all the countries in Africa, plus his travels overseas. This caused some tension in the family and had a long-term impact on the older son, Jonathan, who was most affected by his father's absence from home.[227] In Jonathan's adult life it happened that his wife was

---

226. Bowers, "Byang Kato," 14.
227. Haye, *Byang Kato*, 108–110.

a pastor, and her time away from home on pastoral assignments reminded him of his father, in ways that came to affect their marriage.[228]

Kato was a workaholic. While there are some conspiracy theories about his death,[229] what seems to be a more plausible supposition is that he died of fatigue, owing to his heavy work schedule. Thus, he would have been very exhausted or burnt out when he went swimming that day, even though he was a good swimmer. Despite Kato's zeal for biblical Christianity, there could have been ambiguities in some of his biblical interpretations. This work argues for lifestyle and actions/practice as means for theological insights. The way Kato handled and related to the church establishment on some of the issues, like ecumenism, aspects of pietism and social action were problematic. His experience of ATR could perhaps have been utilized more in engaging ATR worldviews for transformation.[230]

Conclusion

Kato started from humble beginnings, was rooted in "pagan worship" (as he described it)[231], got converted to Christianity, and grew and matured into an outstanding Christian leader before his life ended tragically. Africans live in the context of religious plurality and suffer for their faith, especially in conversion to Christianity from other religions such as Islam and ATR. Also, the African church faces the challenge of syncretism – of mixing ATR with the Christian faith.[232] Mburu states, "While obviously not coded into our DNA, worldview is so embedded in the social fabric that it is transmitted both consciously and unconsciously. We have all acquired the knowledge, values, morals, and skills we need to live harmoniously in our communities."[233] The African traditional worldview can dominate the biblical worldview, and therefore practices and beliefs are not always consistent with the Christian faith or what the Bible teaches.

---

228. In an interview with Deborah Kato-Bature, elder sister of Jonathan, on 23 March 2019 in Kaduna, Nigeria.
229. Breman, "Portrait," 143.
230. Kato's biblical hermeneutics will be dealt with in the next two chapters.
231. Kato, *African Perspectives*, 1.
232. Chalk, *Making Disciples*, 10.
233. Mburu, *African Hermeneutics*, 7.

The biographical sketch of Byang Henry Kato paints a portrait that commands attention. Kato was a true native of Kwoi, in Kaduna state in Northern Nigeria, of Jaba ethnicity and of impeccable social standing. He was raised to be a fetish priest and was married to a princess, the daughter of Kpop Ham. He was a true African from sociological and anthropological perspectives, since he was well enculturated and established among his people.

Kato converted to Christianity and experienced remarkable transformation as a young man, committing himself to the service of God for the rest of his life. With singular purpose, hard work and integrity, he excelled in education and his career. As minister of the gospel and Bible teacher, he was committed to the development of the church. He was elevated to head his denomination and went on to become the first African general secretary of AEA. He was known for his Bible-centredness and Christ-centredness. He was concerned about mixing the Christian faith with African traditional religions – thus his warning message to the church in Africa about incipient syncretism and universalism. He proposed a solution to this theological challenge by promoting sound theological education in Africa. He laid a solid foundation to enable AEA to deliver on this vision through the structures he put in place.

A man of exemplary leadership, Kato became the father of evangelical theology in sub-Saharan Africa. He shared the gospel with his family members so they could come to faith and discipled and mentored other people to grow in their faith and their professions. His passion and pursuits in his Christian faith demonstrated some clear hermeneutical positions. His passion was to spread this faith as in understood it in his quest for sound theological education in the church. In an interview this writer had with Manfred Kohl, he said: "You need to reserve a whole chapter about the integrity of Byang Kato; he was a man of integrity. He meant what he said, did what he said he would do and was an outstanding man of God who gave his all to the service of the church."[234]

Lessons from Kato's life are particularly important for disciple-making in the church and for intergenerational leadership development. With the

---

234. In a discussion with the author and Dr. Manfred W. Kohl who had served the global Church in many senior positions in theological education and who personally knew Kato at the WEA General Assembly, Jakarta, November 2019.

burgeoning youthful population in Africa and the lack of opportunity for young people to ascend to leadership, Kato's story could be an inspiration for young people. Kato's life as a Christian leader and family man, as well as his life in church, community and larger society, all provide important lessons for faithfully engaging with the Bible as Christian Africans. Also, with the pervasive and dominant African religious worldview, Kato demonstrated a life lesson about worldview transformation for African Christians. The genius of Kato's story is his worldview's transformation from ATR to a biblical worldview.

The next chapter explores, in depth, Kato's contribution to three particular areas of theological and biblical understanding: his biblical hermeneutics, his perspectives on the question of African Christian identity and his contribution to evangelical theological education in Africa.

CHAPTER 3

Byang Kato's Theological Legacy in Biblical Hermeneutics, African Christian Identity and Evangelical Theological Education

Introduction

Byang Kato was an established leader and a pioneer of evangelical theology in modern Christianity in sub-Saharan Africa.[1] Kato was a young Nigerian theologian praised by some scholars and castigated by others.[2] Shirik writes: "In spite of his brief career, he has left his imprint on the pages of African Christian history. He is not without his supporters and critics alike. It appears that while his critics have misunderstood him in some respects, his supporters also have not paid enough attention to his theological conviction and articulation."[3] Given the context of Kato's time, his theological contribution was motivated and characterised by his fear of the destruction of the faith of the young church in sub-Saharan Africa. Kato raised a uniquely prophetic voice to alert the church about heresies. He opposed much of the theological

---

1. See Breman, "Portrait"; cf. Turaki, "Theological Legacy," 33.

2. Palmer, "Byang Kato: A Theological Reappraisal," 3; cf. MacDonald, "Critical Analysis," 21; Shirik, "African Christians," 132.

3. Shirik, "African Christians," 131.

innovations of his fellow African theologians, whose aim was to restore African dignity and give a more positive appraisal of the values and systems of ATR than Western missionaries did.[4]

He was critical about what was being taught by other African theologians, concerned that it was syncretistic and universalistic – that is to say, that it mixed the two religions (Christianity and ATR) and believed in the salvation of all people, whether they believed in Christ in this life or not. African traditional religions and concepts of God were being systematised without the Bible, making the Bible irrelevant to this vision of African theology.[5] Ferdinando writes:

> A classificatory system which attempts to distinguish the principal responses taken by Christian writers to this issue, and one which has been widely adopted – albeit with modifications and reservations – identifies three major positions. Briefly, *exclusivist* approaches argue that salvation and/or truth is found only through an explicit knowledge and confession of Christ; *inclusivist* approaches argue that salvation/truth is found only in Christ but may be mediated through non-Christian religions or philosophies apart from any explicit knowledge of him; and *pluralist* approaches see Christ as simply one means of salvation and truth among many others.[6]

Thus, some of the proponents for the positive evaluation of ATR tended to be inclusive or pluralistic – syncretistic and universalistic. For example, Kwame Bediako's approach to ATR "tends towards inclusivism, parallel to his understanding of the approaches of Justin Martyr and Clement of Alexandria toward Greek philosophy. The gospel is saving truth, but that truth was known partially – and savingly – in the pre-Christian worship of African traditional religion."[7] Bediako himself makes a positive evaluation of other African theologians, like Bolaji Idowu, John Mbiti and Mulago gwa Cikala Musharhamina,

---

4. Palmer, "Byang Kato: A Theological Reappraisal". 11; Breman, "Association of Evangelicals," 416–417.

5. Kato, *Theological Pitfalls*, 69–70; cf. Ward, *Christianity, Colonialism*, 71; Maxwell, "Post-Colonial," 402.

6. Ferdinando, "Christian Identity," 124.

7. Ferdinando, 124.

and he singled out Byang Kato as the notable dissenting voice. He states: "Byang Kato was most notable as the dissenting voice in the chorus of positive evaluations of the African pre-Christian religious heritage. . . . In Kato's case, his response was complicated by a theological posture that rendered his appreciation of the heritage from the past problematic."[8]

However, there were some others who believed that Kato laid the foundation for evangelical theology and made important contributions to promote sound evangelical theological education in Africa.[9] Nevertheless, many of those who make a positive appraisal of Kato's convictions appear to do so with some reservations and may not have done much to expound on Kato's legacy. Ironically, it is one of his critics, Kwame Bediako, who has devoted substantial effort to evaluating Kato's theology. A whole chapter is devoted to Kato's theology in Bediako's magnum opus, *Theology and Identity*.[10] Later in this chapter, Bediako's continuing influence will be highlighted, and his articulation of a distinctive brand of African Christianity, which may not be in complete agreement with Kato's views. According to Shirik, "Kato's understanding of Christianity was driven by his conviction that the essential message of Christianity can and should be universally understood and constructed. It should then be adequately communicated using contextual forms; therefore, acceptance or rejection of his contextual approach must consider this aspect."[11]

The historical context in which Kato worked was the late 1950s to mid-1970s, a time of cultural awakening and revolution which had welled up from the struggles for independence and freedom from the shackles of colonial domination. Pan-Africanist scholars had been agitating for independence from colonial rule, and starting with Ghana in 1957, a few African countries had just attained their independence. The colonial experience of suppression, and the lack of understanding and appreciation for the African culture by European colonial officials and missionaries, was rife. In the struggle for independence, the call was to reject European influence and return to African cultural roots as part of the struggle for self-assertion and independence from

---

8. Bediako, *Theology and Identity*, xviii.

9. Tiénou, *Theological Task*, 3; cf. Palmer, "Byang Kato: Theological Appraisal," 3–4; Ferdinando, "Christian Identity," 135–137.

10. Shirik, "African Christians," 132–133; cf. Bediako, *Theology and Identity*, 386–425.

11. Shirik, "African Christians," 132.

colonial domination.[12] The cultural revolution impacted not only political, economic and socio-cultural issues but also impacted the church and theology. African scholars and church leaders began talking about African Christian theology that was open to different interpretations. Palmer observes that this was a period of theological investigation and agitation. Biblical doctrines were being questioned.[13] Many of the established churches with headquarters in Europe or America were less fervent in evangelising and focused more on social justice issues.[14]

The immediate post-independence era was therefore marked by three factors: (1) the resurgence of African consciousness that influenced Christian thought and practice; (2) the effects of the struggle for independence, raising the desire among some African scholars to separate themselves from Western Christianity; and in the case of Kato, (3) the social pressures shaping popular Christianity in the period immediately surrounding Nigerian independence.[15] In Kenya, for example, Githiga observes: "The failure of the Church as an institution to speak against colonial authoritarianism made nationalists to coin the phrase '*Gutiri ngurani ya Mubi na Muthungu*'" (which translated means: 'There is no difference between a settler and a missionary')."[16]

This atmosphere likely played a role in Kato's subsequent endeavours and contributions to conceptions of African Christian identity and to defining the evangelical tradition in the Protestant church in Africa. In other words, Kato's earliest adulthood was at the crossroads of the shaping of African Christian consciousness post-independence. In that respect, he turned out to be a resistant voice among several scholars at that time. While the others advocated for a strand of Christian consciousness that rejected Western missionary Christianity, Kato appears to have prioritised biblical Christianity, which admittedly had been handed down by Western Christian missionaries in Africa. It is that brand of Christianity that Kato had experienced and been nurtured in, and which had transformed his life. Kato saw the need to

---

12. Palmer, "Byang Kato: Rejectionist or Conversionist," 6.
13. Ward, "Chrisitanity," 77–82.
14. Maxwell, "Post-Colonial," 406.
15. Githiga, *Church as Bulwark*, 10; cf. Palmer, "Byang Kato: Rejectionist," 15; Maxwell, "Post-Colonial," 405.
16. Githiga, *Church as Bulwark*, 3.

raise a unique and prophetic voice in reaction to the theological trends in the church in Africa.

He was reputed to hold a radical conservative view of Scripture, different from his contemporaries, many of whom preceded him in the academy. His key message was a warning to the church about the threats of incipient universalism and syncretism, with the message of the uniqueness of the gospel of Christ being lost, and the universalistic theology of the ecumenical movement penetrating and destroying the church.[17] Therefore, Kato used strong and prophetic language to address these concerns, courageously debating the individual proponents of those issues he considered heretical. He singled out John Mbiti and Bolaji Idowu in particular. Kato stated: "There is another way of looking at the relationship between Christianity and African religions. It is not neo-colonialism to plead the uniqueness and finality of Jesus Christ."[18] Kato sought for authentic African identity and for an authentic biblical Christianity.

The debates were extremely important in shaping Kato's own self-understanding, and indeed, in directing his energies to defining evangelical Christianity and what he believed would constitute the propagation and defence of the gospel in Africa. Thus, Kato sought to put in check the perceived theological pitfalls creeping into the church in Africa through the liberal theologies espoused by his opponents. Kato's views were met with equally strong opposition and criticism. Palmer's appraisal of the various charges brought against Kato by other scholars include Kwame Bediako's criticism of Kato's perspective on the radical discontinuity between ATR and the Christian faith and the claim that he was an extremist, a rejectionist of African culture, and an alienated African, one who had lost his Africanness, which were charges brought by Bediako and Mercy Oduyoye.[19] Kato was also portrayed as opposed to contextualisation and as being a naïve theologian.[20] However, Palmer defends Kato and observes that a critical study places Kato in the mainstream of evangelical theology in Africa. He justifies Kato's rejection of the term "African theology" given the context of the debate in his lifetime,

---

17. Palmer, "Byang Kato: Rejectionist," 16.
18. Kato, *Theological Pitfalls*, 16.
19. Palmer, "Byang Kato: Rejectionist," 3–5; see also MacDonald, "Critical Analysis"; Shirik, "African Christians"; Bediako, *Theology and Identity*; and Oduyoye, *Hearing and Knowing*.
20. Bediako, *Jesus and Gospel*, 49; cf. Shirik, "African Christians," 132.

and he defends Kato's stance on contextualization, stating that he was not opposed to it.[21] On the contrary, Kato is credited for being one of the earliest scholars to introduce contextualisation into theological discourse.[22]

Kato's disagreement was not only between himself and the extreme ecumenists to the left but also the extreme conservatives on the right, like the International Council of Christian Churches (ICCC). The ICCC and the National Association of Evangelicals (NAE) have their roots in American fundamentalism, but whereas the NAE emerged as a community of classic evangelicals which collaborates with other evangelical groups around the world, the ICCC remains in the fundamentalists and separatist camp.[23] Kato metaphorically referred to the rather disagreeable position he defended as "meat in the sandwich," caught in the middle of the extreme left liberal ecumenists and the extreme right separatists.[24] Though he shared most theological beliefs with the ICCC, the difference was in the legalistic zeal, aggressive separatism and belief in their own extremist interpretation of Scripture.[25] According to Adeyemo, "Fundamentalism refers to those who resist the liberal distortion of the Gospel through the tendency to modernise the Christian faith in order to make it more compatible with a non-Christian worldview or philosophy of life. Unfortunately, fundamentalism too often – not always – indicates a closed minded, defensive, reactionary theology and Church structure."[26] According to Breman, Kato stated: "We are called names, 'neo-evangelicals' by the right, and 'separatists' by the left. Missionaries have refused to have fellowship with me because I'm too ecumenical, and in other places, I've been called a separatist who has been deceived by American missionaries!" Kato went on to conclude: "Maybe we are in the right place when we are criticised by both sides."[27] Kato clearly rejected the fundamentalist label, as well as the accusation of being a mouthpiece for Western missionaries, or anybody, and asserted his independent thinking. Some of his missionary friends were

---

21. Palmer, "Byang Kato: Rejectionist," 3–5.
22. Bowers, "Byang Kato: "Contextualisation of the Gospel" 4;
23. Hinkelmann, "Founding," 104–105; Stott, *Evangelical Truth*, 19–24; Adeyemo, "What Are Evangelicals," 7.
24. Kato, *Spirits*, 17.
25. Hinkelmann, "Founding," 105.
26. Adeyemo, "What Are Evangelicals," 7.
27. Kato, "Ecclesiastical Structures Today" cited in "Portrait," by Bremen, 146.

opposed to his academic pursuits.[28] Kato may have been shaped by the influence of other people in the missionary enterprise, but it is unlikely that he was indoctrinated. He had a critical mind and was convinced about the direction he wanted to pursue and the influence he wanted to bring to the church.

An outstanding contribution for which Kato is remembered is his lament in his magnum opus about the theological trends – *Theological Pitfalls in Africa* – an edited version of his doctoral thesis published in 1975. In this work, Kato outlined the various factors in the church that he thought would result in syncretism and universalism, and he warned the church to be aware of these. He named and delved into the theology and teachings of various scholars, pointing out where their teachings were heretical or unbiblical. These critiques provide a helpful source of information in articulating Kato's own hermeneutics. Some scholars opined that Kato was reactionary and a complainer who did not offer any theological solution for his concerns.[29] However, Kato did not only raise concerns about the misleading theological trends in the church in Africa; he gave a prescription to address the challenges. Kato tried to contribute to the efforts of the proponents of African Christian theology through another dimension, a way of looking at the relationship between Christianity and African religions from an authentically biblical perspective.[30] According to Kato, the panacea was sound evangelical theological education in Africa, to which he made an important contribution. His objective was to defend the authority of the Bible and the uniqueness and finality of Jesus Christ. "*All* who are not in *Jesus Christ* are lost, in accordance to *Scripture*," and he took seriously the debate about what he called a "theological cancer."[31]

The sustained theological debate in African theological discourse is a marker that Kato had some theological contributions to make and could not be easily dismissed. His theological points are worthy of consideration. This chapter seeks to explore these aspects of Kato's theological legacy through

---

28. See Kato, "We Are."

29. See Bediako, *Theology and Identity*; Oduyoye, *Hearing and Knowing*.

30. Kato, "A Critique of Incipient," ThD diss., 11.

31. Kato, "A Critique of Incipient," 11. Emphasis mine. My emphasis here is to note Kato's obvious accent on being Bible-centred and Christ-centred, which is short of the triumvirate evangelical mantra of Bible-centred, Christ-centred and Spirit-led. This is in no way doubting his encounter and belief in the work of the Holy Spirit, which he testified to at his rededication and transformation.

the lense of the theological debates. Also, the chapter assesses the current situation in the church, forty-five years after Kato's demise, in the light of these three theological variables.

Kato's Hermeneutics

At the core of Kato's biblical Christianity is the place of the Bible in Christian thought, and thus biblical hermeneutics – "the art and science of interpreting the Bible, to uncover the message biblical authors wanted to communicate, and apply it in the context of the reader."[32] The word "hermeneutics" is a derivative from the name of a Greek god, Hermes, who served as messenger in bringing the messages of the gods to people.[33] A key problem with the interpretation of the Bible is the presuppositions or worldview systems people have. These presuppositions may be unreliable for interpreting Scripture, especially when they are incompatible with the biblical worldview.[34]

Kato developed his hermeneutics after conversion to Christianity. He embarked on private study of both the English and Hausa Bibles and chose to pursue and develop a career in teaching and preaching the Bible. He pursued biblical and theological training, from diploma to doctoral level. He saw biblical training, including training in the original biblical languages, as essential for enhancing exegesis. While study of other religions was necessary, Kato's emphasis was inductive Bible study as an exegetical method. He was influenced by the dispensational theology he received from his training in evangelical schools in Africa and America.[35] He would be influenced most by DTS, where he did both his master's and doctoral degrees in systematic theology. Kato also taught at DTS, which is renowned for its millennialist teachings on eschatology, and where the faculty affirm and sign the articles of faith. The seminary affirms the inerrancy and infallibility of Scripture, the incarnation, and the visible and personal return of Christ to the earth.[36] The dispensational hermeneutics of DTS must have influenced Kato's own

---

32. Mburu, *African Hermeneutics*, 1; cf. Baba, *History and Principles*, 3.
33. Baba, 3–4.
34. See Baba, *History and Principles*; Chalk, *Making Disciples*; Mburu, *African Hermeneutics*.
35. Turaki, "Theological Legacy," 133.
36. Kirschner, *Futurist Eschatologies*, 32–34.

hermeneutics. DTS held the view that Scripture consisted primarily of unity in theology with some secondary diversity. This diversity is explained by the progressive dispensational scheme that the seminary espoused. How this hermeneutical stance informed Kato's distinctive approach to engaging the traditional worldview will be explored.

African intellectuals were concerned about the fact that Western missionaries did not understand the value of African thought and introduced the gospel to Africans as a civilising project, imposing Western cultural values. With the coming of political independence, there was the desire for independence of thought and of way of life. Several African theologians tended to look to ATR to inform their Christianity and to find ways within ATR of connecting with and worshipping God – ways which the missionaries had ignored or demeaned. However, Kato's views and approach was to look to the Bible to address these concerns. He elevated the place of the Bible for theologising, and he distinguished between ATR and Christianity. This section explores Kato's hermeneutics in three parts: (1) Kato's attitude to the Bible (biblicism), (2) his exegetical approach and (3) his application of Scripture to issues he confronted.

Kato's Biblicism

Kato held a unique and divergent view on the authority, interpretation and application of the Bible from many African theologians of his day. He insisted that the Bible was the sole source of Christian theology. Of particular interest to Kato was the doctrine and authority of Scripture, God's special revelation; also, God's revelation in the person and work of Jesus Christ; and finally, salvation and the future home of the Christian. Kato's perspective about the Bible was key to his hermeneutics. The assumptions people have about the Bible itself is a critical defining factor in the interpretation and application of Scripture.

Broadly, there are three basic views about the Bible: the orthodox, liberal and neo-orthodox views. The orthodox view is that the Bible is the word of God and came to humans through divine inspiration of the Holy Spirit, who caused it to be written in human language and in a particular context so that its readers and hearers can understand (2 Tim 3:16–17; 2 Pet 1:20–21). Because it is God's word, it is infallible and inerrant in all it affirms. It is the supreme guide for faith and conduct. Some nominal Christians hold a liberal view that the Bible is a record of human religious experience and a history of human interaction with God. They question the veracity of miracles and prophecies. For the liberals, the inspiration of the Bible is not different from other works by people and therefore subject to error and fallibility. They rely on scientific and rational explanations of biblical narratives. The third position is neo-orthodoxy. These may partially affirm orthodox belief and reject liberalism. However, the neo-orthodox do not affirm the inerrancy and infallibility of Scripture and rely on analogical tools for the interpretation of the Bible.

Evangelicals hold the orthodox view and maintain that human reason and tradition should all yield to the Bible, a position Byang Kato subscribed to. The rallying cry of the reformers that led to the split in the church was the doctrine of *sola scriptura*, that is, Scripture alone – the Bible has the sole authority and is the source of knowledge for Christian faith and conduct. Kato held this high view of the Bible and defended it as the supreme source of information for African Christian theologising. According to Kato, liberals accept some parts of the Bible and reject others. The evangelical accepts all sixty-six canonical books of the Bible as God-breathed, without error in the original manuscripts, faithfully transmitted and absolutely trustworthy.[37] Kato enumerates the following as the basis for the infallibility of the Bible: (1) Scripture claims to be "God-breathed" (2 Tim 3:16); (2) humans were used as vehicles to convey God's truth (2 Pet 1:19–21); (3) prophets and apostles spoke that which God gave them (Exod 7:1; Jer 1:9; Ps 2; cf. Acts 1:16; 4:25; and John 16:13, 14); (4) Scripture is quoted by Scripture as God's word (Matt 1:22; 2:15); and (5) Christ authenticates the inerrancy and permanence of the Scriptures (John 10:35; Matt 24:35; 1 Pet 1:24, 25). Kato clarifies that inerrancy refers to the original manuscripts. Evangelicals believe in God's ability and promise to preserve his word, demonstrated by the way the manuscripts have been handed down from one generation to another, and affirm with Christ that "the Scripture cannot be broken" (John 10:35).[38]

According to MacDonald, "Kato sets himself apart as a vigorous biblicist in a field rife with speculative musings, completely willing to speak in opposition to cultural norms when scriptural and communal knowledge seemingly

---

37. Kato, "Challenge of Evangelicalism."
38. Kato.

conflict."[39] Others have referred to Kato's high view of the Bible as bibliology. However, Bediako credits Kato for his biblicism and states: "His great achievement, however, consisted in a persistent affirmation of the centrality of the Bible in the theological task."[40] Many Christians and leaders in the church in Africa may also lay claim to the Bible, but their interpretation and application is dubious because of the dominant influence of traditional worldview systems and the suppositions that preachers bring to biblical interpretation.[41]

"Biblicism" or "bibliology" may not be very favourable descriptions of Kato's position as an evangelical. These terms may be derisive characterisations of believers who take the Bible literally and authoritatively without proper reflection and interpretation. For example, Bomboro, in a review of Christian Smith, states: "Smith identifies American biblicism as the principal encumbrance for missional efforts in our milieu, as well as the reason for pop culture's perception of evangelical Christianity as absurd, anti-intellectual, and indefensible."[42] Some critics label biblicists as naïve, but often these critics do not give the rightful place to the Christian Scriptures. However, Bomboro states the evangelical view of the Bible and writes:

> A truly evangelical reading of Scripture would be a gospel-oriented reading of Scripture, where the Bible's in-built hermeneutic of christocentrism would override special interest interpretations; that self-presenting biblical hermeneutic already stands codified in at least two other extra-biblical sources of authority – "the canon of Truth," and the classic, consensual interpretation of Scripture. These three things, together, preserve the Bible's authoritative witness, nature, and content from fraudulent biblicist manipulations and misappropriations.[43]

Kato's theological goal was faithfulness to the Bible, the uniqueness and lordship of Jesus Christ in salvation and redemption, and the otherness of God as revealed in Scripture. Kato wrote: "The Bible must remain the basic source of Christian theology. Evangelical Christians know of only one

---

39. MacDonald, "Critical Analysis," 6.
40. Bediako, xviii.
41. Mburu, *African Hermeneutics*, 12.
42. Bomboro, review of *Bible Made Impossible*, 83.
43. Bomboro, 84.

theology – biblical theology – though it may be expressed in the context of each cultural milieu."[44] His view of the Bible was that it was not just the book missionaries brought to Africa, but it was God's unique revelation to the world.[45]

Kato's centring on the Bible in theology is consistent with the Reformation doctrine of *sola scriptura*. Christianity is the revelation of God as recorded in the Bible. Doing Christian or biblical theology must start with an understanding and experience of coming to faith in Jesus Christ. Thus, Kato's understanding of theology went beyond an academic exercise. Because of Kato's belief in the Bible and its application, he did away with the African religious worldview.[46] He concluded that general or natural revelation has no salvific effect, that salvation is only through Jesus Christ and that the African religious worldview is to be rejected.

Kato did not only demonstrate his biblicism, but he also revealed some of his concerns and approaches to the Bible and Christian faith. He stated: "Theology in Africa is increasingly turning to African traditional religions rather than the Bible as its absolute source. . . . A continuing effort should be to relate Christian theology to the changing situations in Africa, but only as the Bible is taken as the absolute Word of God can it have an authoritative and relevant message for Africa."[47] The next two sections deal with Kato's exegetical approach to some of the theological issues for which he contended.

Kato's Exegetical Approach

Kato's encounter with Christianity was through hearing the word of God in his adopted indigenous language, Hausa, the *lingua franca* for his region. He recalled this as a critical part of his faith journey and continued to let people know what the Bible said about reality and the various issues he confronted. On a lecturing tour in Switzerland, 10–17 November 1974, a reporter asked Kato a personal question about why he was a Christian. Kato responded: "When I was without Christ, I was of course religious – religious in the sense of worshipping idols. But when Jesus Christ was presented to me, I realised

---

44. Kato, *Biblical Christianity in Africa*, 12.
45. Kato, 12.
46. Ngong, "Material," 116.
47. Kato, *Biblical Christianity in Africa*, 42–43.

that He was the Way, and so I asked Him to come into my heart, in order that when I die, I may be sure of going to be with Him in heaven."[48] Kato's personal testimony is important in trying to understand his exegetical approach.

Kato believed in the literal approach to the interpretation of Scriptures, interpreting words and sentences according to their ordinary and usual meanings.[49] In a diatribe against Mbiti's critique of the literal interpretation method of evangelical missions, such as that used by the African Inland Church (AIC), Kato argued:

> While it is true that the A.I.C. has no "Lambeth Conference" to attend, no Vatican from which to expect pronouncements, it has theological, doctrinal, historical and ministerial connections with the universal church. . . . The literal interpretation of Scriptures binds the A.I.C. with such great names as Ezra, Tertullian, Theodore of Mopsuestia, Erasmus, Tyndale, Luther, Calvin and others.[50]

Defining the literal method of interpretation, Ice states: "This means interpretation which gives to every word the same meaning it would have in normal usage, whether employed in writing, speaking or thinking."[51] This approach is also known as the literal grammatico-historical interpretation of Scripture. According to Kato, "Only by following the normal grammatico-historical interpretation would one be free from extreme subjectivism. To follow the allegorical method or to spiritualise normal concepts necessarily leads to subjectivism and preconceived notions."[52] The literal approach, he said, did not mean a literalistic interpretation but to take the word of God at face value, which is a well-established Protestant tradition.[53]

He held the dispensational view of eschatology, a doctrine with diversity of opinion among evangelical Christians. Regarding belief in the second advent of Christ, opinions are split between postmillennialism, amillennialism and

---

48. Kato, "Critique of Incipient," ThD diss., vi.
49. Kato, *Theological Pitfalls*, 78.
50. Kato, *Theological Pitfalls*, 80.
51. Ice, "Dispensational Hermeneutics," 1.
52. Kato, *Theological Pitfalls*, 78
53. Kato, *Theological Pitfalls*, 78.

premillennialism.⁵⁴ The diversity of opinion even among dispensationalists has caused some reticence about the literal interpretation of Scripture as a defining tenet of dispensationalism and wider evangelicalism. Critics' ridicule of this approach could partly be due to defining literal interpretation differently than dispensationalists do, thus leading to misguided conclusions. However, "many believe that they have been able to satisfactorily interpret the details of Scripture and harmonise their exegetical conclusions into a theology that is the product of consistent literal interpretation. On the other hand, there are many inside and outside of dispensationalism who see problems with such an approach."⁵⁵ According to Ice, dispensationalists owe a more thorough definition of the literal approach to Bernard Ramm. Ice writes:

> This is sometimes called the principle of grammatical-historical interpretation since the meaning of each word is determined by grammatical and historical considerations. The principle might also be called normal interpretation since the literal meaning of words is the normal approach to their understanding in all languages. It might also be designated plain interpretation so that no one receives the mistaken notion that the literal principle rules out figures of speech. Symbols, figures of speech and types are all interpreted plainly in this method and they are in no way contrary to literal interpretation. After all, the very existence of any meaning for a figure of speech depends on the reality of the literal meaning of the terms involved. Figures often make the meaning plainer, but it is the literal, normal, or plain meaning that they convey to the reader.⁵⁶

Ice highlights the confusion about the meaning of the term "literal interpretation" and how unconsciously the term has taken on four different meanings. Citing Vern Poythress, Ice writes:

> First is "first thought meaning," which is said to describe "the meaning for words in isolation." The second kind he calls "flat interpretation," by which he means an a priori commitment to

---

54. Kato, 81–82.
55. Ice, "Dispensational Hermeneutics," 2.
56. Ice, 1–2.

an idea of "literal if possible." Third, the one who uses grammatical-historical interpretation "reads passages as organic wholes and tries to understand what each passage expresses against the background of the original human author and the original situation." His fourth type is "plain interpretation," where one "reads everything as if it were written directly to oneself, in one's own time and culture." This is opposed to grammatical-historical interpretation.[57]

Kato's biblical understanding and interpretation was christocentric. God has ultimately revealed himself to the world through the person of Jesus Christ, in his incarnation, life and ministry on earth, his death and resurrection. The guiding principle for interpretation of Scripture is the "Christocentric Principle, i.e. all hermeneutical decisions are made subject to the centrality and authority of Jesus. His life, death and resurrection, together with his teaching and miracles, form the ultimate criteria for evaluating and re-evaluating all Scriptural interpretations and Christian hermeneutics."[58]

Kato's hermeneutical approach was also informed by his lifestyle and way of living. Manfred Kohl, in an interview, stated: "Kato was more of a practical theologian, putting into practice what he believed and was not persuaded by either the left-wing, liberal theologians, or the right-wing fundamentalist theologians. I always saw him as a man of the middle."[59] To question whether Kato was a theologian is to misunderstand his approach. In addition to his limited academic theological literary work, Kato's theology was lived and observed by those who knew and met him. Reflecting on Kato in an interview, Turaki revealed that Kato's major focus was on humans, whether these had accepted Jesus Christ as their Saviour or not.[60] If not, his first concern was to share the good news of the gospel of Jesus Christ with them. Presentation and proclamation of the gospel was an imperative and great passion for Kato. His practical social life was people-centred. He got to know people and found time to listen, know and stay connected to them. Turaki himself was influenced to

---

57. Ice, 2.
58. Domeris, "Historical Theology," 187–188.
59. Manfred Kohl, interview with author, WEA General Assembly, Jakarta, November 2019.
60. Yusufu Turaki, a mentee of Kato, interview with author at Jos Evangelical Seminary, Jos, Nigeria, May 2019.

commit to serving the Lord after listening to a sermon by Kato. Three other interviewees who were friends and relations of Kato shared similar views about Kato's friendship and his role in motivating them to engage the Bible.[61]

Kato also developed a daily devotional lifestyle for himself and his family. He nurtured a private devotional relationship and fellowship with God. This included a daily reading and study of the Bible, sometimes with study aids like *Daily Guide*, one of the Scripture Union's Bible reading materials. Scripture Union's ministry in Nigeria, and indeed in most of West Africa, contributed greatly to a revival in the church, especially in the late 1950s, through the mid-1980s. The Scripture Union's daily Bible reading plan is a five-step method: Step one starts with prayer, to enter the presence of God and ask for the help of the Holy Spirit for understanding the Scripture portion being read for the day. Step two is a careful reading of the passage, followed by step three, which is meditation, pondering some laid-out questions about the text. This step is backed by carefully exegeted notes or commentary for further insights on the passage, together with cross references to related passages in the Bible to help the reader understand how different parts of the Bible are related to one another. Step four requires the reader's response in prayer, turning the discoveries about God from the exercise into prayer and worship. The reader is encouraged to self-introspect and write down some application about what the word of God means to one's personal life and situation. And finally, step five is application of the lessons learned.[62] The Scripture Union *Daily Guide* takes the reader through the whole Bible every three years and applies the inductive Bible study method for exploring the Bible. The Scripture Union Bible reading notes are interpreted contextually and allow the Scripture to be its own interpreter.[63] This was exactly Kato's approach, and it was a helpful tool for discipleship, with contemporary relevance.

Kato kept a journal where he made entries about some of his reflections as he encountered the Scripture. Kato's encounter with Scripture was experiential, and I will now turn to his application of Scripture in his encounters with other theologians.

---

61. In an interview with researcher in Kwoi, March 2019, the following three interviewees credited Kato for engaging the Bible and coming to faith: Deborah Bature-Kato, Rev. Alimu Kato (daughter and brother, respectively) and Baba Leo, childhood friend.

62. Daramola, *Daily Guide*, i–iii.

63. Daramola, ii.

Application of Scripture to Specific Issues Kato Confronted

This section explores Kato's application of the Bible to life and to issues he confronted. The assumption is that Kato applied his biblical understanding or biblical worldview in his polemics and debate with other theologians in sub-Saharan Africa in his lifetime. The following section explores Kato's engagement with some of the doctrinal and theological issues he defended, which may help to assess and define Kato's hermeneutics and theology. His reflections were mostly reactions to what other theologians were writing and promoting in the church, mostly from the ecumenical community.[64] The themes of these polemics were primarily grounded on the relationship between ATR and Christianity, the authority of the Bible, salvation and questions of identity. Kato took a contrary direction from the other African scholars which put him in strong disagreement with them.

Kato enumerated ten challenges he perceived to be the driving force for theological heresies in the church, then and in the future, which also informed his disputations, namely:

1. Prevailing universalism in the homeland of missionaries to Africa from Europe and America
2. The search for solidarity of the human race
3. The emerging political awareness in Africa
4. Universalism as a tool for uniting people in Africa
5. Syncretism, the practice of more than one religion at the same time
6. The belief that very religious people would surely be saved because of their zeal
7. Reformation of African religions
8. That the new garb of African traditional religions made them respectable and promoted universalism
9. Biblical ignorance in the churches in Africa and inadequate emphasis on theological education on the part of the missionaries

---

64. See Kato, *Theological Pitfalls*; Palmer, "Byang Kato: Rejectionist," 16. Most notably, he responded to John Mbiti (*African Religions; Concepts of God; New Testament Eschatology*), Bolaji Idowu (*Olodumare; African Traditional Religion*) and Harry Sawyerr (*Creative Evangelism*).

10. That the gregarious nature of Africans provided fertile ground for universalism because they like to congregate with others[65]

Kato identified the challenges as theological, and thus he labeled these "theological pitfalls."[66] Analysis of the ten issues highlighted could be categorised as falling under the three areas of Kato's theological legacy in this study: African Christian identity, theological education, and Kato's overarching biblical hermeneutics against universalism and syncretism in the church in Africa. First I turn to his hermeneutics by examining some of the issues for which he confronted other theologians in debates.

African traditional religions and Christianity

Kato used his biblical understanding and worldview to confront and critique ATR and emphasise the uniqueness of the gospel of Christ. He argued that the knowledge of God in ATR was not enough to connect with the Supreme God, except through lesser gods created by humans and with no efficacious means for salvation. Any notion of using ATR or any other religious belief and means, apart from the unique revelation of God in the Bible and Jesus Christ, was rejected. Kunyhiop corroborates this view and writes: "It is too optimistic to think that the perception and understanding of God in the African worldview is exactly the same as the understanding we derive from the Bible."[67] African traditional religions claim to give worship to the Supreme God but are also characterised by ministrations to spirits and ancestors, and worship of the Supreme God included intermediaries. Mbiti, for example, writes:

> Sacrifices and offerings constitute one of the commonest acts of worship among African peoples.... "Sacrifices" refer to cases where animal life is destroyed in order to present the animal, in part or in whole, to God, supernatural beings, spirits or the living dead [i.e. ancestors]. "Offerings" refer to the remaining cases which do not involve the killing of an animal, being chiefly the presentation of foodstuffs and other items. In some cases, sacrifices and offerings are directed to one or more of the

---

65. List drawn from Kato, *Theological Pitfalls*, 11–16.
66. Kato, "Critique of Incipient," ThD diss., 278–281; Kato, *Theological Pitfalls*, 16.
67. Kunyhiop, *African Christian Theology*, 79.

following: God, spirits and living dead. Recipients in the second and third categories are regarded as intermediaries between God and men, so that God is the ultimate Recipient whether or not the worshippers are aware of that.[68]

Although Mbiti did not concede to the possibility of salvation in ATR, he argued for the salvation of all people (i.e. universalism) based on philosophical and allegorical interpretations of a transcendent God, the image of God in humans and God's kindness. He also believed the followers of ATR do offer authentic worship to the same God of Christianity.[69] Thus, the question of salvation and the unique and exclusive claim for the sacrificial death of Christ as the only means of salvation and access to God was placed in doubt.

Kato wrote: "Non-Christian religions prove man has a concept of God but they also show man's rebellion against God (Rom 1:18–23). God has redemptively become incarnate in Christ for the redemption of mankind, but only those who accept His offer of salvation can be saved (Rom 5:17)."[70] Ferdinando re-echoes Kato's stance and writes:

> Conversion itself is an act of radical transformation, and not simply the realisation of a process already underway in the convert's pre-Christian religious experience. The ubiquitous demand on all would-be Christians throughout the NT is to repent, which implies fundamental change from a former Christless, sinful way of life, including abandonment of former religious allegiances.[71]

Thus, Kato's attitude to ATR was to advocate discontinuity. He appealed to Scripture to counter Mbiti's assertion for continuity and wrote:

> In advocating that non-Christian beliefs [like ATR] be left to exist, Mbiti gives the impression that both Christianity and non-Christian (*ATR*) religions are valuable and deserve co-existing. The Apostle Paul declares, "And for anyone who is in Christ,

---

68. Mbiti, *African Religions*, 58.
69. Kato, *Theological Pitfalls*, 56; cf. Mbiti, *Concepts of God*
70. Kato, *Theological Pitfalls*, 181–182.
71. Ferdinando, "Christian Identity," 134.

there is a new creation; the old creation has gone, and now the new one is here" (2 Cor 5:17, *Jerusalem Bible*; cf. Eph 2:1–3).[72]

Kato went on to further expound what Paul meant:

> He was able to say this only because he firmly believed that even the most religious person was considered dead and without God; this included Saul of Tarsus before the experience on Damascus road. . . . It is impossible for a person with Paul's conviction to see no need of scrapping the non-Christian beliefs.[73]

Although Kato was initiated and groomed in ATR, he did not see much value in bringing his experience and understanding of ATR into Christianity and advocated for a separation of the two faiths.

Kato's view has a potent salience to African Christianity even more today. The debates about self-understanding and a distinctly African Christian interpretation of Scripture continue to engage the minds of scholars in Africa. Underscoring the problem of hermeneutics in the African church, Mburu, for example, poses the following questions:

> Why is it that after more than one hundred years of exposure to Christianity, traditional practices such as witchcraft, ancestor worship and polygamy are still found in Africa? Why is it not uncommon to hear of pastors consulting witchdoctors to acquire more "power" for the pulpit and of Christians using witchcraft to grow their businesses? Why, if the statistics on corruption and unethical practices on our continent are to be believed, has there been so very little transformation of society?[74]

In response to these rhetorical questions, Mburu is quick to proffer a response, writing: "Many Christians, including those holding leadership positions in the church, live dichotomized lives. In other words, we as African Christians seem unable to understand how our faith should affect our everyday lives. It is as if we keep faith and life in two separate compartments."[75] The result of this dualism is a weak church with no moral authority or positive influence

---

72. Kato, *Theological Pitfalls*, 70.
73. Kato, 70.
74. Mburu, *African Hermeneutics*, 3.
75. Mburu, 3; see also Chalk, *Making Disciples*.

in society. Mburu argues that part of the problem is in the failure to interpret the Bible accurately and allow it to guide the everyday life of the Christian.[76]

In exploring the challenges of profession and practice for African Christians, Chalk states: "If the churches in Africa are not preaching and teaching the biblical worldview, accepting it as their own, and living accordingly, their members will accept the new religion of Christianity without discarding the old conflicting beliefs. That, in missiological terms, is called syncretism."[77] He goes further to state: "Unless the African Christian's beliefs are structured by a biblical worldview instead of the traditional African worldview, their behaviour will be structured more by traditional beliefs and Africa's culture will not reflect predominantly Christian values."[78] No wonder then that it is popularly said of many majority-Christian nations in Africa, such as Kenya, that it is "eighty percent Christian, eighty percent corrupt," and the rhetorical question is then asked: "Where are the corrupt people coming from?" It would appear therefore that Kato's voice for a hermeneutics which emphasises discontinuity needs to be re-echoed even more today than in his time. Domeris adds his voice and states: "Every reading of Scripture includes hermeneutical principles and rules on one hand, and the artistic or interpretive reading of the text on the other, but takes the help of the Holy Spirit as guide to the true meaning and application of the Scripture."[79]

Kato made clear that he was not against culture. Christianity was birthed in a particular culture and should be expressed in every other culture, but without compromising the biblical intent and need for cultural transformation. Kato wrote:

> I am not denying the fact that natives of a particular culture potentially have more to contribute in their culture than an alien. But this is not necessarily so in all cases. I have benefitted very much from the studies of my culture carefully done by an American. Both natives of a culture and aliens to that culture who are committed to the evangelical gospel should all contribute to the worthy effort of getting the gospel truly rooted

---

76. Mburu, *African Hermeneutics*, 211.
77. Chalk, *Making Disciples*, 5.
78. Chalk, 11.
79. Domeris, "Historical Theology," 178.

in every culture before the Lord of the church comes back to claim His own.[80]

Kato rejected the veneration of ATR and argued that this was not due to lack of patriotism: "It is only to safeguard the unique gospel of Christ, which alone provides the way of salvation. African culture as such is not all bad. But like any other culture it is tainted with sin. It needs to be redeemed."[81] Africa is also not one culture, and regarding the attempt to Africanize Christianity,[82] Kato enumerated the following questions as guidelines for practicing Christianity in the African context, without compromising the faith:

> (1) What is your motive in trying to "contextualize" or expressing Christianity in the context of Africa? Is it due to a reactionary attitude to the white missionaries or you want to do it basically in order to help Africans understand the gospel better? Col 3:7. (2) Is it necessary to make that practice African? 1 Cor 9:20. (3) Is it edifying, making people better Christians and helping in evangelism and church building? 1 Cor 10:23. (4) Does it contradict the ethical teaching of the Scriptures? 1 Thess 5:22. (5) If you are an evangelical Christian, then remember the Lausanne Covenant on the point of culture.[83]

Kato held the view that "Christianity cannot cohabit with any foreign religion" and thought some African theologians were seeking recognition of the "so-called 'common ground' between Christianity and African Traditional religions."[84] This, Kato said, was "where the battle [was] raging," and it was the basis for his confrontations.[85]

---

80. Kato, "Contextualisation of the Gospel: Theological Perspective", 2.
81. Kato, *Theological Pitfalls*, 177.
82. By "Africanize Christianity," Kato meant the expression of biblical Christianity in familiar African forms in the African context. Africans needed to feel at home with Christianity. Kato, Theological Pitfalls, 57; cf. Lausanne Covenant 1974).
83. Kato, "Christianity and Culture", 3.
84. Kato, "Critique of Incipient," ThD diss., 13.
85. Kato, 13.

Universalism and syncretism in the church

Kato battled with Mbiti, a leading proponent of embracing ATR and well-respected African Christian theologian, about eschatology. According to Kato, the sure future hope of Christians was being presented as utopian by the philosophy and eschatological teachings and perspectives of Mbiti.[86] Mbiti's perspective was that Africans did not think of a distant future, and he therefore made the biblical realities about eschatology only symbolic and allegorical.[87] Basically, Mbiti's argument was that because, as he judged it, the Akamba people in Kenya lacked a concept of future time, they, and therefore Africans in general, could not grasp future eschatological concepts such as the resurrection and the judgement. Mbiti's conclusion then was that such NT eschatological concepts needed to be jettisoned to fit the Akamba concept of time. It seemed Mbiti's hermeneutics and application of Scripture started from the African worldview, and sought to adjust biblical concepts to fit it.

However, Kato's hermeneutics were directly opposite – the application of Scripture starts from the Bible, and the African worldview must be adjusted to fit the Bible.[88] He thought that the approach adopted by Mbiti, which prioritised African traditional religious concepts, was tantamount to syncretism and underlined a universalistic notion of salvation. Kato affirmed his dispensational stance and belief in the imminent personal and visible return (the second coming) of Jesus Christ at any time (Titus 2:13; Matt 16:27; 24:30; 25:31). Kato concluded that Mbiti's teachings on the eschatological doctrines, such as the sacraments, regeneration, resurrection and mediatorial judgement were unbiblical, and were views that lead to universalism and to pitfalls that Bible believing Christians would do well to avoid.[89]

Kato's worries about the universalistic tendencies in the church in Africa were not unfounded. Mbiti's department of religion at the Makerere University in Kampala, Uganda – East Africa's premier university of the time – had such an important influence in the region. The tendencies promoted there influenced the thought leaders and decision makers of emerging independent African nations. Thus its theological influence would impact the church

---

86. Kato, *Theological Pitfalls*, 69–89.
87. Kato, 77–85; cf. Mbiti, *African Religions*, 15–27.
88. Kato, *Theological Pitfalls*, 77; cf. Turaki, *Engaging Religions*.
89. Kato, *Theological Pitfalls*, 85.

negatively, at least from Kato's perspective. Similarly, across the continent in West Africa there was the influential Ibadan University in Nigeria, and Fourah Bay College in Sierra Leone, where similar religious philosophies were advanced. Scholars from these universities were among the first generation of African theologians and religious philosophers, and those following them looked up to them for mentorship. Their works were growing in influence in Africa and across the world. Disturbed by these developments, Kato wrote:

> Even some of the most outstanding theologians in Africa have not avoided universalistic tendencies. Professor John Mbiti holds that all men will be saved in the final analysis. He affirms, "There is not a single soul, however debased or even unrepentant, which can successfully 'flee' from the Spirit of God (Psalm 139:1–18). God's patient waiting for the soul's repentance must in the end be surely more potent than the soul's reluctance to repent and turn to him (2 Peter 3:9). The harmony of the heavenly worship would be impaired if, out of the one hundred in the sheepfold, there is one soul which continues to languish in Sheol or the 'lake of fire.'"[90]

The department of religion at Ibadan, under Professor Bolaji Idowu, championed what Kato called "A Theology of Peaceful Co-existence," and that message was carried in an influential journal of theology called *Orita* – which is a Yoruba word meaning "where the ways meet" – and which indicated an intersection or meeting of the three dominant faiths ("ways") on the continent of Africa (i.e. African traditional religion(s), Christianity and Islam). According to Kato: "It is in the contents of this journal the basic philosophy of syncretistic and universalistic approach to the study of religions is best displayed."[91] He noted further that Idowu's theology was based on the philosophy of universalism.[92] Idowu was one of the earliest proponents of African theology, calling African Christian theologians to produce theology that satisfied the soul and spiritual needs of Africans. Professor Bolaji Idowu objected to localising theology, according to Kato. He would also eschew

---

90. Kato, *Biblical Christianity*, 30–31.
91. Kato, *Theological Pitfalls*, 94.
92. Kato, 96.

syncretism.⁹³ However, Kato was worried about Idowu's high view of traditional African religions. Idowu objected to calling ATRs "idolatry," since the ATR objects of worship in essence were ministers of God.⁹⁴ Kato queried: "But if pagan gods are not idols, then what are they? Idowu claims with the adherents that these gods are ministers of the Almighty God. To recognise the reality of these man-made gods is to reject the scriptural view of these 'dumb idols' (Isa 2:8; 40:18–20; 41:7; 1 Thess 1:9; 1 Cor 8:4–6)."⁹⁵ Kato further argued:

> While it is true that the pagan is conscious of the existence of a Supreme Being through general revelation, his vision of the Supreme Being is distorted because of original sin. The image of God in man, though not obliterated, is disfigured to the point that he is considered dead in "trespasses and sins" (Ephesians 2:1), until he receives new life in Christ. His worship of creatures rather than the Creator can be described adequately only as idolatry. What Africa needs is the unadulterated Gospel of Jesus Christ who declares authoritatively and finally, "I am the Way, the Truth, and the Life. No man cometh unto the Father but by me" (John 14:6).⁹⁶

At the core of Idowu's theologising was the belief in the evolution of religions. He believed all religions lead to God and that God is revealed in each culture and religion, in fact, to each person. Idowu argued in favour of the use of idols, as in the Yoruba religion, with its pantheons of gods, in the belief that this practice is inevitable until religion evolves to the point where images are no longer required.⁹⁷

Galadima posits that African culture with its traditional religions must be part of the source of information for African theology. "There are as many sources of African Theology as there are theologians: (1) The Bible and Christian Heritage, (2) African Anthropology, (3) African Traditional

---

93. Kato, *Biblical Christianity*, 30.
94. Kato, 30; see also Idowu, *Olodumare*.
95. Kato, *Biblical Christianity*, 30
96. Kato, *Biblical Christianity*, 30.
97. See Galadima, "Evaluation," for a discussion of Idowu's work. See also Idowu, *Olodumare*, and Idowu, *African Traditional Religion*. Idowu also wrote *Towards an Indigenous Church* and scores of booklets, as well as contributing chapters to books.

Religion, (4) African Independent Churches, and (5) African Realities."[98] On the other hand, Kato's concern was that African theology should be done in ways that protected Christianity from syncretism.[99] Kato raised concerns to let the church know that these teachings were contrary to the Christian core belief that God has definitively been revealed in the person of Jesus Christ, the Son of God.[100]

Kato was critical about the diverse sources of theology. His perspective was that the various sources of theology had the tendency to promote the syncretistic and universalistic approach to the study of religions. In particular, he believed that the other African theologians were looking to ATR sources for doing theology and were using the Bible to support their deductions and systematise ATR itself and wed it with Christianity.[101] The underlying assumption of his opponents was that all religions have a monotheistic concept and the same God in every religion – a God that can be served and approached through pantheons of smaller gods. The goal of Idowu's teaching, for example, as promoted by the *Orita* journal, was also seen as the peaceful co-existence of religions, rather than the "proselytising" approach. The implication was that evangelism, as a tenet of the Christian religion, may have to be shelved.[102] Kato characteristically highlighted the unbiblical and humanistic nature of these theological endeavours. Kato wrote: "With all due respect to non-Christian noble ideas of a Supreme Being, the thesis that they are monotheists in the biblical sense cannot be sustained. The only monotheism the Christian can recognise in the New Testament era is the kind described by the Apostle Paul (1 Cor 8:4–6)."[103]

In an interview, Yusufu Turaki opined that many African scholars placed Christianity on the same level, without priority, with ATR and other religions.[104] This approach tends to root religion in the culture, philosophy and worldview of the people. Thus, Christianity is also rooted in the same social factors of human culture, philosophy and worldview. However, Turaki

---

98. Galadima, "Evaluation," 109; cf. Niringiye, "Prolegomena," 44–45.
99. See Galadima, "Evaluation," 108–109; cf. Shorter, *African Christian Theology*, 14–15.
100. Kato, *Theological Pitfalls*, 91–93:104; cf Galadima, "Evaluation."
101. Kato, *Theological Pitfalls*, 54–55.
102. Kato, 92–93.
103. Kato, 92.
104. Yusufu Turaki, interview with author, in Jos, Nigeria, 27 May 2019.

acknowledged that Kato differed in his understanding of religion. He believed that the values that shaped the formation of religion were rooted in human culture, philosophy or worldview, but Christianity was not produced by these sociological considerations. Kato wrote:

> If it is the same God in all religions, it is only a matter of common logic that all religions should seek a peaceful coexistence rather than a "proselytising" approach. If there should be any desire for influence, it should be sought in the idea of "presence" rather than "proclamation." In the final analysis, evangelism in the Christian Church will have to be shelved away. Admittedly, no one has suggested this, but it is a necessary corollary of a peaceful coexistence approach.[105]

The source of Christianity is the revelation of God as recorded in the Bible. Kato saw this as a foundation for any biblical hermeneutics. He asserted:

> Persecution may not be the area where the battle will be fiercest. The devil has many avenues and he knows where best to succeed. Christo-paganism appears to be the area of attack within the next generation. The battle has started. The unique claims of Christ are regarded as eccentricities. The relativity philosophy is seeking to make the Scriptures only one of many revelations rather than a special revelation. Christianity is not repudiated but is given the largest room in the camp of religions.[106]

Those who argued for a more exalted place for ATRs in the church did so in the name of African cultural revolution and thought that to do otherwise was un-African. Kato argued that this was a misconception of the word "culture." Culture, he said, was people's way of life and covered every aspect of a society's life and their relationship with nature.[107] He argued that "since religion is the heart of culture, a change in religion necessitates a readjustment in culture. Culture is examined considering Scripture and states what

---

105. Kato, *Theological Pitfalls*, 92.
106. Kato, "Critique of Incipient," ThD diss., 262.
107. Kato, *African Cultural Revolution*, 7.

aspects are acceptable or not."[108] How Kato dealt with the two religions at a personal level is instructive.

Conception of sin and salvation

A fundamental issue at the core of Kato's contestation was the essential question of sin, the human need for salvation and the exclusive means of salvation by faith in Jesus Christ: "To be saved in the Judeo-Christian sense presupposes the lost condition from which salvation or deliverance is needed. What one is saved from determines the nature of salvation."[109] So, people's conception of sin is critical for their view of salvation. For some people, sin is conceived from a humanistic or religious perspective, and this may be limited to social ills, thus giving rise to the wrong view of salvation.[110] If an anti-social act is all there is to sin, salvation can be attained by satisfying social demands.

If sin is only societal, the so-called social gospel must be the right solution. Therefore, the wrong conception of sin will result in the wrong remedy for sin and the wrong view of salvation. Describing the religion of his ethnic Jaba people as typical of ATR religions, Kato wrote:

> To be saved in Jaba language is to be accepted. To be accepted is first of all in the community of the living, and then in the city of the dead. The way for the offender to be accepted by his fellow citizens is to pay the fine or take the punishment prescribed for him. It may come in the form of exclusion from the tribal gathering or payment of so many goats and so much wine. Blood sacrifice is used in different occasions. It is usually for deliverance from the power of the evil spirits. . . . For acceptance among the dead ancestors, the relatives of the deceased provide a feast three months after the person has died. Every year some food is placed on his tomb to assure the dead that he is remembered in this life.[111]

Ngong applauds Kato in his opposition to the African theology espoused by his opponents, and insists that a stress on material well-being does not

---

108. Kato, 9–10.
109. Kato, *Theological Pitfalls*, 41.
110. Kato, "Critique of Incipient," ThD diss., 42.
111. Kato, *Theological Pitfalls*, 42–43.

represent a Christian understanding of salvation.[112] Ngong further states that in the salvific discourse of African Christianity there is more emphasis on material well-being than on God, a fulfilment of the vision of traditional African religious culture.[113]

However, Ngong disagrees with Kato's biblical understanding of salvation that deals primarily with eternal salvation, issues of heaven and hell, and that disregards material realities, thereby ignoring the very biblical teaching Kato placed so much emphasis on.[114] According to Ngong, Kato went to an extreme in his defence of what he saw as the spiritual character of the biblical view of salvation. He draws a distinct line between the spiritual and the secular, thus undermining the importance of the material realm.[115] To limit salvation to the hereafter and undermine the importance of the present life was a misconception.[116] This, Ngong says, "may actually serve to confirm the fears of those African theologians who claim that stressing the importance of the hereafter in salvific discourse inevitably leads to the undermining of the here and now."[117] By Kato's own admission, social action and humanitarian considerations were deemed to be secondary to the mission of the church. He saw the mission schools, hospitals and clinics that had been provided over the years by evangelicals as making a contribution to humanity.[118] According to Kato, "Christ puts the soul's salvation in reference to future life above earthly existence (Mark 8:36; Luke 12:5). The serving of tables must be given second place."[119] This could well be one of Kato's own theological pitfalls.

In any case, the nature and practice of holistic mission is still a work in progress in the contemporary church. The church needs to fly on both wings for effective soaring with the gospel. It is important to observe that Kato's rise to evangelical leadership predated the First International Congress on World Evangelization in 1974, an important milestone and turning point in

---

112. Ngong, "Material," 108–109.
113. Ngong, 107.
114. Ngong, 129.
115. Ngong, 109.
116. Ngong, 122.
117. Ngong, 122.
118. Kato, "Critique of Incipient," ThD diss., 272.
119. Kato, 273.

evangelical thought, not only in Africa but also the global church.[120] Predating Lausanne, evangelicals were known for dualism, the sharp distinction made between the sacred and secular, the physical and the spiritual, and that the church's priority and focus was to be on what was spiritual. This started to change somewhat after Lausanne, when the Lausanne Covenant affirmed the integral nature of the gospel and mission of the church as taught by Scripture. The earlier position of dualism was deemed to have come from the cultural influences of Enlightenment philosophy, a non-biblical worldview that was prevalent in the Western world. However, Van der Walt observes that the Lausanne statement only succeeded in adopting the "and-and" viewpoint instead of the earlier "either-or" viewpoint. Van der Walt opines that the dualistic thinking was still inherent in the way evangelicals viewed reality, and dualism itself was not rejected: "As long as these worldview glasses are not replaced by a truly holistic, integral, biblical worldview, their (evangelical) theology will not change."[121]

However, it is to Kato's credit that his social interactions with people, the high and low, were commendable. His leadership in the church and his relief and material interventions during the time of the civil war speak for him in terms of integral mission. What is clear is that Kato showed concern for social action, but his primary concern was to present Christ to everyone as the way to transform people and the means for revolutionising society. In one of his lectures and discussions with students, Kato was asked to respond to the question of whether it was right for Christians to drink beer or wine. He responded, "Every Christian is a priest and as such must refrain from drinking. No drunkard will enter the kingdom of God. The Holy Spirit is the one who leads us to abstain. Proverbs 20:1 says: 'Wine is a mocker.' We are God's temple and so must be holy."[122] Sometimes, Kato's hermeneutics tended towards literalism and the fringes of pietism or fundamentalism, as in this case. While many evangelicals in Africa tend to be teetotallers, a categorical view that condemns the drinking of beer or wine is not necessarily as definitively a biblical position as Kato was here making it to be.

---

120. Van der Walt, "Evangelical Voice," 924; Foday-Khabenje, "AEA Joins."
121. Van der Walt, "Evangelical Voice," 946.
122. Kato, "Youth," 5.

Issues of social concern and social action were another area where some scholars opine that Kato's reading of the Bible was problematic. Kato gives credence to the misapprehensions of his critics about his attitude to social action and biblical teaching on the subject when he posits:

> Social concerns have their place in the Christian mandate. But the serving of tables must be given second place (Acts 6:2, 4). Affluence of the Western World is the best demonstration that for Christians to devote their time to social concerns at the expense of seeking to win souls for eternity amounts to fattening a calf for slaughter.[123]

Many would argue that Christians do not necessarily have to devote time to social concerns at the expense of winning souls or vice versa, but rather that the mission of the church is integral or holistic. The conception of the mission of the church is not either/or but both/and. This can equally be supported by biblical references (e.g. Luke 4:18; 10:25–37; Matt 25:31–46; Mark 12:29–31; Mic 6:8).

Ancestor veneration and worship

Along with ancestor veneration, the destiny of those who died without the gospel, or even before the missionaries came, also became a bone of contention in the theological discourse. The positions of Kato's theological proponents were varied. Some believed their ancestors were in heaven because they were good people and religious.

Kato cited various proponents of ancestor salvation and the reasons they advanced for the salvation of those who died without Christ.[124] Harry Sawyerr, for example, believed that the prayers of African Christians might lead to the salvation of non-believing dead relatives, through the providence of God.[125] He also counted on the omnipotence of God for salvation for all. In an interview with Aloysius Lugira, Kato said Lugira believed the religiosity and goodness of the ancestors on their own was enough reason to avoid hell.[126] J. N. D. Anderson advanced that God's grace and mercy extended to those who

---

123. Kato, "Critique of Incipient," ThD diss., 273.
124. Kato, *Theological Pitfalls*, 179–180.
125. See Sawyerr, *Creative Evangelism*; Sawyerr, *God*; Sawyerr, *Practice of Presence*.
126. Kato, *Theological Pitfalls*, 179.

had never heard the gospel.[127] John Mbiti called for *Sanctorum Communio* in the sense of direct communication between the living and the departed saints.[128] This involved the practice of offering sacrifices to dead relatives or ancestors, a form of ancestor veneration or worship. However, Mbiti argued that these practices did not constitute worship but rather these acts symbolised "fellowship, a recognition that the departed are still members of their human families, and tokens of respect and remembrance for the living-dead."[129] Building on Mbiti's theology of ancestor veneration, Mosothoane states: "With the fellowship retained and nourished, the ancestors, according to African beliefs, both continue their protective, providential and intermediary concern for the living and welcome the ministrations of the latter."[130] Mosothoane continues:

> For Africans, as we have seen, this spanning of the chasm of death is expressed in the belief in ancestors. And in the Lord's Supper there is communion not only between believer and the Risen Lord, not only between believer and believer, but also an "in Christ" communion between living and departed members of the Christian fellowship. Instead of discouraging the idea of ancestors, it seems to us, the church should urge African Christians to communicate with their beloved ones who have departed from this life; and to do this within the context of the Christian Eucharist in particular.[131]

Elaborating further on the cultic act of the ancestor veneration practice, Mosothoane states:

> When a family makes sacrifice and offerings in honour of, and as a symbol of, their fellowship with their departed ones, members of the congregation ought to be invited to the feast and, where possible, the clergyman be invited to bless the animal etc. to be

---

127. Anderson, *Christianity*, 101–102, cited in Kato, "Critique of Incipient," ThD diss., 275.
128. Mbiti, *New Testament Eschatology*, 148–149.
129. Mbiti, 93.
130. Mosothoane, "Communio Sanctorum," 86; cf. Mbiti, *African Religions*, 59.
131. Mosothoane, "Communio Sanctorum," 93.

offered. The entire cult could be "baptized" into the service of the Gospel, and remains of the dread of ancestors be removed.[132]

Mosothoane backs his argument with the following Scripture references: Romans 14:7f; 8:31–39; Hebrews 12:1; and 1 Thessalonians 5:10. The argument is that the implications of the death of Jesus Christ are enough to connect believers in Christ, dead or alive – the communion of saints – and that believers continue to be in fellowship and communication with the dead. With the ancestors who were not in Christ, Mosothoane states:

> No ready-made solution is found in the New Testament, though a few texts may point the direction. 1 Pet 3:18ff seems to interpret the death and burial of Christ as making faith and salvation available to the unbelieving and disobedient dead, specifically those of Gen 6–8. We cannot but ask, however, whether the application of this text does not go beyond the Genesis passage, and we strongly suggest that it does.[133]

"Necromancy" is a term which means conversing or consulting with the dead. In ATR beliefs, the dead people are still very much a part of this life. Some argue that the Catholic churches pray through deceased "saints." "But this is wrong for Christians to do."[134] Kato observed:

> I know that in 1 Samuel 28:7–25 we have the account of Saul consulting a witch doctor of Endor. It is a difficult passage, but let us realize that Saul was a backslider, a miserable and confused person, and when Saul inquired of the Lord, the Lord did not answer him (1 Samuel 28:6). Since the Lord did not answer Saul, he turned to satanic sources. The end result was God's judgment by death for Saul and his sons, and defeat for Israel.

Kato rejected salvation for ancestors on the grounds advanced by these theologians. He was emphatic in his conclusions about those who died before the advent of the gospel or those who died without hearing the gospel and wrote: "The biblical answer to the question concerning those who died

---

132. Mosothoane, 94.
133. Mosothoane, 94.
134. Kato, *Spirits*, 25; cf. Isa 8:19.

before hearing the gospel is to be that they go to hell. No one deserves to be saved in any case."[135] Kato also stated: "There is no scriptural basis either for second chance repentance or for direct communication with the deceased."[136] He continued:

> The more scriptural basis would rather be that if God had been dealing with any person apart from the gospel witness, He would provide the way for that would-be Christian to hear the gospel and accept it to be born again. The case of Cornelius is the precedent (Acts 10:35). . . . The members of the Adamic race are all stillborn (Rom 5:12). Not one of them deserves to live. But the undeserving favour of God has made salvation possible through the death and resurrection of Jesus Christ. . . . Christ is universally available to all everywhere at any time. This is how far biblical universalism goes. But its effectiveness applies only to those who receive the offer.[137]

Kato argued that people are not saved on a humane basis alone, outside what the Scripture reveals:

> For the rest of the heathen who died before the advent of Christian evangelism, it is humanely wished that they found their place in eternal bliss. But the word of God gives no warrant for such view. Humanity does not live in neutrality. Since the original fall, the total race of Adam has been condemned to death (Rom 3:23; 6:23). Salvation in the biblical sense is the passing out of this death dungeon (John 5:24) into the dimension of life.[138]

He concluded that there was no clear optimism for those who died without Christ and that what is certain is hell for them. Nevertheless, some of Kato's hearers may view his response on this subject as unsatisfactory. Kato's objection to his opponents may be based more on what their ATR views espoused, rather than what the Bible says.

---

135. Kato, *Critique of Evangelicalism*, 276–277.
136. Kato, *Theological Pitfalls*, 180.
137. Kato, *Theological Pitfalls*, 180–181.
138. Kato, *Theological Pitfalls*, 180.

Suggestions about animal sacrifice, and indeed to incorporate sacrifices into Christian worship, was another characteristic of some ATR African theology. Kato demystified the practice and wrote: "Blood sacrifice is used at different occasions. It is usually for deliverance from the power of the evil spirits."[139] However, there is no meritorious benefit for use of the blood of an animal, and he concluded that this should only make Christians "appreciate the assurance of rest and finality found in the Lamb of God slain before the foundation of the world (Matt 11:28; Heb 9:26; John 1:29)."[140]

Liberal ecumenism

Another issue that Kato engaged in his hermeneutics was liberal ecumenism in the church in Africa. According to Kato, there were five leading issues in ecumenical theology the church needed to contend with:[141] (1) the Bible becoming relative rather than normative, with experiences and other sources becoming just as important as the Bible; (2) salvation being interpreted in terms of political, economic and social freedom; (3) the kingdom of God meaning a search for common humanity, irrespective of religion;[142] (4) dialogue rather than declaration as the approach to evangelism (to declare the gospel to people of other religions was seen as arrogance; however, many evangelicals see dialogue as an opportunity for proclamation of the gospel); (5) a moratorium on missions as part of the liberation process (there was a call for the cessation of mission activities flowing from the West to the Global South). Regarding these theological aspirations, Kato concluded: "Self-assertion is human, and anthropocentric theology, such as is promoted in ecumenism, fits this innate desire. One may expect the influence of ecumenical theology therefore to spread in Africa, since it makes human experience the basic source of theologising."[143] Kato remarkably admonished: "Evangelicals, for their part, must learn to move beyond the divinely revealed source to the

---

139. Kato, 43.
140. Kato, 43.
141. Kato, *Biblical Christianity*," 44–46.
142. Kato stated, "The old liberal concept of anonymous Christianity is now being revived in the African ecumenical movement. It is held that even non-Christians are already Christians without realizing it. The task of Christian missions is simply to make non- Christians aware of their salvation" (*Biblical Christianity*, 44).
143. Kato, *Biblical Christianity*, 45.

human dimension where the action is. Holding the Bible as their basic source for Christian theology, they must discover how best to relate to the human situation in all areas, including the socio-politico-economic arena."[144]

Contrary to the criticism of opponents that Kato's biblicism had an exclusive focus on the soul and spirit, it is apparent that Kato's emphasis was always on the place and authority of the Bible in every aspect of Christian endeavour or theology. With the post-independence leaning of many Africans towards social communalism, and a strong call for unity in Scripture (John 17:21), one wonders where Kato stood on this matter? Kato devoted three chapters of *Theological Pitfalls in Africa* to this subject. To his credit, he affirmed the need and importance of ecumenism in the non-technical sense that may include the whole inhabited world (Luke 2:1; 4:5; 21:26; Rom 10:18). He traced the technical sense of the word "ecumenical" to the ancient church councils, which were also known as ecumenical councils.[145] However, the objective of the ecumenical councils was for doctrinal purity, which helped to establish classical Christian doctrines.[146] Nonetheless, Kato was concerned that modern ecumenical councils, such as the World Council of Churches (WCC), were a drive for Christian unity at any cost and played down the issue of doctrine. The assumption was that doctrine divides but service unites. Therefore, the establishment of AACC, like the WCC, with "minimal doctrinal basis for membership," was a worrying development; it provided room for easy accommodation of the developing theologies on the continent.[147] AACC's link with WCC became the channel for training African Christians in liberal schools abroad – schools that rejected the doctrine of the infallibility of the Bible, developing what Kato called liberal ecumenism, fuelled by universalism and syncretism.[148]

Kato was opposed to liberal ecumenism but affirmed the spiritual and visible unity of the church, in accordance with the prayer of Jesus Christ (John 17:21). However, the unity should be for those committed to Christ and his word. The objective should not be abolishing the different denominations but

---

144. Kato, 45–46.
145. Kato, *Theological Pitfalls*, 129.
146. Kato, 129.
147. Kato, 138–139.
148. Kato, 139.

for unity in diversity. He encouraged membership in the National Evangelical Fellowships, which constituted the Association of Evangelicals in Africa: "Such fellowship seeks to unite Christians in each country in fellowship and service, and then also unites all Bible-believing Christians in Africa. This kind of unity among those who truly know the Lord and are seeking to serve Him is a biblical unity."[149] He was concerned by the prevailing universalism in the missionaries' homeland churches, the push by the United Nations to unite people of all faiths, ethnicities and political ideologies, and the same goals being pursued by the Organisation of African Unity – the pursuit of anything for universal unity.[150] Therefore, universalistic tendencies were being encouraged in the church, similar to the modern day focus on pluralism and relativism.[151]

It is important to note that Kato's confrontations with other theologians were regarding ATRs co-existing with Christianity in Africa. Kato referred to this as syncretism or "Christo-paganism": "when church people made Scripture to be only one of the many revelations, rather than the special revelation, and gave Christianity the largest room in the one house of religions."[152] He said: "one common error which may also be cited is the lumping together fundamental biblical principles with the western culture, and repudiating both."[153] This was Kato's response to his opponents regarding the oft repeated derogatory charge that Kato was acting as a "Western stooge," as his critique of ATR coincided with similar critiques from some Western missionaries. He also refuted that Christianity was a preserve of the West and underscored the contribution of Africans to early Christianity, that Christianity had a home in Africa even before Europe.[154]

Continuity and discontinuity controversy

In the late 1950s to 1980s, considered to be the post-missionary era, African theologians wrestled with a localised theological construct – African theology. This was in two parts: liberation theology motivated by the South African

---

149. Kato, *Theological Pitfalls*, 170.
150. Kato, 13.
151. Kato, "Critique of Incipient," ThD diss., 3.
152. Kato, 262.
153. Kato, *Theological Pitfalls*, 175.
154. Kato, 175–176.

socio-political situation and apartheid, and the theology of integration. The latter sought to explore the indigenous cultures of African peoples, with particular focus on pre-Christian and pre-Islamic religious traditions. According to Bediako: "the broad aim has been to achieve some integration between the African pre-Christian religious experience and African Christian commitment, in ways that would ensure the integrity of African Christian identity and selfhood."[155] However, the underlying assumptions that Bediako posits are "the foreignness of Christianity and minimalist view of the newness of the Christian faith in relation to ATR, if the Christian gospel brought little that was essentially new to Africa, in religious terms."[156] In other words, the ATR beliefs had some knowledge about God to be able to build on with the coming of Christianity, and therefore there was no need to discard those beliefs. In fact, according to this line of thought, the traditional faith was continuous with the newfound faith in Christianity.

Notwithstanding Kato's deep involvement with idol worship as a youth, he saw no such positive value in continuing with ATR beliefs and practices. On the other hand, there was no suggestion or evidence that Kato sought any special deliverance from the influence of the traditional religion, as is the tendency in some of the newer evangelical and Pentecostal churches in Africa. He demonstrated assurance of liberation from his father's religion and radical commitment to his new faith in Christianity. His critics refer to this as "radical discontinuity" and charge him with impertinence and lack of respect for African culture. Bediako writes: "Basing himself on a radical biblicism, Kato stressed the distinctiveness of the experience of the Christian gospel to such an extent that he rejected the positive evaluation of any pre-Christian religious tradition as a distraction from the necessary emphasis on bible truth."[157] That Kato was enculturated in ATR beliefs cannot be contested. Ironically, his experience of ATR was perhaps more in depth than any of his opponents who advocated for the continuation of ATR.

That Kato's religious worldview changed to biblicism, as has been highlighted, is an important consideration for Christian reflection in the African church. Like his initiation into the fetish priesthood, Kato's inception into the

---

155. Bediako, "Understanding African Theology," 14.
156. Bediako, 16; cf. Mokhoathi, "From Contextual Theology."
157. Bediako, "Understanding African Theology," 16.

church was a critical step for the development of his Christian understanding and biblical worldview. Unlike many of the disputants, Kato articulated a clear testimony of his conversion to Christianity. Kato alluded to drawing inspiration from Scripture for his radical worldview change and wrote:

> It is often forgotten that the twentieth century convert is not the first Christian to burn up the bridges linking him with his past life of idol worship. The first converts in Ephesus went to the point of literally burning their books of magic arts for the sake of Christ, thus breaking with their culture (Acts 19:23–41).[158]

He wrote: "where lies the unique claim of Christ which is supposed to supersede even kin relationships (Matt 11:37–38). Should national pride or cultural heritage come before Christ?"[159] He insisted that culture has to be baptised by Christianity and not the other way around.

On the question of continuity of pre-Christian faith with Christianity, Kato asserts:

> The knowledge of God through nature and conscience is evidenced by the fact that man has shown interest in religion per se. But his worship has only proved that man has turned to the worship of creation rather than the Creator. While it may be rightly claimed that the new revelation in Christ has not been discontinuous in the sense of God's general revelation, it must be added unequivocally that it is also discontinuous.[160]

To a certain extent, Kato affirmed continuity because the "God image" in humans has not been completely obliterated by sin. The saved sinner's life is continuous to some aspects of life that abide, because of the image of God in humans. The witness of our relationship with God and yearning for God (the God-shaped vacuum) could be a basis for continuity when God finds us in Christ. Every person or human community or culture may and ought to manifest godlikeness; however, all like sheep have gone astray and grope in darkness. Kato stated:

---

158. Kato, *Theological Pitfalls*, 174.
159. Kato, "Critique of Incipient," ThD diss., 265–266.
160. Kato, *Theological Pitfalls*, 155.

To say that Africans, or anyone else, still have the vestiges of *Imago Dei*, by virtue of which they are still aware of the existence of the Supreme Being, is one thing. But to systematise the concepts and fill them up with the quality of worship of God "in truth and in spirit" is foreign to Christianity.[161]

Therefore, the doctrine of "continuity" as espoused by the proponents of African theology was rejected by Kato. The only way back to God is by crossing the bridge of the cross of Jesus Christ. This discontinues the fruitless groping and ushers one into a new life; it is as if one is born again, born by the Spirit. The hunger for God cannot be filled by human attempts to find God, such as in ATR or any other religion. Kato saw that some African theologians had embarked upon the task of formulating a theology for Africa. He believed that the fact that Africans had unique contribution to make to theological debates was undeniable. But the brand of theology being proposed included features such as the use of sources other than the Scripture, which gave these other sources equal standing with the Bible, the possibility of salvation in ATRs and a strong emphasis on things African for their own sake.[162]

Kato's rejection of continuity was perceived to be synchronous with Western missionary attitudes, which made others question the authenticity of Kato's African Christian identity and nationalism. This raised significant questions about his self-understanding as an African. Was he really reasoning like a true African? Did he understand what he was defending, or had he been indoctrinated to magnify the voice of the Western missionary? Some scholars believed he was a mouthpiece for Western theologians or missionaries that disdained African culture and religion.[163] Thus, Kato's voice, and by implication his persona and identity as an African, was questioned. He was accused of being a caricature of Western missionaries, who held the same derogatory views about ATRs. The next section will explore Kato's response on the question of African Christian identity.

---

161. Kato, 75.

162. Kato, "Theological Trends," 11.

163. Oduyoye, *Hearing and Knowing*, 62; Bediako, *Theology and Identity*, 386–425; Mbiti, *New Testament Eschatology*.

Kato's Contribution to African Christian Identity

Kato's hermeneutics in the theological debates explored in the previous section offer some insight about self-understanding and Christianity identity. The quest for African identity was at the heart of African intellectual discourse, including theological reflections. The general perception about the impact of slavery and colonialism in Africa was that it resulted in a loss of African identity and human dignity. The perception was that some Western missionaries aided or at least abetted in these colonial activities and contributed to the dilution of African culture and traditional religions, leading to loss and to a search for African identity – thus the importance of African Christian identity in African theological discourse, to which Kato made some contribution. Kato argued:

> The Bible addresses itself to the black man, in his plight. It has done so in pointing out both the dignity and depravity of all men. It is the responsibility of Christian theologians to bring these facts to the knowledge of the public. According to the Bible, believers, under whatever human condition, are already liberated (Gal 5:1).[164]

According to Lowery: "Identity is primary among five key themes in African theology. Identity essentially functions synonymously with self-understanding, or self-concept... specifically an identity that is inculturated, liberating, full of life and shaped by community."[165] The theological discourse on self-identity focused on social or communal identities – African and Christian communal identities. The first modern African theologians who contributed significantly to the African Christian identity debates were Mulago gwa Cikala Musharhamina (1924–2012), a Roman Catholic priest from the DRC, and Kwame Bediako (1945–2008), a Ghanaian Presbyterian, among others. These advocated for a Christian message and community taking an indigenous expression. The basis for their theology was rooted in the character of God and the incarnation and argued that Christian identity must be both universal and inculturated.[166]

---

164. Kato, *Biblical Christianity*, 52.
165. Lowery, *Identity and Ecclesiology*, 46.
166. Lowery, 50.

People's worldview and their assumptions about themselves and their realities are at the heart of their biblical interpretation and theology. Self-identity and Christian identity are factors of a person's worldview or biblical worldview. Western ethnographers and anthropologists were the earlier sources of information and discussion about African beliefs and spirituality before the late 1940s and early 1950s when indigenous Africans entered the field.[167] The way Africa was portrayed tended to be demeaning. Western missionaries tended to have no understanding and respect for Africa's culture and value systems, and thus Africa's dignity and unique identity was in oblivion. As a people, Africans themselves believed what other people said about them.

According to Kuwana, a person's self-identity is linked to three factors – namely, personal experiences, social comparisons and internalisation of others' judgements.[168] The bad experiences of African people in the hands of others who enslaved and colonised them, together with the way other people portrayed them, caused Africans to have a poor self-image. When Africans compared themselves with other races and peoples, they tended to believe they were inferior to others, and internalised the poor judgements of other people about them, believing them to be true. This stereotyping and low profiling of Africans continues to be exacerbated by the media as the world is fed mostly bad news from Africa. This scenario has contributed to negative internal judgements and a perceived loss of dignity and self-identity.

The identity question also evokes the sequential slavery and colonisation of Africans by Arabs, Europeans, Asians and Americans; Africans are a people long subjected to the intellectual guidance and direction of others. Most people recognise the fact that due to colonialism, Africa lost a lot of natural resources, but what is often not quite understood is that the biggest resource that Africa lost was its dignity and self-worth.[169] Colonialism brought with it the enforcement of Western culture: the medium of education was the language of the colonial master, and the European masters' way of dressing and value systems were enforced as the acceptable way of life. There was no regard for African ways and values, and their value system was demeaned and relegated.

---

167. Conteh, *Essays*, 3.
168. Kuwana, "African Leadership," 3.
169. Kuwana, 2.

In the struggle for independence, selfhood and cultural revival were critical elements of the burgeoning Pan-Africanists. Africa was characterised by an overwhelming commitment to self-direction and a revival of interest in Africa's heritage. Bowers observed the need to seek and explicate an African identity and authenticity against the domineering influence of Europe. Along with this came the determination to critique and renounce the West, affirm Africa's traditional way of life and assert African distinctive dignity and worth. This commitment to self-identity and resistance to the West's unwelcome political, economic and cultural embrace became the fundamental force for African self-reflection for much of the second half of the twentieth century.[170]

It would appear however that the quest for authentic African identity, by African intelligentsia, paradoxically resulted in exacerbating the identity crisis. The assimilation of Western culture through education and way of life informed much of their reasoning. And yet politically, they wanted to distance themselves from anything Western, and created a portrait of an "African" that was not truly a true African. A vivid example of the spilt personality and identity of the educated Pan-Africanists is Robert Mugabe (1924–2019), former president of Zimbabwe and a renowned Pan-Africanist known for his opposition to the West. A description of Mugabe by his biographer, David Blair, states:

> Mugabe took great care with his appearance, typically wearing a three-piece suit, and insisted that members of his cabinet dressed in a similar Anglophile fashion. . . . Mugabe spoke English fluently with adopted English accent when pronouncing certain words. He was also a fan of the English game of cricket, stating that "cricket civilises people and creates good gentlemen." . . . This cultivation of British traits suggested that Mugabe respected and perhaps admired Britain while at the same time resenting and loathing the country.[171]

Some will say anecdotally that these Western educated Africans were more European than the Europeans themselves.[172] Ironically, the proponents of

---

170. Bowers, "Byang Kato," 3–5.
171. Blair, *Degrees in Violence*, 25–26.
172. Lowery, *Identity and Ecclesiology*, 60.

African theology, who rejected Western teachings and espoused African traditional views for shaping their understanding of Christianity, were themselves shaped and mentored in Western schools. Although Kato was himself trained in the West, he deferred from most of the other theologians in the way they valued ATR in African Christian discourse and made ATR the basis for "continuity".

The theme of a separate African identity has been a major intellectual engagement in African literature, art, history, sociology, political science, economics, philosophy, jurisprudence, educational theory and theology. In each of these fields of study, much has been written about African self-identity, and it has become the core integrating motif of the African nationalist ideology, which enabled the achievement of independence for much of the continent in the late 1950s and early 1960s.[173]

Where African intellectuals ask questions about what it means to be African, African theology sets itself to respond to the question of what it means to be an African Christian. And where the African intellectual turns to African traditional cultural heritage to explain its distinctiveness, African theology proposes to look to Africa's traditional religious heritage for framing its own distinctive identity.[174] For African theologians like Idowu, Mbiti, Mugambi and Bediako, answering the questions African intellectuals were asking was taken to be the defining task of African theology.[175] The core tenet of these African theologians was that the traditional African belief system was viable for evolving a Christianity that was uniquely African.[176] Mbiti and others argued that African Christian converts did not need to set aside their cultural or traditional beliefs. Their newfound Christian belief system was continuous with their traditional beliefs. According to many of these scholars, conversion to Christianity did not require discontinuity with the pre-Christian past, and they rejected the notion of discontinuity. The desire for African theologians was the quest for an identity that reflected their spiritual and religious heritage. Underneath this quest was the impact on African culture and social structures of colonialism and the mission movement.

---

173. Bowers, "Byang Kato," 6; Crafford, "Church in Africa," 163–175; Viriri and Mungwini, "African Cosmology," 27–42; Wright, "(Im)Possibility of Articulating."

174. Bowers, "Byang Kato," 6; Ngong, "Material," 114.

175. Bowers, "Byang Kato," 6.

176. Mbiti, "Christianity," 30.

Kato saw the quest for the restoration of the African identity differently. In the first place, he questioned the reality of a single African persona. Commenting on the Kinshasa Declaration about "the renaissance of African Personality,"[177] as part of the search for identity and authenticity, Kato wrote:

> One gains the impression that African peoples enjoyed homogeneity and possessed a single ethos in terms of African Personality in the recent past. Now this loss is being recovered in ecumenism, according to the declaration. But apart from the solidarity of the human race, is there any evidence, written or oral, that all 1,000 peoples or tribes of Africa were one united group of people?[178]

According to Kato, "The Scriptures know of only two groups of people, the people of God and the people of the world (Luke 12:30)."[179] He repudiated a return to ATR and proposed "a third race," consistent with his biblical understanding. He believed he was a citizen of heaven. By this he did not denounce his earthly citizenship, in fact advocating for a faithful heavenly citizenship that Christ would be proud of and a loyal earthly citizenship that the national authority would rejoice over.[180]

Those who have given their life to Christ should have no room for any other. He banishes those things humans pursue most from the centre of their lives.[181] The nature of Christian conversion is a call out of pre-Christian culture or belief into a new life – born anew. Abraham's call, paradigmatic of all Christian calling, was a call out of the world of the Chaldeans and Haran respectively (Gen 11:31; 12:1). It was a call to leave his native land and relatives and go to the unknown, at God's instruction.

According to Kato, the perceived goal of rejecting anything European, including the Christian missionary gospel message, was a case of throwing out the baby with the bath water.[182] Kato may appear to have admitted his as-

---

177. "Kinshasa Declaration", following AACC conference held in Kinshasa, Zaire, 18–31 October 1971 cited in *Theological Pitfalls* by Kato, Appendix iii, 201
178. Kato, *Theological Pitfalls*, 156.
179. Kato, 21
180. Kato, "Christian Citizenship."
181. Cockerill, *Christian Faith*, 107.
182. Kato, *Theological Pitfalls*, 175.

similation, but it was not an assimilation with the West but with the Christian message; he was a Christian African. He recognized the Western missionaries as carrying an authentic, life-changing message, but he was not unmindful about the excesses of some missionaries.[183]

The charge against the African theologians was that they were, in fact, themselves espousing Western philosophical views and approaches to doing theology.[184] If indeed the missionaries failed to engage ATR, or at least failed to try to understand it from an African perspective, the same cannot be said of Kato. He was immersed in ATR like no other person among the disputants. Kato was initiated as a fetish priest as a baby and completed the rite of passage to manhood before his encounter with Christianity or the missionary religion. His rejection of certain cultural aspects could well be because of his personal experience and understanding of ATR and cultural belief systems, which is worth exploring. Thus, the subject of Kato's African Christian self-identity is at the core of his theology and sets him apart from his opponents. It is important to explore Kato's Christian self-identity as a key to understanding his hermeneutics and ministry, especially in evangelical Christian theological education in Africa.

Kwame Bediako was one of the leading scholars who had done extensive work on the subject of African Christian identity.[185] Bediako devotes a whole chapter to critically appraising Kato's view on the identity problem of the modern African Christian, which was at variance to other writers. He says,

> Byang Henry Kato came to embody the very antithesis of the basic positions enunciated by the African theologians.... Virtually everything he wrote was intended as a reaction to, and a rebuttal of, much that went to constitute the "African theology" of the last two decades. For this, if for no other reason, Byang Kato's work compels attention.[186]

Kato and Bediako were in the same room at the 1974 Lausanne Congress as part of a group to discuss Kato's two papers presented at the congress on

---

183. Kato, 175.
184. Turaki, *Engaging Religions*, xxviii; cf. Bediako, *Theology and Identity*, xi–xii.
185. Lowery, *Identity and Ecclesiology*, 58.
186. Bediako, *Theology and Identity*, 386–425.

the subject of the gospel, cultural contextualisation and religious syncretism.[187] Kato had outlined the theological challenge of syncretism and contextualisation, thus bringing the subject of contextualisation to the fore of evangelical theological discourse. According to Stephen Knapp, the recorder of the group discussion, Bediako's first reaction, among other comments, was: "What is the relationship between syncretism, exegesis, and hermeneutics (biblical and theological reflection)? I get the impression that the Congress is emphasizing giving of culture back to the Third World. What are the principles of biblical exegesis in relation to culture and contextualization?"[188] In response to comments and questions (including Bediako's) about his paper, Kato said:

> In some circles, this concept [contextualisation] questions the content of the Gospel itself. My understanding is that we should not throw away the word, but just be sure the meaning is good. I would define contextualisation as "expressing the same unchanging Gospel within the context from which the people come." The revelational content is the same [propositional revelation] but communicated so that people will get the message. I would preserve syncretism as undesirable. Contextualisation does go beyond form. It includes, ideas, etc.[189]

This must have been a particularly important interaction between these two theological figures in the African church as would be clear in their ongoing contributions and debates about the relationship between Christian faith and African culture.

In terms of self-identity, Turaki opines that Africans define themselves by their ethnicity, affiliation, religion, culture or geography. He states that people could not claim their ancestry, especially land, if they came from another geographical area:

> Ancestral land is the political geography of traditional Africans. Each ethnic group in Africa has an ancestral land. Associated with this geography are the political ownership, by each ethnic

---

187. See Kato, "Gospel, Cultural Contextualisation"; and Kato, "Evangelism Opportunities."
188. Recorded in Knapp, "Gospel, Cultural Contextualization."
189. Recorded in Knapp, "Gospel, Cultural Contextualization"; cf. Kato, "Gospel, Cultural Contextualisation."

nationality, of its land and its right to control the land and rule itself within it, through its traditional chieftains. Thus, the rights to ancestral land are the rights of self-rule and self-identity.[190]

Hence, Kato himself came from a rich and well-established African ancestry. He hailed from the Ham or Jaba ethnic group, with one of the earliest and richest African cultural heritages – the Nok culture of early Iron-Age civilisation.[191] The Jaba people with their Nok ancestry have lived in the archaeological Nok area for at least two thousand years. Kato prides himself with firsthand knowledge and understanding of the religion of the Jaba people, having been born and brought up in it.[192] Kato's family homestead is located in the Sab-Suro area in Kwoi, Nigeria, where, before her death, the widow lived in her own house with other family members in the homestead. Reverend Adamu Kato, a retired clergyman of the ECWA church and younger brother of Byang, is currently the head of the Kato family and has his own house on the same homestead.

In terms of personal identity – before the technology for personal identification numbers (PINs) or the *huduma namba* (an identifier issued to Kenyans from a single database for all personal information) – Kato bore on his temple the Jaba tribal marks as his identity. According to Rev. Adamu Kato, one could tell the the person's gender, ethnic identity and the type of ritual for inserting the tribal marks done by special persons known as *wanzami*. The *wanzami* was a specialist, trained to do the incision, shaving and circumcision rituals. They used special knives to do the cutting and applied charcoal to stop the oozing of blood and herbs to heal the wound. The ritual involved incantations to the gods.[193]

Byang Kato's marriage to a Jaba princess, Juma Rahima Gandu (a.k.a. Jummai), daughter of His Royal Highness Mal Gandu Maude, the Kpop Ham or king of the Jaba people,[194] further asserted Kato's traditional African nobility, heritage and social standing in the land of his birth. Four decades after

---

190. Turaki, *Tainted Legacy*, 169.
191. Kato, *Theological Pitfalls*, 28.
192. Kato, 27.
193. Rev. Alemu Kato, brother of Kato, in discussion with Researcher in Kwoi, 22 March 2019
194. Biography of Mrs. Jummai Kato, recorded in her funeral booklet, Kwoi, 25 May 2019.

his death, Kato is still remembered by many people among the Jaba ethnic group in Kwoi, as one of their most illustrious sons. The researcher met and interviewed several people in Kwoi, some of whom were contemporaries of Kato and some younger. Among the people interviewed was the current king or chief of the Jaba people, the Kpop Ham, His Royal Highness Dr. Danladi Gyet Maude (OON, JP).[195] The chief revealed he was a classmate with Kato in primary school; he referred to him as his brother and said that Kato was held in high esteem as the top student in class. Kato's spouse would have been the one on the kingship stool (the throne) ahead of the current Kpop Ham, but for the fact that she was a woman and had to defer to the male kin next in line as tradition demanded.

Another respondent was an elderly man in Kwoi who said he did the traditional rite of passage initiation with Kato. Now in his eighties, he praised Kato for his friendship and recalled how Kato influenced his life:

> We parted ways when Kato went to school and rose up to be a world leader but when he came back to the village, and he often did, we spent time together and he taught me many things. He taught me to read the Bible in Hausa and made me to be a good leader in church and a good farmer too.[196]

Both Kato and his friend went to the ECWA church in Kwoi, where the latter currently serves as an elder and sings in the choir.[197]

Some people who never met Kato remember him by one of the most notable events in the community, which they continue to recall to this day. The news of Kato's death by drowning in a foreign land, Kenya, in East Africa, took the community by storm. On the day of Kato's funeral, the people of Kwoi were overwhelmed and awed when in a single day they witnessed aeroplanes flying in and taking off from the small airstrip they had in the community. Never again have they seen the airstrip so busy. My guide remembered this day as the day he first saw Kato's daughter, who eventually became his wife.

---

195. The letters OON stand for Order of the Niger, the third highest meritorious honour conferred on distinguished Nigerian nationals. Simimarly, the letters JP means Justice of the Peace, for work in the community to promote peace.

196. Baba Leon, Kato's childhood friend in discussion with the Researcher in Kwoi in March 2019.

197. Interaction with this respondent was through an interpreter, so the author could not explore further how Kato's influence helped him to become a better farmer and better leader.

Kato was the first of five prominent people buried in the First ECWA Church grounds at the centre of Kwoi. The town authorities in 2010 named a street after Kato: Byang Kato Road. There is also now in Kwoi the Kato International Training Academy, founded by Kato's family and led by his surviving son, Paul. This is both a secondary school and football academy. Therefore, in terms of ancestral land, political geography, ethnicity and nationality, Kato was a true African of noble Jaba ethnicity and Nigerian nationality, born and raised in the culture of his people.

Although Kato's African ancestry and birth is firmly established, the question of "identity" and the charge against Kato of a non-African identity had to do with his views and attitudes towards African religions, culture and worldviews.[198] Even though Kato was being raised to be a fetish priest and a religious leader in the traditional sense, his conversion to Christianity may not necessarily mean a lack of appreciation or understanding of his African culture. However, his conversion to Christianity led to a change in belief and perspective about spirituality and worship of the divine. He turned away from the beliefs and practices of ATR, especially when the rationale and practice was inconsistent with what Kato believed to be the biblical view. Thus, he advocated for discontinuity and embraced the message and teachings of the Bible as the sole authority for his conduct and his understanding of his new faith. This change of religious view had implications for self-identity.

Self-identity for an individual in an African context may be difficult to characterise. For a start, identity in African conception is communal, and one's existence is in relation to others and the community. This way of life or philosophy is known as *ubuntu*, African socialism, and is profoundly relational.[199] The tendency then is to believe as the community does, and the idea of personal freedom and individualism were treated with suspicion.[200] Religion gives direction to people's culture and the whole scheme of life. Turaki states that a person's identity is in her or his religious beliefs, among other factors.[201] Kato looked more to his new community of followers of Jesus Christ for guidance and worship of God, even if Christianity was inherited

---

198. Ngong, "Material," 107.
199. Mbiti, *Introduction*, 175; Mburu, *African Hermeneutics*, 36.
200. Mburu, 37.
201. Turaki, *Foundations of African*, 11.

from the missionaries and was viewed with suspicion as the White man's religion. Kato was lonely in his views about his newfound faith in Christ and argued: "If religion is what gives direction to life, Christianity must necessarily change the life-style or culture of the African. Where such a differentiation is not possible, two alternatives are called for. Either the culture is abandoned or Christianity is compromised."[202] He cited the example of Stonehenge in England, which was used for Druidism in the pre-Roman era, but the shrine remained for cultural reasons when Druidism was outlawed. However, in the eighteenth and nineteenth centuries, the veneration of the shrine was revived and continues today. Using this analogy, Kato questioned whether it is worth preserving the juju[203] after conversion in Africa.[204]

In any case, Kato was not unmindful about the challenges Africans faced in terms of self-worth and identity. His approach to the question was radically different; he portrayed himself as a proud African but unashamedly embraced biblical fidelity.[205] Speaking at an interview abroad, his response to the question on culture and Christianity was as follows:

> But in Africa, the search for personality and the emphasis for human identity is coming out in the way of cultural revolution. Again, I am not being critical altogether of culture. In fact, if it were not for your wonderful winter here, I would probably be wearing my national costume today. I am proud to be an African and I believe Jesus Christ saved me not to be an American Christian, but an African Christian, and I'm proud of that. The Lord wants us to be happy with our society and loyal to our government. I am that way and I feel Christians should be that way, but there is a limit to my understanding of my own culture. Since I am a Christian, Jesus Christ has come into the center of my being now. This same Jesus Christ should be the one to show me what is good and what is bad in my culture[206]

---

202. Kato, "Critique of Incipient," ThD diss., 175.

203. According to Kato, *juju* is another term used to describe African traditional religions, one of the many terms that does not adequately describe ATR. The term is deprecatory and vague and refers to the objects of ATR worship (p. 23).

204. Kato, *Theological Pitfalls*, 175.

205. See Graham, foreword to *Theological Pitfalls*.

206. Kato, "African Prudence and Promise", n.p..

Kato argued that Christian Africans need to give up cultural belief systems that are not consistent with a biblical worldview's understanding and worship of God. A mix of the two belief systems would result in syncretism and universalism. He condemned these practices as unbiblical and unchristian.[207] He believed that true freedom and identity are found in salvation in Jesus. He stated:

> [It] is actually in Christianity that we find the assertion of true humanity. Jesus Christ, in His incarnation, took the form of man and not so much one particular kind of man, one racial kind of man, but man in general. He also was born as an individual and that demonstrates the concern and interest that God has in redeeming man.[208]

The dignity, true identity and value of people is in the fact that we are made in God's image and God, in his incarnation, identified with humanity. Bowers writes: "As biblically-grounded evangelical believers, what our commitments call us to, whether in Europe or Asia or Africa or wherever, is neither to ignore our intellectual setting, nor to accommodate to it, but intentionally to understand and engage it for the sake of the gospel."[209]

Notwithstanding the belief that Africans have lost their identity, a critical challenge to the church in Africa is the dominance of the African worldview. The African traditional worldview, which the Western missionaries disdained and condemned, is ironically more prevalent in the church today than a biblical worldview.[210] Ordinary African Christians continue to address their existential challenges through beliefs and practices informed by the traditional worldviews of ATR.[211] Some theologians have advanced that African worldviews and spirituality must be explored even more. There is then the tendency to look back in time to explore what and how Africans lived before the intrusion of the slavers and colonisers and Western missionaries. So, for things sacred, many proponents of African theology are advocating looking back in time and exploring the religious beliefs and practices that African

---

207. Kato.
208. Kato, "Africa Prudence and Promise", n.p..
209. Bowers, "Byang Kato," 10.
210. See Chalk, *Making Disciples*.
211. Ngong, "Material," 114.

peoples cherished, even if these beliefs and practices are at odds with what the Bible teaches. Or they try to impose these beliefs on the Bible and make believe that these are African interpretations of the Bible:

> As the African has now attained independence, he is asking himself, "Who am I?" He is seeking to assert his identity telling the rest of humanity, I am now a human being. I want to show you that I have arrived. Get off my back. I want my autonomy. I too am a first-class human being and not a second-class human being.[212]

Kato found a new identity when he converted to Christianity. Despite the impact of all the factors that contributed to the loss of African heritage and religious values – slavery and colonialism – Kato found real freedom in Christianity. Kato's concern for biblicism went beyond nationalism. He saw himself first as a child of God in the world but also as a loyal citizen of his country. He wrote:

> A Christian should be the most loyal citizen of his country because he is aware of the fact that God has ordained even a dictatorial type of Neronian rule. Moreover, as a citizen of two dominions, he knows what it means to submit to the higher power. But his belief in the absolute authority of the Word of God also forces him to acknowledge the equality of all men. That being the case, the awareness of the existence of other nations becomes imperative. Blind nationalism of Nazist type should have no place among Christians.[213]

His primary identity was Christian; he was first a Christian before an African. Kato was a typical African son of the soil and was at ease living in his community. Kato was raised to embrace African traditional cultural values in the best possible way. With his conversion to Christianity, he adopted the biblical worldview as his predominant value system. He continued to live in the African context, and by every standard he had the respect of the community and rose to be one of the prominent personalities not only in his community and country but also in Africa and beyond.

---

212. Kato, "Africa: Prudence and Promise", n.p..
213. Kato, "Critique of Incipient," ThD diss., 268–269.

Kato saw himself as a Christian African: authentically African, but saved and transformed by the gospel of Jesus Christ.[214] He was born again (John 3:3). The implication here was that he was now a new person; the old life was gone, and a new life had begun (2 Cor 5:17). He did not stop being a Nigerian African man, but he strove to live his life by biblical values and to unlearn anything that was not consistent with biblical values. Therefore, Kato could have been conscious about the loss of identity, whether this was the traditional African identity or the Europeanised African identity. But he had found a new identity in Christ through new birth (John 3:3; 1 Pet 1:3–5, 23; 3:18–23), and he was now a new person with a new identity, as the Bible teaches. Aware of his African identity, he also was happy and proud of his new citizenship (Phil 3:20; Col 3:17). Kato said: "It is not neo-colonialism to plead the uniqueness and finality of Jesus Christ. It is not arrogance to herald the fact that all who are not 'in Christ' are lost. It is merely articulating what the Scriptures say."[215] Kato's belief in Jesus Christ as Saviour was unshakable.

As for the apostle Paul in the New Testament (Phil 3:8), every other gain or identity was a loss for Kato. In the abstract of his doctoral thesis, Kato wrote: "Christianity is unique. It creates the third race, a race called 'the body of Christ,' made up of people from all cultural backgrounds."[216] Kato argued further: "The gospel content, of course, needs no addition or modification. It is because of this irreducible, immutable message that Christianity has produced the third race which cuts across all races and all peoples."[217] Kato proclaimed: "Let African Christians be Christian Africans."[218] By this he meant, when as an African you accept Jesus as your Lord, the Bible should be the judge for your conduct and culture. If the cultural practices conflict with the Bible, the biblical injunction stands, and one does not have to stick to culture. This, Kato insisted, was not to say that the Christian should abandon her own culture. The emphasis was on the supremacy of the wisdom and veracity of the word of God above any human wisdom, especially when human wisdom contradicts Scripture.

---

214. Breman, "Association of Evangelicals," 366.
215. Kato, *Theological Pitfalls*, 16.
216. Kato, "Critique of Incipient," ThD diss., Abstract (no page number).
217. Kato, 270–271.
218. Quoted in Nystrom, "Let African Christians."

The purpose of Kato's theological engagement was to preserve biblical Christianity, which he believed had become a vital part of the life of Christians in Africa. He wanted to be seen as a defender of the Christian faith in Africa. He figured out that church people were being led away from the truth of the Christian faith because they were prideful about culture and gave undue reverence to African traditional religions. He was not naïve or ignorant about ATR. He understood the nature of ATR from personal experience and doctoral research in ATR. Kato saw himself first as a Christian, then African – a "Christian African."

The plight of Africans in the hands of their White compatriots in apartheid South Africa was one of the key factors that drove the discourse on African Christian identity and African theology, which included Black theology, or liberation theology, from South Africa. Kato was asked about what he would do about the South African question, and his response was:

> We are now in the process to organize a national evangelical fellowship for the whole Republic of South Africa that would be multi-racial and interdenominational. We may come up against a wall, but I have been working in correspondence with both blacks and whites. If Bible-believing Christians pray and keep talking, we probably will achieve more success than a radical approach would. We can leave the radical approach to government and non-church organizations. We see the work of the Church as conciliatory.[219]

Kato's transition from holding a predominantly traditional worldview to a biblical worldview involved hermeneutical keys espoused in the previous section on the application of Scripture. In the quest for identity, Kato prioritized his citizenship of heaven. In an address to Kenyan citizens on Jamhuri Day, the national day celebrated each year on 12 December to mark their independence from British colonial rule,[220] Kato outlined the meaning of a heavenly citizen. Exegeting a text from Romans 13:1–14 on the subject of Christian citizenship, Kato admonished his audience to rededicate themselves to greater involvement in nation building. He reiterated the fact that Christian

---

219. Kato, "African's Christian Future," 16.

220. Kato erroneously referred to this as Madaraka Day, which is celebrated on June 1, when Kenya attained internal self-rule.

citizenship was in heaven (Phil 3:20), but said: "while God should be given the first place in the believer's life, the national government also deserves the loyalty of all citizens, the Christians included."[221] He went on further to state:

> The Bible too expects Christians to play a double role, first as citizens, then as Christian citizens (Rom 3:10). Christians and non-Christians alike are subject to the governing authorities. Authority is not qualified, it is not indicated whether the governing authorities are communistic, or capitalistic. Whether it is multi-party state or one party, whether it is democratic or dictatorial.[222]

The authorities themselves are subject to the rule of God, and ultimately God allows them to be in authority, and God removes them when he wants to do so. The citizen's responsibility is to show and ensure loyalty by teaching obedience and respect at home. Quoting Dorothy Law Nolte's poem, "Children Learn What They Live," Kato added, "If a child learns to walk with the Lord, he will not depart from Him (Prov 22:6)."[223] Loyalty to the government means law abiding and responsible citizenship, not just in fear of punishment but for the sake of conscience. Other obligations include paying dues and taxes in appreciation for all the government does for public services and an ordered society.

However, Kato admonished Christians, as citizens of heaven, to prioritize the moral development of individuals and the nation and to live lives worthy of the call of God, a life of holiness. Highlighting the life of Augustine of Hippo, as an example, Kato wrote:

> For many years he roamed from one university faculty to the other, seeking for the best philosophy in life. He wandered from one drinking bar to the other, from one prostitute to the other – all in search of the One who still says "come to me all who labour and are heavy laden and I will give you rest" (Matt 11:25). With his life completely changed, he followed the warning of these

---

221. Kato, "Christian Citizenship."
222. Kato.
223. Kato.

verses (Rom 13:1–14) and separated his life from the things done in the dark. He learned to live a life transparently honest.[224]

Kato also had the view that the Africanisation of the church was a secularist agenda and especially driven by ecumenism. He wrote:

> In its push for secularization, there has been an urgent call for the Africanization of Christianity. What seems to be the meaning behind this is that African Culture should take precedence over the Bible. There has been a call to change the content of Christian theology, if necessary, to suit the African context.[225]

In summary, Kato saw himself as a true African, who had found Christ and for whom Christ had given true meaning to life. He had been set free from hell bound groping in darkness. He believed this was the plight of every person and he contended for his fellow Africans by doing all he could to safeguard biblical Christianity on the continent. He identified himself as a "third race" citizen, freeing himself from the split or dual personality of the African. He was "Christian African"; his new citizenship identity was superior to his African identity. He was a mainstream conservative evangelical, with dispensational pre-millennial leanings, unapologetically Bible-centred and Christ-centred. He certainly valued his African identity and was never separated from his people; he rather reached out to connect them with Christ. Ngong observes: "There is no doubt that the past is important but to tie anyone's identity essentially to the past is biblically, theologically, and philosophically problematic.[226]

African Christian identity continues to be of interest. There are current debates to decolonise or even Africanise Christianity.[227] Kato's contributions to the question continue to have an appeal. Essentially, Kato's hermeneutical principle is to look to the Bible for the self-understanding of the Christian. He differentiates the message of the Bible from the messenger – the Western missionaries – especially in the African context. He also affirms the missionary intent of the Christian faith, thus, the particularity of the Christian call

---

224. Kato.
225. Kato, *African Cultural Revolution*, 34.
226. Ngong, "Material," 135.
227. See Sakupapa, "Decolonising Content"; Graham, "Decolonising Theology."

and the universal nature and missional intent of the call. His biblical stance was that African Christians ought to be Christian Africans – Christians primarily before ethnically African:

> African Christians must understand and accept the fact that African Traditional Religion (ATR) is not synonymous with Christianity. Even though the two religions share a lot in common, there are other areas in which they are at conflict. These areas of conflict establish the line between true practice of the Christian faith and its syncretistic practice. Syncretism sets in when African Christians ignore these conflict areas and consider them as complementary options to the Christian faith.[228]

Kato believed that the underlying cause for differences in hermeneutics was theological training or its lack. Talking about a church without theology, Bediako said:

> This could only result from allowing, in the first place, for the existence of a pre-Christian memory in African Christian consciousness. For theology presupposes religious tradition, and tradition requires memory, and memory is integral to identity: without memory we have no past, and if we have no past, then we lose our identity.[229]

The suggestion here is that one's identity as an African Christian is defined by one's past in the traditional religions, without which there is no selfhood. Kato proposed a remedy for the misleading theologies or theological pitfalls in Africa: sound evangelical theological education. Underscoring the importance of theological education, Ananng states:

> It is a primary vocation of theological educators to analyse, discern, and critique the forces shaping the socio-religious milieu of the contemporary Church, bring the unchanging truth of the Gospel to bear on illuminating these forces, employ their insights to predict future trends, suggest strategic responses

---

228. Otonko, "Beyond the Rhetoric," 8.
229. Bediako, *Theology and Identity*, 58–59.

and monitor the effectiveness of the implementation of these responses.[230]

The next section catalogues Kato's endeavours for promoting sound biblical education in sub-Saharan Africa.

Kato's Contribution to Evangelical Theological Education in Africa

Kato's particular contributions to African theological discourse were not only polemical, or what he said, but also what he did and set out to do before his untimely death. A more holistic assessment of Kato goes beyond what he wrote or said in his key theological writing, *Theological Pitfalls in Africa*, the content of which was mostly viewed as alarm bells for the syncretism and universalism creeping into the church in Africa. By this, Kato was engaging the academy with contemporary and relevant issues for theological discourse in Africa.[231] His contribution went beyond merely warning the church and included provision of a recipe for overcoming the theological errors he identified. He articulated a vision for sound evangelical theological training on the continent as the panacea for these theological pitfalls.

Kato saw the need for theological education in the church in Africa at all levels, including informal, off-site and home-based education, education for children, and above all, graduate-level theological education. Speaking on the subject of "Christian Higher Education" at the First International Conference of Reformed Institutions for Christian Scholarship, Potchefstroom, South Africa, in September 1975, Kato said:

> A Church without a sound theological basis is like a drifting boat in a storm without an anchor. The wind of every doctrine is blowing against the Church today. The wind of contextualization is testing the relevance of the boat of evangelical theology. The ill-wind of ecumenism with its call for secularization of Christianity is proving very tempting to the average Christian. The wind of Black theology, with its legitimate quest for human

---

230. Asumang, "Reforming Theological Education," 117.
231. See Bowers, "Byang Kato," 8.

dignity but without an adequate term of reference, appears convincing. The wind of African Theology with its rightful search for the African personality yet failing to see the unique nature of Christian revelation, is very appealing. For the ship of evangelical faith to stand the test of the times, it must be grounded on the hope of our fathers.[232]

Thus it was that, through the AEA Theological Commission (AEA-TC), Kato put together a strategic roadmap to lay the groundwork for a robust theological training programme on the continent. According to Kato, the result of a survey conducted by the AEA Christian education coordinator in 1972 revealed a worrying trend. The report showed that only 39 percent of the respondents believed the Bible was the sole authority of the Christian. Also, in response to the question: "What must a person do to receive eternal life?," only 38 percent said one must believe in Jesus Christ.[233] At that time, according to Kato, various estimates put the Christian population of Africa between 60 and 160 million people.[234] Kato was eager to launch robust theological training on the continent to address theological ignorance. The current state of the church in Africa may resonate with Kato's era and its need for theological training. The need for theological training continues to be a critical challenge for the church, underscoring the importance of Kato's contribution.

According to Bangura:

> Recent studies indicate that the Charismatic Movement that began in the late 1970s and early 1980s is gradually becoming the most inviting face of the Christian faith in Africa. However, the pace of growth seen in the Christian faith far outweighs the available theological training institutions that prepare the leaders who will eventually preside over the affairs of these churches.[235]

A 2019 report of the AEA Theology and Christian Education Commission (AEA-TCEC) consultation for theological educators across the continent states:

---

232. Kato, "Creating Facilities for Evangelical Theological Training in Africa," 3.
233. Kato, "Critique of Incipient," ThD diss., 53.
234. Kato, 53.
235. Bangura, "Tracking the Maze," 109–110.

The original purpose and objectives of the Theological Consultation was "to provide a forum where theological educators can develop and implement a strategy to equip and strengthen the grassroots churches of Africa, particularly the leaders and pastors of African churches, where it is estimated that 85–90% of those leaders are untrained and undertrained biblically and theologically."[236]

Corroborating this report, Re-Forma reveals:

Studies show that over 90% of all pastors do not have a formal theological education. According to statistics, that equates to well over 2 million Protestant pastors worldwide. In addition, every year thousands of new Protestant churches are established, very often without a trained pastor or preacher. The biggest crisis facing the evangelical, global church today is the fact that most pastors, missionaries, and Christian leaders are undereducated or not educated at all. Re-Forma has set as its goal to fundamental remedy this situation.[237]

According to Kato, "Bible doctrine or teaching may be considered as theological instruction, perhaps with less philosophical reflection."[238] Thus, theology and doctrine have been part of gospel ministry in Africa,[239] and theological education in Africa has been a critical contribution in the role played by missionaries in the establishment of the church over the years. However, this effort in theological education was not without its shortcomings, especially for the evangelical wing of the church. Kato lamented the missionaries' biblical ignorance and lack of emphasis on theological education. He wrote: "Seminary education is for pastors in North America and the Bible School and Bible Institute is for missionaries. So, a mammoth church has been established without the depth of theology that the church needs. Christian leaders were now vulnerable to the tactics of ecumenism with its

---

236. *Association of Evangelicals Theology and Christian Education Commission (AEA-TCEC) Theological Consultation Report*, 2

237. "Background/Reality Check," Re-Forma: Developing Global Ministry Outcomes, accessed 5 August 2020, https://www.re-forma.global/.

238. Kato, *Problem of Theological Education*, 1.

239. Kato, 1.

basic universalistic premise."[240] It is unsurprising, therefore, that nearly half of his decalogue of proposals for mitigating theological pitfalls in Africa were matters directly related to educational curriculum.[241]

Theological education may not be lacking in the church altogether. Kato enumerated six initiatives he believed constituted the theological teaching programmes in the church, namely: (1) catechetical instructions, (2) Sunday school, (3) women's fellowship, (4) Bible teaching in schools, (5) the family altar and (6) theological institutions.[242] However, these programmes did not go far enough and were not effective. Kato postulated that the shortcomings had to do with the content of curricula and the limited participation of potential learners. For example, Sunday school was seen mostly as programmes for children, leaving out adult members of the congregation. The relevance of training materials for an African context and learning methodology are also highlighted as contributing factors for the low level of theological education. Other challenges were the fact that instructions were done in foreign languages and students learned mostly by rote. The quality of both teachers and students were all possible shortcomings.

Kato stated that the root cause for the dearth in theological education was the influx of new converts. Churches were not able to keep up with training ministers at the pace needed for the rapidly growing number of converts. The method of operation and anti-intellectualism of the evangelical missions, the lack of availability of suitably qualified students and the difficulty of retaining trained students in the ministry of the church were all contributing to the lessening of theological education. Ironically, the indigenisation of theology was also problematic, and left much to be desired, according to Kato.[243] The theological agenda failed to adequately address issues of African traditional religions, culture, polygamy, the Christian home or the spirit world. Reflecting on other parts of the world, Smith points out a characteristic of evangelical theology, writing:

> Due to the pressure to obtain acceptance amongst academic peers, many evangelical scholars adopt approaches that include

---

240. Kato, "Critique of Incipient," ThD diss., 8.
241. Kato, *Theological Pitfalls*, 181–184.
242. Kato, *Problem of Theological Education*, 2.
243. Kato, 4–7.

presuppositions and methodologies that are subtly at odds with core evangelical beliefs. Both in their choice of topics and their selection of methods, evangelicals often conform to the more liberal ways of doing theology.[244]

Kato saw the need for sound biblical and theological education as the church's greatest need in Africa. Kato's vision, or model, for theological education was grassroots upwards. He was concerned about providing commensurate theological education to ordinary Christians, and from that level extending it upwards to higher levels. This was a distinctive of Kato in his generation. He clearly rejected the elitism of the liberal theologians of Africa and seemed more interested in keeping the church's scholars as near to the rank and file as possible. Kato himself exemplified a rigorous pursuit of sound theological education in the church in Africa. MacDonald succinctly summarises Kato's theological educational attainment and writes:

> From his youth onward, Byang Kato was vigorous in his pursuit of education. Despite the protests and gibes of peers, Igbaja Bible College was the path forward for Kato. Even after marrying Jummai during his final year, he still "excelled in the classroom" and juggled many responsibilities. He went on to secure his Bachelor's degree abroad at London Bible College, and by 1970 Kato was at Dallas Theological Seminary (DTS), earning his Master's degree. Due to his incredible persistence, he had his Th.D. from DTS by May of 1974. Supporting Christian education and the church of Africa continued to be his passion. He was a gifted writer with a host of articles – crowned by his greatest work *Theological Pitfalls in Africa*. At his height, he was considered "the most outstanding evangelical theological leader in Africa."[245]

Kato strove hard to acquire the highest level of theological education from world class theological institutions – the famous London Bible College (now London School of Theology) in the UK and Dallas Theological Seminary in the USA – and he was the first to do so in the history of modern

---

244. Smith, *Integrated Theology*, 15.
245. MacDonald, "Critical Analysis," 20.

evangelicalism in sub-Saharan Africa. Kato did not only achieve a doctoral degree in theology but, along with his spouse, was also qualified and certified by the Child Evangelism Fellowship Institute in Paris.[246] In the preface to Kato's booklet, *Biblical Christianity in Africa*, Tite Tiénou highlighted that Kato's whole ministry was directed toward the grounding and growth of biblical Christianity on the continent.[247] As a student of the Bible, he taught others what he learned. Kato was a Bible teacher. He taught his peers and fellow believers in their native Hausa language, at a grassroots level and in formal Bible schools, from basic certificates to graduate level courses in seminaries in Africa and the USA. His Bible teaching was also reflected in his sermons, speeches and writings.

The magnum opus of Kato's writings was *Theological Pitfalls in Africa*, published by Evangel Publishing House in Kenya, which turned out to be the first book of its kind published by an evangelical scholar in Africa. *Theological Pitfalls in Africa* was the book version of Kato's doctoral dissertation. Other equally important works included *African Cultural Revolution and the Christian Faith*, *The Spirits* and *Biblical Christianity in Africa* – a collection of papers and addresses Kato wrote.[248] These contributions were unprecedented at the time and represented a unique evangelical voice in African theological and intellectual discourse. Kato's theological articulations sparked and enhanced theological reflections which continue in current times. He did not only raise an alarm about the incipient syncretism in the church; he astutely envisioned a remedy and put together a plan to address the theological malady in the church in Africa, under the auspices of the AEA.

Kato's first contact with AEA was as a guest speaker. He spoke about Christian education at the AEA First General Assembly in 1969. According to Haye, between Kato's first contact with AEA in 1969 and his next speaking engagement in 1973, he wrote in a letter to the AEA:

> To me, the great need in Africa today is ministerial training, coupled with in-depth teaching in the church. We should make an effort to convince missionaries and Christian leaders that while evangelism should not be neglected, teaching the converts

---

246. Haye, *Byang Kato*, 43
247. Tiénou, preface *to Biblical Christianity in Africa*, by Kato, vii-viii.
248. See Haye, *Byang Kato*, 105.

we already have should be our priority. A well-taught Christian will become an evangelist.[249]

Tiénou suggest that 1973 was a critical turning point in Kato's career with the founding of the AEA Theological Commission and the appointment of Kato as the commission's first executive secretary. Kato was also elected as the general secretary of the AEA before the Second General Assembly in 1973 came to an end. Thus Kato became the first African to lead the AEA as its chief executive officer, and he held the dual position of executive secretary of the AEA Theological Commission and general secretary of AEA.[250]

One purpose of the AEA Theological Commission was to encourage the existing theological schools on the continent and promote more advanced-level training of church leaders on African soil. While the evangelical church's priority was evangelism and winning souls, with little attention to theological training, Kato emphasised sound theological education for ministers as *sine qua non* for effective evangelisation. Kato was especially troubled by evidence of theological indifference and deviation within the church and sought by every means to strengthen theological life in Africa. Evangelical theological education was necessary not only for evangelism but also for the soul of the church. He believed that the battle for the soul of the church in Africa was a theological battle. Some scholars fault Kato as being an alarmist and complainer, without providing any theological solution to the problems he raised.[251] Reviewing Kato's *Theological Pitfalls in Africa*, Bowers cites the following from a newspaper editorial which was reviewing Kato's book:

> A prominent religious newspaper in eastern Africa ran a review which calls *Pitfalls* "alarmist in what it says and colonial in the perspective in which it is written." It goes on to suggest that Kato, through miseducation, permitted himself to become a tool "in the preservation and protection of neo-colonial interests," and goes on to charge: "There is a theological pitfall in Africa from which we must climb out: the reactionary evangelical theology which has a capitalistic birthright."[252]

---

249. Haye, 74.
250. Tiénou, *Theological Task*, 54.
251. Bowers, "Evangelical Theology," 36.
252. Bowers, 37.

These were serious charges especially in the immediate aftermath of colonialism. Kato was threatened with a lawsuit by one of the ecumenical scholars that Kato believed contributed to promoting theological errors in the church in Africa.[253]

The AEA Theological Commission's intention was to consolidate, upgrade and coordinate theological education. AEA had eighty-three theological schools on its mailing list then, but these had low standards and none of these offered programmes on the post-graduate level, such as a master of divinity (MDiv). The Theological Commission, under Kato's leadership, purposed to establish graduate schools that would provide MDiv-level training on the continent.[254]

Kato developed a comprehensive plan for sound theological education in the church in Africa to mitigate the theological malady.[255] Following his election as AEA general secretary, Byang Kato was asked by his missionary colleagues and friends at SIM in Nigeria about his long-range plan for the church in Africa. According to Nystrom, Kato's response was "African Christianity is being consumed by a dreadful disease.... We must find a cure for our theological anaemia." Within the hour, Kato outlined to his three friends his vision to address the theological anaemia. This included four items:[256]

1. Develop African evangelical scholars who would write and publish their theological reflections in the African context.
2. Develop graduate schools on the continent where African leaders can be trained without having to leave the continent.
3. Develop a theological journal for the publication of the theological ideas of African scholars.
4. Develop an accrediting agency to set standards for theological education and monitor the progress of schools to maintain standards.

It is astonishing that even though Kato died two years later, his fourfold plan did not drown with him. Kato's plan for addressing the theological problems in the church in Africa resulted in the establishment of the first

---

253. Bowers, 35.
254. Kato, "Theological Trends," 8.
255. Bowers, "Evangelical Theology," 36–37.
256. Nystrom, "Let African Christians."

two graduate schools for evangelical theological education in sub-Sahara Africa, namely the Faculté de Théologie Évangélique de Bangui (FATEB) in the Central Africa Republic, established in 1977 to serve the francophone regions, and the Nairobi Evangelical Graduate School of Theology (NEGST), established in 1983 in Kenya to serve the anglophone regions of Africa.[257] NEGST is now a fully-fledged university – Africa International University (AIU). FATEB has also grown its programmes with university-level status and has established a second campus in the neighbouring country of Cameroon. The plan also included the establishment of an accrediting body – the Accrediting Council for Theological Education in Africa, now the Association for Christian Theological Education in Africa (ACTEA), established in 1976. ACTEA's mission also includes services in support of the development of theological schools across the continent. Currently, ACTEA has sixty-five theological schools, Bible colleges and seminaries associated with it in seventeen countries across Africa. With regard to Kato's vision for African evangelical scholars writing and publishing, books by evangelical African scholars can now be found on shelves in libraries and bookshops, including the *African Bible Commentary*, edited by Tokunboh Adeyemo, Kato's successor, and with contributions from seventy African scholars.[258] The *Africa Journal of Evangelical Theology* (*AJET*), based at ACTEA-linked Scott Christian University in Kenya, has been a widely-distributed evangelical theological journal for more than three decades. It is published twice yearly and contains articles and book reviews relating to African theology.

The Theological Commission (which later merged with the Christian Education Commission in 1981) also established a centre for the development of sound biblical and contextualised curriculum for children under fifteen years of age – the Christian Learning Materials Centre (CLMC) – in 1981. The CLMC produces curriculum and materials for children aged up to fifteen years and also provides training for Sunday school teachers and caregivers like grandmothers. CLMC now stands for Christian Learning Materials for Children, and it is also a publishing house. The AEA Theology and Christian Education Commission's plan also included theological education by extension (TEE). Extension or non-formal theological education is not only a

---

257. Bowers, "Byang Kato," 1.
258. Nystrom, "Let African Christians."

cheaper way of providing theological education but also makes theological education accessible to students in their home environments. An assessment of the impact of these schools and initiatives in the church in Africa and beyond could well reveal the extent of the important contribution of Byang Kato.

In considering the specific contribution Kato made to address the theological problem of the church, it is noteworthy that he not only strove to have sound education himself, and to establish advanced theological institutions, but he also encouraged, motivated and mentored his peers and younger leaders to grow in biblical education. A renowned African Christian theological educator and a contemporary of Kato, Tite Tiénou, testifies:

> My own introduction to the importance of theology in Africa dates back to the second general assembly of the Association of Evangelicals in Africa and Madagascar (AEAM) in January 1973 at Limuru in Kenya. It was there that Byang Kato became the first African evangelical leader to call attention to theological endeavours in our part of the world. The challenge he gave marked a turning point in evangelical theological development in Africa.[259]

Kato believed the church's primary challenge was theological education or the lack of it and used every opportunity to change the situation. Bowers states:

> He repeatedly charged African evangelicalism with "theological anaemia," and energetically exploited his position as general secretary of the Association of Evangelicals of Africa and Madagascar to try to change the pattern. He travelled and wrote and spoke constantly in the interest of an accelerated development of evangelical theological education at all levels in Africa. He deliberately sought out and encouraged young aspiring African evangelical scholars in their studies and work. He dreamed up programmes to stimulate greater theological involvement among evangelicals, programmes which are still emerging.[260]

---

259. Tiénou, *Theological Task*, 3.
260. Bowers, "Evangelical Theology," 37.

Kato's understanding of sound Christian education was not just about training in theological educational institutions. He advocated for youth development in the church through the work of various parachurch organisations and through Sunday school. He advocated for the inclusion of youth work in seminary curriculum and the training of pastors.[261]

Byang Kato's contemporary, an octogenarian and a respondent in this research, said: "Kato taught me to be a better farmer and a leader in my church, although I did not go to [formal] school."[262] Kato taught the ordinary folks the Bible in the Hausa language since his early days when he started learning the Scripture in Sunday school. He also taught his own children and neighbours' children just as he did with adults everywhere he lived.

Kato's vision for theological education was not limited to the African church only but extended to the global church as well. This is particularly important, given the current state of the church globally. With the secularisation of the West, the church has been declining there, and at the same time the centre of the church has now shifted to the Global South, with Africa in the forefront. Asumang argues:

> The rapid growth of Christianity in the global south, and the simultaneous but equally rapid decline of a secularised Christianity in the global north, are linked, probably causally, but definitely in terms of their future trajectories. I therefore assert that instead of adopting an introverted postcolonialist outlook, as some theological educators essentially propose, seminaries in the global south must rather be consumed by the global dimension of the mantle that the Spirit is placing on them, and so seek to be imbued with his discerning wisdom for forming future leaders capable of steering the pentecostalised Church unto the kingdom's harvest fields and certainly away from theological graveyards.[263]

Thus, Kato's self-understanding of his Christian identity transcended his African identity. He was the first chair of the Theological Commission of the

---

261. Kato, "Youth," 3–4.

262. Baba Leo, contemporary and childhood friend of Kato in an interview with Research in Kwoi, 22 March 2019

263. Asumang, "Reforming Theological Education," 117–118.

World Evangelical Fellowship (WEF), now the World Evangelical Alliance (WEA). Following the 1974 historic First International Congress on World Evangelization in Lausanne, Switzerland, Kato was appointed to several important committees in the global church. He was appointed secretary to the WEF International Council, chair and convener of the WEF Theological Commission and as a member of the Lausanne Continuation Committee. In his capacity as chair of the WEF Theological Commission, Kato shared in the vision of the commission's executive secretary, Bruce Nicholls, for establishing a link among evangelical theological schools at a global level, similar to the services of the ACTEA network at a continental level. This led to the eventual birth of the International Council for Evangelical Theological Education (ICETE).[264] During the official opening of the AEA complex in Nairobi in April 2019, the AEA general secretary paid glowing tribute to Kato's memory and stated:

> Kato earned himself the accolade of father of evangelical theology in Africa. In his brief years as General Secretary of AEA, before his tragic demise by drowning on the coast of Mombasa in the Indian Ocean, Kato prophetically sounded the warning bells in his *magnum opus – Theological Pitfalls*. Even more importantly, Kato articulated a theological vision to address the malaise in the Church. Five decades on, the core of AEA ministry continues to be the strategic objectives Kato outlined.

When FATEB marked forty years of its existence on 25 January 2017, the head of state and president of the Central Africa Republic (CAR), His Excellency Faustin-Archange Touadéra, was guest of honour, and he used the occasion to confer national honours on the leadership of the school and on the AEA in recognition of, and appreciation for, the work of the theological graduate school in CAR and beyond.

Kato's initiative to launch theological programmes was strategic and may have contributed substantially to the growth of the church in Africa and the development of more theological schools on the continent. However, the current state of the church suggests a dire need for theological training. Hadebe observes: "Theological education as part of higher education has not

---

264. Bowers, "Byang Kato," 4.

escaped commodification. African theologians pioneered resistance against the hegemony of western theologies. However, there are additional factors driving commodification, such as high demand for training that outstrip supply because of the phenomenal growth of Christianity and rise in Christian consumerism."[265] The relatively few training schools and programmes are struggling for sustainability, and many have been pushed to rebranding and shifting their focus to become liberal arts schools, further diminishing the number of theology graduates they produce.

Summary of Kato's Theological Legacy

While some scholars are reticent about Kato's theological contributions, and at best credit him for diagnosing theological problems but offering no solutions, a careful analysis of Kato's work reveals important theological contributions. His magnum opus, *Theological Pitfalls in Africa*, indeed sounded an alarm about the dangers of universalism and syncretism. These were not unfounded complaints, the theological thought leaders in the church at that time were making inroads with their writings and academic work in influential universities. A holistic assessment of Kato's writing reveals his commitment to biblical truth, apostolic teachings and the historic witness of the church.[266] In particular, he addressed important theological issues regarding the uniqueness of God's special revelation, the Bible and salvation in Christ. He also demonstrated the witness and presentation of Christ in the context of non-Christian religions and cultures, especially in Africa.[267]

Kato took the study of Scripture seriously and championed the development of Christian leaders in the church. Not only did he assiduously pursue personal growth, but he also endeavoured to create institutions for higher theological education on the continent. Thus, his contribution cannot be discounted but must instead be recognized as an important contribution to the growth and maturing of the church in Africa. Kato's approach to theological education has implications and lessons from which to glean. Theological education has been identified as one of the greatest challenges facing the

---

265. Hadebe, "Commodification," 1.
266. See Turaki, "Theological Legacy," 137.
267. Turaki, 134–150.

global church, justifying calls for different and innovative approaches for curriculum design and teaching methodology. This is very much in tandem with Kato's approach, to evolve a strategy to train people at all levels.

This chapter has explored three aspects of Kato's theological legacy; namely, hermeneutics, African Christian identity and evangelical theological education. On the question of identity, Kato saw himself as a "Christian African," a third race, different both from the identity of his biological birth and from the colonising culture of the Western missionary. Kato refused to be drawn to the conclusions reached by other scholars of his time that the principal task of theology was a call to deal with culturally rooted questions of African Christian self-identity. The main proponents of African Christian identity conceived theology primarily as a response to missionary underestimation of the value of African traditional religions. Thus, it seems proponents of African theology were concerned about establishing how pre-Christian beliefs would lead them to Christ in the same way as the missionary message from the Bible, even if packaged in Western culture. Kato maintained that you cannot throw the child (the biblical message) out with the bath water (Western cultural nuances). Kato saw conversion to Christianity as a rebirth – being born again of the Spirit – and therefore becoming a new creation. His new identity was primarily that of a Christian, a child of God and follower of Christ, and a new creation, in accordance with what the Bible says (John 1:12; 2 Cor 5:17).

This was not a denial of his Africanness nor a lack of understanding of his African culture. As a matter of fact, Kato's position rose out of his profound understanding of his pre-Christian religion and his newfound biblical faith in Christianity. His early assimilation in African traditional religion was unrivalled by his peers in the academy. His radical conversion could well have links with his knowledge of the deep menaces of his pre-Christian religion, so that embracing the message of his new faith served him as a lifeline of salvation and redemption to hold on to firmly. After all, this is the message of salvation; a call to Christianity is a call to come out of the past and even to launch out to the unknown. A positive response to this call is absolute faith in the One who calls and reliance on his goodness, love, infinite power and sovereignty. Thus, Kato's Christian identity was more important than his ethnicity or African identity.

Not everybody holds Kato in high esteem in the theological community in Africa. Even so, several decades after his death, he is remembered in theological education circles with esteem for his contribution to evangelical theological education. A visitor to renowned institutions like the Africa International University in Nairobi would notice the Kato Memorial Chapel as a centre of worship for the university community. At the Faculté de Théologie Évangélique de Bangui (FATEB) in Central African Republic, the Kato Memorial Library is the centre of student life. In Nigeria, at the ECWA Theological Seminary Jos (JETS), the Byang Kato Research Library is the centre of attraction for the seminary community. Also at JETS, the Byang Kato Memorial Lectures are held regularly.[268] Painting a portrait of Kato at the Forty-First Kato Memorial Lectures, Stephen Baba described him as "Rev Byang Henry Kato, PhD, of a special class, a theologian, an erudite scholar, administrator and an exemplary Church leader, an astute facilitator, and promoter of Christian Evangelical Theological Education in Africa."[269]

Kato's firm belief about the state of the church was "an implicit faith in God's word and an absolute assurance in Jesus Christ as the only solution to the sin problem which is responsible for all human ills is the only bulwark and offensive weapon of the Christian."[270] Kato had a high view of the Bible, as the sole authority for faith and conduct. He affirmed the inerrancy and infallibility of the Bible. He demonstrated a biblical worldview and endeavoured to view reality in terms of what the Bible says. Western missionaries may have done things that did not show respect for Africans and their culture, including their religion. However, the evangelical doctrine of *sola scriptura* affirmed Scripture as the sole basis and authority in matters of faith and conduct and allowed no place for tradition to have similar status. If Western missionaries were misguided in applying Scripture through their own cultural lenses, and therefore needed to be corrected, other cultures that have embraced Christianity should not also be misguided in viewing the gospel from cultural lenses in ways that are opposed to the biblical narrative. This is particularly so when African Christianity is becoming influential in global Christianity.

Nevertheless, Kato may not have done much himself in providing tangible methodical approaches or systematised theological reflections for spreading and preserving biblical Christianity on the continent. In any case, Kato's

---

268. Bowers, "Byang Kato," 1.
269. Baba, "Profile of Dr. Byang."
270. Kato, "Critique of Incipient," ThD diss., 277.

actions, and the projects and institutions he sought to establish, continue to make an important contribution for African theological reflections and the spread and preservation of biblical Christianity in Africa and beyond. The church continues to experience phenomenal growth. However, the challenges Kato faced in terms of biblical illiteracy in the church continue to abound. I will now, in the next two sections, turn to Kato's own limitations and weaknesses and to an overview of the current state of the church in Africa four-and-a-half decades after the death of Kato.

Kato's Theological Pitfalls

Kato was human and erred, with feet of clay. This study has a focus on his theological contribution in a limited area of endeavour, but also his life story is explored. Accordingly, his conduct and Christian ethics are equally of interest in responding to the research questions and purpose of the study. Reflecting on the core theological emphasis, a gap in the articulation of some essential evangelical doctrines was noticed, either by his silence or little emphasis in his proclamations or writings. These were considered as downsides of the otherwise positive contributions, as highlighted in the previous sections.

For example, the evangelical triumvirate affirmation of Bible-centred, Christ-centred and Spirit-led may not have been sufficiently articulated. In Kato's teaching, a balanced emphasis on the Trinity, especially on the place of the Holy Spirit, the third person of the Trinity, is not so evident compared to the emphasis Kato had on the place of the Bible and the place of Christ in the believer's life and in the church. Apparently, his pneumatology tended to be inadequate. However, this does not necessarily mean a lack of understanding of the theology of the Holy Spirit, as demonstrated in a later section in this study.[271] In his work on spirits,[272] which addresses what the Bible teaches on the subject of spirits, his discussion of the created and fallen spirits is extensive compared to the time he invests on the Holy Spirit. In his critique of this work, MacDonald hails Kato for his contribution to demonology and writes:

> Overall, Kato's work presents timely contributions for our demonological goals, especially considering the multicultural context.

---

271. See the section on Kato's theology in chapter 5.
272. Kato, *Spirits*, 1–34.

In an increasingly intermingled world, with many backgrounds being represented in multicultural Christian communities, Kato's demonology is a superior model. Human perceptions concerning the demonic are often inseparable from prevailing cultural attitudes, and the temptation to exalt one's own culture must be avoided, especially due to the new norm of multicultural churches, para-church organizations, and seminaries. Kato's demonology gravitates to the biblical material, and thus it delivers both challenges and affirmations to every party.[273]

The study provided a good understanding about demons and evil spirits. Kato goes on to talk about good spirits and angels and the work they do, including "worship of God, doing God's will, looking after God's chosen people, serving Jesus and helping Christians."[274] However, the place of the Holy Spirit in the believer's life and in *Missio Dei* could have been highlighted much more.

I cannot agree more with Turaki for the need to demonstrate here how the biblical worldview could engage the important subject of spiritism and impact on the African worldview. Belief in evil spirits is so pervasive in the African worldview that simply demystifying the belief at a conceptual level may not be enough to bring about a change in worldview. Articulating the biblical teaching about the Holy Spirit would have been helpful, more so than guardian angels, to bring about transformation in the mindset of African believers and in perspectives about evil spirits. In particular, this applies to the place and work of the Holy Spirit in the life of the believer, and that the Holy Spirit is God himself and like no other spirit (which Kato rightly recognises). However, Kato does testify about the work of the Holy Spirit at his conversion which led to his radical transformation from the worship of idols to surrender to the Triune God.

Kato appears to give the impression that the gospel is limited to being a cure for the soul or spirit of the person, and anything else outside the spirit/soul concern is less of a priority for the gospel. This view does not fully express the potency of the gospel for God's *shalom* and redemption of creation and the whole person. If believers in Christ should obey the second great commandment to love neighbour like self, meeting emotional, social and physical needs

---

273. MacDonald, "Critical Analysis," viii.
274. Kato, *Spirits*, 8–12.

is inevitable and an integral part of the good news of Jesus Christ. Often, love for neighbour cannot be about saving their souls only for future salvation, as much as this is of utmost importance. Biblical salvation does point to the eschaton, but justification and sanctification also have implications for life on this side of eternity. Thus, salvation involves the work of Jesus Christ who justifies and the Holy Spirit who sanctifies. The ministry of Jesus Christ, the Lord of the church, demonstrates the balance between saving the soul and bringing people life and life in abundance (Luke 4:18; John 10:10).

However, the priority and immediacy of evangelism over social action continues to be an important debate in the church. The differing perspectives relate to underlying assumptions in regard to hermeneutics. Currently, many evangelical and biblical scholars seem to be in consensus about the integral or holistic nature of the gospel. Important as the salvation of souls is to gain eternal salvation, the gospel does offer wholeness to the existential hopelessness of the human condition and, indeed, to the whole of creation. The nature of what the holistic gospel is – or whether, in fact, the word "gospel" needs a qualifier – is another dimension of the debate.[275]

In any case, Kato vindicated himself through his leadership and actions during the Biafran War in his country, Nigeria. And his emphasis on sound education was unlike the pietism of his day that perhaps saw higher education as a worldly pursuit. His engagement with political leaders in Zaire (now DRC), for example, and the likes of Emperor Bukasa in CAR, were pointers of one who cannot be seen as only caring for the salvation of souls, with no concern about material well-being. Kato may not have considered his actions as gospel work, especially when it seems that he had a Bible in one hand and gave relief items to the people with the other. On reflection, it was lopsided theology to focus on spirituality and be insensitive to the material or physical reality of people. At the intellectual level, soul-winning was prioritised but his action in developing people complimented soul-winning of people that brought about genuine transformation.

Another pitfall of Kato's theology was the extreme pietistic tendencies that he demonstrated. In particular, his attitude towards ecumenism, and especially AACC as an institution, could have been more positive, and he could have encouraged dialogue and collaboration without necessarily compromising his

---

275. Masika, *Mobilising Mindset Change*, 24–30.

doctrinal and biblical positions. His sentiments about alcohol and dancing, or "body twisting," could have been better moderated. The emphatic statements and biblical references and interpretations may not be consistent with mainstream evangelicalism.[276] However, given the context and time of Kato's ministry, the aftermath of the East African revivals and, to a limited extent, West African revival, Kato's sentiments would have been respectful of the evangelical community, even if not sound biblical injunctions.

A balance between work and family needs was a challenge for Kato. Attention to the emotional and social needs of wives and mothers to ensure they can adequately play their role, especially when the father or husband is away, is an important consideration. While Kato may not have excelled in this matter, his experience demonstrates things to avoid and those to embrace. Leaving the family to go abroad for studies is not setting a good example, but endeavouring to reconnect with the family is an example to be embraced. Kato died at an age and time when he was young, and remuneration systems in the church were inadequate, so the family did not have a home of their own, as was to be expected in that context.

Kato's voice was also silent on doctrines like the sacrament, apart from a brief swipe at Mbiti, writing: "Mbiti widens the gates of 'heaven' through the sacraments of baptism and the Eucharist. He declares, 'Christian Baptism is the means of mediating the implication of Christ's Death and Resurrection, both on individual human and cosmic levels.'"[277] Also, Kato's position on the issue of women in leadership in the church was imprecise. His denomination, ECWA, did not ordain women. Kato stated:

> African Christians owe the missionaries a debt that only eternity knows. Through God's providence many a humble young lady from overseas has been used to establish a thriving church. For this we are grateful. Nevertheless, we must face the fact that many missionary ladies until recently outnumbered men 3 to 1; this is a rebuke for the older churches. This state of affairs is contrary to any New Testament precedent. In fact, it contradicts the Apostle Paul's teaching (2 Tim 2:9–15, 1 Cor 14:34); this is not a criticism of the faithful lady missionaries who stepped in

---

276. Kato, "The Youth in the African Church," 5.
277. Kato, *Theological Pitfalls*, 86.

where men refused to go, but it is a fact that the New Testament does not give us a precedent of a church founded by a lady missionary.²⁷⁸

Notwithstanding the fact that Kato had a missionary lady for a spiritual mother and mentor, he held the view that women missionary leaders were a misnomer. While there is no conclusive agreement in the church about women in leadership, current positions tend to be in favour of female leadership as a valid biblical position.

In any case, while Kato was reacting mostly to the theological agendas of other theologians by pointing out the theological pitfalls he saw in their theologies, he did outline his own theological beliefs on the issues he encountered in the process. Thus, there could have been other theological subjects Kato could have deliberated, under a different set of circumstances or had he lived a longer life.

Current State of the Church in Africa in View of Kato's Theological Legacy

During the lifetime of Kato, the church in Africa was experiencing growth. And like the population rate in Africa, the growth of the church has continued at a phenomenal rate to this day. According to Kato, the population of Africa was nearly 100 million with a Christian population of about 20 million.²⁷⁹ However, there was not a single evangelical graduate theological school on the continent. In 2018, Africa's Christian population was 631 million out of a population of about 1.3 billion.²⁸⁰ Thus, Africa became the region with the largest number of Christians for the first time. Despite the phenomenal growth of the church, African society has not experienced the kind of transformation expected in a predominantly Christian society. The gospel does not seem to have much impact by way of transforming the society. "There is the need for authentic emphasis on Christian beliefs and practices. Christianity in Africa must pursue a depth in the context of its shallow profession of the

---

278. Kato, "Theological Trends," 2.
279. Kato, *Biblical Christianity*, 13.
280. Johnson, "Christianity 2018".

Christian faith. By the depth, it must seek to place value on Christian professions of the faith and Christian practices."²⁸¹

Restating an anecdotal comment by an observer, Tiénou wrote: "Africa is the fastest growing church in the world; it may also have the fastest declining church."²⁸² Accordingly, Otonko states:

> This rapid growth in numbers of Christians in Africa does not often correspond with the authentic translation of the Christian faith in the daily affairs of the peoples. This incapacity of the Christian faith is seen in the inability of the growing numbers of Christians to transform the public space. The paradox of growing Christian presence and growing poverty, corruption, bad government, disease, failed service delivery and several dysfunctional states challenge the effective impact of this Christian presence. It seems the rhetoric of numbers has not translated directly into Christian practice.²⁸³

The same challenges of syncretism, universalism and religious relativism the church faced in the first two centuries has continued "to be the same in the twentieth century and will continue to be so in the future."²⁸⁴ Every generation of Christians must be on guard to fight against the world's culture undermining the gospel regardless of where that culture is located. The European or Western Christian has much the same battle as the African Christian. Syncretism is always a danger lurking at the door of every Christian generation. Then what Kato's warning amounts to is constant awareness and vigilance, and Kato's prophetic voice needs to be heard again as a wakeup call, as secularism and syncretism continue to be on the rise.

The theological challenges the church continues to face in Africa are largely a question of biblical interpretation: "The way people understand, translate and apply the message of the Bible in their culture needs to be assessed with care. People are not without presuppositions shaped by historical, social and cultural processes."²⁸⁵ The African traditional worldview is still predominant

---

281. Otonko, "Beyond the Rhetoric," 10.
282. Tiénou, *Theological Task in Africa: Where are We Now*, 3.
283. Otonko, "Beyond the Rhetoric," 1.
284. Kato, *Theological Pitfalls*, 172.
285. MacDonald, "Critical Analysis," 11–12.

in the church. In this regard, Kato's hermeneutics have much to contribute to today. What Kato saw as emerging Christo-paganism in the church in his time has become the more dominant face of the church.

Cole describes the church in contemporary times as New Generation Christianity (NGC).[286] According to Cole, NGC now dominates the landscape of Christianity in Africa. NGC includes Pentecostal and charismatic movements and can be found across all confessional traditions and denominational divides. Some of these churches have had tremendous impact on the church around the world; they are seen to be scratching where people itch, addressing or at least talking about felt human and societal needs and not just about soul and spirit. However, this is not without commodification of the gospel. There is the tendency to unwittingly appropriate ATR worldviews or Western lifestyles; their theologies and practices are expressed in their hymnologies, prayers and proclamations. Some of the older historic churches are also adopting the same worldviews and theologies as part of the competition for numbers. Quoting Edwin Smith, Cole says: "The African is seeking practical ends in both his magic and his religions. He seeks to use the mysterious powers of nature for his benefit, or tries to ward off the harm that may cause him."[287] Almost a century after Smith these observations may still be true in many contemporary African churches. Hiebert writes: "It is all too easy to make Christianity a new magic in which we as gods can make God do our bidding."[288] Many in the church profess faith in Christianity, but their reality and practices are informed by beliefs in ATR. NGC has striking similarities and parallels to ATR. The following table shows the comparison and similarities between NGC and ATR beliefs.

---

286. Cole, "State of Theological," 1.

287. Isaac Cole, professor of Christian Education, Africa International University, Nairobi Kenya, Paper presented at AEA Theological Consultation of Theological Educators, Nairobi, September 2019

288. Hiebert, *Anthropological Reflections*, 201.

Table 1: Drawing a Parallel between ATR and the New Generation Christianity[289]

African Traditional Religions	New Generation Christianity
Religion permeates all of life	Religion addresses the social and material needs – now, not just the future!
Nothing happens by chance	Causality of happenstances, especially adversity, is sought from one's past, including one's ancestors (e.g. "breaking past covenants")
Diviners occupied a prominent role as consultants on a range of life issues – birth, destiny, marriage, sickness, adversity, counteracting known and unknown enemies, etc.	The "man/woman of God" plays the role of a modern-day diviner/consultant and is sought after on a range of life issues (business, family matters, adversity, illnesses, etc.)
Belief in the efficacy of special objects sought from the diviner	Widespread belief in the efficacy of "holy water," special handkerchiefs, "anointing oil," etc., provided by the "man/woman of God"
Fear of malevolent forces, seen and unseen, and the constant struggle to checkmate them	Ongoing fear of malevolent forces and the need to invoke "the Blood of Jesus," the "Name of Jesus," etc.

The table highlights the extent of the challenge of how well integrated the African traditional worldview abides in the psyche and practices of Christians in Africa. Biri writes:

> Many Pentecostal or "born again" church services are characterised by the theology of "deliverance from powers of darkness" that ruin the life of a Christian. Located within the rubric of "powers of darkness" are African traditional religions and culture (ATRs). ATRs have been condemned by Pentecostals as demonic so a "born again" Christian needs a "total break from the past," supposedly achieved through its denunciation.[290]

---

289. Cole, "State of Theological," 4.
290. Biri, "Silent Echoing Voice," 1.

Paradoxically, the practices of the church are sometimes no less than a form of ATR but in the name of Christianity. Biri argues that "the traditional religion and culture inform Pentecostals and continue to be a source of reflection, meaning and purpose, manifesting in their theology and rituals in spite of the adversarial stance."[291] This raises questions about the path for theologians and scholars in promoting authentic African biblical Christianity.

The missionary influence in the church in Africa tends to have waned. Meanwhile, the once heathen sub-Saharan African nations, ripe for evangelisation by European and American missionaries, have become a Christian majority region and a mission force of their own, sending missionaries to the same American and European nations, as well as other parts of the world. Ward observes:

> Ironically, both America and Pentecostals were commonly associated at the beginning of the twentieth century with a new world, an anti-colonial mentality. By the end of the twentieth century America seemed to be the chief bearer of a form of Western, Christian, neo-imperialism. Pentecostalism often does seem unashamedly to promote capitalism in its American expression. The gospel of wealth and prosperity may seem to appeal to crass forms of materialism.[292]

The newer forms of missionary work in African Christianity are characterised by Pentecostalism and American evangelism. The need is for the new majority church to propagate a gospel that is biblical and understood in other cultures. The next section will specifically assess the state of the theological categories of Kato's theological legacy in this study.

Contemporary Resonance of Kato's Hermeneutics, Identity and Theological Education

African theologians continue to debate approaches to the way the gospel of Christ is proclaimed in Africa and the importance of pre-Christian religious beliefs. Turaki opines: "The dominant presence of the African

---

291. Biri, 1.
292. Ward, "Christianity," 87.

traditional religions and their powerful religious worldview have ever posed great challenges to the presentation of the Gospel of Christ and the rooting of Christianity in Africa."²⁹³ Thus, Christianity was mixed with cultural traditions and practices in the church have been syncretistic. Turaki observes further: "The reaction of the non-Christian world is to relativitise Christianity and make it at par with other religions. Plurality of religions and cultures means that none is unique or superior, that all are equal."²⁹⁴ This mentality remains prevalent even among the leaders of the church in Africa.

African Christian theologians' search for identity may lead to the creation of African Christian theology as a separate discipline. The primary goal for proponents of African Christian theology seems to be peeling off the culture of Western missionaries and wrapping theology in African culture, with no serious commitment to the Bible. Byang Kato saw this move as counter-intuitive and perilous to the Christian faith. Kato insisted that sound contextual theology should be consistent with Christian Scripture, the Bible. He was not opposed to Africans theologizing in itself. Kato wrote: "If there is any need in the Church of Christ in Africa today, it is the need for theology expressed in the context of Africa by Africans and for Africans"²⁹⁵ Further, Kato said:

> There are certain issues peculiar to Africa where only African theologians may be able to speak effectively. Such issues include polygamy, family systems, courtship and marriage, liturgy, the spirit world and cultural revolution. In dealing with these issues, the ever-abiding Word of God remains the authoritative source.

Over four decades after the death of Kato, some of the key issues he highlighted continue to be prevalent in the church in Africa. Concerns are still being raised on both sides of the divide between the liberal ecumenists and the evangelicals (as Kato categorised the Protestant church) about the state of theological education on the continent. In the last four months of 2019, both AEA and AACC mounted significant theological consultations in Nairobi in response to the alarming rate of theological heresies on the continent. The AEA Theology and Christian Education Commission's

---

293. Turaki, "Theological Legacy," 135; see also Biri, "Silent Echoing Voice," and Otonko, "Beyond the Rhetoric."
294. Turaki, "Theological Legacy," 139.
295. Kato, "Written Theology."

theological consultation was held 8–13 September 2019. In the invitation letter to participants, the organisers stated:

> One of the greatest challenges facing the Church today is the lack of sound biblical and theological education for ministers of the gospel of the good news of Jesus Christ. In spite of the phenomenal growth of the Church in Africa, the society has not been proportionately impacted. Research studies reveal that 85–90% of pastors and church leaders in Africa have little to no biblical and theological training required to effectively disciple their congregations.[296]

The AACC has also identified what they termed "Misleading theologies on the continent."[297] In a concept note for a symposium to address the issue, the AACC stated:

> The AACC through its theology, interfaith relations and ecclesial leadership development department is preparing this symposium to accompany the churches in Africa in the area of promoting relevant contextual theology in the continent and to engage with churches in *theology that promotes life with dignity*. Also to engage churches in identifying, analyzing and deconstructing misleading theologies on the continent.[298]

Institutional leaders in theological education are equally concerned about the state of theological education on the continent. According to Van Rensburg, "the biggest crisis facing the global evangelical church today is the fact that most pastors, missionaries, and Christian leaders have no formal theological training."[299] The WEA also identifies biblical illiteracy as the leading challenge in the world today.[300] The church in Africa is growing at a

---

[296]. Association of Evangelicals in Africa Theological Training Conference, Nairobi, Kenya,. 9–11 September 2019 Seminar on

[297]. All Africa Conference of Churches "Concept Note", Symposium on Addressing Misleading Theologies, Nairobi, Kenya, 23–27 October 2019, Hardcopy circular Invitation Letter

[298]. All Africa Conference of Churches, "Concept Note," Symposium on Addressing Misleading Theologies, Nairobi, Kenya, 23–27 October 2019. Emphasis mine.

[299]. Van Reinburg, Reuben. *Introducing Re-Forma to the AEA General Secretary in an Email Communication on 18 July 2019*

[300]. https://www.christianpost.com/news/wea-head-biblical-illiteracy-utmost-problem-facing-church.html

phenomenal rate and even though every year thousands of new churches are planted, they are pastored by people without any formal theological or college and seminary training. Assessing the state of theological education fourteen years following Kato's vision for theological initiatives on the continent, Tite Tiénou has made the following assertions:

> Indeed, while all of these initiatives have made laudatory contributions, some perhaps more so than others, not one has yet become effectively settled, not one is yet securely in orbit. And there is still so much else needing to be done. Assuredly as we survey the scene today, ·we are forced to acknowledge that evangelicals have a long way yet to go in achieving Kato's vision for evangelical theological responsibility and maturity in Africa.[301]

Tiénou goes on to enumerate the root causes of the theological malaise. According to Tiénou, part of the reason is that "when we think of theologians, most of us do not automatically think of people of non-European stock. Theology as we experience it in Africa is basically of European origin"[302] He has also highlighted the following factors as causes of the theological malaise:

> Proclamation without reflection and theological responsibility; fragmentation of the church along doctrinal and denominational lines, which prevents evangelicals from working together on a common theological agenda, resulting to many groups working alone, and even when cooperation is agreed, each group wants to participate on its own terms. Other factors include shortage of trained evangelical theologians, and unconstructive instinct for power and control.[303]

He has said the consequences of these lapses were dire in weakening the Church in Africa, and included (1) silence by default – African theology was being constructed without contribution from evangelicals, and there was little contribution of evangelicals in scholarly publications; (2) numerical growth outpaced the spiritual depth and maturity of African Christianity; and (3) the concerns of African theology, with its three distinct branches of

---

301. Tiénou, *Theological Task*, 4.
302. Tiénou, 4–5.
303. Tiénou, 5

inculturation – cultural identity, Black theology, and liberation theology – each dealing with dominant problems experienced by Africans.[304]

However, Tiénou posits that these problems are not perceived as theological issues by ordinary African Christian at the grassroots level; they are generated as theological tasks by academics. Theologians have typically been elite scholars in ivory towers constantly addressing issues of an abstract philosophical nature, which while important, has borne little relevance to the day-to-day Christian witness of ordinary believers. Nonetheless, theology should, he says, fundamentally be concerned with how Africans can be real Christians in the African context, which he refers to as popular theology. Thus, he sees the challenge for bridging the gap between these two forms of theologizing: academic theology and popular theology. Academic theology has been written for international readership. Tiénou admits that even his own works and Kato's must be included in this category of academic theology. Many people in the local church may not be aware of these works or read them, as they are not intended for popular consumption.

Popular theology on the other hand is what takes root in the heart of most African Christians. This is the theology expressed in singing and praising God, in preaching, and in the everyday admonition and counsel of the people's spiritual leaders and pastors. Theologically, a lot goes on at the popular level and little at the academic level in Africa. This situation is alarming because popular theology is not grounded and governed by Scripture. The way many pastors preach and give counsel may be completely at variance with sound scriptural interpretation. Tiénou says the solution to this challenge lies within reach of African evangelicals, who are strategically placed to come up with a third option for theological education – one which does not necessarily disdain academic discussion nor neglect real life daily issues. Quoting David Bosch, Tiénou writes: "Good theology always arises out of an encountering situation; that is to say, in the crucible of actual ministry. . . . So it was for biblical writers – NT theology was not produced in ivory towers."[305]

Pastors need to know how to interpret the Bible correctly and apply it to their context. If a proper interpretation of Scripture takes place at the grassroots level by the pastor, informed by a proper understanding of the context

---

304. Tiénou, Issues in the Theological Task, 5. Cf. Otonko, "Beyond the Rhetoric."
305. Bosch, *Transforming Mission*, quoted in Tiénou, *Theological Task*, 7.

of the people's culture, then such a pastor's preaching and counselling will be demonstrating sound African Christian theology. A Lausanne Occasional Paper states: "The purely academic pursuit of theology is a mis-direction and a distortion of the purpose of equipping of the saints for ministry. We do well to heed Robert Ferris' call to move away from 'theology-as-science,' a legacy of the Enlightenment, to 'theology-as-engagement.'"[306] Asumang proposes "that seminaries in the south be consumed by the global dimensions of the mantle that the Spirit has placed on them to form leaders capable of steering the pentecostalised Church into the kingdom's harvest fields, both north and south, and certainly away from theological graveyards."[307] Asumang goes on to examine the practical outworking of this reforming agenda in six areas; namely, (1) theology of theological education, (2) access to that education, (3) curriculum design, (4) resource development, (5) research and (6) seminary-church relationships.

An assessment of the WEA Mission Commission (WEA-MC) highlights how secularism, or so-called post-Christianity, as a new form of syncretism in the church, is growing in many places, even in the Global South. The WEA-MC's description of the church in the Global South could be emblematic of the contemporary African church, as now the typical face of the contemporary church in the world.[308] The WEA-Mission Commission Report, 2017 highlights the need for a new reformation. According to the report, the fifteenth century Reformation was more of a European reformation, and only secondarily did the Global South benefit from its impact. The Roman Catholic Church had much of an influence in the rest of the world, and later along with Protestant missionary presence, and with local or indigenous religions, continued its influence in receiving countries in the Global South. "We realise that a new reformation is needed. A call to recover the integrity of the Church is heard more in the global South."[309] Further, the report states how the once missionary-sending regions with evangelical zeal were now in need of missionaries from the Global South.

---

306. Theron and Raiter, *Effective Theological Education*, 18; cf. Asumang, "Reforming Theological Education," 121.

307. Asumang, 115

308. Walls, *Cross-Cultural Process*, 85.

309. Ruiz and Ekstrom, WEA-Mission Commission, Presentation at WEA Annual International Leadership Meeting, Bad Blankenburg, Germany, March 2017 "New Reformation."

With the phenomenal growth of the church in the majority world, especially in Africa, there is a need to train leaders to handle God's word with integrity and manage their congregations well. According to Chris Paul, "Most of the emerging churches are made up of first-generation believers. Therefore, they come with totally different sets of worldviews. They lack deep discipleship under the lordship of Jesus Christ in their lives, which would transform their worldviews."[310] The new believers would require informal training, flexible and adaptable learning methods and materials, with sound biblical basis.[311] However, given the challenges associated with national educational accreditation, it may well be necessary for seminaries in Africa to seek ways of supporting two-tier systems. Students of lower academic qualifications could be allowed to pursue good quality theological education, yet be covered by accreditation of an interim character, in preparation for entry to fully accredited programs. Additionally, extension programmes such as church seminars and "taster courses" should be provided, since they increase the access of rank-and-file church members to theological educators. This will also serve to demystify theological education and reduce the often justified suspicions some believers hold against the educational enterprise.

Legacy of Mission and Culture Debates

As mentioned earlier, it was Kwame Bediako who invested some time into his research on Byang Kato. More importantly, Bediako, like Kato, went beyond polemics and established an outstanding institution to continue to advance his vision of theology and theological education. The Akrofi-Christaller Institute of Theology, Mission and Culture (ACI), a postgraduate research university, was established in Ghana in 1987, with Kwame Bediako as the founding rector. The antecedent of ACI was a missionary training seminary, established by the Presbyterians in the 1840s. The name "Akrofi-Christaller" is in honour of two pioneer figures in the "cultural witness of the Church in Ghana, Clement Anderson Akrofi and Johannes Gottlieb Christaller."[312] The university's objec-

---

310. Chrispal, "Restoring Missional Vision."
311. Asumang, "Reforming Theological Education," 131.
312. "Our History," Akrofi-Christaller Institute of Theology, Mission and Culture, https://www.aci.edu.gh/aci/the-institute/about-us.

tive is to promote African innovation, and it is dedicated to the study and documentation of Christian history, thought and life in Africa. The institute affirms Scripture as the word of God, the uniqueness of Jesus Christ as sole Redeemer and Lord, and the regeneration and sanctifying role of the Holy Spirit in the individual, and in the church, and his enabling in the Christian witness to society and the world. The institute is committed to a spiritual view of life, to the spiritual renewal of the church and to socio-political and cultural transformation through the gospel.[313]

Some of ACI's core programmes include African and world Christianity, biblical studies in the African context and Bible translation and interpretation so students from all over the world can undertake studies in "the *forms and traditions of African Christian life and thought emerging as a distinctive strand of non-western Christianity with potential to contributing to world Christianity.*"[314] The research centres and interests include interfaith studies and engagement in Africa, gospel and culture engagement, early African Christianity, and primal and Christian spirituality. Describing the later research focus, it is noted:

> Contrary to the prevailing view among evangelicals, vital Christianity has always been built on a primal substructure. By contrast, Christianity that has lost its primal vision has declined. Where indigenous knowledge is now acknowledged generally to have much to contribute to human enhancement, contrary to earlier negative estimations, the same is true in the area of Christian mission and spiritual renewal, with respect to the primal substructure of religion and culture.[315]

Therefore, it is evident that Bediako's legacy seems entrenched and influential, certainly in some of the research objectives and aims of this institution. But also, with the prevailing secularism and humanism, a newer definition of African evangelicalism may appear to be emerging as the representative

---

313. See the website for the Akrofi-Christaller Institute of Theology, Mission and Culture (https://www.aci.edu.gh/).

314. "Master of Theology (MTh)," Akrofi-Christaller Institute of Theology, Mission and Culture, https://www.aci.edu.gh/academics/programmes/master-of-theology-ac-bti. Emphasis mine.

315. "Centre for Primal and Christian Spirituality (CEPACS)," Akrofi-Christaller Institute of Theology, Mission and Culture, https://www.aci.edu.gh/research/centres/cepacs.

brand. A recent publication of a handbook by the WEA, *Evangelicals around the World*, featured eight personalities from the mid-1800s into the current century in an article titled "Evangelicals You Would Want to Know." Notably, Kato was not among the eight personalities, while Bediako was featured among the eight leading evangelicals from Africa.[316] Thus the importance of exploring Kato, in order to distil and apply his legacy with its contemporary relevance. Notwithstanding the growing challenge, the contribution of Kato's endeavours to address the theological challenges should not be underrated.

Conclusion

Following Kato's conversion to Christianity from ATR, he pursued and excelled in a rigorous programme of biblical and theological training. He demonstrated a biblical worldview and held a high view of the Bible, its inerrancy, infallibility and authority as God's word. The Bible for Kato was the final authority for faith and conduct and sole source for Christian theology.

Based on his biblical hermeneutics, he confronted many of the theological scholars of his time and several issues that he perceived were heresies in the church in Africa. Notably, he endeavoured to draw a distinction between African traditional religions and the Christian faith to avoid syncretism, and he advocated for authentic biblical Christianity from an evangelical perspective. He rejected universalism and affirmed the unique and only way of salvation in Jesus Christ.

Salvation in Christ meant a transformed life and conferred identity and self-understanding, a solution to the elusive search for African Christian identity. Notwithstanding the diversity and pluralities of identities, humans belong to two categories: those saved in Christ and those dead and lost in sin. Thus, Kato believed that being in Christ was far more fulfilling and liberating than ethnic identity, and he therewith affirmed a Christian African identity. In Kato's opposition to the theological teachings of many scholars of his time, he contributed to defining and shaping evangelicalism, especially in the African context.

Kato was perhaps one of the best placed theologians of his time to engage ATR. He probably had more experience in ATR practices than his peers, both

---

316. Hickman, "Evangelicals," 227.

his detractors and those who supported him. However, and despite Kato's efforts, ATR beliefs are still influencing the church in Africa today. The promise of a transformed society through Christian ethics, even in a Christian-majority region, appears to have eluded Africa. Perhaps Kato could have done more about how the biblical worldview could have engaged or confronted the pervasive ATR worldview. Yet the time allowed him for ministry was short. Nevertheless, he did lay the foundation for sound theological education to promote a biblical worldview.[317]

Kato may have argued the evangelical doctrines reasonably well, but that the praxis of many in the church did not align with these doctrines continues as a conundrum. I will now turn to a dialogical analysis of Kato's views against other scholars and materials considered to be mainstream evangelical.

---

317. See Chalk, *Making Disciples*; Mburu, *African Hermeneutics*; Turaki, *Engaging Religions*.

CHAPTER 4

Theological and Biblical Foundations for African Christian Identity, Hermeneutics and Evangelical Theological Education

Overview

This chapter seeks to provide theological and biblical data against which Kato's contribution may be assessed. It traces, though briefly, how classical or orthodox beliefs of the church, consistent with mainstream evangelical understanding, were established. Specifically, Kato's views on the issues of biblical hermeneutics, African Christian identity and theological education will be examined, considering the orthodox teachings and beliefs of the church, rooted in the apostolic teachings in the New Testament church, handed down to the contemporary church, which Kato professed to defend.

No one theologian or person has the final word or flawless theology: "All theology involves fallible human beings interpreting God's word and will. Although we rely on the Holy Spirit to guide us into all truth, our limited knowledge and sinful nature make it possible that our interpretation is incorrect or imperfect."[1] It is possible that some perspectives or stances Kato took, even with the best of intention to be faithful to the Bible, could be unbiblical.

---

1. Smith, *Integrated Theology*, 39.

Aware of this reality, Kato stated in an address to leaders of the National Association of Evangelicals in the USA:

> Then there are all these different relationships. So, when some fear we are too far to the right, some too far to the left, where do we fit in? Well, we need a lot of prudence and perception. And we would appreciate very much your prayers for the evangelical Christians in Africa as we seek to be as wise as serpents and harmless as doves in our day.[2]

Therefore, Kato's defence of African evangelicalism must be weighed against a broader context of biblical and theological foundations of classical Christianity. Thus the materials surveyed include works by scholars from Africa, from the West and from other parts of the world.

The rest of this chapter is divided into four main sections. The first section deals with some essential tenets of mainstream evangelicalism, followed by the way the classical doctrines were established and sustained from the New Testament era to modern times through the medieval and Reformation eras. The theological and biblical foundations of Kato's legacy of (1) hermeneutics, (2) African Christian identity and (3) theological education will be examined.

Tenets of Evangelicalism as Background to Kato's Theology

Given the ambiguity about evangelicalism, some clarity about mainstream evangelicalism is required. Theological texts in the global church have long been the work of Western writers. Current endeavours by scholars in the majority world, especially in Africa, are critical and laudable. Kato's vision to have evangelical theological scholarship in Africa saw the establishment of several institutions. However, Kato's effort at initiating the evangelical theological enterprise in Africa was against the background of the elusiveness and confusion about what evangelicalism is.[3] Evangelicalism grapples with the enigma of popularity and disfavour.[4]

---

2. Kato, "Africa: Prudence," 17.
3. Shiriki, "African Christians," 136.
4. Stott, *Evangelical Truth*, 16; cf. Sider, "Evangelicals and Social Justice."

John Stott expounds on the defining essence of evangelicalism. Stott first makes three disclaimers about what evangelism is not[5]: First, it is not a recent innovation; rather, "evangelical Christianity is the original, apostolic, New Testament Christianity."[6] The Reformers contended for the same thing in the sixteenth century, as they sought to go back in time to recover the authentic original gospel. They were charged with heresy by the Roman Catholic church for invention. In a rebuttal to the charge, Stott quotes from John Jewel's *Apology of the Church of England* (1562): "It is not our doctrine that we bring you this day; we wrote it not, we found it not out, we are not inventors of it, we bring you nothing but what the old fathers of the church, what the apostles, what Christ our Saviour himself hath brought before us."[7] Stott asserts that the same criticisms and charges of being innovators that have been brought against evangelical Christians have been heard in every generation, and the charges have always met similar rebuttals. In Africa, Kato took a robust posture for evangelical or biblical Christianity, writing:

> We are engaged in a battle for survival of sound biblical Christianity in the African continent. Should the revealed Christian faith be sacrificed at the altar of syncretistic universalism, in the guise of contextualisation? Should the church in Africa exchange eternal values of the Kerygma for "one morsel"? Or is the evangelical concern for eternal values nothing more than a "pie-in-the-sky by-and by" theology? These are the issues that require attention in Africa today.[8]

The well-known evangelist, Billy Graham, faced similar charges at the beginning of his ministry. He was said to be "hopelessly out of date, setting back the cause of religion a hundred years."[9] According to Stott, Billy Graham's rejoinder was "I did indeed want to set religion back – not just 100 years but 1900 years, to the Book of Acts, where first century followers of Christ were accused of turning the Roman Empire upside down."[10] Kato had his

---

5. Stott, *Evangelical Truth*, 16–20.
6. Stott, 16.
7. Quoted in Stott, 17; cf. Oden, *Rebirth of Orthodoxy*; Oden, *Rebirth of African Orthodoxy*.
8. Kato, *Biblical Christianity*, 15.
9. Stott, *Evangelical Truth*, 17.
10. Stott, 17.

share of such criticism: "Byang Kato was most notable as the dissenting voice in the chorus of positive evaluations of the African pre-Christian religious heritage.... His own acultural conception of theology in fact, defeated the very purpose of theology as the struggle with culturally-rooted questions."[11]

The second disclaimer Stott states is that the evangelical faith is not a deviation from Christian orthodoxy. Evangelicalism is mainstream Christianity, Christians "who attribute ultimate authority to Scripture and Salvation to Christ crucified alone."[12] Both Kato's supporters and his critics credit Kato for his high view of the Bible, and they respectively either affirm or critique him for his overzealousness to proclaim the resurrected Christ as the only way for salvation. Third, Stott states that the evangelical faith is not a synonym for fundamentalism. The word "fundamentalism" originally referred to publications of Christian truths or affirmations of the Christian faith called "The Fundamentals." However, the word has become a slur which evangelicals reject; they would not accept the fundamentalist label.[13] However, the word evangelical and evangelicalism became current in modern church history, culminating in the beginnings of the World Evangelical Alliance in 1846, albeit as a primarily British endeavour. The WEA reorganised as a global entity in 1951 (with the name World Evangelical Fellowship, but then resumed the WEA name in 2001).[14]

Stott gives a more positive description of evangelical essentials. These, in reality, relate to the three persons of the Trinity – "the authority of God in and through Scripture, the majesty of Jesus Christ in and through the Cross, and the lordship of the Holy Spirit in and through his manifold ministries."[15] This was built on David Bebbington's survey findings of four main characteristics of evangelicalism – conversionism, activism, biblicism and crucicentrism (i.e. a stress on the Bible and the cross, evangelism and conversion).[16] Stott further extrapolates:

---

11. Bediako, *Theology and Identity*, xviii.
12. Stott, *Evangelical Truth*, 18.
13. Stott, 19–20.
14. "Our History," World Evangelical Alliance, accessed 28 April 2020, https://worldea.org/who-we-are/our-history/.
15. Stott, *Evangelical Truth*, 28.
16. Bebbington, *Evangelicalism*, 27.

In seeking to define what it means to be evangelical; it is inevitable that we begin with the gospel. For both our theology (evangelicalism) and our activity (evangelism) derive their meaning and importance from the good news (the evangel). And when we are thinking about the gospel, three fundamental questions and answers are bound to formulate in our minds regarding the origin, the substance and the efficacy of the gospel. They occur in 1 Corinthians 2:1–5, where Paul states his position over against the false teachers who were disturbing the Corinthian church.[17]

Having carefully expounded the passage in 1 Corinthians, Stott concludes his treatise on the tenets of evangelical Christianity as follows:

> I have been at pains to argue that evangelical Christianity is trinitarian Christianity. We hold the three "Rs" – revelation, redemption and regeneration, associating revelation with the Father, redemption with the Son and regeneration with the Holy Spirit. We desire above all else to bear witness to the supreme authority of the Word of God, the atoning efficacy of the cross of Christ and the indispensable ministries of the Holy Spirit.[18]

Underscoring the humility with which the evangelical faith is engendered, in spite of the reputation and the charge by others that evangelicalism is characterised by pride, arrogance, vanity and conceit, Stott states:

> Yet the more the three persons of the Trinity are glorified, the more completely human pride is excluded. To magnify the self-revelation of God is to confess our complete ignorance without it. To magnify the cross of Christ is to confess our utter lostness without it. To magnify the regenerating, indwelling and sanctifying role of the Holy Spirit is to confess our abiding self-centredness without it.[19]

The word, the cross and the Spirit have a very special place in the thinking and mindset of evangelicals, and they are at the core of the worldview

---

17. Stott, *Evangelical Truth*, 28–29.
18. Stott, 145–146.
19. Stott, 146.

assumptions through which they view reality, thus at the heart of their hermeneutics. Given the pride of place John Stott holds in global evangelicalism, his outline here about the fundamental tenets would be representative of mainstream evangelicalism. Much of what Kato pleaded for would resonate with much of Stott's analysis.

Historical Sketch of the Development of Evangelical Orthodoxy

The church in the current era can look back on two millennia of human culture and the grounding of scriptural integrity by objective approaches or methods. This subsection attempts to outline how the classic Christian doctrines were established and handed down to the church from New Testament times. The proper source(s) for constructing orthodoxy was a key pre-occupation of Kato in his arguments with his detractors and is an important aspect of the discipline of historical theology.

Classical Ecumenical Approach to Christianity

In the formative centuries of early Christianity, the worshipping community defined the shape of classic Christianity. In discerning the meaning of Scripture and faith, they established orthodoxy using reliable interpretive methods. Orthodoxy, according to Oden, is the "integrated biblical teaching as interpreted in its most consensual classic period – Classic Christian teaching – and by which truth-claims are assessed."[20] This approach is also referred to as the classic ecumenical method.[21]

It is necessary to explain or define briefly the two words or concepts: "orthodox" or "orthodoxy" and "ecumenical." Simply, orthodoxy is a concept opposite to heresy or heterodoxy or non-orthodoxy.[22] Bebis proffers a concise description of the words orthodox and orthodoxy, and the way related derivatives are used:

> The terms "Orthodox" and "Orthodoxy" (from the Greek orthos, "right," and doxa, "opinion" or "doctrine") appeared in

---

20. Oden, *Rebirth of Orthodoxy*, 33.
21. Oden, 183–207.
22. Porumb, "Orthodoxy and Ecumenism," 9.

the fourth century A.D., and became common to refer to "true doctrine" and "true practice." The term Orthodox Church now refers to those churches also known as the Eastern Orthodox Church, the Orthodox Catholic Church, or the Greek Orthodox Church. Orthodox in this modern sense contrasts with Roman Catholic, Protestant, and Nestorian and Coptic Churches of the east. The Niceno-Constantinopolitan Creed (381) defined the Church as "one, holy, catholic, and apostolic" without the use of the term "Orthodox," because it and other creeds were themselves a definition of what right doctrine was. The terminology of the Orthodox Church arose (e.g. Justinian, Cod. 1.5.214) in contrast to positions defined by the ancient church as heretical.[23]

Biblical orthodoxy refers to the inheritance from and connection to the apostolic era and early centuries of Christianity. The evolution of Christian orthodoxy was based on already established principles, familiar to the worshipping community.[24]

"Ecumenical," like the word "evangelical," has also become a contentious word in modern times.[25] However, according to Oden: "Ecumenism is Christian unity, based expressly upon Christian truth, rather than a union for absolute toleration, allowing anyone to bring to the table any faith-feeling."[26] Kato could not agree with Oden more. He argues for church unity that is based on doctrine, consistent with the early ecumenical councils.[27] Therefore, ecumenism as here defined should not be confused with the ecumenical movement as promoted by the World Council of Churches (WCC).[28] Modern conciliar and bureaucratic ecumenism may not be succeeding in uniting the church.

In the thirteen-chapter *Theological Pitfalls in Africa*, Kato developed three chapters underscoring his concerns about modern liberal ecumenism. He wrote:

---

23. Bebis, "Orthodox Church," 841.
24. Harnack, *Mission and Expansion*, 81–82.
25. Sider, "Still Evangelical"; cf. von Sinner, "Ecumenism," 2.
26. Oden, *Rebirth of Orthodoxy*, 69.
27. Kato, *Theological Pitfalls*, 130.
28. Oden, *Rebirth of Orthodoxy*, 67.

> The basic problem of ecumenicism is the lack of an authoritative source for the meaning of salvation. The word liberal[29] means a person who, among other things, does not accept the absolute authority of the Bible. While evangelicals hold that the Bible is the word of God, liberals advocate that the Bible contains the Word of God.[30]

However, ancient ecumenism's methods of consensual affirmation were a viable means of learning about the Christian faith in the church.[31] Most of the fundamental doctrines of the church, represented in confessional statements or creeds common in the different traditions of the church, came into being through the ancient ecumenical method. Kato stated:

> Early "ecumenical" church councils were very concerned about doctrine. In fact, for the first millennium of the Christian era, every Council condemned a major heresy. For example, the orthodox council meeting in Nicaea 1 (325) condemned Arianism which reduced the deity of Jesus Christ, that exalted the humanity of Christ at the expense of his deity. Although ecclesiastical politics played a major part in some of the struggles, the primary concern of the orthodox church was purity of doctrine. Subsequently, discussion will reveal that contemporary liberal ecumenism cannot rightly claim identity with the early ecumenical councils.[32]

The conciliar practice began in Jerusalem (Acts 15) and "took on formal characteristics in African debates in Carthage, Alexandria, Hippo and Milevis, that would gradually come to define the methods for achieving ecumenical consensus elsewhere."[33] The church looked to the past – to the gospel that was handed down from the prophets, apostles and the early church fathers – to proclaim anew the ancient gospel in succeeding generations.[34] Classic Christianity does not necessarily pitch tradition and the Scripture

---

29. Kato used the terms liberal or liberal ecumenical or modern ecumenism interchangeably.
30. Kato, *Theological Pitfalls*, 141.
31. Kato, 129–130; cf. Oden, *Rebirth of Orthodoxy*, 184.
32. Kato, *Theological Pitfalls*, 129–130; cf. Porumb, "Orthodoxy and Ecumenism," 4.
33. Oden, *Rebirth of African Orthodoxy*, 48.
34. Oden, 204.

against each other. The understanding of tradition is as a way of "right remembering – consensually received throughout all Christian ages and cultures – the earliest testimony of Scripture to God's self-disclosure in history."[35] Asserting any tradition that has no basis in Scripture is less orthodox. The way the early interpreters of the Bible shaped the understanding of the church was articulated by Vincent of Lérins, a French monk:

> Christian teaching, consists in "what you have received, not what you have thought up; a matter not of ingenuity, but of doctrine; not of private acquisition, but of Public Tradition; a matter brought to you, not put forth by you, in which you must be not the author but the guardian, not the founder but the sharer, not the leader, but the follower."[36]

Following the third ecumenical council in Ephesus in AD 431, Vincent of Lérins withdrew to shape the course of Christianity by studying the process the church adopted in arriving at decisions. This is how he described the classic Christian method for understanding and interpreting Scripture: The classic Christian method for orthodox scriptural discernment, guided by objective historical inquiry and with the help of the Holy Spirit, was summed up by the Latin words *ubique, semper, omnibus*.[37] That is to say: *everywhere* – across cultural space; *always* – intergenerational time; *by all* – by fair deliberative processes. That is, that which has been believed and lived out by the faith community in all cultures and believed from the time of the apostolic witness. Also, that which has been accepted by the general consent of both clergy and laity in the whole church, over the whole world, in all generations. This is succinctly stated as universality, apostolic antiquity and conciliar consent.[38]

This standard is not the preserve of any establishment or tradition. It is as diffuse as is the uniting work of the Holy Spirit. Thus, according to Oden, the test of orthodoxy or reliability of scriptural interpretation or opinion must respond in the affirmative to all three following questions:

---

35. Oden, 36.
36. Vincent of Lérins, quoted in Oden, 143.
37. Oden, 83–84.
38. Oden, 190–192.

1. *Universality*: Does this opinion echo out of a particular locale or is it shared generally by the whole community of believers around the world?
2. *Apostolic antiquity*: Is this claim something new or is it grounded in ancient intergenerationally received faith?
3. *Conciliar consent*: Has this teaching been confirmed by an ecumenical council or the broad consensus of ancient Christian writers? Do we have documented tradition of consenting laity generally affirming it? Has it been duly expressed through the liturgy and prayers of the church?[39]

Nevertheless,

> Fourth-century Christianity and the Council of Nicaea have continually been read as a Constantinian narrative. The dominancy of imperial Christianity has been a consequent feature of the established narrative regarding the events within early Christianity. There is a case for a revisionist enquiry regarding the influence of the emperor in the formation of orthodoxy.[40]

Therefore, the only reliable and authoritative source of faith and conduct is indisputably the Bible. Kato's constant insistence on this fact was not unreasonable, as his detractors would make it out to be. "The Bible must remain the basic source of Christian theology. Evangelical Christians know of only one theology – biblical theology – though it may be expressed in the context of each cultural milieu."[41]

Incidences of division, starting with the East-West Schism of the church in the eleventh century, continued to arise when the church experienced crises of confidence, and some dissenting voices broke away from the communion of previously perceived faith. In the New Testament church, the apostles resorted to a council to discern the mind of God regarding the place of uncircumcised believers in the church (Acts 15). Ancient ecumenical councils resolved heretical readings of Scripture and affirmed what is now embraced by the church as orthodoxy. The church's response to safeguarding the truth

---

39. Oden, 191.
40. Rukuni and Oliver, "Nicaea as Political," 1.
41. Kato, "We Are," 2.

of God's word has been the universal body holding against the variability and fragility of the few: "Christian teaching prefers the universal to the particular, the classic to the eccentric, the whole to the part."[42] Nevertheless, tradition and councils and any human method are all subordinate to Scripture.[43]

Sometimes, the opposite scenario of the majority holding onto a heretical view, can cause problems in the church when even the majority may threaten to abandon the historically held faith. The next level of appeal, when the majority errs, is apostolic antiquity which precedes and regulates the newer proposal. If apostolic antiquity itself is questioned, a sound conciliar process with the aid of the Holy Spirit should diligently discern what is consistent with apostolic teaching as generally received cross-culturally and intergenerationally.[44] In the case of Kato, he appeared to be a lone "voice in the chorus of positive evaluations of the African pre-Christian religious heritage" informing hermeneutical discourse in Africa.[45] Kato was an embodiment of the antithesis of the theological positions propounded by the majority of African theologians – theologians like John Mbiti and Bolaji Idowu, whose publications included a number of subjects such as ATR and its relationship to Christianity, salvation and African Christian theology.[46]

The classic ecumenical approach underscores the oneness of the church and dependency on the guidance and enabling of the Holy Spirit, who leads the consenting community of faith to unity as the one body of Christ united by one Spirit, one hope, one Lord, one faith, one baptism, one God and Father of all (Eph 4:4–6). The apostles remembered events accurately and transmitted these reliably in the written word, aided by the Holy Spirit. The received apostolic teaching is trustworthy and entirely reliable for faith and conduct. The Christian community is not a mere human institution, constantly in need of protection by human guarantees; it stands under the protection of God the Spirit, who helps the faithful to receive and remember rightly.[47] Thus, Vincent of Lérins defined ecumenical teaching as an aid to the interpretation

---

42. Oden, *Rebirth of Orthodoxy*, 215.
43. Oden, 190, 194; cf. Mueller, "Donatism."
44. Oden, *Rebirth of Orthodoxy*, 195–197.
45. Bediako, *Theology and Identity*, xviii.
46. Bediako, 386; cf. Breman, "Association of Evangelicals," 367; Kato, *Theological Pitfalls*, 200.
47. Oden, *Rebirth of Orthodoxy*, 206; cf. Zizioulas, *Being as Communion*, 205.

of Scripture under the threefold test of classic Christianity: "that which has been believed everywhere, always and by all."[48] The church as a whole acts as the hermeneutical community. Paul Hiebert reiterates the importance of the church community acting as a hermeneutical safeguard against interpreters going astray from the text and writes:

> The priesthood of believers is not a license for theological "Lone-Rangerism." We need each other to see our personal biases, for we see the ways others misinterpret Scriptures before we see our own misinterpretations. Along the same line, we need Christians from other cultures, for they often see how our cultural biases have distorted our interpretations of Scripture. This corporate nature of the Church as a community of interpretation extends not only to the church in every culture, but also to the church in all ages.[49]

However, Kato had strong reservations about modern ecumenism. According to him, the use of the term "ecumenism" had taken on a new connotation, namely the general idea of brotherhood "based on the feeling that our differences really do not matter so long as we can eat together and talk together."[50] Also this had become an "institutionalised movement incarnated in the World Council of Churches."[51] Thus the concerns Kato raised about what he called liberal ecumenism were not about ecumenism per se, but the basis upon which ecumenism had been forged in modern times. Kato wrote:

> Unity with all "Christians" at any cost is advocated by some. The African solution to a problem of disagreement, as it is said, is to seek compromise. The two parties sink all their differences, gloss over the truth and pretend that all is well. . . . The word of God has some strong things to say regarding disagreement over doctrine and Christian living. "If there come any unto you, and bring not this doctrine, receive him not into your house, neither bid him Godspeed. For he that bids him Godspeed is partaker

---

48. Oden, 103.
49. Hiebert, *Anthropological Reflections*, 91.
50. Kato, *Theological Pitfalls*, 130.
51. Kato, 130.

of his evil deed" (2 John 10, 11). Regarding Christian living, the Word of God commands, "... certain men who, having a form of godliness, but denying the power thereof, from such turn away" (2 Tim 3:5).[52]

Kato feared that the drive for Christian unity was to bring all the church denominations together, including the Roman Catholic Church, under one tent. The preservation of the established doctrines of the church was no longer the focus.

Notwithstanding the need for a *sensus communis*, some evangelical churches believed they should remain outside the WCC structures represented by the AACC in Africa. However, realising the need for unity and that

> Jesus Christ did pray for both spiritual and visible unity (John 17:21), evangelicals should want to pull together as long as it is for unity of people committed to Christ and his Word.... For African evangelicals, the most desirable alternative is membership in the Evangelical Fellowship of each country, and also membership in the African Evangelical Association.[53]

Biblical Orthodoxy in the Reformation Era

In the history of the church, the Reformation era was an important turning point for the biblical hermeneutics that have reshaped the understanding of the church. It was a time when there was discontent and much need for the church to go back to the apostolic doctrines. Martin Luther's action led to galvanising the Protestant movement for the reformation of Christianity. The Reformation, as the movement would be known, was essentially "a theological and spiritual movement and it was, above all else, about the nature of divine communication."[54] Luther and the Reformers believed the Bible to not only be the word of God but the all-sufficient guide for faith and practice, "overriding the authority of pope and council."[55] Patterson states:

---

52. Kato, 169.
53. Kato, 170.
54. Patterson, *Theology of Reformers*, 6.
55. Patterson, 7.

The first Principle of the Reformation is the conviction that God spoke by means of the Holy Spirit to holy ones who wrote the words of God and the Bible as such is the inerrant and sufficient Word of God. As such, the Bible – not the church or the government in any of its forms – was to provide the trajectory for knowing God and serving Him. This conviction of the authority of the Bible led to the second great principle of Reformation – justification through faith alone.

Altogether, the Reformation teachings are summed up in the reformation slogan (what is now commonly referred to as the "five solas"): (1) *Sola Scriptura* (that the Scripture alone is the standard and source for Christian faith, doctrine and practice), (2) *Sola Fide* (faith alone), (3) *Solus Christus* (Christ alone), (4) *Sola Gratia* (grace alone) and (5) *Soli Deo Gloria* (for the glory of God alone).[56] The leaders of the Reformation affirmed the authority of the Bible as supreme and encouraged the inductive study of the Bible. With the emergence of the printing press, the Reformation succeeded in promoting the reading of the Bible and the inductive study of the Bible by all, clergy and laity alike.

The resonance for Kato with the Reformation was not least in the shared focus on the apostolic witness of the Scriptures, handed down to the early Christian believers and transmitted from one generation to another, aided by divine providence. The trusted scriptural witness and the inherited theological traditions are an important continuum for engagement by modern day reforming movements. Even though Kato, with the Reformers, was notably known for contending for Scripture as the sole source of authoritative theology, in step with the Reformers, he embraced the church's traditions of scriptural engagement in its early centuries. In his defence of the received scriptural traditions of the missionary church in Africa, he stated: "One common error which also may be cited is the lumping together of some fundamental biblical principles with the Western culture and repudiating both. The error begins with some early Western missionaries who identified the kingdom of God with Western civilisation."[57] Bediako labels Kato as the Tertullian of the

---

56. Baba, *History and Principles of Biblical Hermeneutics for Beginners*,111; cf. Smith, *Integrated Theology*, 14; Holder, "Reformers and Tradition," 1.

57. Kato, *Theological Pitfalls*, 175.

modern African church and states: "The Tertullian viewpoint of Byang Kato must be given due weight, but so also must the evidence of a firmly established Christian religious commitment in the African church."[58] Kato affirmed the place of the early patristic fathers. He wrote:

> It is often forgotten that the Apostolic Creed, on which most Western church creeds are based, was composed by Europeans, Asians, and Africans. Athanasius, the great architect of the earliest Christian creed and defender of Orthodoxy, arose out of Africa. Other theologians of Africa, Arius and Origen, of course, were not condoned in their false views. Inevitably, many cultural tendencies were passed on to the converts by the Western missionary.[59]

The Reformation itself was not without its own pitfalls and limitations. In the centuries following, the authority of the Bible and the place of tradition continued to be in a state of flux, and a particular stream of Protestants, known as evangelicals, emerged.

Evangelical Hermeneutics

Evangelicalism, as known today, can be traced back to 1521, to the Reformation era. Like the Reformation itself, evangelicalism was a continuation of the contention for NT and apostolic teaching against the corruption of the world. According to Hickman: "Erfurt University rector Johannes Crotus Rubianus, friend of Martin Luther, is the first to call Luther and his followers 'Evangelicals' (Evangelische). The term rapidly gained widespread usage, and a variant is used to mean 'Protestant' in most non-English European languages today."[60] Reformation posture encourages individual assertiveness, justified by the doctrine of the priesthood of all believers (1 Pet 2:5). The liberty to read the Bible for oneself, without dependence on the designated priests, paved the way for various individual emphasis, separate from other leaders' particular emphases.

---

58. Bediako, *Theology and Identity*, xviii.
59. Kato, *Theological Pitfalls*, 176.
60. Hickman, "200 Events," 10.

In the early 1700s, Puritanism and Pietism in Europe and America were more dynamic than other forms of Christianity and challenged what they saw as mere nominal Christianity in the institutional Protestant churches. They called for repentance for past sins, personal conversion to Christ, authentic Christian living and commitment to proclamation of the gospel. This brand of Protestant Christianity gave the word evangelical greater currency. Although evangelicalism itself is theologically diverse, evangelicals "continue to see themselves as inheritors of a tradition of authentic Christianity that can be traced back to the early church, although operating outside of ecclesiastical structures and sometimes in open revolt against them."[61]

Underlying this approach is the principle that the Bible cannot be interpreted like any other book, and one has to depend on the Holy Spirit for guidance. The interpreter must recognize that the ultimate purpose for God's word is a changed life through the Holy Spirit. God continues to reveal himself through the written word and human interpreters, but their interpretations must be consistent with what the Bible says.[62] Thus, Kato embraced the grammatico-historical interpretation of the Bible, free from extreme subjectivism or the spiritualising of normal concepts based on preconceived notions.[63]

A sweep of evangelical history in more recent centuries reveals, according to Heckman, four main categories of events that have shaped evangelicalism in more recent centuries. These include:[64]

1. Revivals, evangelical awakenings and evangelistic crusades
2. The founding of Bible societies, mission societies, denominations and other organisations that were evangelical at the time, even if they are not so now
3. The sending of missionaries
4. Conferences mostly related to missions and/or evangelism

The First International Congress on World Evangelization, held in 1974 in Lausanne, Switzerland, with 2,473 delegates from 150 countries (50 percent from the Global South), was another important turning point in the

---

61. Wolffe, "Who Are Evangelicals," 25–26.
62. Kunhiyop, *African Christian Theology*, 36, 41.
63. Kato, *Theological Pitfalls*, 78
64. Hickman, "200 Events," 10.

history of the global church and especially for evangelicalism.⁶⁵ The Lausanne Movement, born under the leadership of Billy Graham and John Stott, has contributed to the current shape of evangelicalism around the globe. The Lausanne Covenant once again grounded evangelical commitment in the authority and reliability of the Scriptures. It also affirmed that the mission of the church is meant to be integral and holistic, that the evangelistic mission of the church is inclusive of social action.⁶⁶

It is noteworthy that Byang Kato was one of the plenary speakers at the Lausanne Congress and on that occasion brought the subject of contextualisation into the limelight of evangelical theological discourse. It is additionally noteworthy that he was afterward selected as a member of the Lausanne continuation committee and also appointed to the executive committee of the World Evangelical Alliance (WEA), as well as being selected chair of the newly formed WEA Theological Commission.⁶⁷

Following this abbreviated history of the church's engagement with biblical hermeneutics through the centuries, I will now turn to selected works on evangelical hermeneutics in the contemporary church, taking into consideration the African context, the African traditional religious worldview and the priority of missions for the church.

Contemporary Evangelical Hermeneutics

Context, plurality of religions, worldviews and the mission of the church are important considerations impacting hermeneutics. In the African context, Kato's missional endeavour had to contend with ATR. This section seeks to engage some theoretical foundations for biblical exegesis. The three main models selected for review embrace the grammatico-historical, or literal, interpretations, a method adopted by mainstream evangelicalism. Elizabeth Mburu asserts:

> Scripture is meant to be relevant to the context in which it is being taught and applied. And yet millions of believers in Africa are constantly bombarded with foreign ways of approaching

---

65. Hickman, 22.
66. Moffitt, *Evangelicalism without Disdipleship*, 10; cf. Hickman, "200 Events," 22–23.
67. Bowers, "Byang Kato," 4.

the text of the Bible that ignore important aspects of the social, economic, political and theological culture of Africa.[68]

Nonetheless, the history of exegesis reveals that "classic African Christian teaching in the patristic period (100–750 AD) preceded modern colonialism by over a thousand years."[69] According to Oden: "Many young African women and men are now re-examining these roots. They are hungry for accurate information on their brilliant Christian ancestors."[70] Mburu states: "However, in the nineteenth century when Western missionaries brought Christianity to Africa, they also brought their own Western readings of the Bible. Consequently, although some of the approaches to Bible interpretation originated in Africa, Western approaches are prominent in the African church today."[71]

Four decades earlier, Byang Kato made a similar call for contextualisation of the gospel in the African context and wrote:

> "Contextualization" is a new term imported into theology to express a deeper concept than "indigenization" ever does. I understand the term to mean making concepts or ideas relevant in a given situation. In reference to Christian practices, it is an effort to express the never changing Word of God in ever changing modes for relevance. Since the Gospel message is inspired but the mode of its expression is not, contextualization of the modes of expression is not only right but necessary.[72]

Kato further outlines aspects of Christianity for contextualisation and states:

> Contextualization can take place in liturgy, dress, language, church service, and any other form of expression of the Gospel truth. Musical instruments such as organ and piano can be replaced or supplemented with such indigenous and easily acquired instruments as drums, cymbals, and cornstalk instruments. It must be borne in mind, of course, that the sound of

---

68. Mburu, *African Hermeneutics*, 5.
69. Oden, *Rebirth of African Orthodoxy*, 3; cf. Mburu, *African Hermeneutics*, 4.
70. Oden, *Rebirth of African Orthodoxy*, 3.
71. Mburu, *African Hermeneutics*, 4–5.
72. Kato, *Biblical Christianity*, 23.

music must not drown the message. Clergy do not have to wear a "Geneva" gown or even a "dog collar." Not only should the message be preached in the language best understood by the congregation, but the terminology of theology should be expressed the way common people can understand.[73]

Mburu proposes a hermeneutical model that could be particularly helpful in the African context, which she calls the "four-legged stool." Using known African categories of interpretation, this model employs a familiar object in the African context, a four-legged stool, as a theoretical framework for a five-step process. According to Mburu,

> Just as a good stool is stable and supports our weight, so the hermeneutical stool will be one we can put our weight on, confident that it provides a stable or accurate interpretation of the biblical text. To do so, it requires four legs, which in this case are (a) parallels to the African context, (b) the theological context, (c) the literary context and (d) the historical context. These legs support the seat, which represents the final stage of interpretation – the application.[74]

The fifth stage is the application (the seat), supported by the four legs, with each leg representing a critical step in the process of interpretation. The first step (leg 1) has to do with our presuppositions (the African context), or the known before moving to the unknown. The familiar worldview could either stand in the way or prove essential in understanding the text. Mburu states: "Hermeneutics involve moving from the known to the unknown."[75] If the reader does not know her own assumptions, she would not know when these are incorrect or wrong. Mburu writes: "While the Bible stands in a historical context and tradition, so does the reader."[76] Earlier exegetes did not realise this. In oral cultures, as in Africa, a narrator's story must connect with the audience, thus there must be contact with the biblical text.

---

73. Kato, 23.
74. Mburu, *African Hermeneutics*, 65.
75. Mburu, 67.
76. Mburu, 68.

The diagram below demonstrates the four legs of the stool and the seat resting on the four legs. According to Mburu:

> The first leg of the hermeneutical stool is to consciously identify our own context and discover the points of contact between it and the biblical context. In this way, we can identify cues that will allow for a more accurate interpretation of the text through a process of comparing the two contacts and analysing the findings.[77]

The second leg (leg 2) of the hermeneutical stool seeks to understand the theological importance of the text in terms of its genre and the rest of the Bible as a whole:

> Africans tend to be very religious, even in modern Africa. The spiritual dimension of life is always a factor in our interaction with the world around us. Because of this orientation, most African readers initially focus on the theological emphases of the text and allow these to determine their interpretation of it.[78]

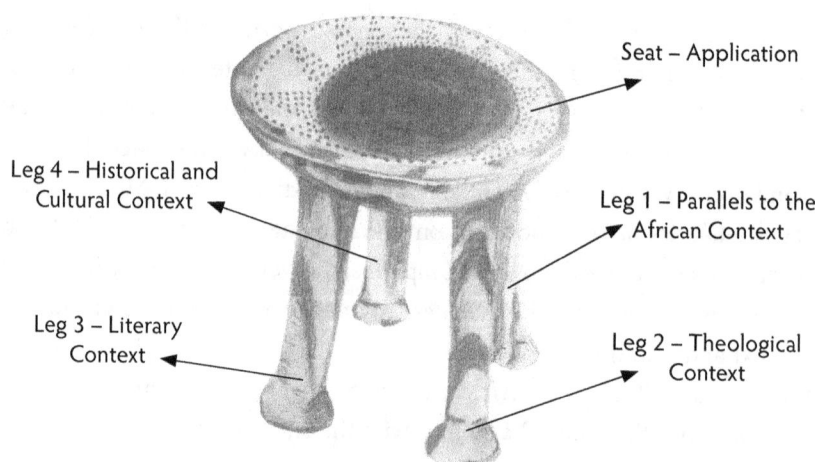

Figure 3: An African Hermeneutic – A Four-Legged Stool[79]

---

77. Mburu, 70.
78. Mburu, *African Hermeneutics*, 70; cf. Mokhoathi, "From Contextual Theology."
79. Image from Mburu, *African Hermeneutics*, 66.

The third step (leg 3 of the stool) represents the literary features or genre of the text, which needs to be identified. This helps in clarifying the interpretations so far, in the previous two steps. Finally, step four (leg 4) is the historical and cultural context of the text. This step seeks to understand the context of the original readers and how they would have understood the message. These approaches are necessary to uncover the intended meaning to the original audience for appropriate application to the African context, the seat of the stool.

Undergirding this approach to African cultural hermeneutics, Mburu's pinpoints the following considerations:

> (1) Africans tend to have an inherently religious or spiritual worldview that is not lost when they become Christians, (2) The philosophy and method used in an African hermeneutic must address issues that are relevant to African Christians, (3) An African hermeneutic must ground abstract thinking in concrete realities and (4) An African hermeneutic must be comprehensible to all Christians and not just to a select group of intellectuals. The goal is millions of believers who live in Africa to truly understand the biblical text and apply it in their lives.[80]

Kato sensitised the church in Africa about syncretism and warned of its negative impact. The need for sound biblical exegesis in the African context is highlighted by Chalk who writes: "Statistically, sixty-five percent of the population in sub-Saharan Africa is professing to be Christian . . . large enough that by this time there should be some Christian shaping of African culture."[81] The lack of transformation has been ascribed to the fact that "Christians are holding on to their African worldview while trying to assimilate new Christian doctrines into it."[82] Thus, the quest for African Christians to deal with the prevailing and dominant traditional cultural and religious worldview.

Turaki proposes a radical approach in African hermeneutics so that Christians can embrace the biblical worldview for transformation. The use of Western hermeneutics on one hand and the use of African traditional religion on the other, as a basis for Bible interpretation, have proved problematic

---

80. Mburu, 7; cf. Kunhiyop, *African Christian Theology*, xv–xvi.
81. Chalk, *Making Disciples*, ix.
82. Chalk, ix.

and inadequate in the African context. Western methods of doing theology have been "too rationalistic, too scientific and too humanistic with too many secularists' ideas. This approach betrays African authenticity. On the other hand, African scholarship has been accused of being too ideological, using the African culture, religion or worldview to portray Africa in a better light."[83] Thus, Turaki proposes a method that takes ATR seriously without undermining the fidelity to biblical Christianity – a method "that engages ATR from a biblical, Christocentric and ecclesiastical perspective . . . to formulate an African Theology that is relevant and biblical."[84]

The goal of this method – which, as his title states, engages religions and worldviews in Africa – is to demonstrate how biblical Christianity can transform traditional cultural and religious mindsets. According to Turaki: "Any teachings and any presentation of the gospel of Christ to people in traditional Africa must bear in mind the great influence of these religious and social beliefs and practices. Christianity cannot provide less than traditional religion offered to Africa."[85] Turaki outlines elements of the worldview or belief system of the African which needs to be understood from a biblical perspective. This suggests enquiry into the following:

1. What do traditional Africans feel about particular religious beliefs, for example, the belief in spirit beings (the spiritual phenomenon) or the belief in mystical, mysterious, unseen and hidden powers and forces (power phenomenon)?
2. What attitudes, behaviours and practices accompany, support and reinforce this belief?
3. What religious and social feelings, attitudes, behaviour and understandings are affected when such a fundamental belief encounters Christianity, Islam or modernity?
4. What is the impact of such a belief as it shapes and moulds the traditional African mind, or the Christian mind in Africa, or modernity in Africa?

---

83. Turaki, *Engaging Religions*, xxvii.
84. Turaki, 231.
85. Turaki, 231.

5. What religious and social practices, rituals, rites and ceremonies of traditional Africa are rooted in beliefs that shape and mould the African response to Christianity and modernity?[86]

These beliefs should not be treated lightly and dismissed as superstitious; they are real to the African. Kato affirmed this and observed:

> God has revealed Himself in two ways – general non-redemptive revelation on the one hand, and special redemptive revelation on the other. In the context of African traditional religions, the worship is merely an indication of an honest craving for God, which can be fulfilled only in biblical revelation through the incarnate Christ who died and rose again. This should be the preoccupation of the church in Africa.[87]

Thus, in what would seem to be a response to these considerations of the African traditional worldviews and practices, Kato stated:

> The written Word of God should be the final test of any action. Always compare every teaching or practice with Jesus Christ. Some questions you can ask are: Does such practice or teaching recognize that Jesus Christ is truly God and truly man? Does it uphold the fact that He was born of a Virgin, died and rose again as the only Saviour of the one who accepts Him? Does it teach that Jesus Christ went up to heaven and that He is now praying for the believers? Does it acknowledge that He is able to take care of all our problems now, whether they have to do with examinations or health? Does it allow for the possibility that Christ may even permit us to fail examinations or be ill and yet He still loves us? Does it recognize that the wicked may even prosper in this life through their dealings with evil spirits but the day is coming when Jesus Christ will put down all principalities and powers, and become Lord of Lords and King of Kings? Only the teaching that answers these questions positively is in line with God's Word.[88]

---

86. Turaki, *Engaging Religions*, 231–232.
87. Kato, *Biblical Christianity*, 9.
88. Kato, *Spirits* 30.

Christianity and the Bible, with their theology of salvation and redemption and God's special revelation to humanity through Jesus Christ, adequately respond to the ATR enquiries. Turaki further writes:

> If we get our methods wrong, we will be liable to misunderstand, misinterpret and misapply theological data. This is what happened in the past when those using comparative and descriptive approaches spent their time looking for similarities or differences between Christianity and ATR and when phenomenologists looked for religious meanings. Any theological discourse apart from God's special revelation in the Bible and in Jesus Christ would merely be an analysis of human theology.[89]

Therefore, the task of Christian theological reflection is not to seek to understand Christianity from the perspective of African traditional culture and religion but to understand African traditional culture and religion from the perspective of a biblical Christian worldview, a method of engagement and interaction of religions and worldviews.[90]

There is a growing number of African scholars magnifying the voice of Kato and taking a stance for the authority and primary place of the Bible in Christian theological reflection.[91] Palmer, quoting Imasogie, for example, states: "The primary objective source of theology is the Scripture. As the inspired words of God, the Bible becomes the authentic objective source of the Christian faith. The Holy Bible becomes the primary objective medium by means of which the Living Lord, through the Holy Spirit, continues to disclose God to us."[92] Palmer agrees with Martin Luther and writes: "reason and natural theology can lead us astray."[93] Natural theology does not tell us about the Trinity, a suffering God and Jesus dying on the cross for our salvation nor the condescension of God in a manger.[94] Natural revelation does not

---

89. Turaki, *Engaging Religions*, 232.

90. Turaki, 232.

91. Turaki, *Engaging Religions*; Mburu, *African Hermeneutics*; Kunhiyop, *African Christian Theology*; Mokhoathi, *From Contextual Theology*; Otonko, "Beyond the Rhetoric."

92. Palmer, *Christian Theology in an African context*, 7, cf. O. Omasogie, *Guidelines for Christian Theology*. 72–73.

93. Palmer, *Christian Theology*, 6. Cf. M. Luther. "The Last Sermon in Wittenberg" in Luther's Works 51:371-80.

94. Palmer, 6.

help us to get a full understanding of God and salvation. Authentic Christian theology is derived from the Bible.

The phenomenal growth of the African church is driven by evangelical activism or evangelism, with a sense of divine vocation and commission in the mission of God. Thus, African hermeneutics could be mission centred. Kato in an address to the Evangelical Alliance in Natal, South Africa, spoke on John 17, among other things, and said:

> In this chapter the Father, Son and Holy Spirit discuss Missions. vv. 15–21. Whom did Jesus send as missionaries? (a) the disciples at that time, and (b) those who would believe through their word. (Unbelievers have no room in this prayer for unity.) Christ wants all Christians to be ONE, and He wants to send them out in MISSION. All Christians are sent, even believers from the Third World. "As the Father has sent Me, so send I you."[95]

Christopher Wright observes that the whole grand narrative of the Bible, from Genesis to Revelation, is about the mission of God and the participation of God's people in the mission of God.[96] Wright writes: "Mission is, in my view, a major key that unlocks the whole grand narrative of the canon of Scripture."[97] With this key, he proposes a framework for reading the Bible and identifies underlying themes as foundational pillars of the biblical worldview and biblical theology. These themes include "monotheism, creation, humanity, election, redemption, covenant, ethics, future hope."[98] He explores each of these themes from their Old Testament roots through to the New Testament to illustrate how they are developed and fulfilled.[99]

Despite the diversity in methodologies, the goal of hermeneutics is always to get to the one true meaning of the original message as understood by the original hearers in their own context. Wright writes:

> It is important to point out here that "plurality in interpretation" is not pluralism as a hermeneutical ideology, nor is it a relativist

---

95. Kato, "Third World Missions," 6.
96. Wright, *Mission of God*; cf. Tennent, *Invitation*.
97. Wright, *Mission of God*, 17.
98. Wright, 17.
99. Wright, 17–18.

> charter. The starting point for understanding the meaning of biblical texts . . . remains a careful application of grammatico-historical tools in seeking to determine as far as is possible their author's and editor's intended meaning in the contexts they were spoken or written. . . . But as we apply those tools and then move to appropriate the significance and implications of these texts in our own context, cultural diversity plays its part in the hearing and receiving of them.[100]

However, the different methodologies and approaches may all have their limitations and be open to critique. Ultimately, it is the text that should govern the methodological framework and not the other way round.[101] Wright counsels to base hermeneutic assessment on its "heuristic fruitfulness" (i.e. clarity and coherence with the Bible's overarching message).[102] It may be difficult to define missiological studies as a theological discipline.[103] Missional endeavours, by nature, involve a wide spectrum of social engagement if the church takes seriously the second most important commandment – loving neighbour as self – and indeed the former – "loving God with all your heart, all your soul, all your mind and all your strength" (Mark 12:30). According to Leffel:

> The gospel's social dimensions have been integral to Christian mission from the beginning. Caring for the poor, naked, homeless, starving, oppressed, and abandoned; "seeking the welfare of the city" – these concerns always have accompanied faithful witness. They also have animated generations of missioners who established schools and universities, hospitals, orphanages, agricultural programs, and relief programs for the poor with great impact throughout the world.[104]

Kato's interpretation and application of Scripture can be deduced by his polemics in part but much more so by his missionary activities, as explored in

---

100. Wright, 40.
101. Wright, 40, 68; cf. Bauer and Traina, *Inductive Bible Study*, 19.
102. Wright, *Mission of God*, 68.
103. Oborji, "Contemporary Missiology," 383.
104. Leffel, "Conference Theme," xiii.

the previous chapters. However, I will now turn to his handling of particular biblical texts as examples of how his hermeneutics impacted him directly or how he exegeted a particular passage in preaching.

Theological and Biblical Foundations of Kato's Theological Legacy

This section explores the theological and biblical basis for Kato's approaches to hermeneutics, African Christian self-identity and theological education. From an evangelical or orthodox perspective, at the core of theology is the appreciation of the Bible and how it is interpreted and applied to one's reality and context. Some selected works demonstrating the historical development of classical approaches to hermeneutics, from the early church to contemporary times, have been discussed in part. These included Thomas Oden's work on Christian orthodoxy in antiquity and early African Christianity[105] and Christopher Wright's *The Mission of God*, which uses the theme of mission as the meta narrative for understanding the Bible. The contributions of Elizabeth Mburu and Yusufu Turaki on hermeneutical approaches in the contemporary African context have also been helpful materials in this task of highlighting theological and biblical foundations.[106] This survey drew a historical sketch of how the early Christians received the Bible, understood, interpreted and applied it. This is how the canon of Scripture was defined and the essentials of classic Christian doctrines were established. How these approaches specifically resonate with each aspect of Kato's theological legacy that are the focus of this study will now be examined.

Foundations of Kato's Biblical Hermeneutics

Kato's biblical worldview was shaped by the Western missionary enterprise, from Sunday school through elementary school and Bible college. His undergraduate and postgraduate studies were also done in Western-based theological institutions in the UK and the USA. Kato was well trained in systematic theology. Kato's perspectives were also shaped by his cultural upbringing and context. In practice, his approach was more pragmatic, and he was essentially

---

105. Oden, *Rebirth of Orthodoxy*; Oden, *Rebirth of African Orthodoxy*.
106. Mburu, *African Hermeneutics*; Turaki, *Engaging Religions*.

a practical theologian, which also took him into the role of a theological polemicist. Kato's own actions were based in the concern that practices in the church should be consistent with what the Bible says. He referred to himself as a conservative evangelical.[107] His doctrinal stance on the Bible and of the uniqueness of Christ was unwavering.

It may be difficult to pinpoint a particular established methodology or theory to describe Kato's way of doing theology. This could well be a distinguishing characteristic of renowned theologians.[108] Smith states that the goal of evangelical theologians is not to construct a theology of their own; their concern is faithfulness to the teachings of Scripture that honour God. Thus, the approach is scriptural, doxological and Trinitarian.[109] This section of engaging the foundations of Kato's biblical hermeneutics is divided into three subsections: (1) biblicism, or the doctrine of the Bible; (2) approaches or methods for the study of the Bible; and (3) the application of Scripture. Some classical works are explored in dialogue with Kato's hermeneutics.

Engaging Kato's biblicism

At the heart of Kato's theological contribution and indeed any Christian theological discourse is the place and authority of the Bible. Mainstream evangelicals believe the Bible is God's word to humans, revealed through the agency of the Holy Spirit who enabled people to write God's message in human language for their understanding. God reveals himself through his word. God has also revealed himself through nature and creation.[110] Ultimately, God revealed himself to the world in the person of Jesus Christ, God's Word made flesh (John 1:14). The Bible, the written word of God, is the supreme source of information about God and the guide for faith and Christian theological reflection and conduct. In his ten-point proposal for safeguarding biblical Christianity in Africa, Kato wrote: "The Bible alone is the final infallible rule of faith and practice. Its verdict cannot be challenged in any court of law since He is the final court of appeal. This propositional revelation is fully inspired, inerrant in the original manuscripts, and faithfully transmitted (2 Tim 3:16;

---

107. Breman, "Association of Evangelicals," 366.
108. Smith, *Integrated Theology*, 13.
109. Smith, 15.
110. Palmer, *Christian Theology*, 6.

John 10:35)."[111] According to Tennent: "The *Missio Dei* is the central message of the Bible. The Bible, like the *Missio Dei*, is the story of God's *redemptive, historical initiative on behalf of His creation*. Missions ultimately must derive its life from that *source*."[112]

The Bible by itself is sufficient for faith and conduct.[113] The canon of Scripture – the sixty-six books of the Bible, comprising thirty-nine books in the Old Testament and twenty-seven books in the New Testament – was established by ancient ecumenical tradition and "explicitly defined for eastern and western Christianity in Africa."[114] Byang Kato asserts the absolute centrality of the Bible for theology and life: "In the African evangelical effort to express Christianity in the context of Africa, the Bible must remain the central absolute source. The Bible is God's written Word addressed to Africans – and to all peoples – within their culture and background."[115] In an interview with Don Smith,[116] he drew a difference between African theology and biblical theology. Comparing Western theology and African theology, Smith said:

> The two theologies were asking and responding to different questions and these discussions may not necessarily provide data from Scripture or the Bible. On the other hand, biblical theology is concerned with what the Bible says, what it meant for its first hearers and the implications for the current era.[117]

He concluded that the difference between Kato and some of his contemporaries was Kato's unique focus on biblical theology and not so much on African theology.

Kato and other scholars both contended for a local theology; the division was (and continues to be) the place of the Bible itself for theologising.

---

111. Kato, *Theological Pitfalls*, 182.
112. Tennent, *Invitation*, 124 (emphasis original).
113. Palmer, "Byang Kato: Theological Reappraisal," 21.
114. Oden, *Rebirth of African Orthodoxy*, 7.
115. Kato, "Theological Issues," 43.
116. Don Smith was a fellow missionary with Kato in Nairobi and members of the Nairobi Baptist Church. Don Smith is also the founder of a private Christian university, Daystar University, in Kenya.
117. Don Smith, Missionary who founded Daystar University in Nairobi, Kenya, who attended the same church, the Nairobi Baptist Church, with Kato, in discussion with the Researcher in February 2019.

Bauckham argues for a hermeneutic "that takes seriously the missionary direction of the Bible itself; embodying a kind of movement from the particular to the universal."[118] Bauckham further states:

> The Bible is a kind of project aimed at the kingdom of God, that is, towards the achievement of God's purposes for good in the whole of God's creation. This is a universal that takes the particular with the utmost seriousness. Christian communities or individuals are always setting off from the particular as both the Bible and our own situation defines it and following the biblical direction towards the universal that is to be found not apart from but within other particulars. This is mission.[119]

How the Bible is understood, interpreted and practiced – hermeneutics – is important for the integrity of the Christian faith. The authority of the Bible in the church determines the way people interpret the Bible: "Hermeneutics is foundational to any theological education."[120] Kato affirmed the high view of the Bible, stating:

> The content of the Bible is inspired. It cannot be changed. "Scripture cannot be broken" (John 10:35). As the Bible moves from culture to culture, it remains the same. It is the culture that must change. If the Bible did not remain the same, Christianity would have changed so much from country to country and generation to generation that it would hardly be recognizable today. Jesus Christ remains the same as He was in the past and will ever be (Hebrews 13:8). His Word remains unchanged in the same way (Psalm 119:89).[121]

Byang Kato contended against what he perceived as an attempt to shift the focus of the church in Africa from the authority and truth of the Bible. According to Kato: "If the Bible is not recognised as the authoritative source, it stands to reason that the biblical meaning may not be adhered to."[122]

---

118. Bauckham, *Bible and Mission*, 11.
119. Bauckham, 11.
120. Baba, *History and Principles*, 19
121. Kato, *African Cultural Revolution*, 37.
122. Kato, *Theological Pitfalls*, 142.

Other theologians did not differentiate between biblical values and the nationalistic values of Western missionaries, and the tendency was to extol African values or traditional religion at the expense of biblical teaching. Bediako expresses his disappointment with Kato for the latter's elevation of Scripture above one's own tradition or culture and writes:

> Whereas most other African theologians felt an inner compulsion to . . . vindicate Africa before a critical European audience, one that is largely without understanding of the continent, Byang Kato, on the other hand, tended to see as his opponents fellow African Theologians, who, perhaps more aware than he was that the Western Value-setting for the Christian faith was no longer tenable, were concerned to seek new foundations for an African Christian self-identity which took account of the African religious past.[123]

Bediako further states: "There is no issue so crucial as the understanding of this heightened interest in the African pre-Christian religious tradition, if Africa's theologians are to be interpreted correctly and their achievement duly recognised."[124] He affirms Mbiti's assertion that the African religious heritage is *praeparatio evangelica*.[125] However, this view can be countered by the historical reality that Christianity sprang from Judaism, but the majority of the Jews have not embraced the gospel of Jesus Christ to date. Overstressing the cultural heritage of people who encounter Christianity would therefore appear to be an error. According to Kato:

> African traditional religious worshippers may claim that their gods are agents of the triune God, Father of the Lord Jesus Christ. But their view must be subjected under the searchlight of the Word of God. Under that scrutiny the traditional religions are found wanting. They highlight the cry of the human heart but the solution lies elsewhere. The natural revelation was never given for the purpose of salvation. . . . Man may get a glimpse of the Supreme Being through natural revelation. But a clear

---

123. Bediako, *Theology and Identity*, 391.
124. Bediako, 1.
125. Bediako, xvii.

picture is impossible. . . . For a clear and final revelation to any people, only the Christ-event will do.[126]

However, Mburu argues for an understanding of both the African traditional worldview and the biblical worldview for even an evangelical reading of the Bible: "If we lack understanding of African worldview as well as the biblical one, how can we understand what the Bible has to say about daily life in Africa?"[127] Between African traditional religion and Christianity, many Christians live dichotomised lives; their Christian faith does not seem to affect their everyday lives.[128] According to Mburu, this has weakened the church, causing it to lose its moral voice in the world. She argues that part of the problem is in the failure to interpret the Bible accurately and allow it to guide the everyday life of the Christian.[129] Similarly, in an interview, Yusufu Turaki[130] opines that most African scholars have equated Christianity with ATR and all other religions. This approach tends to root religion in culture, philosophy and the worldview of the people. Thus, Christianity is also rooted in the same social factors of culture, philosophy and human worldview. Turaki further states that Kato differed in his understanding of religion and believed that the values shaping the formation of religion are not rooted in human culture, philosophy or human worldviews, and in particular that Christianity was not produced by these sociological considerations.

Engaging Kato's hermeneutical approaches

While uncovering the one true meaning of God's word to humans is the intended outcome of hermeneutics, people may miss this. They hear and interpret the same word differaently out of their different contexts or preconceptions. Th task of hermeneutics is to discern the intended meaning of God's word in its original context and how to apply that meaning in a contemporary context.[131] The Holy Spirit is indispensable in the process of discerning the meaning of God's word. The Scripture came to humans by the inspiration of

---

126. Kato, *Theological Pitfalls*, 122–123.
127. Mburu, *African Hermeneutics*, 5.
128. Mburu, 3.
129. Mburu, 211.
130. Prof. Yusuf Turakin in an interview with Researcher in Jos, Nigeria on 27 May 2019
131. Baba, *History and Principles*, 4–5; cf. Mburu, *African Hermeneutics*, 5.

the Holy Spirit, and he aids illumination in the interpretation and application of Scripture. However, while inspiration is inerrant, illumination can be errant, given the role of human disposition in the process.

There is wide ranging scope of methodologies and tools for Bible study and interpretation. "A distinctive feature of biblical studies as an academic discipline is the fact that it employs explicit and transparent methods for researching the Bible."[132] Perhaps the veracity of a particular method could be measured by its acceptability by the church community in different parts of the world and for all times. There may be more that unites the church in terms of orthodoxy than divides it. In this study, three pivotal turning points in the approaches for biblical interpretation, from the time of the New Testament church to the current era, have been touched upon, namely the epoch of early classic Christianity, the period of the Protestant Reformation, and the era of modern evangelicalism.[133] Although the periods and prevailing contexts were different, what emerged are timeless principles that may be common and helpful for the assessment of sound biblical principles for understanding and interpreting Scripture, everywhere and at all times.

While the church has always had disagreement around biblical interpretation, the major split in the church occurred in the Reformation era, about five hundred years ago, when Martin Luther (1517) led a protest against the corruption of the church and advocated for its reformation. Scripture was no longer functioning as the supreme and absolute authority. Tradition, allegorical approaches and deductive interpretation of the Bible had also been embraced, leading to practices that were inconsistent with the Bible. This led to the split of the church, with the breakaway or expelled faction known as the Protestant church and the "remainers" represented by the Roman Catholic Church, the majority church at that time.

This major split was preceded by division of the church by geography – the East-West Schism in the eleventh century AD. This was a break in communion between what is now the Roman Catholic Church and the Eastern Orthodox Church.[134] These splits were marks of the growing discontent in the one church that emerged out of the New Testament church birthed at

---

132. Asumang, "Biblical Studies," 73.
133. Oden, *Rebirth of Orthodoxy*, 2.
134. Porumb, "Orthodoxy and Ecumenism," 34.

Pentecost (Acts 2). Various factions of the divided church pointed to Scripture to support their position. Therefore, biblical interpretations and applications by people in different contexts may continue to be the root cause of division in the church. MacDonald writes:

> Any particular passage can elicit a slew of meanings from two similar people, and the divide can be even greater when age, culture, and training backgrounds differ. Thus, who dictates meaning? Since the Scriptures self-attest to be from God through the superintended authorship of men and, presumably, the divine perspective is more valuable than ours, we should not choose to dictate the meaning.[135]

The evangelical movement itself grew out of the Protestant Reformation movement in defence and promotion of biblical orthodoxy. Thus, it is important to look back at the approaches for understanding and interpreting the Bible and scan how biblical orthodoxy has been sustained in the light of divisions, from the NT church to contemporary times, especially within the evangelical tradition.

Church history reveals that North Africans were among some of the most important early interpreters of the Bible. The list includes church fathers like Athanasius, Cyprian, Tertullian, Augustine and Origen.[136] However, Oden observes: "A demeaning prejudice has crept into historical lore that these great figures were not Africans at all – merely Europeans in disguise."[137] Oden goes on to state:

> This is a fairly recent Western intellectual prejudice. It suggests that the African intellectual tradition cannot even claim its own sons and daughters, especially if they happened to have been articulate, or if they were sufficiently astute as to speak in the common international, academic, commercial and political languages of the day. According to that bias, the greater those competencies, the less African they would be.[138]

---

135. MacDonald, "Critical Analysis," 7.
136. Mburu, *African Hermeneutics*, 4; cf. Kato, *Theological Pitfalls*, 176.
137. Oden, *How Africa Shaped*, 62.
138. Oden, 62–63.

Notwithstanding the cynicism, African Christians of today could turn to their North African ancestors, if indeed they need to look to ancestors for developing their Christian beliefs, and not necessarily to non-Christian ancestors. It is also insightful to note that Christianity has been on the continent for nearly two thousand years, and it thus has a longer history there than in most other parts of the world – and a longer history than Islam. Perhaps the arrival of Christianity in Africa is long enough ago for Africa to lay claim to Christianity as an indigenous religion rather than a foreign one.[139] Also, it is ironic that Kato's theological African identity is apparently in question for his defence of Christian orthodoxy, as if the Christianity he expounded was an invention of Western missionaries in the last two centuries of Christian history in Africa.

Developing theology from an anthropological standpoint tends to undermine exegesis in African theological discourse. "While evangelicals would concur with the idea that God speaks individually to each reader, through the power of the Holy Spirit, they would reject the postmodern notion of the relativity of all truth-claims."[140] The Bible must speak for itself as we seek to address the needs and aspirations of people in the local context. Kunhiyop states: "Insights gained from anthropological study do not have the same revelatory status and authority as the truth of the inherent word of God. Consequently, all insights obtained from such studies must be subjected to the scrutiny of Scriptures."[141] A key pre-occupation of Kato in his arguments with his detractors was biblical orthodoxy.

Engaging Kato's exegesis and application

This section explores how Kato, an eminent evangelical Christian leader, navigated the hermeneutical problem of consistency between practice, belief and biblical orthodoxy in the African context. The discussion in terms of assessing Kato's hermeneutics is limited in scope. Here he is assessed by the conclusions he made regarding certain issues previously highlighted. Kato engaged the church on several matters concerning the application of Scripture in the African context, such as the place of African traditional religions in African

---

139. Kato, *Theological Pitfalls*, 176; Mbiti, *African Religions*, 229.
140. Domeris, "Historical Theology," 187.
141. Kunhiyop, *African Christian Theology*, 80.

Christianity, the continuity or discontinuity of the two faith systems, salvation, the authority of the Bible with regard to culture or tradition, ancestors, ecumenism and social issues. In many ways, Kato held a contrary view from many of his contemporaries in the way they interpreted and applied Scripture to these issues. Kato's perspectives on these matters have been highlighted.

According to Domeris, "There are emic readings of the Bible (people who have a faith investment in the text) and etic readings (people who operate outside of any faith commitment)." Further, Domeris states that when a preacher or a Bible study leader expounds Scripture, which is a hermeneutical task, one of them may focus on a message for today and the other will probably emphasise the meaning of the text. An academic theologian, in a lecture on the Bible, may make the same emphasis but may additionally provide scholarly information and try to respond to academic questions.[142] Kato contended against the church looking to other sources for enriching its understanding of God, especially looking to African traditional religions. Kato regarded these secondary sources, informed by African traditional belief systems in general, to be limited in their ability to guide Christian theological reflection. I will now turn to examining the way Kato interacted with and applied biblical texts. This is an attempt to examine how he used the texts for preaching and how he applied them to his own life.

Kato's application of Genesis 6:9–7:24

This is the passage, according to Kato's biographer Sophie de la Haye, which Kato heard and brought about his conversion to Christianity. Haye narrates:

> One day his Nigerian teacher explained the way of salvation, using the story of Noah and the ark. "God prepared a way of escape from the flood for Noah and his family," the teacher explained. "When the ark was built, God commanded Noah and his family to go in. Then He closed the door. Because they obeyed God, in spite of the laughter and ridicule of all their neighbours, they lived. So for you and me, God has prepared a plan. . . ." Byang realised that he had to choose. That day, standing before the

---

142. Domeris, "Historical Theology," 177–178.

class, he asked Jesus to come into his heart, and received God's free gift of salvation in Jesus Christ.[143]

Kato was still a child at the impressionistic age of twelve when he became Christian, an experience he would remember and recall in his adult years and at the peak of his ministry. In an interview with *Christianity Today* in 1975, and in response to the question about how he was converted to Christianity, Kato said:

> It was through the ministry of a missionary of the Sudan Interior Mission and a Nigerian school teacher. The missionary worked in my town and got me interested in Sunday school. Later, when I was twelve, I started going to school, and it was in the classroom through the ministry of a Nigerian school teacher that I came to know Jesus Christ as my personal Saviour. My pagan parents later gave their hearts to Christ as well.[144]

In another account about his conversion, Kato mentions further details:

> One day the teacher told us the exciting story of Noah and his ark. At the end he solemnly applied the story to us in a personal way, inviting us to accept the Lord as Saviour. I did so with a child's faith and sincerity, little realizing all that was involved.[145]

There may not have been a specific account of Kato's exegesis of this Scripture passage about Noah and the ark. However, it is clear that the text made a substantial impact on him, and it is how he appropriated the text that is the task here. I could not find any sermon or exposition by Kato himself on the passage, except the summary of his Nigerian teacher's exposition of the passage as briefly accounted in the previous paragraph. The Bible story was for Kato not just a fable for entertainment but a story that had a personal application for him.

The story of Noah and the ark is one of the familiar lessons taught in Sunday school. Perhaps it is also the case that the animals trooping into the boat, and the rainbow at the end of that narrative, would make a lasting

---

143. Haye, *Byang Kato*, 19.
144. Kato, "Christian Surge," 12.
145. Kato, "Devil's Baby," 2.

impression on children, but not many leave Sunday school and go home with a story of conversion. Kato's experience compels a fresh look at the passage as evangelistic material. The passage was about the salvation of Noah, a righteous man, and his family, from a wicked world. The rest of the people perished in the flood waters. It took faith for Noah to build an ark on dry land that would turn out to be the means of surviving the flood waters. Kato was able to relate Noah's story to himself, as a sinner, to be saved in Jesus Christ by faith. As Kato recounted, his teacher had "solemnly applied the story to us in a personal way, inviting us to accept the Lord as Saviour. I did so with a child's faith and sincerity, little realizing all that was involved."[146]

It is evident that Kato read the Old Testament through a christocentric NT lens. In this lens, the flood is seen as divine judgement and the ark as a type of Christ. Second, this interpretation of the Noahic flood accords with the NT interpretation of this passage in 1 Peter 3:20–22. And third, Kato clearly believed that Scripture spoke directly into his situation and circumstances. Thus, his exegetical enterprise was not merely at the level of cognitive and abstract apprehension of the text, but as applicable to himself, as if God was directly speaking to him. This accords with the principles of evangelical hermeneutics expounded earlier in this chapter.

Studying Kato's attitude and approach to the Bible in adulthood – that is to say, his high view of Scripture and literal approach – one can observe some consistency with this early encounter with Scripture and how he appropriated texts. His sense of urgency to proclaim the gospel and avoid the looming judgement of eternal damnation also has parallels to the lesson of Noah and the ark. The flood narrative also has echoes of eschatology:

> When the Son of Man returns, it will be like it was in Noah's day. In those days before the flood, the people were enjoying banquets and parties and weddings right up to the time Noah entered his boat. People didn't realise what was going to happen until the flood came and swept them all away. That is the way it will be when the Son of Man comes. (Matt 24:37–39)

The amount of space given to Noah and the ark and flood narrative in the Bible is indicative of the flood's epoch-making importance (2 Pet 3: 3–6).

---

146. Kato, "Devil's Baby," 2.

"The Flood stands out in Scripture as the most general judgement between creation–Fall and the final consummation."[147]

Kato's evangelistic fervour and orientation to save the lost reflect the implications of the flood washing sinners away. "The flood severed the central trunk of human history, the ark-remnant exempted, so terminating the old world and justifying the NT's representation of it as universal in its significance and making the end of one epoch and the beginning of another in God's programme of redemption."[148] There are also some startling similarities between Kato's experience and that of Noah. His *lone voice* and his commitment to the doctrines on which he took a *lone stance* can be likened to Noah (Gen 6:9; 7:1). Even if no one took Noah seriously, building a big boat on dry land, he did not give up. He diligently pursued his objectives and waited for the flood to use the ark (Heb 11:7). Kato was similarly relentless, even if the other theologians viewed him negatively:

> Sometimes obeying God may mean doing the most absurd things in the eyes of other people. It may mean a sacrifice of your prestige, fame, and resources. But when through faith, we obey God – even when it seems foolish to others – we will find favour with God. Obedience through faith takes us above human wisdom into special relationship with God and in his favour.[149]

However, the voyage in the ark was not a voyage alone. Noah brought his extended family into the ark. Similarly, Kato did not only see the need for salvation for himself and his family alone, but he also saw the need for salvation for all whom he met. Notwithstanding Noah's reputation as a righteous man, he was subject to the brokenness of the world. The account of his nakedness and drunkenness (Gen 9:21), and Kato's frustration even after giving his life to Christ, reveal their common mortality and sinfulness – traits shared with all humans with their feet of clay (Dan 2:31–33; see also Rom 3:23; Isa 53:6). Kato could attest to his own experience of slipping back into the old life of sin after giving his life to Christ, writing:

---

147. Kline, "Genesis" in Guthrie and Motyer, *New Bible Commentary*, 88.
148. Kline, 88.
149. Jusu, "Our Identity," 1601.

> One day the teacher told us the exciting story of Noah and his ark. At the end he solemnly applied the story to us in a personal way, inviting us to accept the Lord as Saviour. I did so with a child's faith and sincerity, little realizing all that was involved. The next few years passed in semi-darkness. I was a Christian, but knew constant failure. Youthful lusts held me in their grip, and my testimony was a mockery to the Name of Christ.[150]

Outside of the ark there was no salvation. Salvation inside Christ was the key for Kato and would justify making a commitment at the next opportunity to stay in Christ for life. Recounting his rededication experience at a revival service in the church in his town, he wrote:

> I will never forget the amazing scenes that took place in Kwoi in March 1953, and changed the whole course of my life. . . . Men and women began to weep for their sins. One after another rose to strip off his outer garments and empty his pockets to show that he would keep nothing back from the Lord. Many promised to give their pigs, gramophones, clothes, and other possessions. Thanksgiving continued for a whole week. My own heart was breaking within me. With tears I went to the front of the church to confess my sins before the Lord and His people. It was then that I promised to serve my Lord all the days of my life. He took me at my word. It became clear that He wanted me to go to Igbaja.[151]

Kato made probable connections and corroborated his experience with that of Noah, which shaped his understanding of salvation, and did so while still on this side of eternity.

Kato's application of Philippians 4:13–19

Kato is believed to have used Philippians 4:13–19, in particular 4:13, as one of his favourites and one that he applied to his own life circumstances. Haye reports that Kato said to her: "One day, while working in a missionary's home

---

150. Kato, "The Devil's Baby" 2.
151. Kato, "The Devil's Baby" 2.

I read a wall plaque: 'I can do all things through Christ, who strengthens me.' This became my life's motto."[152]

This is a familiar text and may be recited by many Christians. Often, like any biblical text, people may interpret and apply it incorrectly. For instance, this may be taken to mean that the Christian is empowered to accomplish "anything" in the name of Christ. However, the text is part of a section in the last chapter of Paul's letter to the Philippian church expressing his appreciation for their concerns and financial support for his apostolic ministry. This indeed was the theme of the entire book of Philippians: Paul's appreciation for their support and for their faithfulness. Ironically, he was joyful and lifted the spirits of the Philippians in times of incarceration and challenge. Despite all the challenges, the Lord sustained him through all the difficulties, in good times and in bad times. Thus, Paul could say: "I have learned how to be content with whatever I have. I know how to live on almost nothing or with everything. I have learned the secret of living in every situation, whether it is with a full stomach or empty, with plenty or little" (Phil 4:11b–12). He goes on to say: "For I can do everything through Christ, who gives me strength" (v.13). Paul was confident that "God [would] enable him to do God's will in every situation."[153]

How did Kato understand and apply this to his life? Unlike the life-changing text in the previous analysis, Kato actually spoke on this text. The title of his presentation was "The Joy of Christian Service." The key text of the sermon was Philippians 4:19. First, Kato recalled one of his experiences in his relationship with Jesus Christ:

> In the year 1953 a great revival broke out during a church conference at Kwoi in North Central State. Many people with tears streaming down their cheeks dedicated their lives to the Lord. As a mark of their dedication some gave clothes, money, goats and grain. As a young man struggling to earn his school fees and buy clothing, I did not have much to give. But I dedicated my life to the Lord for whatever thing He would have me do. As a sign of my life dedication, I gave my best of two shirts I had to the church for God's work. God's perfect joy filled my

---

152. Haye, *Byang Kato*, 24.
153. Eaton, *Branch Exposition*, 771; cf. Adeyemo, *Africa Bible Commentary*, 1448.

heart when I surrendered my life, my talents and my best shirt to Jesus Christ.[154]

It is evident that one of Kato's approaches to interpreting texts like these was to relate to the writer, in this case Paul, and seek to appropriate the text to his own circumstances. Like Paul, Kato would say this was the secret of his own life. He recalls the challenges he encountered in his life, even after the encounter with Christ. He was persecuted by his parents and also encountered discouragement and ridicule when he chose to be "a missionary" and go to Bible college instead of seeking a secular career that promised a better life and affluence according to his friends.

> But I have found the Lord not only faithful in meeting my needs. But He has filled my life with joy even at the times my family and I have not had much in the way of material possessions. Although I knew that God wanted me at Igbaja Bible College, I did not know even where I would get money for the train ticket to Igbaja. Neither did I have any money for my school fees. But one week before I left for Igbaja, I got a letter that had gone through the Post Office without the return address. When I opened it, I found exactly enough amount to pay for my train ticket from Kafanchan to Ilorin. Within the same week the pastor of our church also told me that the church would pay my school fees during the first year. These things really encouraged me to trust the Lord and to be prepared to face every situation with confidence in God. I have found Philippians 4:19 true many, many times. It says, "But my God shall supply all your need according to his riches in glory by Christ Jesus."[155]

Kato, like Paul, credited God for meeting his needs and for encouraging him and giving him joy when it seemed the situation was hopeless or dire. Doing all things through Christ who strengthened him did not mean that there would not be challenges. How Kato saw strength from God in all situations is highlighted when he stated:

---

154. Kato, "Joy of Christian Service."
155. Kato.

God has not always given me all the money, clothes and food I have needed. God does not promise that His children will always live in plenty. As a matter of fact, He has warned His children against the idea that material possession is what makes life happy and meaningful. Jesus Christ warned His followers. "Beware! Don't always be wishing for what you don't have." (Luke 12:15 Living Bible). The Apostle Paul did not always have all the money, clothing and food that he needed. Paul was hungry, thirsty and without clothes many times. He says, "Often I have been hungry and thirsty and have gone without food; often I have shivered with cold, without enough clothing to keep me warm" (2 Cor 11:27 LB). While Paul went through poverty, he still believed that God could supply all the needs of His children. He does this not only by giving them material things but by giving them sufficient grace to carry on serving Him happily even at times of material needs.[156]

Apart from material things, the grace of God – "sufficient grace" – is how God keeps his people happy through the challenges of life, with little or nothing or in abundance. He went on to narrate:

When I started serving the Lord full time in 1957 my salary was N10 per month, while my counterparts working elsewhere were getting about N30. There were times when we had to eat only sweet potatoes. But the Lord gave us peace and satisfaction in serving Him. Some preachers mistakenly say that when we become Christians all our physical needs and our troubles on earth will end. But that is not so. God does supply our physical needs as He sees fit. But sometimes He just gives us sufficient grace to go through times of poverty and sickness (2 Cor 12:9).[157]

He admonished his audience, mostly pastors, not to abandon their call for greener pastures nor to live a life of misery, attracting sympathy from others because of poor pay structure in the church.

---

156. Kato.
157. Kato.

Some pastors run away from their calling because of low income. Others stick to the ministry but go about seeking sympathy from other people as if the ministry of the gospel is the saddest vocation one could get. Although the Apostle Paul was despised by some men and suffered poverty and sickness, he still felt that serving the Lord as a full time Christian minister is an honourable job. Paul writes to Timothy, "It is a true saying that if a man wants to be a pastor he has a good ambition" (1 Tim 3:1 LB).

For a true joy in Christian service, certain principles needed to be realized. Kato outlined some principles that keep the Christian or Christian worker joyful. These include a correct view of God and the world, contentment, assurance of God's call for vocation, concern for the fate of unbelievers and joy as the fruit of the Spirit. Elaborating further on these, he pointed out that the attitude of frugality is not asceticism, the wrong notion that in order to serve God one needs to live in abject poverty, physical punishment and self-denial of all good things in life. He said that the right attitude towards wealth, and contentment with what God avails to people, is necessary, and stated:

> "For every creation of God is good, and nothing is to be rejected if it is received with thanksgiving" (1 Tim 4:4 RSV). The correct attitude is to realize that "The earth is the Lord's and the fullness thereof, the world and those who dwell therein" (Psa 24:1). He distributes the wealth of His creation as He wills. He may withhold some material possessions from the pastor, but He will give sufficient grace. "No good thing will he withhold from them that walk uprightly" (Psa 84:11). But it is not for God's people to deliberately inflict God's minister with poverty.

Contentment does not necessarily come with the amount of goods one has. God's Word says, "There is great gain in godliness with contentment, for we brought nothing into the world, and we cannot take anything out of the world. But if we have food and clothing, with these we shall be content" (2 Tim 6:6–8). Discontent only brings sorrow, backsliding and disobedience to God's call, or even self-destruction (1 Tim 6:9). True joy comes from contentment, and the source of true contentment is faith in Jesus Christ for salvation, and obedience to his will and the ministry to which he calls people. The Christian ministry may be difficult and the pay small, but the joy of the

Lord will prove to be our strength. And one must be able to say with Paul, "Woe is unto me if I preach not the gospel" (1 Cor 9:1b). The love of Christ which led him to the cruel tree should so fill our heart that we can truly say:

> Were the whole realm of nature mine, that were a gift far too small. Coupled with this should be the compassion for souls going to hell where they will be tormented eternally. This burning passion should challenge us to serve the Lord. The joy of future reward should also fill us with joy in serving the Lord. It is said of the suffering Christ, "He shall see the fruit of the travail of his soul and be satisfied" (Isa 53:11). Paul calls his converts "my joy and crown" (Phil 4:1). The Christian minister should look beyond the immediate circumstances to the time of reaping the result of his faithful ministry.[158]

Finally, a child of God should be full of the joy of the Lord under any circumstance (Gal 5:22–23), and people around you should see the joy. Kato wrote:

> Remember in the list of the fruit of the Spirit, joy comes next only to love. Joy does not necessarily mean a smiling faith, but a smiling faith speaks a lot about a person's joy. The best way to have J - O - Y is Jesus first and His call to us. Others second in the service we offer. And You last in seeking material benefits.[159]

The exegesis of this passage illustrates Kato's hermeneutical views as outlined in chapter 3. He made several helpful applications to real life situations, drawing parallels from the original context of the Bible to contemporary times. He did that in ways that were understandable and consistent with the classical views of the message of the Bible as highlighted in the foundational and theoretical discussion.

Kato's application of Jeremiah 8:11–22

A final sampling of Kato's handling of biblical texts in his sermons is Jeremiah 8:11–22. The title of the sermon was "The Brave New World." This topic may be alluding to Aldous Huxley's fictional novel by same title, published in 1932.

---

158. Kato.
159. Kato.

The main theme of the novel is that happiness and truth are irreconcilable. Its message and content caused a lot of controversy in the English-speaking world, and it was banned in some countries.

According to Kato, Jeremiah 8:11–22 is about a hope that after all else has failed, there is still hope for the new world. The book of Jeremiah is clearly a prophetic book, and the passage itself is a narrative about God and the people of Judah. God's messenger, the prophet Jeremiah, foretold what God would do with the people then and in the future because of their idolatrous sinfulness and refusal to repent. Jeremiah was announcing the impending calamity that was going to befall the people of Judah because of their sins. They had turned away from God, and it appeared the call for repentance fell on deaf ears – thus the imminent judgement. Instead of them repenting and turning to God, they followed false prophets and teachers who gave them a false sense of security. These false teachers assured them of peace and healing but there was no peace. Instead, they were faced with terror and calamity as prophesied by Jeremiah. They also perceived of ways to run away from the approaching enemy attack, and of ways to flee to safety in more fortified cities and towns, but they could not escape the wrath of God.[160]

Kato starts his exegesis with a brief background of the book. Jeremiah was called to be God's mouthpiece when he was in his early twenties. He compares Jeremiah with Timothy in the New Testament. They were both timid, yet they had a message for the people of their times. Jeremiah realistically confronted the prevailing situation. He condemned the false teachers of his days who were shouting "Peace, Peace" when there was no peace. The false security in Israel was gone.

> Since the days of Amos and Hosea, the children of Israel had a false theology. Because of their material prosperity, they felt God was on their side. The rich were getting richer, and poor were getting poorer. The rich deprived the poor man of his land and felt that since they were rich, God was pleased with it. Religious leaders held that God would never desert his temple. Yahweh

---

160. Adeyemo, *Africa Bible Commentary*, 860; cf. Ndjerareou, "Yahweh and Other Gods," 861.

must defend His temple under any circumstances. Having a form of religion, they denied the power thereof.[161]

The false security the Jews were given by false prophets, and the material prosperity they enjoyed, were in conflict with what the prophet Jeremiah proclaimed. He warned them about the peril of their actions and their need to repent. However, the Israelites were oblivious to the pending danger of the advancing enemy, the troops of King Nebuchadnezzar of Babylon, outside the city wall. The false prophets proclaimed "peace, peace," but there was no peace. They continued to revel in sin and would not listen to God's word that the prophet Jeremiah was giving them. Nebuchadnezzar with his mighty army stood outside the city wall, yet nobody paid any attention. False prophets kept on saying, "Never mind, all will be well. God is a God of love; no judgment will come." So they cheered the hearts of the people.

> The weeping prophet Jeremiah reflected the sad situation of his people. He cried "The harvest is past, the summer is ended, and we are not saved" (Jer 8:20). The time is running out. Hope is fast disappearing. Yet Israel remains stubborn. Jeremiah asks a rhetorical question: "Is there no balm in Gilead? Is there no physician there?" (8:22).[162]

Kato draws parallels with the twentieth century world he lived in. There was so much advancement in science and technology, marked by the invention of things like the steam engine (1763), train engine (1829), aeroplane (1903), radio (1907) and TV (1940). These gave the world some sense of security. And this era of advancement also had its false prophets (theologians), who announced "peace, peace." But apparently this was false security:

> This false philosophy of humanism has gripped Man. Man was spelt with a capital M. Liberal theology taught that man by his own effort could bring about a Utopia. A man called Rauschenbush taught the false view that by working to improve society, Christians would be bringing about the kingdom of God. European theologians Ritschl and Schleiermacher identified Western Civilization with the kingdom of God. Some liberal

---

161. Kato, "Brave New World."
162. Kato.

missionaries went to foreign lands to bring what they believed to be the message of the kingdom of God. These were the type of erroneous teachers shouting peace, peace, when there was no peace.[163]

A careful analysis of Kato's exegesis reveals an understanding of both the biblical context of Jeremiah's world and the twentieth century context of Kato's world. Along with the original context, Kato's worldview and his theological assumptions are in evidence, which constitutes the first leg of the stool according to the African "four-legged stool" hermeneutical model. The title of the sermon, and Kato's "third race" view, would be assumed in his introduction. He clearly draws parallels from Jeremiah's world and the contemporary world of the twentieth century. The Bible's historical context, and the reader's (Kato's) context, find some points of contact and interaction. The theological implications of the passage are also drawn out by Kato, the second leg of the hermeneutical stool. He alludes to God's message through the prophet and false prophets in the Bible on one hand, and the liberal theologies of humanism and the kingdom of God on the other hand, with the false hope in humanism and real hope in the true God, and the implied salvation message, as underlying theological themes. The content itself is more of a historical narrative or story, even though the book is a prophetic book, constituting the third leg of the stool. Kato's exegesis does give a literal interpretation. The historical and cultural character of the text, the fourth leg of the stool, is also seen. Kato lets his hearers know about the author of the message and the context of his prophecies.

Finally, Kato rests his message, the application (the seat) or fifth step in the process, on an appeal for salvation, which Kato deemed important for his audience. Kato proclaimed: "The weeping prophet Jeremiah reflected the sad situation of his people. He cried, 'The harvest is past, the summer is ended, and we are not saved.' (Jer 8:20). The time is running out. Hope is fast disappearing. Yet Israel remains stubborn."[164] Kato then makes a final appeal:

> Jesus Christ is going to make all things new. For the individual sinner there is hope for a brave new world right now. Jesus Christ

---

163. Kato.
164. Kato.

Theological and Biblical Foundations for African Christian Identity 233

says, "I am come that they might have life, and that they might have it more abundantly" (John 10:10). The Apostle Paul says, "Therefore if anyone is in Christ, he is a new creation; the old has passed away; behold the new has come" (2 Cor 5:17). Accepting Jesus Christ now will bring you the following results: 1) You will be at peace with your maker instead of being in conflict with Him. 2) You will receive eternal life and know that you have it here and now in spite of your sinful condition, past or present. 3) You will have the right perspective of this world, helping to make it a better place in which to live and yet realizing that we have no abiding home here. 4) You will live at peace with your neighbours, your family and other people by the enabling power of the Holy Spirit. 5) You will someday enjoy eternity with Christ. This is the new brave world which we invite you to explore.[165]

In this one sermon, Kato's theological disposition, as articulated in much of this study, rings through. More importantly, the treatment and interpretation of the text would be agreeable to normative evangelical approaches. Kato's hermeneutics and application can also be seen in the other two pillars of his theological legacy in this study. I will now turn to some theoretical and theological underpinnings in dialogue with Kato's perspectives on African Christian identity.

Foundations of Kato Contribution to African Christian Identity

The quest for self-identity for the African is an important consideration, with implications for the African race, both on the continent and in the diaspora. In modern times, books and movies like Alex Haley's novel *Roots* (1976) and, more recently, the movie *Black Panther* (2018) have attracted the interest of Africans, Black people and the world in general on this subject. Africans on the continent, and those in dispersion on other continents because of slavery, have struggled to gain some form of independence and unique identity and freedoms. The enslavement and colonisation of Africans seems to have dented

---

165. Kato.

their sense of human dignity and self-worth. Unfortunately, the missionary enterprise in Africa may have also contributed to this sorry situation. One cannot talk about African identity without addressing slavery, colonialism, racism and the indignity the Black race has suffered at the hands of others, even in the church.[166] As a matter of fact, the problem of identity and indeed personhood is not unique to the Black race alone. It is a human problem and indeed a theological question.

For Africa the question that arises is "What does it mean to be an African or a Black person?" This is not just a question about birthplace or provincial identity; it has far more implications for the African or the Black person. The question has to do with slavery and colonialism and African spirituality. Africans have been made out to be the inheritors of Ham's cursed son (Gen 9:20f), even if erroneously.[167] "The black colour of the African skin was criterion used to place Africans at the bottom of the human social scale."[168] The common human ancestry in Adam and Eve, and indeed the humanity of Africans, was questioned by some Europeans. Centuries of demonising and ridiculing "Africanness" have in effect forced some African people to abandon or lose what was once sacred and brought meaning and self-worth. When they try to reconnect with what they perceive as a lost African heritage, it is not clear what that is, and whether they could ever connect with what is left of this heritage, if any is left. Thus, African scholars seek

> to deconstruct a myriad of negative images that denigrate the African continent as dark and seek to place into proper context distortions of the original African creative intellect, twisted by Western hegemony. It further attempts to invalidate the stereotypes that were pervasively consecrated as historical truths in literature, philosophy, religion, and politics.[169]

Some African intellectuals look to traditional African social philosophy as

> a viable framework to shape life in contemporary Africa and as a counter to the widespread individualism threatening humanity

---

166. Viriri and Mungwini, "African Cosmology," 28.
167. Adeyemo, *Is Africa Cursed*, 11–16.
168. Viriri and Mungwini, "African Cosmology," 38.
169. Viriri and Mungwini, 27; cf. Kato, *Theological Pitfalls*, 50.

in the world of today, in order to show how African indigenous systems that were condemned as irrational and backward can inform life today in a much more beneficial way by shaping a unique African modernity.[170]

According to Viriri and Mungwini:

> The philosophy of ubuntu is basically an indigenous philosophy of social existence that defines the relationship that ought to obtain between members of the society. The distinguishing features of this philosophy are its welfarism, altruism, universalism and basically its utilitarian outlook. Central to it is the near universal lessons that "to be human is to affirm one's humanity by affirming the humanity of others." . . . While Western scholars have gone to length to demonstrate that there is nothing worth noting from the African continent besides its vast forests and wild animals, the philosophy of ubuntu stands out clearly as one aspect of the African cosmology that has to be salvaged to promote a humane social existence.[171]

Africa's problem with self-identity may not just be the multiple calamities of slavery and colonialism and not just Western economic imperialism, impactful as each of these have been, but rather a principal problem may also be a dominant intellectual ideology that has lost its efficacy.[172] The African identity question has occupied the mind of African scholars in all intellectual endeavours, whether literature, art, history, sociology, political science, economics, philosophy, jurisprudence, educational theory or theology.[173] Africans themselves have contributed to negative profiling and to an identity crisis. According to Hendriks:

> An American president's reference to African countries as "shithole countries" is only one in a long history of racially tainted, derogatory remarks and characterisation aimed at our

---

170. Viriri and Mungwini, 27
171. Viriri and Mungwini, 39–40.
172. Bowers, "Byang Kato," 7.
173. Bowers, 6; cf. Ngong, "Material," 114; Viriri and Mungwini, "African Cosmology," 27; Mengara, *Images of Africa*, 1–2.

continent and its people, remarks that hurt and humiliate. What makes these remarks even more mortifying is that, in some cases at least, if we are honest with ourselves, we have to admit that we are responsible for making such terms quite accurate characterisations.[174]

The involvement of some Africans in the slave industry for financial gains and ongoing corruption and nepotistic and despotic rule by the political class in collusion with foreign powers characterise too many countries in Africa. Even the humane social construct of ubuntu – "a person is a person through other persons"[175] – touted as a fine defining characteristic of the African value system and way of life is put to the sword by limiting it in practice to one's own tribe and not the wider society.[176] In the church, "blood of ethnicity, tribe, racialism, sexism, caste, social class, or nationalism seems to flow stronger than the waters of baptism and the confession of Christ."[177]

Similarly, there was a quest for African church people to do theology in a distinctly authentic African way, unique to their context. The emerging proponents were nationalists across the linguistic divide of Anglophone and Francophone Africa. The early African scholars were concerned with disputing Western stereotypes and extolling African culture and religious beliefs, devoid of any Western ascription. Among the Western educated clergy were Vincent Mulago of Zaire, Alexis Kagame of Rwanda, Harry Sawyerr and Edward Fashole-Luke of Sierra Leone, E. B. Idowu of Nigeria, John S. Mbiti of Kenya and Cardinal Francis A. Arinze, Archbishop Stephen N. Ezeanya and E. C. Ilogu of Nigeria.[178] For about three decades these scholars, among others, continued to attempt to reconcile Christian thought with African belief systems.

Many would assume that the quest for African theology was simply about giving an African face to theology, providing Christian truth with contextually sensitive illustrations and applications. However, the aspirations of African theology were more complex and diverse than contextualisation. It was an

---

174. Hendriks, "Public Theology and Identity," 49.
175. Tutu, *God Is Not Christian*, 21.
176. See Maigadi, "Christian Faith."
177. Rice, *Reconciliation*, 5.
178. Conteh, *Essays*, 4.

attempt by some to identify a correlation between Christianity and African culture, Christianity and African traditional religions or Christianity and an implicit African worldview (from a philosophical perspective). "Ecumenists have pursued not a correlation of Christianity with Africa's past so much as an activation of the Christian community in shaping Africa's future, towards greater liberation and humanisation."[179] Commenting on the lack of Christian impact on society, notwithstanding the growth of the Christian population in Africa, Otonko writes: "The revival of cultures and the attendant theological enterprise in inculturation have often legitimised the importance of African cultural expressions on Christian beliefs, but also with tendencies of distorting the purity and integrity of Christian faith as a result of misunderstanding."[180]

The principal proponent of a theology of identity, framing African Christian theology in terms of a doctrine of self-identity and as a biblical hermeneutical question, was Kwame Bediako in his seminal work, *Theology and Identity*. This work was essentially Bediako's PhD thesis at the University of Aberdeen in 1983, eight years after the death of Byang Kato. The underlying theme of Bediako's work was about how one's own Christian self-understanding is rooted in the gospel and culture. Bediako states: "I have felt the need to seek a clarification for myself of how the abiding Gospel of Jesus Christ relates to the inescapable issues and questions which arise from the Christian's cultural existence in the world, and how this relationship is achieved without injury to the integrity of the Gospel."[181]

Thus it would appear that both Kato and Bediako were concerned and interested in the authenticity of African biblical Christianity. However, the two approached this question from different perspectives. Kato's approach was the centrality of Scripture and the need to "baptise culture"[182] when culture was not consistent with biblical values. In his *Theological Pitfalls in Africa*, Kato stated:

> The primary purpose of this book is to sound an alarm and warn Christians on both sides of the argument concerning the dangers of universalism. These dangers are theological pitfalls

---

179. Bowers, "African Theology," 110.
180. Otonko, "Beyond the Rhetoric," 1.
181. Bediako, *Theology and Identity*, xi.
182. Kato, *Theological Pitfalls*, 174.

indeed.... The noble desire to indigenise Christianity in Africa must not be forsaken. An indigenous theology is a necessity. But must one betray Scriptural principles of God and His dealing with man at the altar of any regional theology? Should human sympathy and nationalism override what is clearly taught in Scripture? Many voices in Africa and outside the continent are answering these questions in the affirmative. Their number is increasing rapidly. This is why I wish here to alert Christians to these pertinent dangers.[183]

Bediako on the other hand grounds his reflections on self-identity and writes:

The basic argument which underlies the various chapters is that the development of theological concern and formulation of theological questions are closely linked as inevitable by-product of a process of Christian self-identity. In this sense, how certain problems assume a priority of a group of writers is illuminated by the view of Christian self-identity that a particular writer takes, or which is shared by that group of writers.[184]

Thus proponents of African theology tended to look towards African traditional religion as a source for doing theology, defending ATR as not being a religion of animism or of devil and idol worship. Therefore, the objective was not an emphasis on the authority of Scripture that was associated with the Western missionary endeavor. The intention here was to look into the Bible for ideas that would support the value of ATR by analogical deductions. This was the critical tension between Kato and the other theologians: African traditional religions existing alongside biblical Christianity, without syncretism.

Kato's view was not unsympathetic to the concerns of other theologians – the association of the inhuman acts of Western slavery and colonialism with Christianity and Western missionaries. Kato stated: "Admittedly biblical Christianity does not favour this type of inhuman practice.... However, the Western world is steeped in Christianity, so the two appear identical."[185] However, Kato believed the African quest for freedom and selfhood still lay

---

183. Kato, 16.
184. Bediako, *Theology and Identity*, xv.
185. Kato, *Theological Pitfalls*, 13.

in Christianity: "In fact, it was Christians such as William Wilberforce who helped to abolish slave trade."[186] Authentic Christian faith would require a critical appraisal of African theology. Thus Kato saw many of the teachings of his contemporaries as an affront to the unique claims of the Bible and salvation by Christ alone. He argued:

> The relativity philosophy is seeking to make the Scriptures only one of many revelations rather than a special revelation. Christianity is not repudiated but given the largest room in the camp of religions. It is claimed that the difference lies not in kind but in qualitative teachings. "Thus said the Lord" as a propositional revelation is reduced to merely a segment of general revelation or a fulfilment of other revelations. By this process it cannot dislodge other revelations but only improve upon them. That being the case, salvation is no monopoly of Christianity. It is just as possible to be saved through other religions as it is possible through Christianity though the later may bring salvation faster. Such is the kind of thought prevailing today. These are *theological pitfalls* that only a discerning Spirit-filled Bible-believer can see and refute.[187]

Therefore, Kato was very concerned about what he perceived as universalism and syncretism creeping into the church in Africa. This formed the basis of his main work – *Theological Pitfalls in Africa* – in which he was critical about the direction of African theology.

Commenting on the work of an early church father, Tertullian, Bediako said:

> Tertullian's major concern was not so much how the Christian Gospel might be made relevant to the world, as how Christian truth was to be defended and protected from the world conceived as "demonic." Tertullian, therefore, represents "negative" response of the Christian to the cultural tradition in which he stands.[188]

---

186. Kato, 13.
187. Kato, 173–174. Emphasis mine.
188. Bediako, *Theology and Identity*, xvi.

In this respect, Bediako labels Kato as the Tertullian of the modern African church. Bediako concludes: "The 'Tertullianic' viewpoint of Byang Kato must be given due weight, but so also must the evidence of a firmly established Christian religious commitment in the African church."[189] Bediako further asserts: "African theology in the post-missionary era, therefore, is as much a response to missionary underestimation of the value of African pre-Christian religious tradition, as it is an African theological response to the specific and more enduring issues of how the Christian Gospel relates to African culture."[190]

Accordingly, African theology tended to exalt Africa's pre-Christian religious traditions as authentic religion with perhaps the same claim as Christianity or with a rationale to synthesize the two, rather than emphasise the authority of Scripture, which was associated with the Western missionary endeavor. Accordingly, Kato wrote:

> Africa stands to gain by becoming more creative than by expending energy on cultural demythologisation. It is childish to water down or compromise the gospel in order to impress the world with African contribution. The Spirit-filled believer bathed in the study of God's word has great contribution to make to the universal Church of Christ.[191]

Acknowledging the religious confrontation and cultural challenge that Christianity faces in any culture, Kato stated: "The test for Christianity, however, was going to be whether it would survive as a unique faith, as the only answer to the human dilemma. Would it baptize cultures or would it be polarised and enmeshed by the multitudes of cultures it would invade?"[192] Oden asserts:

> Afro-centrism must be rejected as an ideological bias contrary to the catholicity of the faith. Africa was the continent in which the concept of catholicity was first tested. Global vision is essential to catholicity. The aim of catholicity in Christian teaching is to reflect the wholeness of apostolic truth to the whole world,

---

189. Bediako, xviii.
190. Bediako, xviii.
191. Kato, *Theological Pitfalls*, 176.
192. Kato, 174.

not simply the uniqueness of African Christianity to Africa. . . . The gospel is not for or from Africans only. Classic African Christianity was attuned to a global citizenry.[193]

Nonetheless, some missionaries may have had dominant cultural worldviews and assumptions in their interpretation of Scripture which were unbiblical and also offensive in the African context. What other people or the community think about Africans could give them a diminished sense of self-worth or worthlessness based on a fear/honour-shame culture. This is an important consideration for one's identity. Guilt, fear, honour and shame play an important role in shaping identity in human cultures. There are dominant traits of these factors in different cultures. Anthropologists generally agree that the Western culture is mostly guilt-based, whereas African and Asian cultures are shame/honour and fear based.[194]

Tennent posits that "a more biblical understanding of human identity outside of Christ is framed by guilt, fear and shame that should be able to stimulate a more profound appreciation for the work of Christ on the cross and perhaps which has not been well articulated by Western missionaries."[195] A negative reaction to the attitude of those who demean African culture was inevitable. However, should the negative reaction to the misapplication of Scripture be tantamount to rejection of the good news itself, the Bible? Kato's response to this was in the negative. Human philosophy or rationalism should not "override what is clearly taught in Scripture."[196]

However, the subject of identity is not just about the demeaning of Africans; it borders on the whole question of "personhood and being" that occupied the minds of patristic fathers as they envisioned the being of God.[197] According to the Orthodox theologian John Zizioulas,

> Respect for man's "personal identity" is perhaps the most important ideal of our time. The attempt of contemporary humanism to supplant Christianity in whatever concerns the dignity of man has succeeded in detaching the concept of the person from

---

193. Oden, *Rebirth of African Orthodoxy*, 25.
194. Tennent, *Theology*, 77–82; cf. Mburu, *African Hermeneutics*, 68.
195. Tennent, *Theology*, 92.
196. Kato, *Theological Pitfalls*, 16.
197. Zizioulas, *Being as Communion*, 18.

theology and uniting it with the idea of an autonomous morality or with an existential philosophy which is purely humanistic. Thus, although the person and "personal identity" are widely discussed nowadays as a supreme ideal, nobody seems to recognize that *historically as well as existentially* the concept of the person is indissolubly bound up with theology.[198]

People's reality is never apart from God, our Creator. Zizioulas further notes: "Humanism or sociology could struggle as much as they wished to affirm the importance of man. The existentialist philosophers . . . have shown the person who has an absolute ontological freedom remains a quest without fulfilment."[199] The Bible says: "For in him we live and move and have our being" (Acts 17:28). Indeed, the quest for true identity is being in Christ.

In the new birth, people can have a new identity in Christ. "For the Christian, the work of Christ on the cross is the most fundamental place where our new identity is formed. In Adam we became identified with guilt, fear, and shame. In Christ we are now identified with forgiveness, confidence, and honour."[200] Further, Tennent writes:

> The apostle Paul uses the expression "in Christ" or close equivalents (e.g. "in him") 165 times in his letters. He declares, "I have been crucified with Christ and I no longer live, but Christ lives in me" (Gal 2:20). For Paul the cross is the place where our new identity is formed.[201]

Thus, Kato suggests a "third race" identity – an identity that is neither African nor Western, nor a split identity between the two. In any case, followers of Christianity, like Judaism, in earlier centuries were considered a strange and abnormal kind of people who did not bow to worship the emperor and other deities:

> They stood alone by themselves amid all the other races who were included in, or allied to, the Roman empire. . . . This very uniqueness of character was taken to be a defect in public spirit

---

198. Zizioulas, 27. Emphasis in original.
199. Zizioulas, 18.
200. Tennent, *Theology*, 92.
201. Tennent, 92.

and patriotism, as well as an insult and a disgrace. . . . In the case of Christians, some of the sources of offence peculiar to the Jews were absent; but the greatest offence of all appeared only in heightened colours, viz, reprobates, belonging to an unlawful group.[202]

The Christians were not considered as belonging to any of the recognised social classes, having fallen from being Greek or Roman, or even Jew, but a classless Christian, something worse than Jew.

> So monstrous, so repugnant are those Christians (of whose faith and life Cæcilius proceeds to tell the most evil tales), that they drop out of ordinary humanity, as it were. Thus Cæcilius indeed calls them a "*natio*," but he knows that they are recruited from the very dregs of the nations, and consequently are no "people" in the sense of a "nation."[203]

Thus the Christians were considered a "third race." According to Harnack, Tertullian, "in his two books: *Nationes* and *Apology*, states that Christians were called '*genus tertium*' (the third race) by their opponents."[204] Drawing from Scripture, Harnack further writes:

> In classifying mankind Paul does speak in one passage of "Greeks and barbarians" alongside of Jews (Rom. i. 14), and in another of "barbarians and Scythians" alongside of Greeks (Col. iii. 11); but, like a born Jew and a Pharisee, he usually bisects humanity into circumcised and uncircumcised –the latter being described, for the sake of brevity, as "Greeks." Beside or over against these two "peoples" he places the church of God as a new creation (e.g., 1 Cor. x. 32, "Give no occasion of stumbling to Jews or Greeks or to the church of God"). Nor does this mere juxtaposition satisfy him.[205]

This new conception of identity leads to higher unity: Jews and Greeks coming together as one in Christ.

---

202. Harnack, *Mission and Expansion*, 204–205.
203. Harnack, 204.
204. Harnack, 207.
205. Harnack, 187.

> The people of Christ are not a third people to him beside their neighbours. They represent the new grade on which human history reaches its consummation, a grade which is to supersede the previous grade of bisection, cancelling or annulling not only national but also social and even sexual distinctions.[206]

The concept of "third race" identity was quite rife in the early twentieth century among European politicians, especially when the Jewish and Gentile roots of Christianity became a very hot and contested issue in Germany, with the anti-Semitic sentiments of Nazism.[207] Kato's application of this terminology therefore has very potent resonance to that of the NT church. Just as theologians from the time of Paul sought to overcome the totalizing effects of their cultures on their Christian theology by asserting that the Christian is in essence a member of a new race, Kato was attempting to do the same in applying this concept. The third race identity is the "new life in Christ" (2 Cor 5:17), apart from African and Western identities or a split between the two.

Turaki states: "Our Lord Jesus himself made some categorical statement about his message of salvation within the context of Jewish monotheism and the plural religions and cultures of the Roman Empire. The Apostles' message was about the uniqueness of Christ."[208] The third race is profoundly biblical, supported by orthodox evangelical understanding of the being and otherness of the Christian. Conversion is not passivity and assimilation of a new belief into the old. Becoming a Christian is being born anew of the Spirit (Rom 8:5–17; Eph 4:21–24). Christian identity is what the Christian is, in Christ.

> Romans 2–11 describes who the believer is in Christ: our identity consists of what God has done and made us to be – our very nature and essence in Christ. The passage suggests that God has chosen, elected, justified and saved us from the penalty and power of sin. So we are new creations, no more living under condemnation but living as children of God and joint heirs with Christ (Rom 8:14–17). No longer are we fallen and hopeless before God. Instead, we are victorious in Christ. . . . This identity

---

206. Harnack, 187; cf. 1 Pet 2:9; Col 3:11; 1 Cor 10:32; Gal 3:28; and Rom 9–11.
207. Harnack, *Mission and Expansion*, 279.
208. Turaki, "Theological Legacy," 137.

does not depend on our gender, tribe, education or nationality. It is purely how God has created us and what he has given us.[209]

There are many references in the Bible that talk about the identity of the believer. Human identity is in God, and without God all humans are lost, and yearn for a true identity.

> When humankind chose to be in charge of their own little gardens (Gen 3), when they chose to construct cities with high walls and impressive towers to make a name for themselves (Gen 11), paradise was lost. God then called Abraham and took him on a journey (Gen 12). In the same way that God had created the world and blessed it, he now called this man and blessed him so that he could be a blessing to the nations of the world. . . . Abraham's journey was the first "long" walk to freedom.[210]

Hendriks further states: "If God calls and the Holy Spirit empowers, there is no ethnic, class, gender, age or any other human or natural barrier that prevents a person from becoming a vehicle for the coming kingdom of God. That, rather than their human circumstances, is what is their identity."[211]

At the heart of the question of Kato's African Christian identity was his theology – *Theologia Africana*. *Theologia Africana* is a concept which defines the quest for African theology as distinct from that of missionary Christianity. This is a quest for an African theology of post-missionary Christianity. According to Kato, the challenge of the church in Africa was biblical ignorance and lack of emphasis on theological education on the part of missionaries.

> Many pastors in the churches in Africa have swallowed the pill of incipient universalism without knowing the premise nor the end result. While the work of interdenominational missions in Africa, which still make up the core of evangelical Christianity, is highly commendable, nevertheless it is a fact that most of the missionaries lacked sound theological education. So a mammoth church has been established without the depth of theology

---

209. Jusu, "Our Identity," 1601.
210. Hendriks, "Public Theology and Identity," 51.
211. Hendriks, 53.

that the church needs. Christian leaders are now vulnerable to the tactics of ecumenism with its basic universalistic premise.[212]

Bediako insists that the question of African theological identity is "the key to understanding the concerns of Christian theology in modern Africa and in the Second Century AD."[213] He asserts that the primary agenda of "modern African Theology" is "the meaning of the pre-Christian heritage as a prime concern." He further states: "There is no issue so crucial as the understanding of this heightened interest in the African pre-Christian religious tradition, if Africa's theologians are to be correctly interpreted and their achievement duly recognized."[214] To the credit of Kato, Bediako states: "Kato's achievement was in his persistent affirmation of the centrality of the Bible in the theological task. . . . Kato thus contributed a viewpoint of cardinal importance . . . even though his own cultural conception of theology in fact defeated the very purpose of theology as the struggle with culturally-rooted questions."[215]

However, Kato in turn insisted that African Christians can only fulfil this quest in Christ. The answer is not to turn to culture and traditional African religion for identity. Against the background of the African Christian identity debate, it is important to note the perspective of Andrew Walls, a mentor of Bediako. Walls writes:

> Throughout Christian history there has been another force in tension with this indigenising principle, and this also is equally of the Gospel. Not only does God in Christ take people as they are: He takes them in order to transform them into what He wants them to be. Along with the indigenising principle which makes his faith a place to feel at home, the Christian inherits the pilgrim principle, which whispers to him that he has no abiding city and warns him that to be faithful to Christ will put him out of step with his society; for that society never existed, in East or West, ancient time or modern, which could absorb the word of Christ painlessly into its system. Jesus within Jewish culture, Paul within Hellenistic culture, take it for granted that there will

---

212. Kato, "Danger." 2
213. Bediako, *Theology and Identity*, 1.
214. Bediako, 1.
215. Bediako, xviii.

be rubs and frictions – not from the adoption of a new culture, but from the transformation of the mind towards that of Christ.[216]

The quest for a balance between an authentic African worldview and biblical worldview, without mixing the two, continues to be an illusion. On the place of Christ in theology, Mugambi and Magesa write: "Theology is not Christian at all when it does not offer Jesus Christ of Nazareth as the answer to the human quest."[217] However, some scholars argue that because the Western missionaries who introduced Christ in sub-Saharan Africa were also compatriots, and in some instances allies, with those who suppressed the African, christological discourse has been tainted The ambiguity about African Christology has also been complicated with the quest for African identity.

In any case, the notion of an African identity, even from a non-theological view, has been a conundrum. Many writers may only paint a skewed version of what that "Africanness" is. There is hardly any one particular religion called African traditional religion. Rather there are as many religions as there are different African traditional societies, each with its own particular religious practices, even though these could have similar elements or characteristics. Underscoring the ambiguity about the African context, Palmer asks: "But what is the African context? Is it the traditional world of Chinua Achebe? Or is it the modern urban context of half of the population of Africa?"[218] In response to this query, Turaki states:

> Modern Africa is a mixture of the old African traditional values, institutions, religion, culture, and worldview; of Western colonialism, Christianity, modern Western values and philosophies, and the secular forces; and of new values, social structures, and institutions generated as a result of the interaction between civilizations such as the West, Christianity, and Islam. A modern African therefore has a new identity forged out of modernity. This African could be a Christian, or a non-Christian,

---

216. Walls, *Missionary Movement*, 8.
217. Mugambi and Magesa, introduction to *Jesus in African Christianity*, x.
218. Palmer, *Christian Theology*, 1.

or a traditionalist. Others might be neither traditionalist nor Christian nor Muslim."[219]

Nevertheless, the quest for identity has some validity, certainly under the current sociological strains of globalization. The fact is people always have some form of identity, for identity is the basis upon which we define self to others. Those who refuse to self-define their identity will have other people defining it for them. In any case, for the Christian, we only bear witness based on our identity. Evangelism cannot be successful except evangelicals inhabit the identity for which they preach. So, really, the question is not whether identity is important or not, but what sort of identity Christians in Africa ought to assume and project.

The challenge is that there are no literary forms of ATR to return to and examine for established orthodox concepts to find parallels to the Christian religion. What the beliefs were may merely be conjectures by scholars who themselves have not had a full immersion experience of ATR. If anything, experience is varied and superficial. A typical African person is so different from the imaginary traditional African before the arrival of the gospel. The Kenyan Maasai in a three-piece suit and tie, on Zoom in his air-conditioned office in Gigiri and arguing passionately about traditional Maasai values, is so different from his kinsman who had his rite of passage by surviving a contest with a lion in the Maasai Mara.

According to Turaki: "The 'Africanness' ideology in scholarship must be put to one side as it will only divert our attention from engaging and interacting with the traditional mind."[220] Turaki rejects both African and Western ideologies and their styles of theological discourse, especially the dominant approaches of African scholarship. The "Africanness" of the African person comes out in the way they live, sing African songs, serve the interest of others, dance in church, pray as they do and in other expressions which happen effortlessly. Kato wrote:

> The disturbed traditional life must be re-examined. Culture is what binds a people together and gives them a sense of identity as a community. The call for cultural revival is therefore right

---

219. Turaki, *Engaging Religions*, xxiii.
220. Turaki, xxvi.

and necessary. But no culture is static. Every culture is changing. So the Romans influenced English culture, Arabs influenced Spanish culture. Africans influenced early American culture, and recently Americans have been influencing European culture. Borrowing from other cultures and revisions of traditional lifestyle is what makes a culture alive and dynamic.[221]

Kato argued that religion is the heart of culture for Africans, and if there is a change in religion it would require a re-adjustment in culture. Short of this is to deny the person freedom of religion, a fundamental human right.

If Christians, for example, refuse to be involved in dancing, they cannot be charged with throwing away African culture. Their deep respect for the older people, parents, and authorities is certainly more important than body twisting, which may have immoral intentions. Because they have assumed a new religion, Christianity, they have to abide by the principles laid down in the Book of their religion, the Bible. The Bible becomes the final judge of their culture.[222]

An authentic African Christian is one who will authentically live as an African in authentic Christian ways, as Christ did. About Christ, the people in the community asked: "Isn't this the carpenter's son? Isn't his mother's name Mary, and aren't his brothers James, Joseph, Simon and Judas?" (Matt 13:55 NIV). One's identity in the society is unmistakable; but also, there is a sense in which one's identity is infused with the community. Jesus could not be distinguished from his disciples; he had to be identified by a kiss in order to tell him apart from the rest of the disciples (Mark 14:44). Distinct Christian identity then does not necessarily distance the believer from the community or people around them.

A model of the church as the one family of God, rooted in agape love, is the answer for the quest for self-understanding for the African Christian. The choice of this model is also based on its relational element, a core value in African cultures. However, more than the African practice of *ubuntu*, the "Christian African" should have no place for divisive ethnicity. "God is

---

221. Kato, *African Cultural Revolution*, 6.
222. Kato, 7.

glorified when Christians view themselves as members of one family, an attitude of voluntary surrender is generated, and God's children are compelled to learn each other's cultures."[223]

Defining a Christian identity distinct from the culture in which Christians find themselves is critical to the Christian faith. In the past, scholars explained identity construction without taking into consideration changes in group dynamics over time. However, sociologists' current social identity theory teaches that identity is a complex social construct. Afterall, Christian identity may not be monolithic and unchanging as previously held.[224] Perhaps Christian identity is much more complicated than we tend to think.

> People can belong to several different groups at the same time; people could hold multiple social identities. Different people represent their multiple social identities in different ways. Within the same group, for instance, there might be people who simultaneously belong to particular groups each of a different nature (intimacy groups, loose associations, religious groups, and so forth), but in their own mind, and in a particular context, they might view a certain group (and loyalty to that group) as being more important than another group.[225]

With the help of social identity complexity theory, social scientific models have been proposed to support Christian identity construction and ethos, which transcend and transform social and cultural boundaries, rather than maintaining the social hegemony of the day.[226] From social scientific perspectives, social identity can be construed and structured in many ways. People's social identity can be high or low in social identity complexity. People with a high level of social identity complexity tend to be more inclusive of outgroups, according to Roccas and Brewer.[227] Accordingly, Kok writes:

> From a cursory analysis of the Pauline texts as a case study, it seems that Paul had a high level of social identity complexity

---

223. Maigadi, "Christian Faith," ii.
224. Kok, "Social Identity Complexity," 1.
225. Kok, 2; cf. Roccas and Brewer, "Social Identity Complexity," 88.
226. Kok, "Social Identity Complexity," 8.
227. Roccas and Brewer, "Social Identity Complexity," 7.

that enabled him to transcend social boundaries and facilitate a higher level of inclusiveness. Paul was rather critical of Peter at one stage in history, as a result of Peter's compartmentalisation that functioned in a dominating way and brought about re-segregation rather than reconciliation. Paul's baptismal unity formula in Galatians 3:28, which states that all believers are one in Christ, irrespective of whether a person is a Jew or a Greek, free person or slave, created new language and metaphors, like, "new creation," "brothers and sisters," "all of you are one"; and he rejects language and practices that break down this unity (cf. Gal 3:38; 1 Cor 12:13; Col 3:11; cf. 1 Cor 9:19–23).[228]

In other words, "identity" is always being negotiated, debated and asserted and is always changing; whether personal identity or ethnic, racial or national identity, all are always being revised. Human identity requires redemption; one dies to the old and is raised with Christ in baptism.[229]

There is a difference between assimilation, inculturation and sanctification. The newly born-again Christian's aspiration is for Christian living. This should not be negritude, colonialism or inferiority of African cultural values; it is indeed a judgement on all human cultures. Kato wrote:

> The search for authenticity through culture remains a desirable element in many African societies. The attitude of Christians toward cultural renaissance need not be negative. Culture as a way of life must be maintained. Christ became a man in order to save men. In becoming incarnate, he was involved in the Jewish culture – wearing their clothes, eating their food, thinking in their thought patterns. But while he went through all that, he was without sin, addressing both Jewish and Gentile people authoritatively as the Son of God.[230]

Furthermore, Kato wrote:

> Jesus would not have come to make Africans become American Christians nor to cause Europeans to become Indian Christians.

---

228. Kok, "Social Identity Complexity," 8.
229. Otonko, "Beyond the Rhetoric," 8.
230. Kato, *Biblical Christianity*, 41–42.

It is God's will that Africans, on accepting Christ as their Saviour, become Christian Africans. Africans who become Christians should therefore remain Africans wherever their culture does not conflict with the Bible. It is the Bible that judges the culture. Where a conflict results, the cultural element must give way.[231]

The story of the Tower of Babel in Genesis 11 was an attempt by fallen humanity to seek an identity without God and his purpose. But in the New Testament, this was reversed at Pentecost; at Pentecost, God reverses the curse of Babel. The Pentecost narrative affirms ethnic and linguistic diversity as part of the renewed people of God. At Babel, people sought homogeneity outside God's intended purpose; Pentecost restored unity-in-diversity as God intended.[232]

It is worthwhile to state that Christ is not against any culture. What he does is to eliminate elements of culture that are opposed to the will of God, thereby raising the culture to God's standard. As a transformer of culture, Christ (or the Christian faith) permeates cultures to heal people of practices that hinder them in fulfilling the will of God. The neglect of this important dimension of Christ's relationship with all human cultures – that he is the *transformer* of culture – has made Africans carry the Christian faith and African traditional religion on the same voyage. This is, indeed, the crisis of the Christian faith.[233] Yes, there are basic unchangeable aspects of identity – physical and geographic characteristics. But there are also adjusted elements which undergo repeated changes depending on several factors.

Therefore, Kato's argument with his detractors was extremely important at the time. In fact, Kato offers some lessons for the contemporary church that are even more important today than in his generation. If Africa is to take seriously the mantle God is handing over to the African church, to be his mouthpiece of the gospel to the world, the introspective identity some scholars are once again suggesting is actually the opposite of what the church must assume. In global Christianity, the evangelical church in Africa cannot hope to evangelise Europe by insisting on projecting our Africanness, as if we believe that the European missionaries were after all correct in their colonization of

---

231. Kato, "Contextualisation and Religious," 2.
232. Tarus and Lowery, "African Theologies," 306.
233. Otonko, "Beyond the Rhetoric," 5–6.

Africa.²³⁴ We must, on the contrary, assume "third race" Christian identity in order to be able to evangelise the world.

Kato's contribution towards theological education also had theoretical and theological bases, to which I now turn.

Foundations of Kato's Contribution to Evangelical Theological Education

Kato recognised the importance of the top giftings that the Holy Spirit bestows on the church for solid grounding, expansion and maturation. These are the prophetic, apostolic, and teaching-pastoral ministries.²³⁵ While he was concerned about teaching the Scripture at all levels in the church, he was particularly concerned about the training and development of leaders for prophetic, apostolic and pastoral roles. The Christian faith is sustained and passed from one generation to another through Christian education. Education with the aid of the Holy Spirit grounds believers in the faith and provides direction for every area of life.

Theology is the soul of the church; therefore, "theological education is an intrinsic and intentional part of our participation in God's mission."²³⁶ Formal and informal theological education "belong to the biblical category of 'teaching.' It is for the Church, to serve the life, growth and mission of God's people, both in training its pastors and leaders and in helping all believers to be 'transformed through renewal of their minds' – to have the mindset of the Spirit."²³⁷ The goal of theological training is to strengthen the church, so the church can transform the world. Therefore, theological education must be characterised by missional intent to shape the character and behaviour of people, by the worship of the one true God in a world of religious pluralism and by the maturing of the church.²³⁸Kato was concerned about the state of theological education in newly independent African countries during his time. He observed that Islam and Socialism were doing more to brainwash Africans

---

234. Asumang, "Biblical Studies," 60–62.
235. Kato, "Power"; cf. Eph 4: 1–16.
236. Wright, "Effectiveness and Impact," 2
237. Wright, 2.
238. See Col 1:6, 9–11; Eph 4:11–16.

by enticing Africans with offers of scholarships from Islamic, socialist and communist nations but little was done for theological education; stating:

> African Independent churches number 6,000 movements, claiming 7,000,000 adherents, and are growing by 100,000 each year. Their theology varies from strong belief in fresh visions by priestesses and priests, to a syncretism that places their founder e.g. Simeon Kimbangu in Zaire, in equal position with Jesus Christ. A strong emphasis on things African will bring about a repudiation of traditional Christianity as presented by the missionaries. The philosophy of doing things African per se will help the growth of the Independent Movement. Theology, that is where the action really is.[239]

Kato went further to assess the kind of training offered on the continent then, and to underscore the need for theological training:

> By sheer number of trained theologians, liberalism presents a real threat. Although only about 1% of all students in Africa go to University as compared to 4.6% the world average, these university-level people are the elite of the continent. They will be the administrators, financiers, military rulers, decision makers in every department of life including the church. Theological education available so far for any of these varsity grads, has a strong view of African religions and culture. Almost all the 68 universities of the continent have a department of religions, where one can obtain up to a Ph.D. A search for peaceful co-existence among religions seems to be the basic concern of these religions. Thus, the graduates have come out with a call for softer and friendlier approach to Islam, African Religions and other faiths.[240]

Thus, evangelicals in Africa saw this as a challenge; the need to battle for the mind and the training of the leadership, the decision makers, to match the intellectual formation of these others for the survival of biblical Christianity

---

239. Kato, "Africa: Facts," 1–2.
240. Kato, 2.

in the church in Africa. This is how the theological commission of the then AEAM was established. Kato wrote:

> In their triennial conference, the 165 delegates of the Association of Evangelicals of Africa and Madagascar from 27 countries, expressed a deep concern on the theological trends in Africa. A Theological Commission under the AEAM was set up to encourage the few existing theological schools in the continent. It was noted with regret that nowhere in the continent could a college graduate get a theological education at a graduate level. It was therefore resolved that an M.Div. level of training be started in the continent.[241]

According to Domeris and Smith: "The task of studying theology at tertiary level is a complex one, because this is not just an academic exercise – it involves our faith, indeed our whole reason for living."[242] Ultimately, the theological training programmes must produce graduates who are fit and committed to participate in God's mission, faithful to worshipping the one true God of the Bible and growing in maturity in their understanding, obedience and endurance in faith. Kato wrote: "It is absolutely essential that church leadership in Africa delve into the discipline of theology before the queen of sciences is relegated to the second-rate status and the Christians left undernourished and confused."[243] He advocated for the church to reach out to young people, especially in secondary school and university. Kato underscored the importance of theological education not only for evangelisation, but for discipling the young. He encouraged Christian education programmes for the youth in the church and wrote:

> Christian Education encourages the growth of various youth organizations in the church as well as those of the older people. A strong Sunday School, Youth Fellowship, Boys' Brigade, Girls' Brigade, Young Sword League, and other similar clubs that promote Christian teaching are given impetus by Christian Education. . . . Youth centres in cities to be established by NEFs

---

241. Kato, 2
242. Domeris and Smith, "Preface" in A Student's Guide" 8.
243. Kato, "Written Theology," 1

as not every single church should do so, Bible colleges to train in youth work. Encouraged parents to do the same.... A good Christian home should be the foundation of youth work.... Involve youths in activities of the church. Sunday school, library for them to read, games and sports. Discover their talents.[244]

The task of making disciples emphasizes the educational aspect of the great commission given to the faith community. "It is discipleship unto life transformation – a process of growth and development of the total person, spiritual, intellectual, volitional and emotional, to the end that the disciple is made fit for life here and in the hereafter."[245] Theron and Raiter further stated: "The church has a missional purpose, which is enhanced through education, both of her leadership and of the generality of her membership."[246] Jesus Christ himself spent three years teaching, coaching and mentoring the apostles. Similarly, the apostle Paul invested time in teaching and mentoring leaders for the churches he planted in his ministry (Acts 20:27).

The church is divided on the place for theological education in the mission of the church. The evangelical movement has placed priority on evangelism and church planting tasks, with speed as a core value, to the neglect of investing time and resources for theological education as a core component of the great commission. The church is starved for not being fed with the whole counsel of God's word. The goal of evangelical theological education is to turn out a graduate who is a thinking practitioner: "one who thinks deeply about theology, but who is also actively engaged in Christian ministry of some sort. They reflect deeply on the great questions and challenges facing the church in their context, develop theological responses that seek to show God's viewpoint so as to help the people of God to respond in ways that are faithful to the Lord."[247]

In a review of a book by Tite Tiénou, Carson highlights what Tiénou perceived as the theological challenge and task of the church in Africa. According to Carson, Tiénou pinned the challenge to "the relationships between biblical Christianity and African culture, and between biblical Christianity and

---

244. Kato, "Youth," 3.
245. Theron and Raiter, *Effective Theological Education*, 12.
246. Theron and Raiter, 17.
247. Smith, *Integrated Theology*, 13.

African religion; and the nature of and need for proper contextualization of theology in Africa today."[248] However, what Tiénou saw as threats to the evangelical church were internal. Unlike Kato's external threats from liberal ecumenists, Tiénou draws attention to "dangers within the evangelical church." These include: (1) mistrust of theology; (2) the persistent tendency of African evangelicalism to follow their leaders blindly without thinking biblically and theologically and thus contribute to their errors (Tiénou called this "sacerdotalism"); (3) the danger of an ahistorical faith and the need for some awareness of two thousand years of Christian tradition and reflection; and (4) denominational individualism. Tiénou's call or prescription was the need to develop "positive theology." A theology that does not merely criticise other developments, or merely follow leaders, African or Western, but that thinks "God's definitive revelation" for itself and in its own context. This should be done without sacrificing the authority of Scripture or the counsel of tradition, but equally without adopting undigested theological formulations that bear no consequences for Africa and its needs, cultures and categories.[249]

Tiénou also urged that theological reflection should be in the context of prayer, and he called for African evangelicals to aim for a balance between theological unity and denominational and personal identity and freedom. Furthermore, Tiénou admonished African evangelicals to advance their numbers in the developing departments of religion in the new universities instead of withdrawing. He highlighted the need to establish "two or three" more graduate schools of theology. He urged the church to proceed cautiously with theological education by extension (TEE) programmes. He called on evangelicals to befriend wherever possible the leaders of the many independent churches in Africa, in the hope of influencing their direction to strengthen ACTEA and ETSA (Evangelical Theological Society in Africa) and more.[250]

As the immediate successor to Kato as the executive secretary of the AEA Theological Commission,[251] Tiénou's musings here are important. Tiénou's observations may be a fair assessment of the situation in the church, but perhaps his concerns are more of leadership issues than theological issues per

---

248. Carson, review of *Theological Task*, 119–120.
249. Carson, 120
250. Carson, review of *Theological Task*, 120.
251. Bowers, *Theological Education*, 9.

se. Also, these challenges are not so much in tandem with Kato's perspective on theological advancement, even if both agreed on the need for theological education. One wonders whether Tiénou's concern was more of quelling the feud and diffusing the line Kato had clearly drawn between liberalism and what was the beginning of the evangelical wing in the emerging African theological discourse. Bowers notes: "The average educated African evangelical would probably resonate with many of the themes and preoccupations of African Theology, even if he would expect to modify the answers given on these issues."[252] Thus, Tiénou's proposal could well be the genesis of the "middle-ground" posture many of the budding evangelical theologians took. Carson observes: "Tiénou reflects a healthy catholicity: he draws from western and African writers, conservatives and otherwise, without in the slightest veering from his biblical moorings."[253] By contrast, Kato maintained his stance: "I have heard some key leaders warn against 'the hardening of lines between liberals and evangelicals,' and this we can appreciate. But can we realistically wipe out the line without compromising the evangelical faith if the liberals stick to their theological stance and practice?"[254]

The nature and goal of theology is not simply to apply the gospel in the diverse contexts of human life. It also aims to create understanding of the unchanging nature of the gospel – the absolutes that transcend time and cultural pluralism.[255] Kato's remedy included establishing an academic service for providing standards, accreditation, curriculum and faculty development, in addition to establishing two graduate evangelical theological schools in sub-Saharan Africa. Kato insisted on training Christian leaders on African soil to avoid liberalisation in Western institutions, among other reasons.

However, the faculty in the evangelical African seminaries at the time were mostly Western missionaries. The approaches and curriculum were shaped by Western standards, and subjects like African traditional religions were also taught by Western missionaries. Harries asserts: "The categories of 'African Traditional Religions' (ATRs) and 'world religions' (WRs) turn

---

252. Bowers, "African Theology," 121.
253. Carson, review of *Theological Task*, 119.
254. Kato, "African Perspective" in Evangelical Mission Quarterly, No. 10, 308
255. Hiebert, *Anthropological Reflections*, 102.

out to be Western inventions with an incomplete grasp of reality."[256] Drawing from his personal experience of mentoring an African colleague who took over his teaching responsibilities in ATR, Harries opines that what is written and communicated about ATRs is on Western terms and forms, and in fact, originally written by Westerners and Africans who followed the same patterns of communication that would gain acceptance in the academy. "Without a doubt, my African colleagues knew African religion, in the sense of what Africans do and believe, better than I did. What they did not know was how to communicate this information in a form that is acceptable to Western scholarship."[257]

Kato himself taught ATR at Igbaja Seminary. Rev. Norman Lohrenz, a missionary colleague, observed that the students got a better understanding of the subject under Kato's tutelage than under any other faculty member.[258] He was forthright in spelling out the difference between ATR beliefs and Christianity. According to Haye, Kato said: "In the context of African traditional religions, the worship is merely an indication of an honest craving for God, which can be fulfilled only in biblical revelation through the incarnate Christ who died and rose again."[259] He also argued that Africans should be made to feel that Christianity was an African religion and not any more foreign than it is in Europe or other parts of the world.

Kato's unique and contrary theological views became a cause for hot debate in theological circles in Africa. Aspersions were voiced that Kato's stand was not African, and the authenticity of his Christian beliefs was questioned.[260] Yet Kato's theological perspectives were not innovations. Similar to the way classical doctrines of Scripture were established, Kato contended for what had been known and practiced from antiquity, and what represented contemporary mainstream evangelicalism.[261] Kato's theological perspectives were grounded in classical Christian beliefs. The contentions against Kato in contrast arose from what were more novel and localised theological instincts.

---

256. Harries, "Overcoming Invented Ogres," 171.
257. Harries, 172–173.
258. Cited in Haye, *Byang Kato*, 50.
259. Haye, 50.
260. Ngong, "Material," 109.
261. Otonko, "Beyond the Rhetoric," 6.

Summary and Conclusion

While Kato's theological perspectives stood in contrast with the views of many of his fellow Africans with whom he debated, there seems to be resonance with other evangelical theologians and with scholars from the past and from other parts of the world, as well as some African scholars. Some people could argue that Kato's views did not resonate with the African context because Christianity tends to be cloaked in Western civilisation rather than being authentically African. However, Kato contended that the answer to getting rid of the Western cloak was not to then cloak the gospel in African culture or ATR. Instead, Kato advocated for a biblical Christianity that both has a home in Africa and is understandable for others from other regions of the world.

Byang Kato's theological interpretative stance and approach to the Bible was dispensationalism and the inductive method. In the inductive Bible study approach, it is acknowledged that all have blind spots, and therefore the help of others is needed.[262] In endorsing Kato's *Theological Pitfalls in Africa*, Billy Graham stated: "Paul, Peter and Jude would have approved of the theme of this book, for they too were on guard against the destructive effect of heretical ideas (Gal 2:4; 2 Peter 2:1; and Jude 4). Dr Kato provides us here with an update in the perennial concern the Christian Church ought to have against what he calls 'unhealthy trends' in theology."[263] Graham went on to state:

> Much of the world, including Africa, today still reveals entrenched idolatry. In addition, the awakening consciousness of nationalism provides the temptation of fabricating a faith to be embraced mainly because of what it can do for people materially. Dr Kato properly suggests however that there should be no conflict between nationalistic loyalty and biblical faith. The Scripture teaches clearly that a believer is by definition a citizen of two worlds.[264]

Charles Ryrie, in his introduction to *Theological Pitfalls in Africa*, was equally affirming of Kato's theological direction. Ryrie stated:

---

262. Bauer and Traina, *Inductive Bible Study*, 26.
263. Graham, foreword to *Theological Pitfalls* iii.
264. Graham, iv.

Byang Kato is uniquely qualified to say what is said in this important work. His background is in Africa; his training has been thorough; and he has no cause to champion except that of the truth of the Scripture. . . . The author's case against syncretistic universalism is fully documented and well-reasoned. He has issued a scholarly challenge to those who follow these false teachings.[265]

Kato's theology has had an appeal to other scholars in other parts of the world.[266] He may have been a solo voice in vigorously defending the gospel against several opponents, but what he stood for had resounding resonance with mainstream Christianity. Kato's contribution, to make Christianity understandable in all cultures, is particularly important in contemporary Christianity where the African church is now the majority in the global church. As part of this research inquiry, the next chapter attempts to analyse in detail what constituted Kato's theological legacy as a whole – and in particular in relation to the areas highlighted in the preceding chapters, including this one.

---

265. Ryrie, introduction to *Theological Pitfalls*, ii
266. See Shirik, "African Christians."

CHAPTER 5

A Model for Biblical Fidelity in African Evangelical Christianity

Introduction

As a pioneer evangelical theologian in Africa, Kato has a unique place in the church and theological circles in global Christianity. Kato's life and ministry in the academy, in the pulpit and in the community, not to mention his leadership roles in his own church body, in Africa as a whole and indeed within global Christianity, established him as a theological leader. He is acclaimed as the father of evangelical theology in modern sub-Saharan Africa. His theological legacy is very much alive in the church in Africa. His name is revered and remembered in many parts of the church today. Kato's life story is itself a theological means for reflection.[1] His conversion from African traditional religion to Christianity and how he lived as a Christian with a dominant biblical worldview is of theological interest.

Nevertheless, Kato has been criticized by some people, and it has been said that he has no theology of his own.[2] Kato's critics may be referring to academic theology, and therefore limiting his theological contribution to the scholarly work of his doctoral dissertation and its published version, *Theological Pitfalls in Africa*, which sparked heated theological debates that

---

1. See 1 Thess 5:12–13; Heb 11; 13:7.
2. Bediako, *Theology and Identity*; Ngong, "Material," 109; Palmer, "Byang Kato: Rejectionist"; Oduyoye, *Hearing and Knowing*, 62.

continue to date. Kato's work was a critique of the theology of other scholars, who were mostly concerned with the integration of African traditional religions with Christianity. Kato's aggressive critique of African theology for embracing syncretistic and the liberal tendencies of universalism was his major scholarly undertaking before his untimely demise. He warned the church and named the drivers of these theological pitfalls. Further theological contribution would be cut short by his sudden and tragic death.[3]

What is considered theology in the academy is generally limited to the traditional disciplines of "biblical exegesis, church history, systematic theology, pastoral theology."[4] Thus Kato's critics credited him for little or no theology of his own, but branded him as a complainer, thus making him seem infamous. Kato is charged with being a pawn in the hands of Western theological masters, intent on undermining attempts at promoting the dignity of Africans.[5] Kwame Bediako, one of Kato's fiercest critics, writes: "Virtually everything he wrote was intended as a reaction to, and a rebuttal of, much that went to constitute the 'African theology' of the last two decades. For this, if for no other reason, Byang Kato's work compels attention."[6] Bediako further charges Kato with retaining the Western model of theologizing, stating that Kato was "trained in theology on a Western model like his fellow African theologians of modern time, yet unlike them, he retained that model for his theological reflection in his African context."[7]

So, while Kato is charged as a rejectionist of African theology,[8] it is implied that the other theologians had rejected whatever they had been taught in their own training in the West. One wonders what in fact had been rejected or retained from the West by these other theologians. Bediako also acknowledges the fact that Kato's views represented his deep roots in conservative evangelical tradition.[9] While Kato's engagement with other people's theologies was indeed a critique of what was wrong, that was itself one category of theologising. However, a careful assessment also reveals that Kato's life history

---

3. Haye, *Byang Kato*, 91; cf. Ngong, "Material," 127.
4. Oborji, "Contemporary Missiology," 393.
5. Ngong, "Material," 132.
6. Bediako, *Theology and Identity*, 386
7. Bediako, 386; cf. Bediako, "Understanding African Theology," 16.
8. Kato, *Lift Up Your Hearts*.
9. Bediako, *Theology and Identity*, 386.

and his zealous polemics accented and defined what he perceived as biblical Christianity, and close examination can reveal some theological constructs that characterised his theology and for which he was known and remembered.

Theology itself is born out of mission, the mother of theology.

> The missionary commission, which has its source in the *Missio Dei*, cannot appear only in the specifically theological sphere but also embraces liturgy, prayer, proclamation, communication of the faith in all its forms. All of this, of course, needs thorough theological reflection, especially in the cultural context, but must not be confined to it.[10]

However, theological reflections did not necessarily have a prominent place in the development of a discipline of systematic reflection on mission, according to Oborji.[11] Oborji quotes Bosch:

> Christianity is missionary by its very nature and it is the intrinsic nature and mission of the church to proclaim the message of salvation in Christ to the ends of the earth. To neglect this mission is for the church to deny its very *raison d'être*. But this does not mean that missiology as a theological discipline is a neutral or disinterested enterprise; rather, it seeks to look at the world from the perspective of commitment to the Christian faith. Such an approach implies as well a critical examination of every manifestation of the church's missionary activity to rigorous analysis and appraisal, precisely for the sake of the Christian mission itself.[12]

For many centuries, theology was a single discipline, the knowledge of God, without subdivisions. According to Oborji, theology came to be subdivided into two areas with the emergence of the Enlightenment:

> Theology as practical know-how necessary for clerical work, and theology as one technical and scholarly enterprise among others (theology as practice and as theory). From here, theology

---

10. Oborji, "Contemporary Missiology," 390.
11. Oborji, 385.
12. Bosch, *Transforming Mission*, 9, quoted in Oborji, 384.

evolved gradually into what Farley calls the "fourfold pattern": the disciplines of the Bible (text), church history (history), systematic theology (truth), and practical theology (application). Each of these had its parallels in the secular sciences. "Practical" theology became a mechanism to keep the church going, whilst the other disciplines were examples of "pure" science.[13]

However, missiology, as a discipline which takes into consideration the diverse aspects of mission and the work of the church, is a form of theological discourse. Smith posits, "We do theology by thinking and speaking about God's word and our faith. Scholars use four important words to describe the way theologians reason and discourse: hermeneutical, critical, correlational and dialogical."[14]

Thus, there is firm theoretical foundation for exploring the life histories of missionaries and their activities in the church for theological reflection, apart from and in addition to their contributions to the academy or seminary. Therefore, this study has sought to explore the missionary activities of Byang Kato, a prominent African church leader, and his contributions in the academy. The discourse in this research has been hermeneutical, critical, correlational and dialogical. It has been "a word about God."[15] It is not so much about studying God, as God cannot be a direct object of study, but "divine revelation and people's faith are two direct objects of theology," and indirectly we get to know God's nature and will through the systematic study of divine revelation and human faith.[16]

The lively debates and abiding impact that Kato ignited continue to date, more than four decades after his sudden death. One could argue that the ongoing debate in African theological discourse, especially about the relationship between African traditional religions and Christianity, is itself an important theological contribution. Following Kato's death, a number of his written contributions, although largely unpublished, were recovered and collated and made available as an important resource of information about Kato. Consequently, as important as *Theological Pitfalls in Africa* is, there are other

---

13. Oborji, *Contempoarary Missiology*, 387; cf. Smith, *Integrated Theology*, 35–38.
14. Smith, *Integrated Theology*, 38–39.
15. Smith, 3.
16. Smith, 18.

written sources that provide biographical information about Kato's life and theological reflections. Oral sources of information from family, colleagues and friends who have survived Kato for over four decades – despite being a depleted group of people – can provide vital information about Kato's life and ministry. During this study, for example, Kato's widow passed away only two months after the researcher met her and forty-four years after the death of Kato. Kato's contributions are also immortalized in at least three theological institutions that Kato helped to found in different regions of Africa.

The various sources highlighted above were used in this research to collate information to respond to the research questions. Bowers observes:

> Discussion about Kato needs to be reformulated, by setting him within the larger framework of his agenda and accomplishments. Much of the conventional treatment of Kato has repeatedly taken his measure almost exclusively in terms of his distinctive input to the African Theology debate. Kato is then interpreted either by critiquing or by defending that input. To the extent that this has become a common framing of the entire Kato discussion, it can prove reductionist and hence misleading.[17]

Therefore, this study was designed to explore data from the life history and biography of Kato and his theological legacy in three areas – hermeneutics, African Christian identity and evangelical theological education – as described in preceding chapters. In this penultimate chapter, I set out to construct a theological system that uniquely characterised Kato's contribution, which I have called the "Kato theological construct" – a distillation of Kato's legacy as an account of his theological vision which has relevance for contemporary evangelical scholarship in Africa. Kato himself did not claim any theology of his own, other than what the Bible says. The beliefs and practices that Kato's life and message conveyed could be a helpful model for the African Christianity of our day

Kato's message may seem to have been drowned with his body in the Indian Ocean on the eastern coast of Africa and interred with his bones in Kwoi on the western coast of Africa. This study is an attempt to resuscitate or resurrect that message for reflection in the contemporary church in the African

---

17. Bowers, "Byang Kato," 7.

context. As it were, this is a rebirth of Kato's *Theological Pitfalls in Africa*. The life and ministry of Kato – his birth and the context of his birth, his conversion and spiritual journey, his message, his rise as a global evangelical Christian leader and his tragic death – provide some important theological lessons with spiritual and practical value for Christians. The task is to assess Kato's effort to sustain biblical Christianity in Africa through teaching, the training of leaders and the development of discipleship programmes in the church.

Data from the study, drawn from the preceding four chapters, was the material for reflection and analysis in order to identify the themes that characterised Kato's theology. The themes identified were based on frequency of occurrence and the emphasis Kato placed on them. The themes were coded and categorised in the simple and understandable language Kato used, but that is perhaps not always as easily recognised as theological constructs crafted in technical theological language. Kato believed "Theology should be expressed in the context of every people for their understanding and practice, but Christian Theology does not need polarization, which has a tendency of adding to or subtracting from the gospel of Christ."[18] I have also attempted to set these out in standard or classical theological categories, which would make it easily comparable and contrastable with others. Thus, the following is the outline of the theological constructs or themes that I have identified as particular to Kato's theology. Each theme highlighted has subthemes, as outlined and described below.

Outline of Kato's Theological Construct

The following outline sets out what I deduce as Kato's theological emphases, even if he himself did not set these out in a systematic account in his writing. Kato was concerned about the historic or classical doctrines of the Christian faith and wrote: "Unless the church in Africa wants to isolate itself from historic Christianity, it should take a position on these vital doctrines."[19] This comment was in reaction to those who wanted unity of the church at all costs, and who avoided talking about doctrines to avoid division. However, from his messages, writings and polemics, the following could be distilled as the

---

18. Kato, "Jesus Christ Frees," 30.
19. Kato, *Theological Pitfalls*, 149.

theological and doctrinal positions that Kato affirmed, contending for a historic Christianity that could be understood and applied in different contexts.

1. Soteriology (personal conversion)
   - Own personal salvation from world of sin or Adamic nature (Gen 6–8; Rom 3:23; 6:23; Eph 2:1; Col 1:21)[20]
   - Lostness of all humans and need for salvation (John 5:24; Rom 3:23; 5:12, 15; 6:23; Eph 2:1; Col 1:21)
   - Vicarious death of Jesus Christ as the only way for salvation (John 5:24; Acts 19:23–41; Rom 5:12, 17; Phil 3:8)
   - Uniqueness and otherness of Christ in salvation (Rom 5:17)
   - Salvation is more than physical liberation; both the oppressed and oppressor (all people) need salvation (John 3:16)
   - Conviction of sin, repentance and acceptance of Jesus Christ by faith (John 1:12; Eph 2:8–9; Phil 2:5–11)
2. Christian formation (disciple-making)
   - Discipleship through consciousness/consistency in learning to follow Christ as taught in Scripture (Matt 28:19; Acts 1:8).
   - Children and youth programmes (Prov 22:6; Eccl 12:1; 2 Cor 2:16; 2 Tim 1:5)
   - Family altar
   - Contending for the faith (Jude 3)
   - Holism in discipleship
   - Christian education
3. Bibliology (Bible-centred)
   - Doctrine and high view of the Bible as God's special revelation; inspired, inerrant and infallible (Acts 10:35; Heb 1:1; 2:3–4).
   - Biblical worldview (Exod 25:40; Heb 8:5)
   - Conservative, consensual and contextual
   - Authoritative and sufficient guide for faith and conduct; content unchanging (the 66 books of the OT and NT) but mode of expression contextual
   - Only foundational source for Christian theological reflection

---

20. Scriptural references are to the relevant Bible passages Kato used in connection to the themes related in this outline.

4. Christology (Christ-centred)
   - Incarnation and virgin birth
   - Personhood and divinity
   - Vicarious death and resurrection
   - Uniqueness of Christ as the only way for salvation
   - Return of Christ to earth as the glorious hope of followers of Christ
5. Ecclesiology (Christian African identity)
   - Identity in Christ
   - Third race citizenship (Rom 13:1–14)
   - New citizenship/one body of Christ (Acts 17:26)
   - Discontinuity (Matt 11:7–24; Eph 2:15)
   - Christian African – true freedom and self-understanding for the African Christian
   - True unity in diversity, and in Christ and his word (John 17:21)
6. Missiology (safeguarding biblical Christianity in Africa)
   - Strategic leadership development and establishing evangelicalism (Acts 13:1–2)
   - Theological education
   - Growth and maturation of the church (evangelism and disciple-making and leadership development)
   - Children and youth and family (roles in the ministry of the church)
   - Evangelical activism (evangelism)
7. Eschatology (the second coming or return of Jesus Christ)
   - Pietism – tendencies on the fringes of mainstream evangelicalism
   - Dispensationalism/premillennialism (Rev 20)
   - Second advent of Christ (Matt 16:27; John 1:14, 17; Titus 2:13)
   - Glorious hope of the church
8. Pneumatology and demonology (the Holy Spirit and demons)
   - "The second experience" (Acts 2; 4:8–31; 10:46; Eph 19:1–6)
   - Receiving the Holy Spirit, and the evidence (Luke 24:49; Acts 1:8; 2:1–13)

- Baptised and sealed and being filled with the Holy Spirit (Acts 6:3–5; 7:55; 9:17)
- Spiritual gifts (Rom 12:3–8; 1 Cor 12:4–14:40; Eph 4:1–16)
- Demons and angels and their impact on Christian life and missions

Each one of these constructs will be further described in the following subsections below.

Description of Kato's Theology

This section will now give a fuller description of each of the eight theological categories outlined in the last section. The description reflects the discussion in the previous chapters, and as much as possible uses Kato's thoughts, re-echoing his perspectives, reflecting his voice and including words he used and how these were understood.

Soteriology (Personal Conversion)

Kato's conversion to Christianity from African traditional religion, as a Jaba fetish priest and the "devil's baby" (Kato's words in alluding to his dedication as a fetish priest to the tribal god as a baby), is key to his understanding of salvation. Kato got saved at an impressionistic age of twelve years old and would continue to recount the experience for the rest of his life. Asked in an interview how he would respond to the question of how he was saved, Kato said:

> My reply will be, well, when I was without Christ. I was of course religious – religious in the sense of worshipping idols. But when Jesus Christ was presented to me, I realized that He was the Way of Life – not just a way, but the only Way, and so I asked Him to come into my heart, in order that when I die, I may be sure of going to be with Him in heaven.[21]

His personal experience of salvation was futuristic and foundational to his understanding of salvation, his theology and indeed his soteriology. Understanding the need for salvation requires an understanding of what is

---

21. Kato, "African Perspectives," 1.

at stake, which is to say, the right conception of sin and its eternal consequences. Kato observed:

> There has never been such great confusion concerning the meaning of salvation. The number one problem for not attaining the truth is the rejection of the authoritative Word of God. Since the Bible is not the authoritative source of teaching, the ecumenists are left to devise their own concept. The basic concept held by liberal ecumenists is social and economic liberation. To stress the idea of personal salvation and declare hell judgement is considered eccentric and dehumanizing. The concerted effort is for universal deliverance of all people everywhere from any kind of oppression by fellow human beings.[22]

Kato believed in the original depravity of human beings and their need for salvation. Humans were dead and lost in sin, estranged from God (Eph 2:1; Col 1:21) and hell bound.

> Since the fall, the total race of Adam has been condemned to death (Rom 3:23; 6:23). Salvation in the biblical sense is the passing out of this death dungeon (John 5:24) into the dimension of life. The members of the Adamic race are all stillborn (Rom 5:12). Not one of them deserves to live. But the undeserving favour of God has made salvation possible through the death and resurrection of Jesus Christ. The death and resurrection of the second Adam is described as to only "abound to many" (Rom 5:15). Christ is universally available to all men everywhere at any time. This is how far biblical universalism goes. But its effectiveness applies *only to those who receive the offer*.[23]

Thus, Christ, the God-Man, died for all, but only those who accept his offer through faith and repent of their Adamic nature and sinful life can be saved (Rom 5:17). Salvation does not come through following a religion, philosophy or liberation movement nor from liberation from the oppression of other peoples or systems. Expressing concern about liberation and Black theology on the question of salvation or soteriology, Kato wrote:

---

22. Kato, "Danger," 2–3.
23. Kato, *Theological Pitfalls*, 180–181. Emphasis original.

> To use New Testament terms like "salvation," "freedom," "deliverance," in a context of political liberation is semantically incorrect and leads to a misrepresentation of Christian truth. Questions of social justice are ethical, not soteriological. This in no way lessens the importance of these questions for the Christian but seeks to place them on a theologically-adequate foundation.[24]

Kato understood the demands of true Christianity regarding other religions: "A Christian is a person who believes in Christ and who by faith in Him has received remission of sins and everlasting life."[25]

Kato relates the salvation of Noah and his family in the flood reported in Genesis 6–8 to the salvation of people as a whole in the world. Just as people had to get into Noah's ark to be saved from perishing in the flood, people in this world need to be in Jesus Christ to be saved from eternal destruction without Christ.[26] Kato's main theological concern was salvation for people through faith in Jesus Christ. However, salvation for Kato was more of a future reality. He believed the essential mission of the church was to warn people about future condemnation and eternal suffering in hell through the proclamation of the gospel. Nevertheless, Kato stated: "It is a gospel that salvation of the individual soul begins here and now, and that eternal life qualitatively influences the whole dimension of life."[27]

Like the apostles in the Bible, Kato's message was what he had personally experienced. For example, the apostle John writes: "We proclaim to you the one who existed from the beginning, who we have heard and seen. We saw him with our own eyes and touched him with our own hands, He is the Word of life" (1 John 1:1). Kato claimed no apostolic authority, but the prayer of Jesus Christ confers similar standing on those who believe in him through the apostolic message. Jesus prayed for the disciples before going to the cross and ascending to heaven: "I am praying not only for these disciples but also for all who will ever believe in me through their message" (John 17:20). Therefore, Kato appropriated this and stated his own experience:

---

24. Kato, "Jesus Christ Frees," 70.
25. Kato, "Challenge of Evangelicalism."
26. Haye, *Byang Kato*, 19.
27. Kato, *Theological Pitfalls*, 153.

> While the NT Christianity respects human dignity and calls for justice, liberation in terms of what Christ came to do must be understood as meaning liberation primarily from man's fundamental dilemma, which is sin. When Christ talked of freedom, the Jewish leaders thought of political freedom. But He made it plain that He meant freedom from sin (John 8:31–38). Both the oppressed and the oppressor need this message. The liberated person must, therefore, see his fellow men as equal before God. The heart of Paul's social ethics is summed up in Galatians 3:28: "There is neither male nor female; for you are all one in Christ."[28]

Many people in the church in Africa today would base their membership in the church on reasons other than conversion in the biblical sense – the born-again experience or new birth in the Spirit. The burgeoning church membership could be motivated by African spirituality or religiosity and result in syncretic practices and not real conversion as understood by evangelical orthodoxy. Some Christians could be described as nominal or cultural Christians, relying on culture and tradition for their faith, and taking salvation to be political or social action. Kato wrote:

> While justice and social improvement are the results of salvation, they are not salvation. Both a slave and his master in the New Testament needed and enjoyed the salvation of the Lord (e.g. Philemon). It was possible for both the rich and the poor to be happy in the salvation of the Lord in the New Testament (Luke 16:19–31; Acts 16, 14, 15). Both the oppressed and the oppressor today need the gospel (Romans 3:23; John 1:12).[29]

Until people can confess being in Christ as the Bible teaches, and as demonstrated by Kato, in word and deed, their profession of the Christian faith is not authentic. Kato stated:

> Exploitation, disease, abject poverty and deprivation of the basic necessities of life have been the lot of the majority of African people. But what is the root cause of these human tragedies? Would man's problems be solved after alleviation of physical

---

28. Kato, *Biblical Christianity*, 51.
29. Kato, *African Cultural Revolution*, 32.

suffering and material deprivations? Is putting clothes on man's back and food in his stomach the way to solve man's basic need? Is political liberation the final answer? History negates any answers to these questions. Philosophical reflections show that man's root problem is beyond these issues here noted.[30]

Conversions start with conviction, confession and then forgiveness and repentance, based on Christ's substitutionary and sacrificial death on the cross:

> The Holy Spirit is absolutely necessary for rebirth (John 3:1–6). Anyone born of the Holy Spirit has the Spirit taking His abode in him from the time of that conversion experience onward (Rom 8:9). Even such carnal Christians as those in the Corinthian church, possessed the Holy Spirit (1 Cor 16:19–20).[31]

Forgiveness is appropriated by faith in Christ. Life in Christ means a complete turnaround and a new identity in Christ. It is not just a change of religion but a change in religious beliefs, values and practices from previous religions, which were always sinful and inconsistent with what the Bible teaches.

It is the person of Jesus Christ, and not the religion or culture, that is being presented, if Christianity is to be faithful to the mission and message of its Lord. Nominal or cultural Christianity may also be one of the reasons for misleading theologies based on human philosophies and not the Bible, God's special revelation. True conversion demands the lordship of Jesus Christ in every aspect of the Christian's life, above anything else, any person, religion, culture or nationality. Arguing the case for evangelism as distinct from social action, Kato wrote:

> The Messiah came as both the Messenger and the content; the "*eungelion.*" The incarnation as a whole was good news to the cursed Creation (Rom 8:23) but the "saving of souls" was the primary purpose of God condescending to the lowest depth of humanity (Phil 2:5–11). The Son of Man truly came to serve, but that service was the atonement made possible on the cross (Mark 10:45; 8:36). When it is announced intelligently to the hell-bound sinful soul that God gave His Son to die in his place

---

30. Kato, "Theology of Eternal," 1.
31. Kato, 2.

and that the choice is now left with him, a choice that will determine destiny, evangelism has taken place (John 1:12; 3:16, 36; Acts 4:12; 16:31; 1 Peter 1:23–25; Eph 2:8, 9).[32]

Kato goes on further to argue:

> While it is true that the Old Testament concept of salvation was physical deliverance from whatever problem the people of God had (Exodus 15:1, 2; Psalm 34:6; Isaiah 43:11), the New Testament assumed the meaning primarily as deliverance from sin (Luke 19:10). Sin is the fundamental dilemma of man. Christ died to save man from that dilemma (Ephesians 2:13–18). The outcome of salvation, of course, calls for social concerns here and now. But that in itself is no salvation.[33]

Kato's definition of evangelism is important for the church, even as the debate about the definition of evangelism and social action continues in the church. Kato believed that salvation was not political liberation or social development but eternal redemption.

Christian Formation (Radical Discipleship)

Following Kato's conversion to Christianity, he saw the need to learn and grow in his faith. Being a Christian meant learning about and following Jesus Christ as a disciple. Kato believed the only reliable source of information about Christ and his newly found faith was the Bible. He took seriously what the Bible said, made time "for the inductive study of God's word"[34] and was diligent in availing himself of biblical teaching in the church. Kato asserted: "Know the truth and defend it, with all at your disposal, including your life's blood. Our Lord appeals to us to 'contend for the faith which was once delivered to the saints' (Jude 3)."[35]

Like his conversion experience, Kato began his discipleship journey with fundamental biblical vision, learning to be a disciple. Kato was an adolescent when he converted to Christianity, a period of life when he was still open and

---

32. Kato, *Theological Pitfalls*, 153; cf. Leffel, "Conference Theme," xiv.
33. Kato, *Theological Pitfalls*, 163–164.
34. Kato, 183.
35. Kato, *Biblical Christianity*, 37.

willing to learn anything that would stay with him for life. He went through biblical instructions in the church before he was baptised. He developed a keen interest in Sunday school, where he followed the lady missionary teacher to hear and learn more of the gospel message. He also went to the regular missionary school in the village. Kato was accorded the opportunity to learn about what it means to follow Jesus. He consciously and consistently availed himself of the opportunity for learning and Christian growth. He took advantage of the opportunity to teach others what he was taught in Sunday school and the normal school. Applying what he learned by teaching others was a way of integrating the message in his own life.

Kato was an enthusiastic member of the Boys' Brigade. He achieved the rank of sergeant, a leader of his company, and won the Proficiency Star.[36] The Boys' Brigade accorded him the opportunity to develop disciplines and life skills based on Christian values. He was also involved with Youth for Christ, a non-denominational international Christian youth ministry. As an elementary school pupil, he continued working on the family farm and doing chores for missionaries to earn his livelihood.[37]

Kato understood that following Christ meant a change of worldview and identity, with far-reaching implications for his direction and way of life. Thus, he wrote: "Following the steps of the New Testament church, Christians in Africa should be prepared to say, 'For me to live is Christ, and to die is gain' (Phil 1:21). Africa needs her Polycarps, Athanasiuses, and Martin Luthers, ready to contend for the faith at all cost."[38] He went on further to state: "The Lord of the Church, who has commanded Bible-believing Christians to 'contend earnestly for the faith' (Jude 3), has also said, 'Yes, I am coming quickly' (Rev 22:20). May we give the reverberating response, 'Amen, Come Lord Jesus.'"[39] Kato was indeed a radical follower of Jesus Christ and led others to follow Jesus.

Kato was a strong voice for discipling children and youth in the church. Underscoring the importance of children and youth in an address to church leaders in Africa at the First General Assembly of the AEA, Kato stated:

---

36. Haye, *Byang Kato*, 23.
37. Haye, 22.
38. Kato, *Theological Pitfalls*, 184.
39. Kato, 184.

"A reliable survey has indicated that 75% of Africa's 260,000,000 population is under 20. If children and young people form the majority of our population then they deserve our whole attention. But it is not the size alone that makes this age group very significant. This is a very significant age for conversion."[40] The scriptural injunction in Proverbs 22:6 is apt: "Train up a child in the way he should go; and when he is old, he will not depart from it" (KJV). The Scripture further urges: "Remember your Creator in the days of your youth, before the days of trouble come and years approach" (Eccl 12:1). Young Timothy was commended for his sincere faith inherited from the grandmother and mother (2 Tim 1:5). Kato wrote: "There is nothing for the youths to remember that has not been made known to them. Here we want to see if the Church of Christ in Africa is fulfilling its task in filling the minds of the youth with something to remember."[41] Further admonishing the church leaders, Kato stated:

> A sound Christian Education programme in every local church should be pursued. A great deal of evangelism has been done but little teaching has followed. The great commission is "Go ye therefore, and TEACH all nations. TEACHING them to observe all things whatsoever I have commanded you." A sound Christian Education would mobilize our young people into active participation of the church life.[42]

He admonished church leaders to prioritise involving young people in the ministry of the church and to take seriously their needs for growth in their faith:

> Many young people today feel neglected. It is a fact that some old pastors look at the youth as sinners who cannot have hands in the holy things of God. But "who is sufficient for these things?" (2 Cor 2:16). "If thou Lord, shouldest mark iniquities, O Lord, who shall stand?" (Psa 130:3). We should sympathize with our young people in their stormy period, bearing in mind that we were once in that stage. We should give our young people

---

40. Kato, "Youth," 1.
41. Kato, 1.
42. Kato, "Youth", 3.

something to do after they have committed their lives to Christ. Sin, of course, must be dealt with. But let us avoid pharisaic attitude.[43]

Kato outlined some programmes for consideration in the churches, like youth centres in the urban cities, libraries, family altars that seek the salvation and discipleship of children, social activities for young people, pastors writing letters to their youth when they are away in school and involving them in church programmes like special youth Sundays where they are solely in charge of the service. Kato himself had a "family altar" and led his three children to Christ before they turned ten. They prayed daily as a family and also had individual quiet times, reading and studying the word of God and doing personal prayers daily. Kato also reached out to neighbourhood children by organising children's clubs. He commended the work of parachurch organisations like Scripture Union, Intervarsity Christian Fellowship, and the Boys' and Girls' Brigades, but opined that young people needed to be grounded in the local church in order to sustain them in the faith.

Kato's consistency and conscientiousness in the pursuit of his life goal of serving God as a preacher and Bible teacher was demonstrated in the way he strove to gain sound theological education and in his diligent service to the church at all levels: national, regional and global. His outlook on life was to engage all of life, and he was an exemplar in standing up for biblical principles as a church leader. His goal was to make everyone a disciple of Christ, in obedience to the commandment and commission of Christ (Matt 28:19–20).

While Kato did not create any theology of his own, he learned from the wider evangelical Christian community. His framework was intentionally consensual. He recognised God's action and human faith in the history of the church. His discipleship experience was also holistic, embracing every area of his life, in community and through the local church. His ministry was also engaging, and always had the goal of making and encouraging disciples of Christ.

Kato was known for his integrity and faithfulness to his call as a disciple of Christ and minister of the gospel. He built a reputation for keeping his word: "He did what he said he would do."[44] He demonstrated a dualistic belief

---

43. Kato; cf. Leffel, "Conference Theme," xiv.
44. Manfred Kohl, interview with author, WEA General Assemby, Jakarta, November 2019.

at the conceptual level; that is, he believed in the dichotomy of the spiritual and physical, or material, aspects of a person, and he believed that the spiritual was more important and was the priority for salvation. However, his actions showed some level of holism. In other words, he did show concern for the whole person, integrating the spiritual and physical in his ministry. He probably inherited the holistic view of the person from his Africanness, which accorded with biblical values. Kato's pietism was also a hallmark of his discipleship. In the early part of his Christian journey, Kato felt the conviction of the Holy Spirit to rededicate his life and all he had to Christ at a revival meeting. Haye records Kato's confession: "With my heart breaking within me, and tears streaming down my face, I went forward to confess my sins before the Lord and His people. As a symbol of my sincerity, I took off my shirt and laid it alongside the other gifts. Oblivious to everyone, I knelt in prayer."[45] The shirt was what Kato had to contribute to the gift basket where others were putting cash as support for sending out missionaries. Kato narrated his encounter with Jesus in his prayer. According to Haye, Kato revealed:

> "It is not only your shirt I want," Jesus said to me. What do You mean? "I want your life, son." Lord, I give you my life. I don't know what you want me to be, but I dedicate myself to You. Do whatever You want with me. "Now I can use you," Jesus said, as He accepted my small gift like He'd accepted the few loaves and fishes from the young boy.[46]

Kato loved God with fervour, a characteristic of evangelicalism.

Bibliology (Bible-centred Christianity)

Kato was known primarily for his high view of Scripture and the eminent place he gave it in the life of the Christian and the church. He insisted that the sole authority for theology was the Bible, all sufficient for faith and conduct. He affirmed the Bible as God's special revelation, the very word of God, inspired, inerrant and infallible. Clarifying what he meant by inerrancy, Kato stated:

---

45. Haye, *Byang Kato*, 20.
46. Haye, 22.

> We should realize that inerrancy refers to the original manuscript originally given by God. But as we believe in God's ability and promise to preserve His Word, and as we note the very careful way by which the manuscripts have been passed on from one generation to another, we definitely believe that the Scriptures as we have them today are absolutely reliable. So we can affirm with Christ that "the Scripture cannot be broken" (John 10:35).[47]

Kato was not unmindful about how the word of God was written by humans, through the inspiration of the Holy Spirit. And by inspiration he did not mean a verbal dictation from God, nor was this in the same way people are inspired to write other books that are not in the canon of Scripture. The Bible was God's special revelation and the supreme authority for judging every aspect of human life, truth and wisdom. It is superior to any other source of information or inspirational writing. Where there is conflict between the Bible and other sources, especially culture, the Bible takes precedence. Kato's embrace of the Bible as the truth from God radically changed his perspective about reality and certain practices informed by African traditional worldviews, especially those that were not in line with biblical views.

Kato's discipleship experience and theological training all contributed to integrating his faith and understanding of the Bible to life's realities and experiences holistically. In rebuttal of the charge that he was against contextualising the gospel in the African context, Kato stated:

> We believe that the content of Scripture is inspired, but the mode of expressing this is not inspired. By this I mean the instrument played rather than the music. Or, in the method in preaching, I don't see anything inspired in insisting on a three point sermon in order to communicate. We can tell stories; we can hold dramas. We can find effective methods which can communicate adequately to people, but when we are doing this, we dare not tamper with the content of God's message to man. Because it is inspired and is unchanging to whatever culture it goes, the

---

47. Kato, "Challenge of Evangelicalism."

Word of God remains forever. "O Lord your Word is settled in heaven."[48]

He went further to state:

> We evangelicals appreciate the sentiment, the desire and the need to contextualise. By contextualise, we mean to make Christianity truly relevant in our situation and to make the African view himself welcome in the church. By that we are not dealing with the content, we are only dealing with a mode of expression.[49]

While some of Kato's opponents affirmed the uniqueness of Christ, they were not so affirming of the authority of Scripture. Kato wrote:

> The uniqueness of Christianity must cover more than the uniqueness of Jesus Christ. How can I know for sure about Jesus Christ in an errant Bible? The Scriptures that speak about Jesus Christ must be accepted as God's final and special revelation. Inerrant authoritative Scriptures alone can give us reliable facts about Jesus Christ and man's relationship to Him.[50]

The Bible and Christianity itself are sometimes portrayed as belonging to the "White man" and the "White man's religion," respectively. Some believe the Bible and Western Christianity were part of the system of the exploitation and demeaning of Africans. Thus, Kato observed:

> Many intellectuals are beginning to see that it makes sense to them, that "because white man and his theology have exploited us," they say, "it is now time for us to pay him back." They forget that God is true even if all men are unfaithful. Christianity is more than what people profess it to be. It is an objective fact, a revelation from God, and regardless of what white men have done, or have not done, the Bible stands true. So, we must tell them to stay with the Bible and find true evangelical teaching.[51]

---

48. Kato, *Theological Pitfalls*, 19
49. Kato, *Spirits*, 20; cf. Kato, "Africa's Battle," 53.
50. Kato, "Theological Trends," 5
51. Kato, "Africa: Prudence," 20; cf. Otonko, "Beyond the Rhetoric," 2.

Kato's perspective and doctrine of the Bible informed his approach to the interpretation of the Bible. His views and approach to the Bible were mainstream and conservative evangelical positions. Kato emphasised the inductive study of the Bible and the literal interpretive approach or grammatico-historical method for interpretation and application of the Bible. Without this method, the tendency is "extreme subjectivism" in Bible interpretation, thus deducing the wrong intent or meaning.[52]

In assessing his views, outlined in this study, and in comparing these with the biblical and classical theological materials highlighted in the previous chapter, there is an appreciable level of consistency. Kato's "radical biblicism" or "bibliology," as Bediako calls it,[53] is a major characteristic of his theology. "If the Bible is not recognised as the authoritative source, it stands to reason that biblical meaning may not be adhered to. . . . The rejection of the authoritative Word of God is the number one problem blocking the attainment of the truth about salvation."[54] Nevertheless, Kato affirmed contextualisation of the Bible and stated: "But this biblical theology should be expressed in terms that are meaningful to every people in their own situation to meet their peculiar needs."[55] Kato's biblicism is extremely relevant today, not just in Africa, but also in wider global evangelicalism, where postmodern tendencies have raised questions about whether the biblicist approach is theoretically, let alone practically, tenable.

While Kato himself may not have provided systematic arguments to contribute to the current debate, examining his biblicist theology in both theory and practice resonates with other evangelicals around the world. For example, Shirk writes:

> That Byang Henry Kato was a man of the Bible and the Church, even his critics accept. That he was also a man of vision, many affirm. That he was a man of a particular context, who faced specific challenges in a particular manner, even some of his sympathizers admit. However, that he was an evangelical Christian whose theological understanding arose from deeply held

---

52. Kato, *Theological Pitfalls*, 78.
53. Bediako, *Theology and Identity*, 11.
54. Kato, *Theological Pitfalls*, 142–143.
55. Kato, "Written Theology."

convictions about the Bible, the world, and humanity that are very much consonant with the fundamental evangelical ethos, his critics deny, and some of his sympathizers misunderstand.[56]

Shirki further states:

> Kato's strength also lies in that he was able to speak beyond the confines of Africa. I, as an Asian, more than four decades separated from Kato, and with very different challenges and struggles, can affirm many of the things he affirms. He and I can read the Scripture together to come to a common understanding. In this aspect too, he has bequeathed to his readers a compelling argument that all theologies must not be contextual to the degree that they have no universal resemblance and application.[57]

Kato advocated strongly for the preaching and practice of the unadulterated word of God in the church in Africa, and he could not have emphasised more that the Bible was the sole source of information for Christian theologising.[58]

Christology (Christ-centred Christianity)

Kato's theology and message were primarily Bible and Christ-centred. This was based on the uniqueness of God's revelation in the written word and in the Word made flesh, who lived on earth as human:

> It must be maintained that Jesus Christ became incarnate as a particular person in time and history. John's use of Logos (John 1:1–7) was in that particular sense. The Word became flesh by assuming not only the form of man in general (Philippians 2:5–8), but by being born as a particular person in Bethlehem. This was necessary in view of the work He was going to do. He could be crucified in time and history only as a particular man. He died and rose as an individual to save each individual sinner.[59]

---

56. Shirik, "African Christians," 132.
57. Shirik, 150.
58. Kato, "Written Theology," 1.
59. Kato, *Biblical Christianity*, 21.

Christ did not only reveal God to humans in incarnation but also died on the cross as a ransom for the sins of the world and accomplished his work of salvation by his resurrection and ascension into heaven. Thus, Kato affirmed the divinity and personhood of Christ, his incarnation and substitutionary death on the cross to atone for the sins of every sinner "everywhere at any time."[60]

Kato emphasised the centrality of the Bible and of Christ, and he affirmed as non-negotiable the doctrines of Christ – that is, the virgin birth, his vicarious death, his bodily resurrection and his pending personal return. Elaborating on the christological doctrines further, Kato wrote:

> The Virgin Birth – that Jesus was born of a virgin who never knew a man becomes a problem only if one questions God's ability to create life out of nothing and the truth of the inspired Word of God (Matt 1:22–25). His Vicarious Death presupposes the fact that man's fundamental problem is that he is a sinner by nature and practice (Gen 3; Romans 3:23; 5:12). Jesus Christ, who knew no sin died in place of sinners (Mark 10:45; Romans 5:17–21; 2 Cor 5:18, 19). Bodily Resurrection – the reality of Christ's physical resurrection is the basis of believer's resurrection (1 Cor 15:3–8, 20–22) and The Personal, Visible Future Return of Jesus Christ is taught in the Scriptures and is believed by all those who take Scripture as truly God's eternal Word for all generations (Matt 24:30; John 4:3; Acts 1:11).[61]

Appraising the AACC statement of faith, Kato said it was not enough to affirm Jesus Christ as Lord, Saviour and Second Person of the Trinity as a statement of faith. Thus, he wrote:

> The statement is commendable in what it says. But the greatest problem and dangers lie in what it does not. Who is this "Lord Jesus Christ as God and *only* Saviour"? Should a statement about His supernatural birth, life, death and resurrection not be mentioned? Is His second coming so insignificant that nothing need to be said about it?[62]

---

60. Kato, 21.
61. Kato, "Challenge of Evangelicalism."
62. Kato, "Written Theology."

The uniqueness of Christianity is in the person of Jesus Christ. Religious leaders and government authorities were puzzled about this Son of God and Son of Man.[63] Commenting on the christological controversies about the divine and human nature of Christ, dating back to the time Christ lived on earth, Kato noted that it took the special grace of God the Father to get to know who Jesus was:

> It was only through the Holy Spirit that men like Peter could declare, "Thou art the Christ, the Son of the Living God" (Matthew 16:16). Even after the Father had authenticated the ultimate claims of the Incarnate Christ by raising Him from the dead and exalting Him at His right hand, the Person of Christ was still a real problem to his followers and to pagans of the early centuries of Christianity.[64]

Kato asserted: "If biblical Christianity is to survive and flourish in Africa, we must hold fast that salvation is only through Jesus Christ."[65] It is a heresy to seek salvation elsewhere, outside "the uniqueness of Christian revelation through the written Word and through the Living Word."[66]

The meaning people attached to religious practices in the African context was a threat to the Christian faith. The new faith in Jesus Christ, through the Holy Spirit of the convert from ATR, is based on the Bible. "The Christian will have to examine his whole life-style or culture by the Bible. The Bible is the final judge of every culture."[67] Furthermore, Kato asserted:

> The judgement of individuals will be entirely Christological. It is a biblical absolute truth that 'he who believes in the Son has eternal life; but he who does not obey the Son shall not see life, but the wrath of God abides on him' (John 3:36). The proposition of accepting or rejecting Jesus Christ here and now settles the question for eternity.[68]

---

63. Kato, *Biblical Christianity*, 20.
64. Kato, *Biblical Christianity*, 20.
65. Kato, 22.
66. Kato, 22
67. Kato, *African Cultural Revolution*, 23.
68. Kato, *Theological Pitfalls*, 104.

Christ is the only way for salvation. Kato argued:

> If the best that religious pluralism can do is to locate the thirst in the human soul, it stands to reason that Special Revelation in Jesus Christ alone can save. Besides making fantastic claims about Himself – The Way, The Truth, The Life, The Door, The Good Shepherd, One with the Father – and justifying all of them, the Son of God also invites all men to come to Him for salvation (Matt 11:28, 29). His closest friend, Peter, through the Holy Spirit declared, "And there is salvation in no one else; for there is no other name under heaven that has been given among men, by which we must be saved" (Acts 4:12). The Apostle Paul affirms, "Therefore also God highly exalted Him, and bestowed on Him the name which is above every name, that at the name of Jesus every knee should bow, of those who are in heaven and who are on earth and under the earth" (Phil 2:9, 10).[69]

Jesus was not only a religious leader; he is God, and he is the only way for salvation for the whole world – for any who would repent of their sinful state and accept Jesus Christ as saviour and Lord.

On the centrality of Jesus Christ as the historical fulcrum, Kato stated:

> Without Him, history has no meaning. For all history is His story. Generally, calculation of history today is divided into B.C. and A.D. in the Christian era. Jesus Christ is historically central in terms of time. His coming is central historically, in terms of events and circumstances. He is central in man's quest for reality in life.[70]

The incarnation and birth of the Son of God into the human world was an important event anticipated in BC, and his second coming is much anticipated to mark the consummation of time.

Ecclesiology (Christian-African Identity)

Kato may have been lonely in his theologizing in his time. However, the *ecclesia*, the body of Christ, the church as a whole, was not lost on him. As an

---

69. Kato, "Theology of Eternal," 6.
70. Kato, "Historical Fulcrum."

African, his personhood was tied to his community, especially the Jaba ethnic people of Kwoi. However, as a Christian, his selfhood went beyond his tribe and, indeed, his Nigerian African heritage. Kato's sense of community went beyond *unbuntu*, the highly appreciated African way of relational life, the collectivist culture of interdependence of most African peoples. The search for a true African identity is often skewed to vindicate the African or the Black person. The call has been to turn to a Black theology of liberation or an integrated theological synthesis of ATR beliefs with Christianity – "African theology" – as espoused by some theologians in Kato's time. However, the more that has been written about the subject of self-understanding or identity, the more elusive the identity question has become. Kato's identity in Christ was his answer to the daunting quest for identity.

According to Kato: "From the biblical point of view all people of the world are divided into two groups: the people of God, and the people outside the covenant relationship with God."[71] The distinction does not depend on one's race, tribe, culture or geography (Luke 12:30). Addressing the social concerns of African indignity, Kato stated:

> The question of social concern also raises the burning issue of justice, especially in southern Africa. As an evangelical, I believe the Christian has the basic task of bringing about the ministry of reconciliation to all men. Racial and tribal discrimination of any kind is sinful. The Christian should speak out the truth "in love." Prayer for both the oppressed and the oppressor is necessary. Action by peaceful means, stressing the equality of all men, seems to be the pattern the New Testament Church followed. This is the method the Apostle Paul took to bring about a reconciliation between a Christian slave and his Christian master (Eph 6:5–9; Philem 17). As an African Christian, I am a citizen of two countries. My Christian commitment requires me to seek to bring through peaceful means a reconciliation between all parties in Africa. But I also owe my national legitimate government a loyalty.[72]

---

71. Kato, *Theological Pitfalls*, 21
72. Kato, "Evangelical Cooperation."

Kato's solution to the identity problem is his understanding of the "third race" or "Christian African" identity in Christ. This describes an identity that transcends the confused split personality between the authentic traditional African and the de-Africanised person by foreign or Western cultures – indeed, that transcends the defaced image of all humanity without Christ, regardless of race, status or origin. Kato's conception of the Christian African identity satisfies the yearning and quest for human dignity and self-worth, not only for the African or Black person but for the whole of humanity, lost and dead in sin. Kato believed he had attained a new identity in this life and the life to come – that of a Christian African. Kato stated:

> Dehumanisation is the socialist slogan commonly employed to ridicule the soul-salvation concerned believer. But is it not in the Bible that true humanisation can be seen? A person without Christ has not attained the ideal status God meant him to have. Man was made in the image of God. The image has been defaced and the unbelievers are considered dead and estranged from the living God (Eph 2:1; Col 1:21). Humanisation comes only when one becomes a Christian.[73]

Christianity, Kato said, is "unique, it creates the new race, a race called 'the body of Christ,' made up of people from any cultural background."[74] Based on scriptural injunction, faith in Christ confers new citizenship (2 Cor 5:17; Rom 13:1–14). The quest is no longer an identity but a pilgrim's yearning for a glorious homeland (Rev 21–22). The search for identity is not just an African problem; it is a problem for all of fallen humanity, groping in the dark for meaning. That emptiness can only be filled when humans find rest in Christ through faith. "The Word of God does teach that our true citizenship is in heaven (Phil 3:20). But does that mean we have no responsibilities to fulfil in the earthly land in which we live?"[75]

By "Christian African," Kato was primarily highlighting the priority of his new self-identity over the natural or cultural identity, an identity that was fallen, broken and lost and that needed redemption. This did not deny

---

73. Kato, *Theological Pitfalls*, 179; cf. Porumb, "Orthodoxy and Ecumenism," 104.
74. Kato, *Biblical Christianity*, 30.
75. Kato, "Christian Citizenship."

the reality of the old life, as a citizen of Kwoi, Nigeria, and as truly African. Kato travelled the world but always returned to Kwoi and connected with his people. He sought to be a part of the community without compromise to his Christian beliefs and way of life. He connected with his boyhood friends from his traditional society. At least one of these childhood friends confirmed that Kato taught him the Bible and how to be a better person in their own language and context. Kato's social relations and interactions in the village were of a piece with his behavior and relationships in postgraduate school, which earned for him the Four-Way Test Award, an award for personal relationships, in and outside the school, consistent Christian life and leadership promise.[76] This is further evidence of his practices being holistic.

Kato emphasised the importance of living in this world according to Christian values as taught by the Bible. He purposed to discontinue any aspect of life that was not consistent with biblical values. While there are some cultural values that are unique to Africa, and ethnic contexts which are consistent with God's truth and can continue to be part of the Christian life, generally the ways of the world are opposed to God's ways as revealed in the Bible. So, Kato's bent was generally, discontinuity. This did not mean discontinuity with aspects of culture consistent with biblical values. There was also an understanding of the common image of God in all people, although God's image is marred by sin and all are in need of the redemption that only comes through faith in Jesus Christ (Rom 3:23; Eph 2:15; 4:17–19).

The Christian African identity also meant membership in the Christian community – the body of Christ, which includes all believers in Christ everywhere, regardless of other identities, such as race, gender, nationality, tribe or social status (Gal 3:28).

> As evangelical Christians we realize that Christ has called us to be nothing other than African Christians. William Barclay has rightly stated, "But it is not Jesus' purpose that we should turn all men into one nation, but that there should be Christian Indians and Christian Africans, whose unity lies in their Christianity. The oneness in Christ is in Christ and not in any external change." (Commentary on Ephesians p. 136). Evangelical Christians are

---

76. Breman, "Association of Evangelicals," 41.

not opposed to the call for a return to African culture.... It is in the area of syncretism, that is, importing pagan elements into Christianity, that cultural revolution poses as a threat to evangelical Christianity. The Christians answer in such a situation should be that Christianity must judge every culture.[77]

The self-understanding of the church is multi-cultural, multi-ethnic and multi-racial: "one body, one Spirit, one glorious hope for the future, one Lord, one faith, one baptism and one God and Father of all."[78]

The implications of the new community meant that Kato had brothers and sisters from everywhere around the world, including missionaries from countries that colonised Africa and destroyed its culture. Kato recognised that these Western missionaries came from cultures that were also fallen, like all human cultures. The Western missionary church may have been the means and cradle for his new birth and encounter with Christianity, but like any authentic follower of Christ, Kato demonstrated a call out of both traditional African religion and Western cultural trappings – a call out of human culture. He demonstrated this by his opposition to ATR, his promotion of developing Christian leaders on African soil and his criticism of the ignorance of Western missionaries. According to Bowers, "Kato called vigorously for contextual theology attuned to the cultural realities of Africa, but he also affirmed the normative role of Scripture for authentic Christian theology in every context."[79] His understanding of the two religions of ATR and Christianity was evident, and he was clearly convinced of the claims of the gospel as unique and as the only means for salvation. He was a true disciple and disciple maker. His own parents embraced Christianity before their deaths. His children all accepted Jesus as their saviour under his watch. In terms of the unity of the church, Kato repudiated unity at all cost:

> Unity with all "Christians" at any cost is advocated by some. The African solution to a problem of disagreement, as it is said, is to seek compromise. The two parties sink all their differences, gloss over the truth and pretend that all is well. But how long can such

---

77. Kato, "Challenge of Evangelicalism."
78. Eph 4:4–6; 2 Cor 5:17; cf. Turaki, *Engaging Religions*, 398–399.
79. Bowers, "African Theology," 120.

> a brittle unity last? . . . Unity is desirable but not at the expense of truth. Political compromise may be in order for Africa, but glossing over spiritual absolutes is suicidal.[80]

Kato admonished evangelical Christians to follow the true light even when it meant separation from a family member.

Kato's emphasis and basis for unity was partnership in the gospel (Phil 1:5). His opposition to the ecumenical movement was not about ecumenicism per se. His criticism was about the humanistic basis for unity, with its low view of the Bible and basic Christian doctrines and ambiguity about the meaning of salvation, among other issues.[81]

> Realising that Jesus Christ did pray for both spiritual and visible unity (John 17:21), Evangelicals should want to pull together as long as it is unity of people committed to Christ and his word. Unity is strength even in the Lord's work. But, also realising that people have different tastes, including those relative to the type of church worship and the form of church government, Evangelicals do not see the need of abolishing church denominations. Unity in diversity is also strength.[82]

At a time when many church leaders, as a way of enhancing selfhood, were calling for a moratorium on the sending of Western missionaries and money to Africa, Kato advocated for collaboration and partnership.[83] At the beginning of 1974, Kato spoke in a series of radio broadcasts on Voice of Kenya (VOK) titled *Lift Up Your Hearts: The Future of the Church*. He spoke on different themes, such as church and government, awakening and renewal in the church, unity, the moratorium, youth and the imminent return of Jesus Christ. While Kato lauded the effort at autonomy, he observed that efforts to achieve self-sustainability, especially in developing leadership in the African church, were too little. Kato argued that because of the potential for the growth and development of the church in Africa, it was necessary to have

---

80. Kato, *Theological Pitfalls*, 169.
81. Kato, 129–170.
82. Kato, 170.
83. Kato, *Lift Up Your Hearts*.

every Christian on board to help nurture the church by accelerating leadership training and building the capacity to tap into local resources.

Stressing the scope of the work of the church and the need, Kato said:

> Perhaps half of the people of the world have no gospel witness. That's about two billion people. And literally thousands of people right here are unreached. God has sent his people throughout the world to these thousands and millions and billions of unreached people. All the available resources of all of God's people everywhere must be put to the task – now.[84]

Kato saw evangelism as the task of the church across denominations and across the world. He was particularly optimistic about the future growth of the church following the inaugural and historic Lausanne Congress in Switzerland in 1974:

> More than 3,000 leaders from 150 countries and every kind of church were together for ten days dealing with this. They talked about what the good news is and what it means in one's life. They discussed the need to getting this good news out to every person in the world in the next 25 years. . . . I was impressed with the widespread commitment to this task.[85]

Continuing to share his experience at Lausanne, Kato stated in the radio broadcast:

> This was a conference of evangelicals, but while there I joined others in a press conference interviewing five catholic priests who were there as observers. Even these men were talking about spiritual renewal. . . . They said they could agree with much of what was being said about evangelism at this Congress . . . that the best road to Christian unity is around the cross of Jesus Christ. These priests talked about the power of the Holy Spirit in one's life, and stressed the need for Bible study and prayer and fellowship. They spoke about the "dynamic proclamation of the person of Jesus Christ" as the core of evangelism. One said that

---

84. Kato.
85. Kato.

"for the Catholics the final goal is the breaking in of God into one's life and fellowship with God established" and that this is an ongoing process that continues "till Christ returns."[86]

It is noteworthy that Kato made the above observation, underscoring what defined his relationship with other traditions, especially Catholicism, and his perspective on the unity of the church. He then went on to state about the "disgrace of divisions" and the need for church unity. People were confused with so many different groups; Christians ought to speak with one voice. He observed that there were ongoing conversations about the churches coming together as one. However, Kato said, "This has to be scriptural unity – one body in Christ – a united approach to the world is scriptural. But there is considerable confusion about what that means among Christians. There is disagreement about just how that is to be achieved." He continued,

> Unity – one voice – does not necessary mean everyone saying the same thing and doing the same thing in the same way at the same time. That's military regimentation, which is not spiritual and quite deadly to the life and vitality of the church. Unity – in any human society – does not mean that everyone is to lose his identity, casting aside his individualism, veneering over the differences. Unity in Christ is not assuming the same name, same forms of worship, the same attitude and feelings and reactions.[87]

Kato likened unity of the church to a family where every member is different in a multitude of ways, with their own uniqueness, their own personalities and talents, but is still a member of the one family. There is unity and oneness that holds them together in warm fellowship and purpose. Similarly, a nation of diverse people groups, tribes and cultural backgrounds holds together as one nation, working for one common good and purpose. In the family, or nation, there must be freedom to develop individual personalities and abilities and to meet individual needs: "This kind of freedom brings tension, but even that can have a healthy effect on growth and maturity. . . . The diversities

---

86. Kato, "Lift Up your Hearts": Radio Broadcast, Voice of Kenya.
87. Kato.

within a family or a church or a nation do not nullify unity for there still can be oneness and togetherness."[88]

Missiology (Apologia for Biblical Christianity in Africa)

At the heart of Kato's theological concerns and reflections was his personal faithfulness to the word of God and his ministry focus on establishing and defending biblical Christianity in Africa and maturing the church (Eph 4:12).

> Two things are necessary for the survival of the ship of our faith. On the one hand, there must be an uncompromising confidence in God's revealed Word. On the other hand, there must be the intelligent communication of this faith to the contemporary African mind. Along with this two-fold commitment, there must be another pair of oars: the head and the heart.[89]

Kato's missionary endeavour was marked by the authority of the Bible – thus the effort for biblical and theological education – and a pastor's heart for people. He believed that the church had a mission, and that every Christian was a missionary. Kato taught that God himself was a missionary. God the Father sent Christ to the world and Christ himself sent out his apostles. The church was established to call all followers of Christ for the same purpose – to be missionaries to the rest of the world.[90]

He outlines the nature of the mission of Jesus as follows:

> 1). A Mission with a Vision of the world in sin. Without vision, the people suffer, together with the "watchman" who keeps silence (Ezekiel 3). 2). A Mission with Compassion. Matt. 9:35–38. People are sheep without a Shepherd. We must see them with the Compassion of Jesus. 3). A Mission of Sacrifice. Mark 10:15 "to minister and to give His life a ransom." Yes, be prepared to be a martyr, "who takes up his cross and follows Jesus." In the past, persecution has often come to the church. . . . And I know that as I expose error, I too will suffer danger. We must be prepared to suffer in Christ's Mission. 4). A Mission of harvest. Is. 53:11, 12.

---

88. Kato.
89. Kato, "Creating Facilities," 3.
90. Kato, "Written Theology."

"Let us not be weary in well-doing, for we shall reap if we faint not." 5). A Mission that does not end until we leave this earth.[91]

Thus, missiology as a theological discipline is all-embracing and is a subject of debate among scholars. Oborji states: "As a theological discipline, missiology is to distinguish itself as that whose primary objective is to explore the origins, concepts and goal of the Christian mission in relation to the missionary activities of the evangelising church."[92] Although missiology has struggled to be accepted as theology, it is now established and given the necessary recognition as a theological discipline. According to Oborji:

> As a theological discipline, missiology must realise its dependence on the other theological disciplines and avail itself of their help. For example, missiology must allow itself to be enriched by modern scholarship on biblical exegesis, church history, systematic theology, pastoral theology, liturgy, and so forth. The missiologist should by no means claim to be an expert in exegesis, church history or systematic theology as well.[93]

Therefore, it is upon this foundation that Kato's several missionary endeavours could be described as part of Kato's theological contribution and that a case can be made for missions from the Global South.

Kato felt at home among his people and the evangelical church in Africa and beyond. He wanted Christianity to have a home in sub-Saharan Africa, a far cry from Christianity being a foreign religion. His approach and strategy for the task was to delineate and clarify what evangelicalism was, against the backdrop of a church that had been established and influenced by Western missionaries but whose members were in practice being informed by traditional religious views. In pointing out the errors some theologians were advancing, Kato set out the mission of his organisation, the AEA:

> The Association of Evangelical in Africa and Madagascar feels that we have a responsibility to exist. Our prudence, our wisdom, our understanding of this is that we now realize the need for safeguarding biblical Christianity and biblical methods.

---

91. Kato.
92. Oborji, "Contemporary Missiology," 395.
93. Oborji, 393.

Therefore, in speaking of relationships between evangelical Christians, we see that Christians in Africa ought to find their own method of coming together and their own method of fellowship and association.[94]

The syncretistic and universalistic ideas or practices were being promoted by thought leaders in the church. Kato reflects: "In the search of the African church for theological identity, evangelicals have a great potential for keeping the church biblical. Practically all the churches started out evangelical, and many of them are still evangelical. If adequate leadership is produced now within the evangelical sphere, the church in Africa will have a proper biblical perspective to hand on to forthcoming generations of African Christians."[95] However, Kato stated: "Biblical Christianity in Africa is being threatened by syncretism, universalism and Christo-paganism. The spiritual battle for Africa during this decade will be fought, therefore, largely on theological grounds. But the church is generally unprepared for the challenge because of its theological and biblical ignorance."[96] He emphasised theological education including basic doctrinal teaching programmes of the church at all levels. Kato observes:

> The word doctrine, which simply means teaching, has been part of gospel ministry in Africa. Bible doctrine (teaching) may be considered theological instruction perhaps with less philosophical reflection. The word theology is of course more appropriate as it is a pregnant word (theo-logos) while doctrine could mean the collection of any system of teaching e.g., government, social club. Nevertheless, Bible doctrine, which is identical with theology, has not been altogether lacking.[97]

Kato thus endeavoured to define what evangelical and biblical Christianity was. He was strategic in his approach and mapped out a clear vision of what he wanted to see in the church. The key for his prescription was the development of leaders and the promotion of sound evangelical theological education

---

94. Kato, *Spirits*, 19.
95. Kato, *Biblical Christianity*, 52.
96. Kato, 11.
97. Kato, *Problem of Theological Education*, 1.

in Africa. He exemplified this through his own personal development and through laying the groundwork for theological institutions and structures for training leaders on the continent. Bowers affirms Kato's strategic leadership:

> Kato was nothing if not a visionary, and his lasting contributions were firmly rooted in that characteristic of the man. But Kato was more than a visionary; he was to an extraordinary degree, an innovative implementer of fresh vision. That is what he was most about, that is what was so tragically cut off by his death. It is this larger perspective on Kato that I believe we need to re-energise.[98]

Kato articulated a comprehensive missional agenda, asserting its necessity for preserving biblical Christianity in Africa. This was a decalogue – a ten-point proposal – for the survival of biblical Christianity in Africa.[99]

1. Adhere to the presuppositions of historic Christianity. The shape of this adherence includes God's general revelation through the *imago Dei*, conscience and creation. Recognise that non-Christian religions may have a concept of the Creator God but also demonstrate people's rebellion against God. Christ came to save all, but only those who accept his offer will be saved. The principle of continuity is present in the sense that God's image in humans is not obliterated, and God continues to reveal himself generally. But running parallel to this is also discontinuity, in the sense that God is now producing a new person, in the formation of the body of Christ, and that the Bible alone is the final infallible rule of faith and practice.

2. Christianity should find a home in the African cultural setting by transforming the culture, and not the other way around. This can be done by expressing theological concepts in terms of the African context rather than pursuing an "African Theology," as proposed by some. The squabbles of Western Christianity do not have to be the pattern for the younger churches. While the Bible content remains unchanged and authoritative, the final word has not

---

98. Bowers, "Byang Kato," 7.
99. These ten points are from Kato, "Critique of Incipient," ThD diss., 278–281.

yet been said in expressing Christianity. Evangelical theology in Africa should scratch where it itches, by providing answers for issues like polygamy, family structures, the spirit world, liturgy etc.
3. Concerted effort should be undertaken for biblical training, including training leaders in the biblical languages to enhance their exegesis.
4. Careful study of ATR as well as other religions is proper, but as secondary to the inductive study of the Bible.
5. Launch an aggressive programme of evangelism and missions, so that the fate of the church in North Africa in earlier centuries will not befall the sub-Saharan church in our day. Kato believed the undoing of the church in North Africa was owing to doctrinal strife.
6. Consolidate organisational structures, based on doctrinal agreements, as in the formation of the AEA and national evangelical fellowships and alliances.
7. Attend to careful definition and concise expression of theological terms. This is necessary to safeguard against syncretism and universalism.
8. Develop apologetics relating to unbiblical systems that are creeping into the church.
9. Christians in Africa should not stay aloof from social ills, while maintaining a primary focus on the salvation of individuals who in turn will revolutionise the society.
10. Follow the steps of the New Testament church to contend for the faith at any cost, even to death.

In enumerating these concerns, Kato not only demonstrated his biblicism, but he also revealed some of his concerns and his approach to the Bible and to the Christian faith. He concluded:

> Theology in Africa is increasingly turning to African traditional religions rather than the Bible as its absolute source. . . . A continuing effort should be made to relate Christian theology to the changing situations in Africa, but only as the Bible is taken

as the absolute Word of God can it have an authoritative and relevant message for Africa.[100]

What is clear here is that Kato was a reflective theologian, applying his theological beliefs to actionable plans for the maturing of the church. He had the courage to institute a different direction for doing theology – biblical theology – in Africa, to stem the direction in which most other theologians of his time were heading – toward the "liberal tendencies" of African theology.[101]

Kato's single mindedness, clarity of focus and determination to accomplish his life goals were remarkable. He was very strategic and foresighted. This was demonstrated in the way his vision has been implemented by those who followed after him, especially in his role as general secretary of AEA. After his sudden and tragic death, between him and his immediate successor there was a three-year gap. However, it was exceptional that Kato's successor continued implementing the plan conceived by Kato, and forty-five years later, Kato's blueprint for AEA continues to be relevant. Bowers observes:

> It is one thing to have vision, and entirely something else to achieve parts of that vision. In Kato's case we live amidst major examples of vision achieved, ongoing powerful blessings to evangelicalism across the continent still in our own day, deriving directly from Kato's personal vision. I speak of NEGST, FATEB/BEST, and ACTEA. One must not fail to note as well in this respect his foundational contribution which underlies the vitality that AEA has continued to represent, not to mention his parallel contribution to WEA, and to the WEA Theological Commission, all still significant movements for good among us; and as well the global movement for which I presently work, ICETE, a direct derivative of Kato's energetic vision. By no means can the significance of Kato in our own day be reliably assessed without taking these exceptional, enduring contributions into account. The thriving publications of scholarly work by African evangelicals were also part of Kato's aspirations.[102]

---

100. Kato, *Biblical Christianity*, 42–43.
101. Turaki, *Engaging Religions*, 65.
102. Bowers, "Byang Kato," 5.

There are some lessons here for succession planning and how to lead institutions. Vision needs to be so clear and compelling that, when the need arises, another person could implement it even without the leader.

Kato believed that the basis for investing in theological education was missions. He wrote:

> The Bible training we give should be with a view to Missions. Teach not only Mission history, but relevant Missiology and Anthropology. (Some of the courses taught in Bible schools do not prepare the students for the REALITIES they will meet.) Technology is a help. Develop a strategy for Urban evangelism, and Bush evangelism. Church-Mission relationships must choose between fusion or partnership. Missionaries must work through the Church already there, and new missionaries should come through the existing Church. We must help the Churches already established to have a missionary vision, sending (as some churches are doing) one Sunday's offering per month to support missionaries. Do "soil research" of areas to ascertain how many live churches there are, where the pagan pockets still persist. Focus attention on responsive areas. WE ARE PARTNERS TOGETHER. Find out how God can use you. Support His work. Let us do God's MISSION TOGETHER![103]

These are important considerations and particularly relevant currently, as the church in Africa sees itself as a mission force and is preparing and sending missionaries to other regions of the world.

Focus on children was also an innovation for Kato's theological work in Africa. The foundation Kato laid for the AEA Theology and Christian Education Commission was strategic and continues to contribute to the growth and maturation of the church in Africa at all levels. The Christian Learning Materials for Children (CLMC) provides Sunday school materials and other resources for children and promotes publication of Christian literature. Kato told his personal testimony to remind his listeners about the

---

103. Kato, "Written Theology."

need to minster to children for their salvation, just as he had experienced. He said, "Church begins in the home."[104]

Kato outlined the following recommendation for Christianity as an authentic African religion:

> (1) Know the truth and defend it (Jude 3). (2) Discern the voices; get your marching orders from the Word of God and not from peoples' voices. (3) Reject moratorium but promote self-reliance. Both the <u>missionaries and the nationals should work together as workers with Christ (2 Cor 6:1) and prioritize the training of leaders in the national church. (4) Evangelise or perish (1 Cor 9:16). (5) Contextualise without compromise</u>. Let Christianity truly find a home in Africa (1 Cor 10:31). (6) Pray for and be prepared for revival; plead with God for more Joshuas and Timothys for the future of the church. (7) Become more missionary-minded; look beyond the borders of your country and further afield.[105]

Eschatology (Second Coming of Christ)

Kato's theological leaning was dispensational premillennialist evangelicalism. Kato was aware of the diversity of opinion on the doctrine of eschatology among Christians. According to Kato:

> There are those placed in the camp of postmillennialism, that view of the last things which holds that the kingdom of God is now being extended in the world through the preaching of the Gospel and the saving work of the Holy Spirit, that the world eventually is to be Christianised, and that the return of Christ will occur at the close of a long period of righteousness and peace, commonly called the millennium. Then there are those holding amillennialism. They believe that the Scripture teaches that good and evil will continue side by side, but eventually there will be a sudden personal eruption of Christ into the midst of

---

104. Haye, *Byang Kato*, 46–48
105. Kato, *Biblical Christianity*, 37–39.

the world's scene of conflict, with a swift sifting and separation of souls at the final judgement.[106]

Kato highlighted yet another view – premillennialism. Citing Carl Henry, Kato stated: "This is a view of last things which insists that the millennial passage in Revelation 20 must be interpreted literally and the Second Coming of Christ will inaugurate His reign as King in person on the earth."[107] This is the position Kato affirmed as an illustrious alumnus and adjunct faculty of Dallas Theological Seminary, a leading premillennial dispensationalist school.

Nonetheless, what Kato affirmed as the absolute was the consensual position. He stated: "One common denominator among orthodox Christians is the belief in the future, visible personal second coming of Jesus Christ. It is agreed by all who take the Bible as the inspired, infallible Word of God seriously, that the second coming is the hope of the Church."[108] Drawing from Arnett, Kato went on to outline the scriptural basis for the second coming of Christ.

> The explicit teaching of Holy Scripture is that Jesus Christ will come a second time from heaven to earth personally, bodily, and visibly. This marvellous and climatic event is called the "blessed hope" of the Christian Church by the Apostle Paul (Titus 2:13). Christ appeared once on earth in grace (John 1:14, 17; Titus 2:11). He will appear a second time in glory (Matt 16:27; 24:30; 25:31; Luke 21:17).

Further elucidating on the return of Christ, Kato stated:

> The second coming means that Jesus Christ will come again to this world in His personal and bodily form, glorified and deathless. The word *Parousia* is used frequently in the New Testament as a technical term to denote the return of Christ at the end of the age (Matt 24:3, 27, 39; 2 Peter 3:4, 12; 1 John 2:28). His second appearing will be personal (Acts 1:11; John 14:3; 21:20–23), unexpected (Matt 24:32–51; 25:1–13), sudden

---

106. Kato, Theological Pitfalls, 81.
107. Kato, 81.
108. Kato, *Theological Pitfalls*, 82.

(Matt 24:27; Luke 17:24), visible (Matt 24:30, Rev 1:7) and glorious (Mark 8:38; Luke 9:26).[109]

In a radio broadcast series in Nairobi, Kenya, in 1974, Kato spoke about the imminent return of Jesus Christ:

> Christians talk about living in the last days and the imminent return of Jesus Christ to the world again. Jesus said he would be coming back again, and I for one expect this. It may be immediately or it may be a thousand years yet. Many see signs that we are in what is called "the last days." Well, I just don't think anyone knows, except God himself. But I would like to suggest that we may not be in the "last days of time" in this world, but rather that we may be in the beginning days of real church history. We may be about to see an awakening and renewal among God's people such as the world has never seen before."[110]

Elaborating further on his biblical understanding of the second coming, Kato said:

> The irreducible minimum of an evangelical belief concerning the life to come includes: (a) Personal, physical return of Jesus Christ at a time not known by any created being, not even the Son during His earthly life (Mark 13:32). (b) Personal, physical resurrection of all people as individuals. (c) The judgement of the living and the dead and retribution on the basis of the acceptance or rejection of Jesus Christ. (d) Reality of Heaven and Hell. The righteous will enjoy heaven eternally, while the unrighteous will be tormented in hell forever.[111]

In assessing Mbiti's eschatology, which critiques the traditional evangelical understand of Jesus's literal second coming and asserts that the events described in the Bible were only symbols and words, Kato gave his own perspective. The eschatological symbols and words Mbiti enumerated, according to Kato, included Gehenna, fire, treasure, city, country, eating and

---

109. Kato, 82.
110. Kato, *Lift Up Your Hearts*.
111. Kato, "Jesus Christ Frees," 1.

drinking, tears and pain (hell), and heaven.[112] According to Kato: "Christ's use of Gehenna was definitely a reference to future judgement, albeit the terrible condition of unbelievers now (Matt 5:22, 29, 30; 10:28; 18:9; 23:15, 33; Mark 9:43, 45, 47; Luke 12:5). The only place Gehenna is used figuratively, and it is quite clear, is James 3:6."[113] These so-called "symbols and words" were major doctrines of the Bible, and contrary to the systematic repudiation of these, Kato affirmed them as future realities, stating:

> Space does not allow a fuller treatment [of the eight doctrines]. But it is a fact that the reality of heaven and hell is a fundamental teaching of biblical Christianity. The twofold teaching of future reward and future punishment was what the early church understood their Lord to teach in the New Testament.[114]

Regarding future resurrection, Kato stated: "That believers are mystically risen and seated with Christ in the heavenlies (Col 3:1–4) no Bible-believing Christian would deny. But this does not remove the real future, personal resurrection."[115] Kirschner observes: "The strong focus on hell and condemnation in Kato's eschatology is prevalent in Kato's writings for two reasons. It derives from a so-called literal interpretation of biblical images used to describe the eschaton or eschatological events. Secondly it goes along with a theology that centres on atonement."[116]

Kato's beliefs about eschatology may have been influenced by his own empirical studies and assessment. Kato stated: "I conducted a survey in 1967 in Igbaja, Nigeria, among some 500 college students, and discovered that 90 per cent found Christ through a message concerning the second coming of Christ."[117] He believed that Africans were futuristic and able to grasp eschatological teachings and the glorious hope of the church. Rebuffing Mbiti, he defended his own dominant futuristic view of eschatology, which was also the view of the Africa Inland Church (AIC) in Kenya, in which Mbiti had his background:

---

112. Kato, *Theological Pitfalls*, 83–85.
113. Kato, 84.
114. Kato, "Critique of Incipient," ThD diss., 133.
115. Kato, 135.
116. Kirschner, *Futurist Eschatologies*, 35.
117. Kato, *Theological Pitfalls*, 77.

> It is a fact that the AIC does not teach all three aspects of the end – past, present and future – under the same doctrine. But do they need to? It is an accepted and workable practice to approach eschatology in a future sense, which is a valid understanding of *eschaton* (the last events).[118]

Kato held a strong futuristic view of salvation or soteriology.

Pneumatology (Power of the Holy Spirit and the Spirit World of the Cosmos)

In Kato's writings and speeches there is not as much emphasis on pneumatology as there is on the Bible and life in Christ. Three factors could have been responsible for this: (1) his personal experience of spirits and the place this had in ATR; (2) this relative silence was generally the case among evangelicals in his era; and (3) the teaching of others about African spiritism, which was the basis of his *apologia*. Also, with the emergence of Pentecostal and charismatic teachings, perhaps with some excesses at the time, Kato had a cautious and conservative approach. However, Kato's theological reflections on this subject were teased out in an undated, typed, fourteen page paper titled "The Power of the Holy Spirit in the Christian."

The apparent lack of emphasis on the Holy Spirit had been observed by people around him, and Kato narrates a particular encounter with an American pastor friend as he lays out his perspective on this subject. This is particularly important to highlight and reflect upon within the current context of the pentecostalisation of Christianity in Africa. Kato wrote:

> One day I met an American negro preacher in the USA who asked me "Have you had the experience?" I asked him what experience. He replied, "You mean you are a preacher and don't know the experience I mean? Have you spoken in tongues?" I told him that I truly know the Lord, and that I realised my need of walking with the Lord daily but that I had never spoken in tongues. But he insisted that speaking in tongues was the mark of spirituality.[119]

---

118. Kato, *Theological Pitfalls*, 81.
119. Kato, "Power," 1.

This experience is familiar for many people in the contemporary church. Accordingly, Kato noted: "Many young Christians today are being urged to seek a 'second blessing', 'second baptism' and 'new experience'. Let us examine the issue which at different times may be called Pentecostalism or Charismatic movement. Is speaking in tongues a spiritual thermometer to measure the spiritual life of a Christian?"[120]

Kato then went on to respond to his own question, and his teachings on this subject provide a comprehensive summary of his pneumatology. He outlined the following: Jesus Christ was conceived, born and did his work through the Holy Spirit. He taught his followers that they could not work in their own strength and commanded them to wait in Jerusalem until the Holy Spirit came upon them (Acts 1:8). It is necessary that a Christian receives the Holy Spirit and is controlled by the Holy Spirit before the Christian can bear effective witness for Jesus Christ. No amount of head knowledge or clever speech can take the place of the power of the Holy Spirit in a person's life:

> A dry, well-articulated sermon may cause listeners to applaud. But only a sermon borne on the oven of prayer, produced through the burning power of the Holy Spirit, can produce lasting results in the church. Cold, dead orthodoxy only hardens the hearts of sinners, making them immune to the gospel of Christ. We need reviving power of the Holy Spirit in our dead churches.[121]

However, Kato reiterated that the power Jesus promised his followers was the initial outpouring of the Holy Spirit on the day of Pentecost. In Acts 1:5 Jesus called it baptism with the Holy Spirit, which was to take place "not many days from now." In fact, the event took place only ten days after Jesus promised the occurrence of the event and ascended into heaven.

> The event of Pentecost (Acts 2:1–13) was going to be of such a historic significance that the Lord commanded his followers to wait in Jerusalem for it. This is the only case in the NT where Christians were ever commanded to "tarry" in the city of Jerusalem (Luke 24:49). Any suggestion by anybody today for

---

120. Kato, 1.
121. Kato, 1–2.

> "tarrying" for any spectacular event such as the Pentecost has no basis in the Bible.[122]

The historic outpouring of the Holy Spirit was marked with some physical signs, including violent sound, tongues of fire and the ability to speak in foreign languages, but none of these was the power itself. The Holy Spirit himself was the power and the giver of the power. As he filled the 120 disciples, he then gave them the ability to work in an unusual way. This marked a new era in which Jews and Gentiles could be brought together into one church of Jesus Christ.[123]

> Since the physical signs were not the power itself, but only a manifestation to the power, they were not a necessary part of the power Jesus promised would come upon his followers. It is true that physical manifestations were given at certain occasions of the outpouring of the Spirit. On the Day of Pentecost (Acts 2), in Cornelius' house (Acts 10:46) and at Ephesus (Acts 19:1–6) speaking in tongues accompanied the filling of the Holy Spirit. Probably because each case was a significant landmark for the expansion of Christianity into a new territory. However, we must note that the filling with the Holy Spirit was NOT ALWAYS accompanied by the physical sign of wind, fire or tongues.[124]

All the apostles were filled with the Holy Spirit (Acts 4:8–31) but tongues did not accompany the events. The seven deacons (Acts 6:3–5), Stephen (7:55), Saul (9:17) and Barnabas (11:24) were filled with the Spirit, but physical signs were not given as the evidence of this filling. We cannot, therefore, take speaking in tongues or any other physical sign as evidence of being filled with the Holy Spirit, or the sign of power in a believer's life. Kato asserted:

> It is clear in the Bible that everyone who has accepted Jesus Christ as their personal Saviour has received the Holy Spirit. The Holy Spirit dwells in every believer. "If a man does not possess the Spirit of Christ, he is no Christian" (Rom 8:9b NEB). The receiving of the Holy Spirit is an act of faith that brings about

---

122. Kato, 2.
123. Kato, 2.
124. Kato, 3.

a spiritual new birth or establishes new relationship with God through Jesus Christ. If therefore you have put your trust in Christ, take God at His Word that you already possess the Holy Spirit. "But as many as receive Him to them gave he the power to become the sons of God" (John 1:12). At the moment of conversion, all believers are baptised and sealed (1 Cor 12:13).[125]

However, while the phrases "indwelling by the Holy Spirit," "sealing with the Holy Spirit" and "baptising with the Holy Spirit" apply to all believers, there is one phrase that cannot be so applied. "Being filled with the Spirit" is commanded to be a continuous act. Being filled with the Spirit, according to Kato, means to continue to be controlled and guided by the Holy Spirit. This is contrasted with the drunkard who is under the influence of alcohol (Eph 5:18). This calls for a life of dedication to the cause of Christ (Rom 12:1). A life that is separated from sin. Sin grieves the Holy Spirit (Eph 4:10). A person, therefore, living in sin is not filled with the Holy Spirit. When sin is confessed, a believer's life becomes a channel for the filling of the Holy Spirit. When sin is confessed, interrupted fellowship is mended. The Spirit fills and flows through one's life. This also calls for a continuous walk in the Spirit, dependence on the Holy Spirit always. This rules out arriving at any point of perfection in life (Phil 3:13–14). While it is true that we have the precedents in Acts where being filled with the Holy Spirit is accompanied by speaking in tongues, that is not always the case (Acts 4:31). The passage that commands the believer to be filled with the Holy Spirit makes no reference to tongues as evidence of the filling. The whole context of Ephesians 5, where the call for infilling is recorded, is the matter of walking with Christ and manifesting the life of Christ in our daily relationship within the church. The evidence of a Spirit-filled life may be summed up as follows: It is a Christ-like character which brings out the fruit of the Holy Spirit (Gal 5:22–23; cf. Eph 5:18–21).

A different aspect of the outworking of the Holy Spirit is called the gifts of the Holy Spirit. Kato also addressed the nature and place of spiritual gifts. The word for gifts is *charismata* which means "grace gifts" or gifts given to believers by the Holy Spirit purely out of grace (Rom 12:3–8; 1 Cor 12:4–14:40; Eph 4:1–16). Kato outlined some principles about spiritual gifts:

---

125. Kato, 3–4.

1. There is a difference between natural gifts and spiritual gifts. The Christian's natural gift(s) can become spiritual gifts as well. However, only those who have the Holy Spirit and are born again can talk of spiritual gifts.
2. Spiritual gifts are by God's grace, and it is only by God's own free-will that he bestows the favour.
3. Every Christian has a spiritual gift, some have more than one, but no one has all the gifts (1 Cor 12:11). No gift is obligatory for every believer or a mark of spirituality. All are commanded to use their gift(s) in love (1 Cor 12:31).
4. The purpose of the gift is not merely for the private edification of the person except as this contributes to the maturation, unity and growth of the church (Eph 4:12–13). The gifts are listed in order of importance (Eph 4:11). This is not because of the person exercising them but simply because God lists them that way. Apparently, the gifts at the top are those with greater potential for greatest contribution to the church. The first major gifts are those of apostles, prophets and teachers (1 Cor 12:28). The original apostles were necessary for the foundation of the church and made up a unique class not to be succeeded (Eph 2:20). The prophets predicted future events as well as declared the message of God to the people of their generation. There are no apostles or prophets today in the same sense.[126]

However, by application, missionaries may be called the sent-out ones, or apostles, but cannot claim succession to the original apostles. In a sense, a gifted preacher may be said to have a gift of prophecy. But there are no prophets today who predict future events. God's revelation is found in the Bible. The reference to teachers may refer to people in the church with a specific gift for expounding the word of God. In Ephesians 4:11 the gifts of teaching and pastoring go together as pastor-teacher, the kind you would look for in order to pastor a church. The gift of evangelism is among the leading gifts to the church. If the apostles and prophets laid the foundation of the church, then teachers, pastors and evangelists are necessary for the continuation and

---

126. Kato, "The Power of the Holy Spirit in the Christian" Sermon/Teaching Notes, archived at AEA Offices in Nairobi, Kenya, 11

expansion of the church. Other gifts include miracles, healings, helping, governing, tongues and interpretation of tongues (1 Cor 12:27–28). Christians are called upon to "earnestly desire the higher gifts" (1 Cor 12:31).[127]

However, although tongues are not to be sought, they should be tolerated (1 Cor 14:39–40) and need to be taken into consideration with the guidance given in 1 Corinthians 14. Speaking in tongues is one of the temporary gifts.

> In 1 Cor 13:8 prophesies and knowledge "will pass away." . . . Tongues will cease, that is they will come to a stop at one time. The time when tongues will cease to function is not, however, indicated. But it is not unreasonable to suggest that they have already ceased, since the truth God wants to communicate to man is in the Bible. However, this is one area I cannot be dogmatic as many eminent Bible scholars do not all agree on this.[128]

Finally, Kato points out that the prophecy of Joel quoted in Acts 2:17–21 can be used to support the possibility of tongues being a gift still in use. The last days in Scripture may refer to the whole period of grace from the time of Christ's first coming until the end of this age at his second coming. The widespread charismatic movement today may include both genuine and counterfeit experiences. But the word of God, and not the experience itself, should be the standard for judgement (Matt 13:24–30).[129]

It is noteworthy to mention Kato's teaching on the other spirits, the demonic spirits. According to MacDonald:

> [Kato] frames the discussion of the demonic in the attributes of the Creator. The spirits are created spirits, far diminished in quality, ability, and power to the Author of spirits. Kato rips away the fear which surrounds the subject by establishing the supremacy of the uncreated Spirit. Kato also resists any and every action that would exalt, worship, or empower the demonic. All forms of false worship and seeking the assistance of spirits is opposed and repudiated. In keeping with the Scriptures, only

---

127. Kato, "The Power of the Holy Spirit," 11–12
128. Kato, "The Power of the Holy Spirit," 13.
129. Kato, 13

God is elevated as the proper source of supernatural assistance for life and death.[130]

Given the contemporary growth of "New Generation Christianity,"[131] with widespread belief in the efficacy of spiritual forces, Kato's teaching on these spiritual forces, and clearly distinguishing them from the Holy Spirit, is important, especially in the African context. Kato gave not only his personal insight on the occult but also his biblical understanding of the spirits. He narrated some of his childhood experiences about the spirit world, which continued to make an impact on him in his adult life, such as his fear of the graveyard highlighted earlier in this work. He wrote about the ATR belief about the spirits of the dead coming back to haunt the living, giving his biblical perspective about this subject.[132]

Kato also reflected on the world of spirits in the cosmos generally. God is spirit but very different from other spirits (John 4:24). The other spirits are created like everything else and are finite, unlike God. God's purpose for creation is for his glory (Ps 148:2–3; Col 1:16; cf. Gen 1:31). In the first place, Kato pointed out:

> God as Spirit is not a vague substance such as energy. He is a Person. In fact, there are three Persons within the Godhead, although there is only One God. There is God the Father, God the Son, and God the Holy Spirit. We call this "Trinity." God as Spirit does not have a body. So in order to be seen by man, God revealed Himself in Jesus Christ. That is why Jesus Christ said, "He who has seen me has seen the Father" (John 14: 9). In Jesus Christ, God who is Spirit has been revealed to man. Because Jesus Christ is fully God and fully man, He was able to die, to be buried and to rise again for our sins. As God He is Spirit, therefore He dwells in the believer today. The Apostle Paul is very fond of the expression "Christ in you," or Christ who "lives in me" (Galatians 2:20). The third Person of the Trinity is

---

130. MacDonald, "Critical Analysis," 204–205.
131. Cole, "State of Theological," 3.
132. Kato, *Spirits*, 2.

called the Holy Spirit. God's nature is holiness and all the three Persons are absolutely holy.[133]

In speaking about demons and cosmological spirits, Kato was not in any way comparing the Holy Spirit to the spirits of the cosmos.

> God as Spirit is absolutely different from all other classes of spirits. He is the Creator. Every aspect of His character is infinite; that is, without limit or comparison. He alone knows everything. He also can do everything that is not against His nature. God alone can be everywhere at the same time. He, therefore, belongs to a distinct category of the spiritual world, though He is Spirit.[134]

However, because of the apparent confusion in the church in the name of charismaticism regarding aspects of God's gifts to the church, there is need to understand the difference between the Holy Spirit, and his work in the life of believers, and other spirits. Also, the operations of the cosmological spirits have their limitations.

> God is the Creator of all that is. He has no beginning and no end. "In the beginning God created the heavens and the earth" (Genesis 1:1). God who always IS, created the heavens and the earth and everything in them. So in our dealing with the origin of spirits, we must exclude God.[135]

Although God created the cosmos and everything that exists (Ps 148:2, 5; Col 1:16), he is not the author of evil. Evil is inconsistent with God's nature and who God is. Part of creation is the invisible spirit world, made up of both good and evil angels. Rebellion against God is the cause of evil. Rebellious angels are demons, with Satan, or Lucifer, being the chief devil (Isa 14:12). This raises the question about why God allows evil. Kato responded:

> You may ask why, if God was good and all-powerful, did He allow evil to come into His beautiful universe? This question bothers me too. It has bothered philosophers and religious leaders. The ultimate answer lies with God. "The secret things belong

---

133. Kato, 4.
134. Kato, 3–4.
135. Kato, 4.

to the Lord our God; but the things that are revealed belong to us and to our children, for ever, that we may do all the words of this law" (Deuteronomy 29:29). So we do not know fully why God allowed sin to spoil His beautiful creation. But we must remember that the spirits are intelligent, personal beings with the ability and privilege to choose. The same thing applies to man.[136]

Some angels left their place of perfection, their proper dwelling place (Jude 6), and led by Lucifer, they rebelled against God and sinned. Apparently sin first occurred in heaven with some of the angels. Satan's pride and ambition were the root cause of sin. Satan was the first sinner. Although he was a "commander-in-chief" of God's armed forces, the angels, he aspired to make himself like God. The result was that he was driven from the presence of God. Other angels who followed Satan in sinning were also expelled from the presence of God. They lost their original holiness. The fallen angels became unclean spirits or demons.[137] Jesus sent his disciples to cast out unclean spirits (Matt 10:1). Some of them are still bound in a place called Tartarus until the day of judgment (2 Peter 2:4). Others are free to roam about. But all the evil spirits will be judged and finally cast into the lake of fire (Matt 25:41; 1 Cor 6:3).

There are good cosmological spirits in our world as well. "Angel is the term used in the Bible to describe the created spirits, and the words 'angel' and 'spirit' can be used interchangeably. The word 'angel' means a messenger or agent of some higher being."[138] Kato briefly surveyed the reality of good angels or spirits in the Bible:

> Daniel describes the multitudes of angels serving God in heaven. "A stream of fire issued and came forth before him; a thousand thousands served him" (Daniel 7:10). Jesus said God could send more than twelve legions of angels at one call for help (Matthew 26:53). One legion of Roman soldiers was between 3,000 and 6,000. So Jesus could call upon between 36,000 and 72,000 at one time and that would not be all the angels there were at God's

---

136. Kato, 7.
137. Kato, 7–8.
138. Kato, 8.

service. In Hebrews we read of "innumerable hosts of angels" (Hebrews 12:22). The Word of God mentions several kinds of good angels.[139]

The good angels are messengers of God and do serve in various functions, including:

> The worship of God (Isaiah 6), working out God's will (Job 33:23; Dan 7:16; Acts 12:23), looking after God's chosen people (Dan 3:28; 10:13, 21), serving Jesus: Predicted and celebrated the birth of Jesus Christ (Matthew 1:20; Luke 1–11). They served Christ in His temptations and sufferings (Matthew 4:11; Luke 22:43). Announced His resurrection and going to heaven (Matthew 28; John 20:12; Acts 1:10, 11), and they will announce the coming of Jesus Christ (1 Thessalonians 4:16). Jesus Christ will send the angels to gather together God's children in the final day of judgment (Matthew 24:31). They will also help sort out the believers from the unbelievers (Matthew 13:49, 50) and help Christians (Acts 5:19; 12:11; Heb. 1:14).[140]

Kato shared a personal experience of receiving help from angels:

> The fact that God's good angels guard and deliver believers from danger should be a great consolation to us. One day I was driving from Kagoro to Kaduna with other pastors in the car. I was driving in a thick fog on the road I had never driven before. At a sharp bend I missed the turning and headed into the bush. There was a huge tree right in front of us. A fellow pastor sitting with me in front offered the shortest prayer he has ever offered. He simply said in Jaba language, "Oh Nom" repeatedly, which means "Oh God." The car stopped just before it hit the tree. We pushed the car back to the road and drove on after a prayer of thanks. I am convinced that the Lord sent his angel to stand between my car and the tree for protection.[141]

---

139. Kato, 8–9.
140. Kato, 11–13.
141. Kato, *Theological Pitfalls*, 13.

Not many people would have attributed their protection in this way to angels or spirits. However, Kato stated: "Let me give a note of warning here. Nowhere in the Bible are we told to pray to the angels or even ask God to send us His angels to deliver us. As a matter of fact, angels themselves rightly feel unqualified to be worshipped since they are creatures."[142]

The demons or fallen angels roam around to cause harm to people in various ways, ultimately under the permissive will of the All-Sovereign God. However, the devil and the demons are creatures, and therefore, they are limited. The devil cannot be everywhere at the same time but does have his agents, the demons, all over the world. However, since Satan and demons are real, their activities must be taken seriously. Some of the happenings people hear about may be true. For example, it is possible for evil spirits to put on the appearance of a dead person and come back to communicate with living people. Satan can perform miracles (Exod 7:10–12). God may allow Satan to do mighty things, but there is a boundary beyond which God will not allow him to go.[143]

The Christian should believe in the reality of the world of demons but should seek no contact with them whatsoever. The Bible condemns any dealings with evil spirits. Evil spirits are behind the activities of witches and diviners. As children of light, we should have no dealings with the works of darkness (Deut 18:10–12; 1 John 1:6). It is sin to consult a witch doctor who in turn consults the spirits to tell the future or to help one in any way. The Christian should not take part in idol worship in any way. Demons are behind the objects that pagans worship (Deut 18:10–12; Isa 8:19). Kato noted:

> I know that in 1 Samuel 28:7–25 we have the account of Saul consulting a witch doctor of Endor. It is a difficult passage, but let us realize that Saul was a backslider, a miserable and confused person. And when Saul inquired of the Lord, the Lord did not answer him (1 Samuel 28:6). Since the Lord did not answer Saul, he turned to Satanic sources. The end result was God's judgment by death for Saul and his sons, and defeat for Israel. Let this serve as a warning to those seeking help from demonic forces.[144]

---

142. Kato, 14.
143. Kato, 22.
144. Kato, 26.

The Christian should be alert all the time, realizing that Satan never takes time off from trying to persuade the Christian to do wrong: "Be sober, be watchful. Your adversary the devil prowls around like a roaring lion, seeking someone to devour" (1 Pet 5:8). The Christian must actively resist Satan. "Resist the devil and he will flee from you" (Jas 4:7). The Christian should be well armed by depending on the Lord for victory over Satan and his forces. "Put on the whole armour of God, that you may be able to stand against the wiles of the devil" (Eph 6:11).

There is a difference between demonic influence and demon possession. The unbeliever does not have the Holy Spirit of God, and therefore can be possessed by demons. The Christian is a temple of the Holy Spirit (1 Cor 6:19). The Holy Spirit and an evil spirit cannot both dwell in the same body at the same time. The believer may be influenced by an evil spirit, as happened to Paul himself when "a messenger of Satan" harassed him (2 Cor 12: 7). But demons cannot possess the body of the Christian. Even at death they still have no claims on a Christian's body (Jude 9). Every spirit should be tested to confirm if it is of God.[145]

Summary

This chapter has endeavoured to consolidate some theological constructs that were pertinent to Byang Kato's theology at both the conceptual level and the level of praxis. The forgone sections established eight key theological categories or doctrines that defined Kato's contention for biblical Christianity in the church in Africa. These covered the believer's new birth in the church (soteriology) through the life of the Christian (missiology) and last things (eschatology). These were deduced from the life history of Kato himself, his conversion, ministry, and his particular perspectives or beliefs about these aspects of theology. The themes highlighted were deduced from Kato's defence of the gospel, among several other African theologians whose work tended to blend African traditional religious beliefs with what the Bible teaches. The assessment also included material from Kato's writings, sermons and speeches surveyed in this study.

---

145. Kato, *Spirits*, 31; cf. John 4:2–3; 2 Tim 1:12.

The theological doctrines outlined above cover essential classical doctrines of the church. The findings have been fitted into eight main theological categories that are mostly practical, mainstream biblical and christocentric evangelical beliefs. Therefore, this corpus of theological material underscores the important contribution Kato made in defining biblical Christianity for the church in Africa.

Kato did not attempt to propose a new particular theological construct, to be rendered in cryptic language like that of his peers, such as *Orita* (Idowu), *Communio Sanctorum and Praeparatio Evangelica* (Mbiti), ancestor veneration (Sawyerr) or African theological innovation/identity (Bediako). In any case, what has been demonstrated in this study is that Kato's notable lone and dissenting message was *ubique, semper, omnibus*. That is, Kato's theological articulations were intended to conform to what was applicable within the Christian community everywhere (across cultures), always (across time), and to all (universal consent). Reiterating Thomas Oden's succinct description of consensual classical theology:

> Christian teaching consists in what you have received, not what you have thought up; a matter not of ingenuity, but of doctrine; not of private acquisition, but of Public Tradition; a matter brought to you, not put forth by you, in which you must be not the author but the guardian, not the founder but the sharer, not the leader but the follower.[146]

Thus, Kato's theology was intended to be in coherence with the tests of universality, apostolic antiquity and conciliar consent.[147]

---

146. Oden, *Rebirth of Orthodoxy*, 143.
147. Oden.

CHAPTER 6

Summary, Conclusion and Recommendations

Introduction

This study is an analytical biography of Byang Henry Kato (1936–1975). Kato was renowned as the father of evangelicalism in the modern history of the church in sub-Saharan Africa. Kato was the first African general secretary of the Association of Evangelicals in Africa (AEA), and he doubled as the executive secretary of the AEA Theological Commission. He is remembered for his unique voice in the theological debates of his time and for his vision for the theological initiatives and institutions he helped create before his tragic death.

Kato's faith journey from a follower of ethnic Jaba traditional religion to an outstanding evangelical Christian witness and leader was exceptional. Kato's assimilation of a biblical worldview was critical in the strides he made and for his achievements in ministry. A critical mass of Christians with practices that are consistent with a biblical worldview is essential for gospel transformation in Africa. However, the practice of many professed Christians in Africa is still often informed by traditional worldviews. Thus, Kato's transformative experience is exemplary.

The purpose of this study was to analyse Kato's life, ministry and theological contributions. It specifically explored Kato's theological legacy in the realms of biblical hermeneutics, African Christian identity and evangelical theological education. The hypothesis was that Kato's theological legacy and lived experiences would be commendable lessons for leadership development and for growth of the church in Africa. Kato's purpose was to contend for biblical Christianity in the church in Africa and safeguard it from syncretistic universalism. He helped to shape evangelical Christianity and laid plans for encouraging sound theological education at all levels, especially for founding advanced-level evangelical theological institutions in Africa.

I used qualitative analytical methods to respond to the research questions. This final chapter summarises the findings of the preceding five chapters and concludes with the research's main findings, how it answers the research questions, its particular contributions and some recommendations for further research.

Summary of the Study

The following sections offer concise overviews of the content of each chapter in turn, starting with chapter 1.

Summary of Chapter One

The first chapter is an introduction to the study, highlighting the nature, importance and theoretical framework of the study and justifying the biographical study of theologians as an academic discipline within historical theology. Byang Kato's importance lies in the fact that he is believed to be the father of evangelicalism in the history of modern Christianity in sub-Saharan Africa. He played a principal role in shaping contemporary African evangelicalism. The study explores his life and his theological legacy in three critical areas in African theological discourse; that is, (1) biblical hermeneutics, (2) African Christian identity and (3) theological education.

The life of one person may not be adequate to serve as normative. However, many people can appreciate and relate to Kato's experiences in the African context. The socio-economic, cultural and political context in which Kato was raised is fairly typical for many Africans. His adult life and ministry were extensive in scope and their sphere of influence. Kato epitomised the kind of life and challenges an average African goes through. That he was able to demonstrate transformation and radically change from holding an ATR worldview to a biblical worldview is worth emulating.

In order to explore Kato's life and theological legacy, the research was framed to respond to this main question: What theological contribution can be made to contemporary biblical Christianity in sub-Saharan Africa by an analytical study of Byang Kato's life history, his legacy and his message about biblical hermeneutics, African Christian identity and evangelical theological education? To respond to this main question, the research sought to respond to four sub-questions, as follow: (1) Who was Byang Kato and what social, cultural, political and theological contexts and influences shaped his theological formation and views? (2) How did Kato's message on biblical hermeneutics, African Christian identity and Christian education impact evangelical Christianity in Africa during his lifetime? (3) What are the biblical and theological foundations for Kato's message on hermeneutics, African Christian identity and evangelical theological education? (4) What can the contemporary sub-Saharan church learn from Kato's life and his theological contribution to sub-Saharan African biblical hermeneutics, Christian identity and evangelical theological education about shaping an African evangelical theological agenda today?

To answer these questions, a design and methodology were crafted to carry out the research. The design described the type of research needed and outlined the different steps sequentially followed to accomplish the goal. The methodology described the instruments used to collect the relevant information required to respond to the research questions. I used this section also to provide the philosophical justifications and framework which shape the design and methodology. The main approach was a qualitative single case study, an in-depth biographical study of Kato's life and theological contribution. It was argued how a single case could be a learning tool, presenting narratives of the lived and real experiences of an African church leader who rose from a traditional background to contribute to the shaping of evangelical Christianity, which others could vicariously apply in the contemporary African context. The study was also exploratory, descriptive, qualitative and, to a limited extent, ethnographic. The researcher is one of Byang Kato's successors at the Association of Evangelical in Africa (AEA), even though several decades exist between us. Nevertheless, access to information, and the fact that the researcher is going through similar experiences, enhanced in-depth exploration of the subject.

The tools used included a literary review of Kato's published and unpublished works, as well as other biographical materials such as the Kato Memorial Lectures and a comprehensive biographical tool put together by

ACTEA. Also included were field interviews of people who knew Kato and could provide relevant information about his life and ministry. A purposive sample of ten persons, from various backgrounds, including his family members, were interviewed. It was providential that the researcher was able to meet for a personal interview with Kato's spouse who had survived him as a widow for forty-four years. The interview took place in Kaduna, Nigeria, at the home of her daughter. Mrs. Jummai Kato died less than two months later, at the age of eighty.

Summary of Chapter Two

The second chapter is a biographical sketch of Kato's life history, covering his birth, childhood, adult life, conversion from a fetish priest to Christianity, education, family, career and death. The context of Kato's birth in the rural town of Kwoi in Northern Nigeria, and the influences that shaped Kato there, are highlighted. The roadmap for Kato's meteoric rise to becoming a globally recognised evangelical Christian leader is described. The chapter crafted a portrait of Kato, from the cradle to the grave, underscoring his theological and spiritual milestones and pitfalls.

Kato was destined to follow his father's footsteps as a fetish priest. He was dedicated to the tribal god a few days after his birth and nurtured in that environment as a child until he underwent the rite of passage to manhood at the age of ten. At the tender age of twelve, Kato converted to the Christian faith. He first got attracted to the church through the ministry of a missionary lady who occasionally came to the village square to preach the gospel in the local Hausa language. Kato followed her on Sunday to the local SIM church in the village and expressed interest in enrolling in the local elementary school to the strong objection of his father. After much persuasion, pleas from the missionaries and the intervention of his grandfather, Byang eventually enrolled in school one year after his first attempt and under very strict conditions which ensured that he continued working on his father's farm while attending school.

It was in school, when Kato heard the story of Noah and the ark told by his teacher, that he felt the need to "jump in the ark of Jesus" to be saved from the "flooding judgement of eternal death" on account of sin. This act would make more sense to Kato when he attended revival services in the church some time later. He was under conviction and recommitted his life, covenanting

Summary, Conclusion and Recommendations

to follow and serve Jesus for the rest of his life. This was a significant turning point in Kato's Christian formation.

Kato went from elementary school to Igbaja Bible College in Nigeria to train for a ministerial career. In his third and final year at Igbaja Bible College, Kato got married to a local princess, Jummai, the daughter of the king of the Jaba people in his home area, and they began a family. He worked as a Hausa Bible teacher, farmed to supplement income and did private studies to sit the O and A Level exams to enter university. He moved to Lagos to start a career in Christiaan media but left to enter London Bible College in the United Kingdom for more advanced theological studies, which led to a coveted BD degree from the University of London.

When Kato returned to Nigeria from studies in the UK, he was elected general secretary of his denominational church, the Evangelical Church of West Africa (ECWA). His tenure coincided with the breakout of the Nigerian Civil War. After three years in this position, Kato proceeded to the USA in quest of more advanced theological studies. He did both his STM and DTh in record time, between 1970 and 1973. By the time Kato was graduating from Dallas, he had already been appointed both general secretary of the AEA and executive secretary of the newly formed AEA Theological Commission.

Kato is remembered for the way he rose from what he called a "devil's baby" to being a great servant of God. He contended for biblical Christianity on the continent. Most of the theologians during Kato's time wanted to decolonise Christianity by integrating ATR beliefs to support African culture and thought. The demeaning of African values and culture by European colonisers was associated with the Christianity brought to Africa by European missionaries. Kato uniquely differentiated the biblical message from the messenger and debated the other theologians, charging them for views he perceived to be syncretistic universalism. His counter arguments helped to shape African evangelicalism.

Kato endeavoured to promote sound biblical teaching in Africa by planning the establishment of theological training institutions up to the post-graduate level, as well as an accreditation service to encourage and sustain high quality in such programs. He also proposed the establishment of an academic journal to encourage and promote the publication of scholarly theological work by African scholars. In these years, Kato was simultaneously engaged with the global evangelical Christian family. He was a plenary speaker at the inaugural International Congress on World Evangelization in 1974 and was selected to serve on the continuation committee of the Lausanne Movement. The same year, Kato was elected to the International Council of the World Evangelical Alliance (WEA) and appointed as chair of the newly-formed WEA Theological Commission.

His tenure in all these roles and initiatives was cut short by his tragic death by drowning in the Indian Ocean near Mombasa, Kenya, in December 1975. However, his achievements remained substantial. The projects and institutions he helped to establish continue to play an important role in theological education and the church in Africa as a whole. Kato, like every human being, was not without shortcomings. The final section of this chapter outlined both Kato's accomplishments and his limitations and failures.

Summary of Chapter Three

The third chapter focused on Kato's theological contributions, especially in the areas of hermeneutics, African Christian self-identity and evangelical theological education in Africa. Also explored were the different theological constructs Kato had to contend with as he brought into the conversation a unique voice which was contrary to many of the scholars of his time. He sparked a lively theological debate on the continent by establishing a clear theological divide between liberal Protestant theologians and evangelicals. Several theologians in Africa advocated linking ATR with Christianity in ways that Kato thought were syncretistic. Kato contended for what he considered to be the biblical position on some essential doctrines, including salvation, the Bible, the uniqueness of Christ as the only way for salvation, ecumenism and ancestral veneration.

Kato's critics charged that he was known for "what he was opposed to, but not what he stood for."[1] Kato's seminal work, *Theological Pitfalls in Africa*, was meant essentially to warn the church about the kind of theology that was becoming prevalent in Africa, and which he perceived to be harmful to the church in Africa. The question was whether he had any theology of his own or was only focused on pointing out error in the theology of others. It needs therefore to be highlighted that, in advancing his theological critiques, Kato also articulated his own theological perspectives. Kato had a high view of the

---

1. Breman, "Association of Evangelicals," 384–385.

Bible. That is to say, he believed that the Bible is God's word and is therefore inspired, inerrant and infallible. He argued for the Bible as the only source of Christian theology and rejected African traditional religions as a valid source for Christian theology, especially as espoused during Kato's time by proponents of African theology. He sought to give an emic and literalist reading and interpretation of Scripture from a conservative evangelical point of view.

Kato helped to define African evangelicalism and to establish it within mainstream global evangelicalism. His views about authentic African biblical theology were clear and unambiguous in relation to African theology, which was based mainly on anthropocentrism. Therefore, he argued that for authentic Christian faith and life on the continent it was essential that the African traditional belief system should be completely transformed and replaced by the biblical worldview. What Kato saw as the task of African theology was to scan the message of the Bible in its original context and learn to apply that within the African context, without the distractions of deductive presuppositions or allegorical interpretations.

On the question of authentic African Christian identity, Kato prided himself on being a Christian African. Of prime importance was his commitment to his faith in Christ. Then, where Christ had chosen to plant him in terms of tribe or nation, he could embrace that too as part of his true identity. He was a proud Christian Nigerian African. African intellectuals had given high priority to the subject of African identity in every area of endeavour. The key assumption was that the influence and maltreatment of their slave masters and colonisers had led to a split personality or loss of identity for Africans. In the quest for African believers to deliver themselves from this identity challenge, Kato argued for use of the "third race" concept that had sustained believers in the first centuries of Christianity, the perception that salvation in Christ provides the primary identity. It is only in Christ that the African can find true liberation and lasting identity – authentically Christian and truly African – a Christian African. This was essential for the resolution of the so-called identity crisis and an important consideration for Africa's aspirations.

Kato not only complained about encroaching deviations in the church but also envisioned guidelines for addressing the resulting challenges. He prioritized theological education and the training of pastors, church leaders, children and lay members of the church in sound evangelical theology at every level. Kato's contribution to theological education was not limited to his own personal development, his ministry or the institutions he envisioned for establishment, but he also contributed to enhancing theological discourse in several ways. His plan resulted in the establishment of the first two evangelical post-graduate theological schools or seminaries in sub-Saharan Africa. The Association of Evangelical Theological Schools in Africa (ACTEA) was also established to help set standards and offer support for seminary faculty and curricula development. Kato promoted evangelical theological scholarship and publication. The theological institutions and projects he helped to establish continue to this day to make significant contributions.

Chapter 3 also highlights the contemporary state of the church in Africa. Theological distortions of the sort that concerned Kato often continue unabated. The role of ATR beliefs is still prevalent among believers, and with the additional impact of globalisation and secularisation on Africa, there is indeed a need to contend earnestly for biblical Christianity in the church. The growth of new generations in the church requires this. Indeed, sections of pentecostal and charismatic churches have sacralised ATR beliefs in more tangible and visible ways than what Kato had to contend with. The growth of the church is not matched by trained and qualified pastors to lead the churches. The overwhelming need that continues to exist in the church does not diminish the importance of the institutions that Kato helped to found but is rather a measure of their continuing importance.

Kato's theological work was groundbreaking. However, in the current era his theological educational institutions and initiatives must also contend against challenges for their survival. Among AEA-related institutions and other ACTEA-affiliated evangelical theological schools in Africa are some that have been converted into universities under the jurisdiction of national educational authorities. The universities mount and operate courses approved by these authorities and comply with the authorities' guidelines, which are informed by values other than biblical or Christian ones. Theology or Christian studies become only one among several subject options, and the intake of students and appointment of faculty may not be limited to Christians. There could be important lessons to learn from Kato when he faced the non-existence of evangelical theological institutions at a tertiary level in sub-Saharan Africa. The church needs to explore innovative ways of continuing to advance sound theological preparation for its leaders and members.

Summary of Chapter Four

While chapter 3 was about polemics, attending to opposing views between Kato and some African theologians on various biblical and theological doctrines, chapter 4 was dialogical and comparative, reconciling Kato's views with established evangelical orthodoxy. It critically engages the biblical and theological basis for Kato's theological themes explored in this study. Brief summaries of selected texts and evangelical biblical materials are outlined as a backdrop against which Kato's theology can be assessed for authentic evangelical orthodoxy. The study first explores evangelical tenets for which Kato contended, and then explores how these orthodox beliefs were established. The texts were extensively reviewed for ancient approaches to biblical hermeneutics and orthodoxy, from the earliest centuries of Christianity through the Protestant Reformation and into modern times. The Scripture has been affirmed, its integrity sustained and handed down to the church from New Testament times, through ancient classical methods guided by objective historical inquiry and with the help of the Holy Spirit. The approach is succinctly summed up by the Latin phrase *ubique, semper, omnibus*. Thus the outcome of these foundations works to establish the criterion of universality, apostolic antiquity and conciliar consent.[2]

Given the missional intent of the evangelical reading of the Bible, Wright's *Mission of God* was also examined. The thesis of this work is that the basis for understanding the Bible is the perspective of God's mission on earth. The assertion is that reading the Bible should be done in a way that takes seriously the missionary direction, moving from the particular to the universal, aimed at the kingdom of God.[3] Wright proposes an approach for reading and interpreting the Bible, one that identifies core themes which are foundational pillars of the biblical worldview and biblical theology. These themes include monotheism, creation, humanity, election, redemption, covenant, ethics and future hope.[4]

For contextual relevance, the presentation in this chapter also includes two African Christian scholars with methodologies that focus on the African context. Elizabeth Mburu's *African Hermeneutics* presents a five-step approach

---

2. Oden, *Rebirth of Orthodoxy*, 190–192.
3. Bauckham, *Bible and Mission*, 110.
4. Wright, *Mission of God*, 17.

visualised by a familiar object in the African context: a stool. She calls this approach a four-legged approach, with each of the four legs representing a distinct step in the hermeneutical process, and with the seat itself being the fifth and final step, the application within the hermeneutic cycle. As a good stool is stable and supports weight, so the hermeneutical stool should confidently provide a stable, or accurate, interpretation of the biblical text. The four legs are (1) parallels to the African context, (2) the theological context, (3) the literary context and (4) the historical context. These legs support the seat, which represents the final stage of interpretation: the application.

The other hermeneutical approach is that proposed by a second African evangelical scholar, Yusufu Turaki. Turaki proposes a method of "engaging religions and worldviews in Africa" (the title of his text). This takes seriously the underlying questions ATR adherents are seeking answers for. Turaki asserts that these ATR questions can be engaged from a biblical standpoint without undermining the fidelity to biblical Christianity. He shows how this can be done from a biblical, christocentric and ecclesiastical perspective. The goal is to demonstrate how biblical Christianity can transform traditional cultural and religious mindsets. Presentation of the gospel of Christ to people in traditional Africa cultures must bear in mind the great influence of African religious and social beliefs and practices. Christianity cannot afford to offer less than what traditional religion offers African Christians. To a less extent than the works mentioned, other works, commentaries and the Bible itself are all sources of information for evangelical orthodoxy.

Kato's hermeneutics in reading, interpretating and applying Scripture was demonstrated by exploring several biblical texts which he engaged, including the text that led to his conversion. The account also explores Kato's Christian self-understanding against the theoretical and biblical foundations for Christian identity, and finally, it explores evangelical theological education.

Evidently, Kato's perspectives are in resonance with many of the scholars mentioned in this study, and indeed with mainstream evangelicalism. Kato's theological propositions are dominantly consensual and understandable to Christians in global contexts other than his own; Christians could readily relate to his teachings. This is an important consideration if the church in Africa, in pursuing its own calling, will take seriously the concurrent call to reach out to other regions of the world with the universal Christian gospel.

Summary of Chapter Five

In the final step, in response to the main research question concerning the relevance of Kato's theological legacy for contemporary challenges facing Christianity in sub-Saharan Africa, the research formulates a model of Kato's theological contributions as practical guidelines toward achieving a faithful and integrated representation of biblical beliefs. The chapter distils the information in preceding chapters to outline and describe the perceived themes that characterise Kato's theology.

Kato's life history – from a childhood immersed in traditional culture and ATR to his conversion to Christianity, education, family life and vocation – has been explored in this study. Kato was well trained in the evangelical tradition and held eminent positions in the church in Nigeria, Africa's most populous country, and in the broader African evangelical community as general secretary of the Association of Evangelicals in Africa (AEA). He was also appointed to important positions in the global evangelical movement, such as in the Lausanne Movement and the World Evangelical Alliance (WEA). Thus, reflections on Kato's life and his theological work hold important lessons for evangelicals in Africa.

Kato's life, apologia, writings and ministry have been explored in this study to identify themes of his theological contributions. There are "very few contemporary African theologians who emphasise the discontinuity between the Christian faith and the traditional African religions and cultures. The great majority are in line with some form of synthesis, pleading for various degrees of continuity between the gospel and traditional African beliefs."[5] Thus, the unique but mainstream evangelical articulations voiced by Kato would constitute a helpful model for the evangelical church in Africa.

The eight themes that were identified as characterising Kato's theology are (1) personal conversion (soteriology); (2) radical discipleship (Christian formation); (3) Bible-groundedness (bibliology); (4) Christ-centredness (Christology); (5) Christian African identity (ecclesiology); (6) safeguarding biblical Christianity in Africa (missiology); (7) the second coming of Christ (eschatology); and (8) the power of the Holy Spirit (pneumatology).

These themes have been explored through their sub-themes. The core themes and sub-themes are defined and described, drawing out relevant

---

5. Van der Walt, *Evangelical Voice*, 928.

theological implications for the church, especially in the African context. I name these the "Kato theological construct." Thus, in response to the research question, Kato provides a corpus of theological constructs that are important learning material for the contemporary church, particularly in sub-Saharan Africa, for discipleship, leadership development and the maturation of the church.

Conclusions of the Study

Byang Kato's life was a short span, yet it was also fulfilling and impactful. The historical context in which Kato was born and raised reflected a typical African traditional culture. He demonstrated how the Christian African could live out the Christian faith without compromise. He was hardworking and consistent, and he conducted himself with integrity and godliness. Kato rose from very humble beginnings to a position of global influence in the church and to the very epitome of his career as a true churchman.

Though Kato became an international figure, he did not neglect his local community, and he maintained an active relationship with his not always so privileged peers. He was able to engage his traditional culture without compromising his biblical beliefs. He embraced traditional values that were not against biblical injunction and rejected those that he perceived to be contrary to what the Bible teaches. He did not reject his Africanness and was well respected by his ethnic community. Vital participation in the community lets individuals live out their creed as their religion. According to Tarus and Lowery:

> These beliefs and practices are not written but handed down from one generation to the next and exist in the heart of the individual. . . . Each [individual] is himself a living creed of his own religion. Where the individual is, there is his religion, for he is a religious being. It is this that makes Africans so religious: religion is in their whole system of being.[6]

Kato's witness was demonstrated both by proclamation of the word and by the way he lived.

---

6. Tarus and Lowery, "African Theologies," 312.

The forefront of Kato's career was his dual role as general secretary of AEA (then AEAM) and executive secretary of the AEA Theological Commission. These roles matched his strengths and skills and passions. He seamlessly understood the theological challenges facing the evangelical church and was able to outline adaptive strategies and goals which continue to be foundational for AEA's work. Nearly all the objectives he outlined have been implemented and continue to be major interventions of AEA. Africa needs visionary Christian leaders in the church, and in the nation in general, to bring about transformation for Africa's renaissance.

The church in Africa continues to grow exponentially, with the Christian population now at least four times larger than in Kato's time. But the provisions for theological formation cannot keep up with the rate of new church plants and the number of trained pastors required to lead these churches. Also, the theological institutions engineered by Kato have focus on academic training. These, and the approach to theological training, may not be adequate to correct the theological malaise in the church in Africa. Some theological seminaries have also transitioned to becoming full-fledged universities, with a diminishing number of students opting for theological or biblical courses. Christian students tend to choose course options they perceive could lead to a more lucrative career than the ministries of the church. Kato was an inspiration for many people who testify to his influence for developing themselves for service in the church and in theological education.

The abiding interest in keeping up theological discourse about "African identity" can itself become a captivation, ironically enslaving the mind with fixations about past suppressions. This can prove a mentality that the church in Africa needs to supersede if it is to play a meaningful role in global Christianity, as indeed it must in this twenty-first century. Pan-Africanist preoccupations and Western cultural impositions cannot be cultivated as the basis for responsible theologising. If indeed the packaging of the good news of the gospel in Western clothing is condemned, repackaging it in African clothing simply continues the same underlying defect. Surely God's revelation to any people group is by God's own means, calling from out of the old into a new life, using circumstances and people in spite of their imperfections. The call of Abraham in Genesis 12 is paradigmatic to the call of every Christian. A faith response requires a coming out of old commitments into the new faith of Christianity. The call is from the particular to the universal. "The church is rooted in localities and is at the same time a global movement. In a world in which, more than ever before, global developments override both nation states and local communities, the Christian church is both an international movement and essentially rooted in localities."[7]

Knowledge of the past and how the evangelical church in Africa was shaped is important. Therefore, this research endeavoured to understand what a notable figure like Byang Kato believed and taught. Experiential pedagogy is an important learning process for missional engagement. Therefore, the biographies of those who have had similar experiences and have creditably acquitted themselves provide important lessons for reflection for those who follow after them. Examples to follow is what the faithful provide. God's people in the Old Testament came to understand God by seeing how he revealed himself to Abraham, Isaac, Jacob and other Old Testament people. Similarly, we follow their examples of trust and obedience and avoid the pitfalls exposed by their failures.[8] Cockerill states three principles for understanding the Old Testament in particular: (1) the example principle (what the faithful do); (2) the picture principle (what God has done) – God's redemption of his people in the OT is a sketch of the deeper redemption provided for his NT people through Christ; (3) the pattern principle (what the law says) – God gave his law at Sinai to show the kind of life he wanted his people to live in fellowship with him and in community with one another.[9] In the New Testament, the apostle Paul encourages following our leaders who follow Christ, and he uses himself as an example to follow.[10]

God has always used human agency, through the help of the Holy Spirit, to reveal himself to humans. He has done so through the patriarchs, the prophets, the apostles and the written word of God, the Bible. The incarnation of Christ was God's ultimate self-revelation. Christ established his church, and he calls and equips people to serve in the church for its growth and maturation (Eph 4:1–16). How that has been unfolding, and how it continues to unfold, is the basis for sound theologising. It is not so for the efficacy of religions created by humans, trapped in their rebellion against the God of the

---

7. Bauckham, *Bible and Mission*, 111.
8. Cockerill, "Bible-Authority," 2.
9. Cockerill, 4.
10. 1 Cor 4:16; 11:1; Phil 3:17; 2:12; see also Heb 13:17; 3 John 1:11.

Bible, whether this is a European religion, or an African religion, or an Asian one. The meaning and effects of the cross are mediated to the community of believers through the Holy Spirit and the Scriptures.

Kato's portrait of Christian African identity is indeed the biblical solution to the African identity crisis. While Africa's identity problem may be particularly acute and daunting, the identity challenge is ultimately a human problem. All humans without Christ are lost and groping in the dark, yearning for some form of self-identity that is illusive. However, Kato's de-emphasis on traditional religion and cultural identity did not highlight the positive theology of politics and economics and leadership in the African context. Turaki's vision of engaging African realities from a biblical mindset builds on Kato's theology to develop a political theology for freedom and emancipation in order to realise the "Africa we want" – a phrase used by the African Union in articulating their aspirations for the continent. The "Christian African" doctrine of Kato does not only resolve the African Christian identity question but lays a foundation for a theological articulation of development and the socio-political and economic transformation of Africa.

Kato's perspectives or hermeneutics on the issues he contended for were consistent with orthodox Christian views. History correctly judges him as the father of evangelicalism in modern Africa. Evangelicalism recognises the imperfection of humans; the best of humanity has feet of clay. Kato did have his own theological pitfalls. For instance, the tendency for pietism or fundamentalism may be noticed in some of his views and attitudes. Getting a right balance between ministry responsibilities and family responsibilities was also difficult. Kato was aware of some of his own limitations, which in itself indicates commendable theological reflection.

The research here presented has focused particularly on a brief biography of Kato, his biblical hermeneutics – the way Kato read, interpreted and applied Scripture – his view of African Christian identity, and the contributions he made to evangelical theological education in Africa. Together, these constitute the theological legacy that this study has sought to highlight. These theological views and actions were weighed against biblical and classical orthodox evangelical views to discern a corpus of Kato's theological content that is a useful model to learn from – the "Kato theological construct" – in support of biblical Christianity in the African context. Kato's theology focused on an apologetic defence of the historic Christian faith. He defended the integrity and authority of the Bible and the unique person of Jesus Christ – the incarnate, crucified, resurrected, ascended and soon-returning Son of God as the only way for salvation. He defended the distinctiveness of the Christian faith from African traditional religions and called for maintaining the clarity of the gospel message while pursuing responsible contextualisation.

Contributions of the Study

This study is essentially a biography of an exceptional pioneering church leader whose context, life experiences and challenges typify those of many people in Africa. Therefore, in exploring Kato's life and theological legacy, the research findings make an important contribution to African theological discourse and missionary activities in global Christianity. This is particularly important, given the status of the African church, which is largely evangelical in persuasion, as the majority church in global Christianity.

The study makes a contribution to scholarship and the mission of the church in the following main ways: (1) It paints a portrait of Byang Kato, an important theological leader, to be visible and accessible as a mirror for reflective practice, especially in the African context. Kato's journey in overcoming prevalent traditional religious worldviews is a useful example for applyingthe transformative power of the gospel of Jesus Christ. (2) It identifies a corpus of theological material, constituting the core of Kato's theological constructs, as a legacy. The nature of this theological corpus is consensual and mainstream evangelical beliefs, and it is therefore relevant not only to the church in Africa but to the global church as a whole. (3) Given Byang Kato's stature, this may not be the last word on exploring Kato, and therefore the study provides a substantial bibliography for future studies on Kato. (4) Kato's theological corpus highlighted in this study helps describe and define evangelicalism in Africa.

As alluded to above, the study does not cover all there was to Kato's life and ministry. His life as a student in the UK and then in the USA, covering a total of seven years in his thirty-nine-year life span, was an important period of his life that needs to be explored more fully. Finally, Kato's polemics explored in this study were mostly about the relationship between the Christian faith and African traditional religions. However, African Christianity has also contended extensively with Islam, especially in Nigeria and particularly in the North, where Kato comes from. Not much is known about what Kato thought about this important relationship and cause of conflict in Nigeria.

Recommendations of the Study

Kato's life offers the church important lessons to explore in disciple-making and contending for the faith in pluralistic and multi-religious twenty-first century societies, especially in the African context. The pragmatic and innovative approach for doing theology (popular theology) and the grassroots training of pastors and laity to read, understand, interpret and apply the Scripture in their own contexts, in response to real problems on a day-to-day basis, is commendable. This kind of approach to doing theology may not necessarily be provided by theological schools or seminaries, which traditionally are residential academic programmes. Therefore, various other means to increase access to theological training, through open and distance learning, using internet technology or online learning, informal and innovative approaches, need to be identified to scale up the training of the large percentage of untrained and unqualified pastors. More importantly, the biblical message needs to be lived for others to learn from the way leaders live their lives. The goal of disciple-making is to embrace the biblical worldview demonstrable in both what Christians say and what they do.

Kato's theological corpus identified in this study could be useful material for training church leaders and disciple-making in the church. These provide understanding for growth in the Christian faith, enabling African Christianity to avoid syncretistic universalism and allow the gospel to transform society for the better. Kato's book, *Theological Pitfalls in Africa*, which has been talked about a lot by the theological community over the past years, is out of print. The AEA needs to undertake reprinting this work to make it accessible to theological bookshops, universities and evangelical scholars.[11]

The seeming controversy Kato sparked in theological circles in Africa has not gone away. Even those theologians of an evangelical persuasion, who hail Kato for the defence of a biblical worldview, tend to hold a middle position. Many do not seem to have a clear stance on the uniqueness of biblical claims and may be straddling between the opposing positions – between the ideas

---

11. Bowers, "More Light," 14.

espoused in ATR and the uniqueness of the biblical message as the supreme and all sufficient premise for authentic biblical Christianity (which is what Kato contended for). The proposal here is for an orderly consenting process, like the ancient church councils whose deliberations have bequeathed to the church classical doctrines and creeds that the church has held through history and across the various church traditions. A good example of this in modern times is the Lausanne Covenant and Cape Town Commitment, which have become more or less creedal among evangelicals globally. "The covenant proclaims the substance of the Christian faith as historically declared in the creeds and adds a clear missional dimension to our faith."[12] The tendency to leave contemporary issues that border on doctrine, such as sexuality and same sex marriage, to subjective judgment is a deviation from the history of the faith. Perhaps the evangelical church could develop a way of building consensus on essential doctrinal subjects that are proving divisive. AEA as the premier representative body for evangelicals in Africa could provide a forum for consensus building.

It is worth taking note of how early African councils provided a practical model for discussion and conflict resolution towards shared theological discernment.[13] This process may have resembled contemporary practices in some African cultures, such as the *Indaba* in South Africa, *barray* (likened to a "town hall" meeting) in Sierra Leone, West Africa, and *baraza* in East Africa. These practices require stakeholders in the community to come together to debate or discuss matters in the open and come to definitive conclusions that are binding on all. One wonders how the church lost this practice.

These traditional African practices are perhaps a wake-up call for African theologians in their quest for African authenticity. If we should look to ancestors and traditional cultures for authenticity, why not turn to the early church, our ancestors in the faith from North Africa, instead of the non-Christian traditional religions? The North African church fathers made important contributions to shaping classical doctrines that informed Western and global Christianity. According to Oden, "African Christianity has arisen out of distinctly African experience on African soil. Those who have most suffered for its genuine depth and continuity have been born as Africans

---

12. Theron and Raiter, *Effective Theological Education*, 2.
13. Oden, *How Africa Shaped*, 48–55.

and have struggled in African cultures nurtured within many generations of indigenous African experience. They are not from outside."[14] This is contrary to the myth of Christianity being a "White man's religion." African theology, though contextual, needs also to be consistent with the Bible and with mainstream Christian theologies. This can only happen if the Bible and the mission of God, in which believers in Christ are privileged participants, are at the heart of our reflection.

The outstanding issues not covered in this study, as mentioned above, could be possible topics for future research. Assessment of the impact of the theological institutions Kato helped to establish could be useful information for the church in Africa. Before his untimely demise, Kato made a ten-point proposal to advance biblical Christianity in Africa. These points are captured in this study and are worthy of scholarly assessment. Generally, Kato's success in advancing evangelical theological education, and its impact on the church in Africa, tends to be anecdotal, and it deserves more empirical assessment.

---

14. Oden, 13.

Bibliography

Abar, M. Emmanuel. "Islam, Christianity, Traditional Religions and Power Politics in Northern Nigeria since Pre-Islamic Period." PhD diss., Seventh-Day Adventist Theological Seminary, Andrews University, 2019.

Adamo, David T. "Christianity and the African Traditional Religion(s): The Postcolonial Round of Engagement." *Verbum et Ecclesia* 32, no. 1 (2011): 1–10. doi:10.4102/ ve.v32i1.285.

Adeleye, Femi B. "The Development of the Thought of Samuel Ajayi Crowther Concerning British and African Culture in the Context of the Church Missionary Society in the Period 1821 to 1891." A thesis presented to Akrofi-Christalle Institute of Theology, Mission and Culture, Akropong-Akuapem, Ghana. 2012.

———. *Preachers of a Different Gospel: A Pilgrim's Reflections on Contemporary Trends in Christianity*. Nairobi: HippoBooks. 2011.

Adeyemo, Tokunboh, ed. *Africa Bible Commentary: A One-Volume Commentary Written by 70 African Scholars*. Nairobi: WordAlive, 2006.

———. "Byang Kato: The Man." Unpublished Byang Henry Kato Memorial Lectures. ACTEA Lecture, 1986/7 (AEA archives).

———. *Is Africa Cursed?: A Vision for Radical Transformation of an Ailing Continent*. Revised and updated ed. Nairobi: WordAlive, 2009.

———. "What Are Evangelicals?" A series of four lectures delivered at the General Council Meeting, Freetown, Sierra Leone, 7–8 November 1989. Pamphlet Archived at the AEA offices,

All Africa Conference of Churches. "Concept Note." Symposium on Addressing Misleading Theologies, October 23–27, 2019, Nairobi, Kenya. Pamphlet.

Anderson, J. N. D. *Christianity and Comparative Religion*. Downers Grove: InterVarsity Press, 1970.

Asumang, Annang. "Biblical Studies." In *A Student's A–Z of Theology: Evangelical Theology in Outline*, edited by Bill Domeris and Kevin Smith. South Africa: SATS, 2014. 53–76

———. "Reforming Theological Education in the Light of the Pentecostalisation of Christianity in the Global South." Special issue, *Conspectus* (December 2018): 115–148.

Association of Evangelicals Theology and Christian Education Commission (AEA-TCEC) Theological Consultation, compendium, Christian Learning Materials for Children, Nairobi, 2019.

Baba, Stephen Oluwarotimi Y. *History and Principles of Biblical Hermeneutics for Beginners*. Revised and enlarged edition. Ilorin: Amazing Grace, 2016.

———. "The Profile of Dr. Byang Henry Kato, Former Lecturer at ECWA Theological Seminary, Igbaja, Nigeria." An opening ceremony address delivered at the 41st Byang Henry Kato (Ph.D) Memorial Conference, 4th April 2017. https://babastephen.wordpress.com/2017/05/14/the-profile-of-dr-byang-henry-kato-former-lecturer-at-ecwa-theological-seminary-igbaja-nigeria/. Accessed 25 January 2018.

Bangura, Joseph Bosco. "Tracking the Maze of Theological Education in Sierra Leone: An Evangelical Perspective." *Africa Journal of Evangelical Theology* 34, no. 2 (2015): 109–126.

Barnes, Roscoe, III. "F. F. Bosworth: A Historical Analysis of the Influential Factors in His Life and Ministry." PhD diss., University of Pretoria, 2009.

Barrett, David B., George Thomas Kurian, and Todd M. Johnson, eds. *World Christian Encyclopaedia: A Comparative Survey of Churches and Religions in the Modern World*. 2nd edition. 2 vols. New York: Oxford University Press, 2001.

Barron, Bruce, ed. "'Scripture and Tradition' and 'the Church in Salvation': Catholics and Evangelicals Explore Challenges and Opportunities; A Report of the International Consultation between the Catholic Church and the World Evangelical Alliance (2009–2016)." *Evangelical Review of Theology: A Global Forum* 42 no.2 (April 2018): 100–130.

Bauer, David R., and Robert A. Traina. *Inductive Bible Study: A Comprehensive Guide to the Practice of Hermeneutics*. Grand Rapids: Baker Academic, 2011.

Bauckham, Richard. *Bible and Mission: Christian Witness in a Postmodern World*. Milton Keynes: Paternoster, 2005.

Bebbington, D. W. *Evangelicalism in Modern Britain: A History from the 1930s to 1980s*. London: Unwin Hyman, 1989.

Bebis, George S. "Orthodox Church." In *Encyclopaedia of Early Christianity*, edited by Everett Ferguson. New York: Garland, 1998.

Bediako, Kwame. *Jesus and the Gospel in Africa: History and Experience*. Theologies in Africa Series. Maryknoll: Orbis Books, 2004.

———. *Theology and Identity: The Impact of Culture on Christian Thought in the Second Century and Modern Africa*. Oxford: Regnum Books,1992.

———. "Understanding African Theology in the 20th Century." *Themelios* 20, no. 1 (October 1994): 14–20.

Biri, Kudzai. "The Silent Echoing Voice: Aspects of Zimbabwean Pentecostalism and the Quest for Power, Healing and Miracles." Supplement, *Studia Historiae Ecclesiasticae* 38 (August 2012): 1–12. http://uir.unisa.ac.za/bitstream/handle/10500/6609/biri.pdf?sequence=1.

Blair, David. *Degrees in Violence: Robert Mugabe and Struggle for Power in Zimbabwe*. London: Continuum, 2002.

Bomboro, John. Review of *The Bible Made Impossible: Why Biblicism Is Not a Truly Evangelical Reading of Scripture*, by Christian Smith. *Concordia Journal* 40, no. 1 (2014): 83–85. http://scholar.csl.edu/cj/vol40/iss1/21.

Bosch, David J. *Transforming Mission: Paradigm Shifts in Theology of Mission*. Maryknoll: Orbis Books, 1991.

Bowers, Paul. "African Theology: Its History, Dynamics, Scope and Future." *AJET* 21, no. 2 (2002): 109–125.

———. "Byang Kato and Beyond: The 2008 Byang Kato Memorial Lectures 1." Jos, Nigeria, March 2008. 3–21.

———. "Christian Intellectual Responsibilities in Modern Africa: The 2008 Byang Kato Memorial Lectures 2." *AJET* 28, no. 2 (2009): 91–114.

———. "Evangelical Theology in Africa: Byang Kato's Legacy." *Evangelical Review of Theology* 5 (1981): 35–39.

———. "New Light on Theological Education in Africa." *Evangelical Review of Theology* 14, no. 1 (1990): 57–63.

———. "More Light on Theological Education in Africa." *EAJET* 8, no. 2 (1989): 11–18.

———. *Theological Education in Africa: The ACTEA Story; Questing for Excellence and Renewal, 1976–2016*. Anniversary edition. Nairobi: ACTEA, 2016.

———. "Theological Education in Africa: Why Does It Matter?" *AJET* 26, no. 2 (2007): 135–149.

Brekus, Catherine. "Forum, Region and the Biographical Turn." *Religion and American Culture: A Journal of Interpretation* 24, no. 1 (2014): 1–35.

Breman, Christina M. "The Association of Evangelicals in Africa: Its History, Organization, Members, Projects, Localization and Message." PhD thesis, Utrecht University, 1995.

———. *Byang H. Kato: A Bibliography*. ACTEA Tools and Studies 16. Ndola, Zambia: Theological College of Central Africa, 1997. https://www.acteaweb.org/downloads/tools/Tools%20and%20Studies%2016.pdf

———. "A Portrait of Dr. Byang H Kato." *AJET* 15, no. 2 (1996): 135–151.

Brewster, Dan. *Child, Church and Mission*. Revised edition. Colorado Springs: Compassion International, 2011.

Bush, Luis. "4/14 Window New Mission Focus." Speakers note, 4/14 Window Global Summit 11, Promise Church, NY, 2–5 September 2010.

Byimui, Umaru Thaddeus. "Toward Christian-Muslim Dialogue and Peace-Building Activities in Northern Nigeria: Theological Reflection." PhD thesis, University of Glasgow, 2013.

Carson, D. A. (1982). Review of *The Theological Task of the Church in Africa*, by Tite Tiénou. *Trinity Journal* 4 (1983): 119–121.

Chalk, Jack. *Making Disciples in Africa: Engaging Syncretism in the African Church through Philosophical Analysis of Worldviews*. Carlisle: Langham, 2013.

Chrispal, Ashish. "Restoring Missional Vision in Theological Education." International Orality Network. https://orality.net/content/restoring-missional-vision-in-theological-education/.

Cockerill, Gareth Lee. "The Bible: Authority, Integrity and Practice." Morning Bible session, 43rd EFSL Convention, Bo, Sierra Leone, 23–26 September 2002.

———. *Christian Faith in the Old Testament: The Bible of the Apostles*. Nashville: Thomas Nelson, 2014.

Cole, Victor Babajide. "The State of Theological Education in Africa." Paper presented at the AEA Theological Education Consultation, Nairobi, Kenya, 8–13 September 2019.

Conteh, Prince S. *Essays in African Religion and Christianity*. Accra: All Nations University, 2014.

Crafford, D. "The Church in Africa and the Struggle for an African Identity." *Skrif en Kerk* 14, no. 2 (1993): 163–175.

Creswell, John W. *Educational Research: Planning, Conducting, and Evaluating Quantitative and Qualitative Research*. 4th ed. Boston: Pearson, 2012.

Cullivan, Lauren. "The Meanings behind the Marks: Scarification and the People of Wa." Digital Collections: African Diaspora Project ISPS. School for International Training, 1998. http://digitalcollections.sit.edu/african_diaspora_isp/4.

Danielson, Robert. "About the Association of Professors of Mission." In *Social Engagement: The Challenge of the Social in Missiological Education*, i. The 2013 Proceedings of the Association of Professors of Mission. Wilmore, KY: First Fruits, 2013.

Daramola, Olaniyi, ed. *Daily Guide: Daily Bible Reading Guide for the Whole Year*. Ibadan: Scripture Union, 2020.

Domeris, Bill. "Hermeneutics." In *A Student's A–Z of Theology: Evangelical Theology in Outline*, edited by Bill Domeris and Kevin Smith. South Africa: SATS, 2014. 177–190

———. "Historical Theology." In *A Student's A–Z of Theology: Evangelical Theology in Outline*, edited by Bill Domeris and Kevin Smith. South Africa: SATS, 2014.191-205

Domeris, Bill, and Kevin Smith, eds. *A Student's A–Z of Theology: Evangelical Theology in Outline*. South Africa: SATS, 2014.

Eaton, Michael A. *The Branch Exposition of the Bible: A Preacher's Commentary of the New Testament*. Carlisle: Langham Global Library, 2020.

Edre, Enosh Anguandia Adia. "Christian Nominalism within Church Membership: A Case Study of the Church in the Town of Bunia in the Democratic Republic of Congo." PhD diss., SATS, 2015.

Evangelical Alliance and Christian Research. *21st Century Evangelicals: A Snapshot of the Beliefs and Habits of Evangelical Christians in the UK*. Evangelical Alliance, 2011.

"Evangelism Is Most Effective among Kids." Barna: Research Releases. Barna Group, 2009.

Ewell, C. Rosalee Velloso. "What Evangelicals Believe." In *Evangelicals around the World: A Global Handbook for the 21st Century*, edited by Brian C. Stiller, Todd M. Johnson, Karen Stiller, and Mark Hutchinson, 48–52. Nashville: World Evangelical Alliance, 2015.

Ezigbo, Victor I. *Re-imaging African Christologies: Conversing with the Interpretations and Appropriations of Jesus Christ in African Christianity*. Princeton Theological Monograph Series 132. Eugene: Picwick, 2010.

Ferdinando, Keith. "Christian Identity in the African Context: Reflections of Kwame Bediako's Theology and Identity." *JETS* 50, no. 1 (March 2007): 121–143.

———."The Legacy of Byang Kato", Africa Journal of Evangelical Theology, 26.1. 2007. 3–16

Ferguson, N. (2008). Review of *T. F. Torrance: An Intellectual Biography*, by Allster E. McGrath. *New Blackfriars*, 89, no. 1019 (January 2008): 131–133.

Ferris, Robert. "The Role of Theology in Theological Education." In *With an Eye on the Future: Development and Mission in the 21st Century*, edited by Duane Elmer and Lois McKinney, 103–105. Monrovia: CA MARC, 1996.

Foday-Khabenje, Aiah. "AEA Joins a Cloud of Witnesses to Wave 'Kwaheri' to Billy Graham." Association of Evangelicals in Africa, 27 February 2018. https://aeafrica.org/aea-joins-a-cloud-of-witnesses-to-wave-kwaheri-to-billy-graham/.

———. *Competencies for Leading in Diversity: A Case Study of National Evangelical Associations in Africa*. Carlisle: Langham Monographs, 2016.

———. *Synopsis and Historical Sketch of AEA: 1966–2016*. Nairobi: AEA 2016.

Fuller, W. Harold. *People of the Mandate: The Story of the World Evangelical Fellowship*. Grand Rapids: Baker Book, 1996.

Galadima, Bulus. "Evaluation of the Theology of Bolaji Idowu." *Africa Journal of Evangelical Theology* 20, no. 2 (2001): 105–131.

Githiga, Gideon Gichuhi. *The Church as the Bulwark against Authoritarianism: Development of Churches and State Relations in Kenya with Particular Reference to the Years after Political Independence 1963–1992*. Oxford: Regnum, 2001.

Glissmann, Volker. "Grassroots Theological Education." *InSight Journal* 5, no. 1 (November 2019): 53–67.

Graham, Billy. Foreword to *Theological Pitfalls in Africa*, by Byang H. Kato. Kisumu: Evangel Publishing, 1975. i–ii.

Graham, Ward. "Decolonising Theology." *Stellenbosch Theological Journal* 3, no. 2 (2017): 561–584.

Green, Gene L., Stephen T. Pardue, and K. K. Yeo, eds. *Jesus without Borders: Christology in the Majority World*. Carlisle: Langham Global Library, 2015.

Greggs, Tom. "The Confessions of Stanley: Accounting for a Human Life Lived Before God." *Modern Theology* 28, no. 2 (April 2012).l, 167–363.

Kline, Meredith G. "Genesis." In *New Bible Commentary* edited by Guthrie, D., and J. A. Motyer, eds. 3rd ed. Grand Rapids: Eerdmans, 1988.

Hadebe, N. M. "Commodification, Decolonisation and Theological Education in Africa: Renewed challenges for African theologians." *HTS Theological Studies* 73, no. 3 (2017): a4550. https://doi.org/ 10.4102/hts.v73i3.4550.

Hanciles, Jehu J. *Beyond Christendom: Globalisation, African Migration, and the Transformation of the West*. Maryknoll: Orbis, 2008.

Haokip, Jangkholam. *Can God Save My Village?: A Theological Study of Identity among the Tribal People of North-East India with a Special Reference to the Kukis of Manipur*. Carlisle: Langham Monographs, 2014.

Harnack, Adolf. *The Mission and Expansion of Christianity in the First Three Centuries*. Grand Rapids: Christian Classics Ethereal Library, 2005.

Harries, Jim. "Overcoming Invented Ogres: African Traditional Religions and World Religions in African Christian Perspective." *Evangelical Review of Theology: A Global Forum* 42, no.2 (April 2018): 171–184.

Haye, Sophie de la. *Byang Kato: Ambassador for Christ; Biography of Dr. Byang H. Kato*. Achimota: African Christian Press, 1986.

Heise, David. *Expressive Order: Confirming Sentiments in Social Actions*. New York: Springer, 2007.

———. *Surveying Culture: Discovering Shared Conceptions and Sentiments*. New York: Wiley, 2010.

Hendriks, H. Jurgens. "Public Theology and Identity." In *African Public Theology*, edited by Sunday B. Agang, H. Jurgens Hendriks, and Dion A. Forster. Carlisle: HippoBooks, 2020: 49–64.

Hickman, Albert W. "Evangelicals You Would Want to Know." In *Evangelicals around the World: A Global Handbook for the 21st Century*, edited by Brian C.

Stiller, Todd M. Johnson, Karen Stiller, and Mark Hutchinson, 227. Nashville: The World Evangelical Alliance, 2015.

———. "200 Events in Evangelical History." In *Evangelicals around the World: A Global Handbook for the 21st Century*, edited by Brian C. Stiller, Todd M. Johnson, Karen Stiller, and Mark Hutchinson, 10–24. Nashville: The World Evangelical Alliance, 2015.

Hiebert, Paul G. *Anthropological Reflections on Missiological Issues*. Grand Rapids: Baker Books, 1994.

Hinkelmann, Frank. "The Founding of the European Evangelical Alliance as a Counter-Movement to the World Evangelical Alliance." *Evangelical Review of Theology* 44, no. 2 (2020): 101–114.

Hirsch, Karen. "Culture and Disability: The Role of Oral History." In *The Oral History Reader*, edited by Perks Robert and Alistair Thomson. London: Routledge, 1998. 1–27.

Holder, R. Ward. "The Reformers and Tradition: Seeing the Roots of the Problem in Teaching the Reformation." *Religions* 8, no. 6 (2017):105, 1–11. https://doi.org/10.3390/rel8060105.

Horowitz, Mardi. "Self-Identity Theory and Research Methods." *Journal of Research Practice* 8, no. 2 (2012). 1–11.

Howard, Kevin L. "Kwame Bediako: Considerations on the Motivating Force behind his Theology and Identity." *Global Missiology* 3, no. 10 (April 2013). http://ojs.globalmissiology.org/index.php/english/article/view/1186/2735.

Ice, Thomas D. "Dispensational Hermeneutics." Scholars Crossing: The Institutional Repository of Liberty University. Pre-Trib Research Center: Article Archives (115), 2009. https://digitalcommons.liberty.edu/cgi/viewcontent.cgi?article=1114&context=pretrib_arch.

Idowu, Bolaji. *African Traditional Religion: A Definition*. Maryknoll: Orbis, 1973.

———. *Olodumare: God in Yoruba Belief*. London: Longmans, 1962.

———. *Towards an Indigenous Church*. London: Oxford University Press, 1965.

Ikwuagwu, Onwumere A. "Initiation in African Traditional Religion: A Systematic Symbolic Analysis with Special Reference to Aspects of Igbo Religion in Nigeria." Inaugural dissertation, Julius Maximilian University, Würzburg, Germany, 2007.

Ikwubuzo, Iwu. "Rites of Passage in Ogbalu's Novel, Obiefuna: An Archetypal Analysis." *Lagos Notes and Records* 15, no. 1 (January 2009): 138–158.

James, Aaron. "Tony Campolo: I Refuse to Call Myself an Evangelical Anymore." *Premier Christian News*, 19 September 2016. https://premierchristian.news/en/news/article/tony-campolo-i-refuse-to-call-myself-an-evangelical-anymore.

Janssen, Diederik F. "Initiation and Passage: Multilingual Encyclopedic and Bibliographic Approach." *World Cultures eJournal*, 16, no. 2 (2008): 1–9. Retrieved 29 July 2020.

Jenkins, Philip. *The Next Christendom: The Coming of Global Christianity*. 3rd ed. New York: Oxford, 2011.

Jonson, Todd M., Gina A. Zurlo, Albert W. Hickman, and Peter F. Crossing. "Christianity 2018: More African Christians and Counting Martyrs." *International Bulletin of Mission Research*. 42 (1); 20–28

Jusu, John, ed. "Our Identity in Christ: Acts 11." In *Africa Study Bible*, 1601. N.p.: Oasis International, 2016.

———. "Rites of Passage: Hebrews 13." In *Africa Study Bible*, 1838. N.p.: Oasis International, 2016.

Kabongo, Luc. "The Africanisation of Missiology: The Work of InnerChange South Africa to Raise Up Local Missionaries and Decolonise Black African Minds (Part 1)." *Global Missiology* 4, no. 15 (July 2018): 1–10.

Kaeser, Marc Antoine. "Biography, Science Studies and Historiography of Archaeological Research: Managing Personal Archieves." *Complutum* 24, no. 2 (2013): 101–108.

Kagabo, Liboire. "Alexis Kagame: The Trail of an African Theology." In vol. 2 of *African Theology in the 21st Century: The Contribution of the Pioneers*, edited by Benezet Bujo and Juvenal Ilunga, 13–43. Nairobi: Paulines, 2006.

Kapteina, Detlef. "Formation of African Evangelical Theology," *African Journal of Evangelical Theology* 25, no. 1 (2006): 61–84.

Kato, Byang H. "Africa's Battle for Biblical Christianity." *Moody Monthly*, November 1974, 53–56.

———. "Africa's Christian Future: Interview with Byang H. Kato (Part 2)." Interview. *Christianity Today*, 10 October 1975.

———. *African Cultural Revolution and the Christian Faith*. Jos: Challenge, 1976.

———. "African Perspectives". Based on original text of interview and edited in accordance with the German text in Idea Number 44/74, Special Edition on World Mission, 6–12. 18 November 1974.

———. "An African Perspective." *Evangelical Missions Quarterly* 10, no. 4 (October 1974): 307–312.

———. "Africa's Evangelicals and the WCC." *Target*, 23 November 1975.

———. "Africa: Facts that You Should Know or Help Train Leaders for Africa." Lecture notes, 1973.

———. "Africa: Prudence and Promise; A Candid Survey of Current Opportunity and Dangers Facing Evangelicals and Missionary Strategy in Africa." *United Evangelical Action* 34, no. 2 (Summer 1975): 17–20, 34.

———. An Open Letter to the Christian Reader in Today's Africa, in Byang H. Kato.

———. *Biblical Christianity in Africa: A Collection of Papers and Addresses*. Theological Perspectives in Africa 2. Accra: Africa Christian Press, 1985.

———. "Black Theology and African Theology." Public Lecture Delivered at the University of Nairobi, 27th September 1975.

———. "The Brave New World (Jer. 8:11–22)." Typescript.

———. "Call for Decision: Address at Igbaja Theological Seminary and Bible College." *African Challenge*, 1969, 16–17.

———. "The Challenge of Evangelicalism in Contemporary Africa." Public lecture, ECWA Theological Seminary, Igbaja, Nigeria, 8 February 1974.

———. "Christian Citizenship (Rom. 13:1–14)." Sermon notes.

———. "Christianity and Culture." Unpublished Manuscript, October 1974.

———. "The Christian Surge in Africa: Interview with Byang H. Kato (Part 1)." *Christianity Today*, 26 September 1975.

———. "Contextualisation and Religious Syncretism in Africa." In *Biblical Christianity in Africa: A Collection of Papers and Addresses*. Theological Perspectives in Africa 2. Accra: Africa Christian Press, 1985.

———. "Contextualisation of the Gospel: Theological Perspective." 1–2. Typescript manuscript, dated 1975?

———. "Creating Facilities for Evangelical Theological Training in Africa." In *Christian Higher Education: The Contemporary Challenge; Proceedings of the First International Conference of Reformed Institutions for Christian Scholarship, Potchefstroom, 9–13 September 1975*, 1–4.

———. "A Critique of Incipient Universalism in Tropical Africa." ThD diss., Dallas Theological Seminary, 1974.

———. "A Critique of Incipient Universalism in Tropical Africa: A Study of the Religious Concepts of the 'Jaba' People of West Africa." *The International Journal of Theology and Philosophy in Africa* 1, no. 1 (January 1989): 55–84.

———. "Danger: Men at Work." *Africa Now*, March–April 1976.

———. "The Devil's Baby." *Africa Now*, January–March 1962.

———. "Evangelical Cooperation in Contemporary Africa." Speech, n.d. Evangelical Fellowship of Zambia, 1974.

———. "Evangelism Opportunities and Obstacles in Africa." In *Let the Earth Hear His Voice: International Congress on World Evangelization*, 147–158. Minneapolis: World Wide Publications, 1975.

———. "From Juju to Jesus Christ." *African Challenge*, 1962, 13.

———. "The Gospel, Cultural Contextualisation and Religious Syncretism." In *Let the Earth Hear His Voice: International Congress on World Evangelization*, edited by J. D. Douglas, 1216–1228. Minneapolis: World Wide Publications, 1975.

———. "The Historical Fulcrum." Lecture, Nairobi University, November 1975.

———. "How I Won My Son to Christ." *Today's Challenge*, May 1975, 15.

———. "Joy of Christian Service." Sermon notes, n.d. Archived at AEA Offices in Nairobi, Kenya

———. *Lift Up Your Hearts: The Future of the Church*. 6 parts. Radio broadcast. Voice of Kenya (VOK), 1975. Archived at AEA offices in Nairobi.

———. "The Power of the Holy Spirit in the Christian." Sermon/teaching notes, n.d.

———. "Presentation at meeting of leaders of the National Evangelical Association of USA." Washington, January 1975.

———. *The Spirits: What the Bible Teaches*. Achimota: African Christian Press, 1975.

———. "Theological Anemia in Africa." In *Biblical Christianity in Africa: A Collection of Papers and Addresses*, 11–14. Theological Perspectives in Africa 2. Accra: Africa Christian Press, 1985.

———. "Theological Issues in Africa." In *Biblical Christianity in Africa: A Collection of Papers and Addresses*, 40–53. Theological Perspectives in Africa 2. Accra: Africa Christian Press, 1985.

———. *Theological Pitfalls in Africa*. Kisumu: Evangel Publishing House, 1975.

———. "Theological Trends in Africa Today." *Theological News Monograph*, April 1973.

———. "The Theology of Eternal Salvation." *Perception*, no. 14 (October 1978): 1–8.

———. "Third World Missions." *Evangel Lens* 5, no. 4 (1981).

———. "Today in Africa." *East Africa's Christian Gazette*, February 1976, 6–7.

———. "The Youth in the African Church." Presentation at First AEA General Assembly in February 1969, Limuru, Kenya, and Christian Leaders Conference, Ilorin, Nigeria, May 1969. 1–7

———. "We Are at a Turning Point in Africa's Church History." *Africa Now*, September–October 1974, 6–7.

———. "The Problem of Theological Education in Africa." Presented at Meeting of Professors of Mission, Kansas City, USA, November 1973. 1–9.

———. "Written Theology." Paper delivered at Ibadan University, Jos Campus, 9 March 1974. 1–7.

Kelsey, David. *Between Athens and Berlin*. Eugene: Wipf and Stock, 2011.

Kenyatta, Jomo. *Facing Mt. Kenya*. New York: Vintage Books, 1956.

Kimilike, Lechion Peter. "An African Perspective on Poverty Proverbs in the of Proverbs: An Analysis for Transformational Possibilities." PhD diss., University of South Africa, 2006.

Kirschner, Thorsten-Marco. *Futurist Eschatologies in Africa and Europe: Pannenberg, Moltmann, Mbiti and Kato*. MTh thesis, University of KwaZulu-Natal, Pietermaritzburg, 2008.

Knapp, Stephen. "The Gospel, Cultural Contextualisation and Religious Syncretism." Notes on group discussion of the Theology of Evangelism Study Group, ICOWE, Lausanne, Switzerland, 22–24 July 1974. Recorded by: Stephen C. Knapp, Partnership in Third World Ministry, 1564 Edge Hill Road, Philadelphia, Pa.19001, USA.

Kok, J. "Social Identity Complexity Theory as Heuristic Tool in New Testament Studies." *HTS Theological Studies* 70, no. 1 (2014). http:// dx.doi.org/10.4102/hts. v70i1.2708.

Kunhiyop, Samuel Waje. *African Christian Theology*. Bukuru: HippoBooks, 2012.

Kuwana, Patrick. "African Leadership: What Is the Missing Link?" Paper presented at AEA Leadership Engagement Seminar, Nairobi, 24–27 September 2018.

Lassig, Simone. "Toward a Biographical Turn? Biography in Modern Historiography – Modern Historiography in Biography." *GHI Bulletin, no.35* (Fall 2004): 147–155.

Leffel, Gregory P. "Conference Theme." In *Social Engagement: The Challenge of the Social in Missiological Education; The 2013 Proceedings of the Association of Professors of Mission*. Wilmore, KY: First Fruits, 2013, xiii–xvi.

Lim, David S. "Jubilee Realised: The Integral Mission of Asian House Church Networks in Contexts of Religious Pluralism." In *Jubilee: God's Answer to Poverty*, edited by Hannah J. Swithinbank, Emmanuel Murangira, and Caitlin Collins, 79–94. Oxford: Regnum Books International, 2020.

Lowery, Stephanie A. "Ecclesiology in Africa: Apprentices on a Mission." In *The Church from Every Tribe and Tongue: Ecclesiology in the Majority World*, edited by Gene L. Green, Stephen T. Pardue, and K. K. Yeo, 74–92. Carlisle: Langham Global Library, 2018.

———. *Identity and Ecclesiology: Their Relationship among Select African Theologians*. Eugene: Pickwick, 2017.

MacDonald, Scott Douglas. "A Critical Analysis of Byang Kato's Demonology and Its Theological Relevance for an Evangelical Demonology." PhD diss., University of South Africa, 2017.

MacKinnon, Neil J., and David R. Heise. *Self, Identity and Social Institutions*. New York: Palgrave, 2010.

MaClean, William. "The Second Coming of Christ: Three Main Views." *Free Presbyterian Magazine*, January 2000.

Madigan, Kevin, and Carolyn Osiek, eds. *Ordained Women in the Early Church*. Baltimore: Johns Hopkins, 2005.

Maigadi, Barje S. "The Christian Faith and Divisive Ethnicity in Africa: A Case Study of the Evangelical Church of West Africa (ECWA) in Nigeria." PhD diss., Asbury Theological Seminary, 1997.

Masika, Titus. *Mobilising Mindset Change for Community Transformation*. Nairobi: Christian Impact Mission, n.d.

Massey, John David. "Theological Education and Southern Baptist Missions Strategy in the Twenty-First Century." *Southwestern Journal of Theology* 57, no. 1 (Fall 2014): 5–16.

Maxwell, David. "Post-Colonial Christianity in Africa." In *The Cambridge History of Christianity: World Christianity c. 1914–2000*, edited by Hugh Mcleod, 401–421. Cambridge: CUP, 2008.

Mbiti, John S. *African Religions and Philosophy*. Nairobi: Heinemann, 1969.

———. "Christianity and African Culture." *Journal of Theology for Southern Africa* 1 (September 1977): 26–40

———. *Concepts of God in Africa*. New York: Praeger, 1970.

———. *Introduction to African Religion*. New York: Praeger, 1975.

———. *New Testament Eschatology in an African Background*. London: Oxford University Press, 1971.

Mburu, Elizabeth. *African Hermeneutics*. Carlisle: HippoBooks, 2019.

Mengara, D. M., ed. *Images of Africa: Stereotypes and Realities*. Trenton, NJ: Africa World Press, 2001.

Meserve, Harry C. "Biography as Theology." *Journal of Religion and Health* 14, no. 4 (Oct. 1975): 227–230.

Moffitt, Bob. *Evangelism without Discipleship: The Consequences of Neglecting Jesus' Command to Disciple*. 2nd ed. Phoenix: Harvest Foundation, 2019.

Mokhoathi, Joel. "From Contextual Theology to African Christianity: The Consideration of Adiaphora from a South African Perspective." *Religions* 8, no. 12 (2017): 266.

Mosothoane, Ephraim K. "Communio Sanctorum in Africa." *Missionalia: Southern African Journal of Missions Studies* 1, no. 2 (August 1973): 86–95.

Mueller, Steven P. "Donatism." The Encyclopedia of Christian Civilization. Oxford: Blackwell Publishing Limited, 2012. https://doi.org/10.1002/9780470670606.wbecc0443.

Mugambi, J. N. K., and Laurent Magaesa, eds. Introduction to *Jesus in African Christianity: Experimentation and Diversity in African Christology*. Nairobi: Acton Publishers, 1998.

Musasiwa, Roy. "The Quest for Identity in African Theology: A Necessary Dimension in the Quest for the African Renaissance." *Journal of African Christian Thought* 6, no. 2 (December 2003): 6–13.

Mwiti, Gladys K. *Parenting with Purpose and African Wisdom*. Nairobi: Arba, 2016.

Ndiaye, Mamadou. "An Investigation into Pauline Church Leadership and Ministry towards a Reduction of the Clergy/Laity Gap in a West African Sahelian Context." PhD diss., South African Theological Seminary, 2013.

Ndjerareou, Abel. "Yahweh and Other Gods." In *Africa Bible Commentary: A One-Volume Commentary Written by 70 African Scholars*, edited by Tokunboh Adeyemo. 861. Nairobi: WordAlive, 2006.

Ngong, David Tonghou. "The Material in Salvific Discourse: A Study of Two Christian Perspectives." PhD diss., Baylor University, 2007.

Nigeria Baptist Church. "Jesus Christ Frees." *Themelios* 1, no. 3 (Summer 1976): 66–75.

Nihinlola, Emiola. *Theology under the Mango Tree: A Handbook of African Christian Theology*. Lagos: Fine Print and Manufacturing, 2013.

Niringiye, David Zac. *The Church: God's Pilgrim People*. Carlisle: Langham, 2014.

———. "Prolegomena to an African Theology: An Examination of the Sources and Methodology of Mbiti's Theology." MA thesis, Wheaton Graduate School, 1987.

Nyende, Peter. "The Church as an Assembly on Mt. Zion: An Ecclesiology from Hebrews for African Christianity." In *The Church from Every Tribe and Tongue: Ecclesiology in the Majority World*, edited by Gene L. Green, Stephen T. Pardue, and K. K. Yeo, 136–152. Carlisle: Langham, 2018.

Nystrom, Carolyn. "Let African Christians Be Christian Africans." *Christianity Today*, 4 June 2009. https://www.christianitytoday.com/history/2009/june/let-african-christians-be-christian-africans.html.

Oborji, Francis Anekwe. "Contemporary Missiology in Theological Education:Origins and New Perspective Missiology." *An International Review* 34, no. 3 (July 2006): 383–397.

Oden, Thomas C. *How Africa Shaped the Christian Mind: Rediscovering the Africa Seedbed of Western Christianity*. Downers Grove: IVP, 2007.

———. *The Rebirth of African Orthodoxy: Return to Foundations*. Nashville: Abingdon, 2016.

———. *The Rebirth of Orthodoxy: Signs of New Life in Christianity*. St. Davids: ICCS, 2015.

Oduyoye, Mercy. *Hearing and Knowing*. Maryknoll: Orbis, 1986.

Ogunbado, Ahamad Faosiy. "Impacts of Colonialism on Religions: An Experience of South- western Nigeria." *IOSR Journal of Humanities and Social Science* 5, no. 6 (Nov.–Dec. 2012): 51–57.

Oladipo, Emmanuel. *Exemplary Christians in the Nigerian Public Square: Mini-Biographies of 15 Nigerians*. Ibadan: CNMS, 2018.

Omulokoli, Watson A. O. "The Priority of African Christian Biography in Authentic Christianity." *Africa International University: 34th Graduation*, 2019.

Osei-Mensah, Gottfried. "Why PACLA." In *Facing the New Challenges: The Message of PACLA*, edited by Michael Cassidy and Luc Verlinden, 19–23. Kisumu: Evangel, 1978.

Otonko, Jake. "Beyond the Rhetoric of the 'Next Christendom'?: An examination of the Integrity of the Christian Faith in Nigeria." *Scriptura: Journals for Contextual Hermeneutics in Southern Africa* 117, no. 1 (2018): 1–12.

Pak, G. Sujin. The Protestant Reformers and the Jews: Excavating Contexts, Unearthing Logic. *Religions* 8, no. 4 (2017): 72.

Palmer, Timothy. "Byang Kato: A Theological Reappraisal." *Africa Journal of Evangelical Theology* 23, no. 1 (2004): 3–20.

———. *Christian Theology in an African Context*. Bukuru: African Christian Textbooks, 2015.

Parker, David. *"Discerning the Obedience of Faith": A Short History of the World Evangelical Alliance Theological Commission*. World of Theology 3. Hamburg: Verlag für Kultur und Wissenschaft, 2005.

Parratt, John. ed. Introduction to *A Reader in African Christian Theology*. London: SPCK, 1997.

Patterson, Paige. "The Theology of the Reformers." *Southwestern Journal of Theology* 60, no. 1 (Fall 2017): 5–13.

Perks, Robert, and Alistair Thomsom, eds. *The Oral History Reader*. Routledge: London, 1998.

Porumb, Razvan. "Orthodoxy and Ecumenism: Towards Active Metanoia." PhD thesis, Anglia Ruskin University, 2014.

Ramm, Bernard. *Protestant Biblical Interpretation*. Boston: Wilde, 1956. 89–92.

Rice, Chris. *Reconciliation as the Mission of God: Christian Witness in a World of Destructive Conflicts; A 2005 Paper from 47 Christian Leaders across the World*. Durham, NC: Reconciliation Network, 2005.

Rieger, Joerg. *Christ and Empire: From Paul to Postcolonial Times*. Minneapolis: Fortress Press, 2007.

Roccas, S., and Brewer, M. B. "Social Identity Complexity." *Personality and Social Psychology Review* 6, no. 2 (2002): 88–106.

Rukuni, R., and E. Oliver. "Nicaea as Political Orthodoxy: Imperial Christianity versus Episcopal Polities." *HTS Theological Studies* 75, no. 4 (2019): a5313.

Rutayisire, Antoine. "God's Heart for the Poor." In *Jubilee: God's Answer to Poverty*, edited by Hannah J. Swithinbank, Emmanuel Murangira, and Caitlin Collins, 9–20. Oxford: Regnum Books International, 2020.

Ryrie, Charles C. Introduction to *Theological Pitfalls in Africa*, by Byang H. Kato. Kisumu: Evangel Publishing, 1975. v.

Sakupapa, Teddy Chalwe. "The Decolonising Content of African Theology and the Decolonisation of African Theology: Reflections on a Decolonial future for African Theology." *Missionalia* 46, no. 3 (2019): 406–424.

Sawyerr, Harry. *Creative Evangelism: Towards a New Christian Encounter with Africa*. London: Lutterworth, 1968.

———. *God: Ancestor or Creator? Aspects of Traditional Belief in Ghana, Nigeria and Sierra Leone*. London: Longman, 1970.

———. *The Practice of Presence: Shorter Writings by Harry Sawyerr*. Edited by John Parratt. Grand Rapids: Eerdmans, 1996.

Seidman, I. E. *Interviewing as Qualitative Research: A Guide for Researchers in Education and the Social Sciences*. New York: Teachers College Press. 1991.

Semenye, Lois. *Let the Children Come*. Nairobi: Taptok Limited, 2007.

Sensing, Tim. *Qualitative Research: A Multi-Methods Approach to Projects for Doctor of Ministry Theses*. Eugene: Wipf and Stock, 2011.

Shana, Goodwill. "Our Evangelical Identity and Role in the Africa We Want." Keynote address, AEA Jubilee Theological Consultation, Nairobi, November 2016.

Shaw, Mark R. *The Kingdom of God in Africa: A Short History of African Christianity*. Katunayake: New Life Literature, 2006.

Shirik, Sochanngam. "African Christians or Christian Africans: Byang H. Kato and his Contextual Theology." *The Asbury Journal* 74, no. 1 (2019): 131–156.

Shorter, Aylward. *African Christian Theology: Adaptation or Incarnation?* New York: Orbis Books, 1986.

Sider, Ron. "Evangelicals and Social Justice." In *Evangelicals around the World: A Global Handbook for the 21st Century*, edited by Brian C. Stiller, Todd M. Johnson, Karen Stiller, and Mark Hutchinson, 128–133. Nashville: The World Evangelical Alliance, 2015.

———. "Still Evangelical in Spite of President Trump's Evangelical Supporters?" *Ron Sider Blog*, 17 Jan. 2020. https://ronsiderblog.substack.com/p/still-evangelical-in-spite-of-president.

Simango, Daniel. "There Is a Great Need for Contextualisation in Southern Africa." *Studia Historiae Ecclesiasticae* 44, no. 2 (2018): 1–11.

Smith, Kevin Gary. *Integrated Theology: Discerning God's will for our World*. Johannesburg: SATS, 2013.

Stott, John. *Evangelical Truth: A Personal Plea for Unity, Integrity and Faithfulness*. Leicester: IVP, 2003.

Sulaiman, Folasade R. "Internationalization in Education: The British Colonial Policies on Education in Nigeria 1882–1926." *Journal of Sociological Research* 3, no. 2 (2012): 84–101.

Tarus, David Kirwa, and Stephanie Lowery. "African Theologies of Identity and Community: The Contributions of John Mbiti, Jesse Mugambi, Vincent Mulago, and Kwame Bediako." *Open Theology* 3, no. 1 (2017): 305–320.

Tennent, Timothy C. *Invitation to World Missions: A Trinitarian Missiology for the Twenty-First Century*. Invitation to Theological Studies Series. Grand Rapids: Kregel, 2010.

———. *Theology in the Context of World Christianity: How the Global Church Is Influencing the Way We Think about and Discuss Theology*. Grand Rapids: Zondervan, 2007.

Theron, Pieter, and Michael Raiter, eds. *Effective Theological Education for World Evangelization.* Lausanne Occasional Paper 57. Lausanne Committee for World Evangelization, 2005.

Tiénou, Tite. "Problems and Issues among the Rural Population of Africa." In *Facing the New Challenges: The Message of PACLA, December 9-19, 1976,* edited by Michael Cassidy and Luc Verlinden, 37–40. Kisumu: Evangel Publishing House, 1978.

———. *The Theological Task of the Church in Africa.* Achimota: Africa Christian Press, 1982.

———. "The Theological Task of the Church in Africa: Where Are We Now and Where Should We Be Going?" *Africa Journal of Evangelical Theology* 6, no. 1 (1987): 3–11.

———. "Understanding African Theology in the 20th Century." In *Issues in African Christian Theology,* edited by Samuel Ngewa, Mark Shaw, and Tite Tiénou. Nairobi: East African Educational Publishers, 1998.

Turaki, Yusufu. *The British Colonial Legacy in Northern Nigeria: A Social Ethical Analysis of the Colonial and Post-Colonial Society and Politics in Nigeria.* Jos: ECWA Productions, 2017.

———. *Christianity and African Gods: A Method in Theology.* Potchefstroom: Potchefstroom University for Christian Higher Education, 1999.

———. *Engaging Religions and Worldviews in Africa: A Christian Theological Method.* Carlisle: Langham, 2020.

———. *Foundations of African Traditional Religions and Worldview.* Nairobi: International Bible Society Africa, 2001.

———. *Tainted Legacy: Islam, Colonialism and Slavery in Northern Nigeria.* McLean: Isaac Publishing, 2010.

———. "The Theological Legacy of the Reverend Doctor Byang Kato." *Africa Journal of Evangelical Theology* 20, no. 2 (2001): 133–155.

Tutu, Desmond Mpilo. *God Is Not a Christian: Speaking Truth in Times of Crisis.* London: Rider, 2013.

Van der Walt, Barend Johannes. "An Evangelical Voice in Africa: The Worldview Background of the Theology of Tokunboh Adeyemo (1 October 1944–17 March 2010)." *In die Skriflig* 45, no. 4 (2011): 919–956.

Van Tonder, Helene. "Towards an Adequate Methodology for Church and Theological Historiography: in Conversation with Paul Ricoeur." *Studia Historiae Ecclesiasticae* 37, no. 1 (2011): 239–253.

Viriri, Advice, and Pascah Mungwini. "African Cosmology and the Duality of Western Hegemony: The Search for an African Identity." *The Journal of Pan African Studies* 3, no. 6 (March 2010): 27–42.

von Sinner, Rudolf. "Ecumenism in the 21st Century: Theses for Discussion." Paper presented for the Continuation Committee on Ecumenism in the 21st Century, Bossey Ecumenical Institute, 19 November 2007.
Walls, Andrew F. *The Cross-Cultural Process in Christian History*. Maryknoll: Orbis, 2002.
──────. *The Missionary Movement in Christian History: Studies in the Transmission of Faith*. Maryknoll: Orbis, 1996.
Ward, Kevin. "Christianity, Colonialism and Missions." In *The Cambridge History of Christianity: World Christianity c. 1914–2000*, edited by Hugh Mcleod, 71–88. Cambridge: CUP, 2008.
WEA Mission Commission. "The New Reformation: WEA Mission Commission Report." A Presentation of the WEA Mission Commission, WEA International Leadership Forum, Bad Blankenburg, Germany, 2017.
Wolffe, John. "Who Are Evangelicals? A History." In *Evangelicals around the World: A Global Handbook for the 21st Century*, edited by Brian C. Stiller, Todd M. Johnson, Karen Stiller, and Mark Hutchinson, 25–33. Nashville: World Evangelical Alliance, 2015.
Wright, Christopher J. H. "Effectiveness and Impact in Theological Education from a Biblical Perspective." Paper Presented at ICETE Conference, Antalya, Turkey, November 2015.
──────. *The Mission of God: Unlocking the Bible's Grand Narrative*. Downers Grove: IVP Academic, 2006.
Wright, Handel Kashope. "(Im)possibility of Articulating Continental African Identity." *Critical Arts: A Journal of South-North Cultural and Media Studies* 16, no. 2 (2002): 1–18.
Wunti, Musa Adamu, and Md Moniruzzaman. "Ethnocentrism and Ethno-Political Conflicts in Northern Nigeria." *A Critical Analysis Journal of Political Science and Leadership Research* 2, no. 2 (2016): 10–23. www.iiardpub.org.
Young, F. Lionel, III. "A 'New Breed of Missionaries': Assessing Attitudes toward Western Missions at the Nairobi Evangelical Graduate School of Theology." *International Bulletin of Missionary Research* 36, no. 2 (2012): 1–6.
Zizioulas, John D. *Being as Communion: Studies in Personhood and the Church*. Crestwood: St. Vladimir's, 2002.

Langham Literature, with its publishing work, is a ministry of Langham Partnership.

Langham Partnership is a global fellowship working in pursuit of the vision God entrusted to its founder John Stott –

> *to facilitate the growth of the church in maturity and Christ-likeness through raising the standards of biblical preaching and teaching.*

Our vision is to see churches in the Majority World equipped for mission and growing to maturity in Christ through the ministry of pastors and leaders who believe, teach and live by the word of God.

Our mission is to strengthen the ministry of the word of God through:
- nurturing national movements for biblical preaching
- fostering the creation and distribution of evangelical literature
- enhancing evangelical theological education

especially in countries where churches are under-resourced.

Our ministry

Langham Preaching partners with national leaders to nurture indigenous biblical preaching movements for pastors and lay preachers all around the world. With the support of a team of trainers from many countries, a multi-level programme of seminars provides practical training, and is followed by a programme for training local facilitators. Local preachers' groups and national and regional networks ensure continuity and ongoing development, seeking to build vigorous movements committed to Bible exposition.

Langham Literature provides Majority World preachers, scholars and seminary libraries with evangelical books and electronic resources through publishing and distribution, grants and discounts. The programme also fosters the creation of indigenous evangelical books in many languages, through writer's grants, strengthening local evangelical publishing houses, and investment in major regional literature projects, such as one volume Bible commentaries like the *Africa Bible Commentary* and the *South Asia Bible Commentary*.

Langham Scholars provides financial support for evangelical doctoral students from the Majority World so that, when they return home, they may train pastors and other Christian leaders with sound, biblical and theological teaching. This programme equips those who equip others. Langham Scholars also works in partnership with Majority World seminaries in strengthening evangelical theological education. A growing number of Langham Scholars study in high quality doctoral programmes in the Majority World itself. As well as teaching the next generation of pastors, graduated Langham Scholars exercise significant influence through their writing and leadership.

To learn more about Langham Partnership and the work we do visit **langham.org**

www.ingramcontent.com/pod-product-compliance
Lightning Source LLC
Chambersburg PA
CBHW061704300426
44115CB00014B/2562